AF743398

Philosophy and Science of Risk

What is risk? How do we assess risk? What are the ethical implications of risk? The concept of risk is important – sometimes even crucial – for many philosophical domains, from philosophy of science and technology to ethics and sustainability.

Philosophy and Science of Risk is a clear, wide-ranging introduction to this urgent and fast-growing subject. It covers the following key topics:

- The philosophical and historical background to understanding and interpreting risk
- The meaning of risk and how it differs from closely related concepts, such as uncertainty or dangers
- The social construction of risk
- Risk perception and risk as an object of scientific study
- The measurement of risk, its probability and severity
- Risk and scientific modeling
- Risk, value judgments, and expertise
- Risk management, including cost-benefit analysis and the precautionary approach
- Risk communication, including deliberative models
- Ethics of risk, including duties toward nonhuman animals and future generations
- Risk and sustainability
- Decision-making under risk

Including helpful additional features such as text boxes, chapter summaries, review, and discussion questions, *Philosophy and Science of Risk: An Introduction* is an ideal textbook for students of the philosophy of risk. It is also suitable for students studying the conceptual questions surrounding risk in related subjects, such as sociology, psychology, economics, politics, geography, sustainability, and environmental studies.

Isabelle Peschard is an associate professor emerita and lecturer faculty in the Philosophy Department at San Francisco State University, USA.

Yann Benétreau-Dupin is a division editor at *PLOS ONE* for the Behavioral and Social Sciences, Neuroscience, Mental Health Team, and a visiting scholar at San Francisco State University, USA.

Christopher Wessels is a lecturer faculty in the Philosophy Department at San Francisco State University, USA.

Philosophy and Science of Risk

An Introduction

Isabelle Peschard, Yann Benétreau-Dupin, and Christopher Wessels

Routledge
Taylor & Francis Group
LONDON AND NEW YORK

Cover image: © Tanes Ngamsom / Getty Images

First published 2023
by Routledge
4 Park Square, Milton Park, Abingdon, Oxon OX14 4RN

and by Routledge
605 Third Avenue, New York, NY 10158

Routledge is an imprint of the Taylor & Francis Group, an informa business

© 2023 Isabelle Peschard, Yann Benétreau-Dupin, and Christopher Wessels

The right of Isabelle Peschard, Yann Benétreau-Dupin, and Christopher Wessels to be identified as authors of this work has been asserted by them in accordance with sections 77 and 78 of the Copyright, Designs and Patents Act 1988.

All rights reserved. No part of this book may be reprinted or reproduced or utilised in any form or by any electronic, mechanical, or other means, now known or hereafter invented, including photocopying and recording, or in any information storage or retrieval system, without permission in writing from the publishers.

Trademark notice: Product or corporate names may be trademarks or registered trademarks, and are used only for identification and explanation without intent to infringe.

British Library Cataloguing-in-Publication Data
A catalogue record for this book is available from the British Library

Library of Congress Cataloging-in-Publication Data
Names: Peschard, Isabelle F., author. | Benétreau-Dupin, Yann, author. | Wessels, Christopher, author.
Title: Philosophy and science of risk : an introduction / Isabelle Peschard, Yann Benétreau-Dupin, and Christopher Wessels.
Description: Abingdon, Oxon ; New York, NY : Routledge, 2023. | Includes bibliographical references and index.
Identifiers: LCCN 2022022970 (print) | LCCN 2022022971 (ebook)
Subjects: LCSH: Risk. | Uncertainty.
Classification: LCC HB615 .P3937 2023 (print) | LCC HB615 (ebook) | DDC 658.1/1—dc23/eng/20220805
LC record available at https://lccn.loc.gov/2022022970
LC ebook record available at https://lccn.loc.gov/2022022971

ISBN: 978-0-367-08643-5 (hbk)
ISBN: 978-0-367-08644-2 (pbk)
ISBN: 978-0-429-02352-1 (ebk)

DOI: 10.4324/9780429023521

Typeset in Times New Roman
by Apex CoVantage, LLC

A ma mère et mon père. Et à notre étoile montante, Clémence.

– IP

To my child, Alice, who better look carefully before crossing the street.

– YB-D

For Aunt Becky, Aunt Connie, and Scott Cox – the book lovers in my life who, each for different reasons, made it possible for me to write one. For Pat Miller, my fellow risk-seeker and intently supportive friend. And for my mother, Ruth, who has spent countless sleepless nights worrying about risks that she, in her selfless love and wisdom, encouraged me to take.

– CW

Contents

Acknowledgments

This book is born from teaching a course on Philosophy of Risk for several years at San Francisco State University. This course is part of the General Education curriculum for students from all the sciences as well as the humanities. While there were many sources to draw on, in articles, monographs, and anthologies, there was no single book to use as textbook for the course. There are many branches of knowledge in which risk is studied, many practices in which risk is assessed or managed, and much about risk every day in the news: pandemics, road design, food safety, natural disaster response, allocation of scarce medical resources, long-term implications of artificial intelligence, to mention a few. Thinking about risk requires deep conceptual work to define, assess, and manage it and its ethical implications. Controversies abound, as do conceptual conflicts, puzzles, and needs for clarification, in the many publications now devoted to risk and its analysis.

The process of writing this textbook led us far beyond what could be presented in any single course, with the advantage that different instructors will be able to select the chapters, issues, and depth of coverage that they deem most important for their discipline, most relevant to the curriculum, closest to their own interests.

We want to thank the philosophy department at SFSU, and especially Anita Silvers, for encouraging the development of this course, and the students for helping us, through their participation and feedback, to develop, clarify, and refine the content of the course to the point where we could start thinking about turning it into a book.

We want to thank, enthusiastically, anonymous reviewers and Philip Ebert for their constructive reactions and suggestions along the way, all extremely helpful in organizing the content and developing different parts of the book. Special, heartfelt appreciation to Philip Ebert for his exceptionally close reading and commentaries.

We are very grateful to our editors, Adam Johnson and Tony Bruce, for their constant support and their patience.

Finally, we want to express our deepest gratitude to Bas van Fraassen for his multifaceted contribution to this project, from helping to clarify some ideas through countless hours of private conversations, to being the first reviewer of several versions of each of the chapters, to helping research and write some of the case studies, in particular in the chapter on risk assessment, to suggesting the idea of putting some parts of the text into frames and participating in writing some of them.

General introduction

The topic of risk is as fascinating as it is ordinary. Risk is both subjective and objective, individual and societal, personal and general. Dealing with risk is, for a large part, what life is about, and also what politics is about. Risk is about the world, but nothing that is in the world yet. There is risk only with regard to possibilities. Moreover, these possibilities are concrete, as opposed to theoretical or identifiable "in abstracto." Indeed, there is only risk when someone or something is *exposed* to the possibility. And that possibility is something "bad," something that "we" who see a risk there perceive as bringing about some form of harm or loss. Thus, risk is an outgrowth of human anticipation. If we did not look to the future and desire for things to turn out one way or another, we'd have no need for the concept of risk. So what we see as risks and what we do about them say a lot about "us," about what and whom we care about.

The risks we identify at the individual and societal levels, and the ways we perceive and manage them, shape our lives and the societies we live in. They permeate all areas of life and are objects of study for a myriad of disciplines, including social and physical sciences, philosophy, psychology, business, and economics. Risk, or more precisely, our composite experience with risk, raises questions for each of these disciplines.

This book provides an interdisciplinary overview of these questions. It is born from teaching a good part of the content, and it seeks to offer a unified, coherent picture of the fast-growing field of risk-related studies, its dynamic, and its diversity. Risk as a topic of research is in its adolescence, and there is much more being done than is shown here. Our relationship with risk and the many dimensions that it comprises is such an important part of how we inhabit the world, how we relate to our environment and others, people and other animals, that this domain of research still has lots of room to grow. We hope that this integrated overview of the research done on the different aspects of our experience with risk, at the individual, scientific, and governance levels, will contribute to making risk more visible as a field of academic study.

Each of the five chapters in this book focuses on a different aspect of risk – namely, the ontological, rational, epistemological, psychological, and

DOI: 10.4324/9780429023521-1

ethical – and explores questions that are particular to those aspects. One theme that consistently emerges from these explorations is the ineliminable tension between the objective and the subjective dimensions of risk, and we make efforts throughout the book to highlight the importance of this tension in connection with our composite experience with risk. Specifically, each chapter is guided by a particular question that speaks to this tension.

The first chapter, "What is risk?" represents an *ontological* approach in which we attempt to clarify what risk is. We address this question from a conceptual angle by identifying the essential conditions in which people apply the concept of risk. The leading question for this chapter is how the concept *itself* can be rightly described as both subjective (in some ways) and objective (in others).

The second chapter, "Decision-making under risk," represents a *rational* approach. We consider rational models of decision-making. The leading question is whether there is – or, merely, whether there can be – an ideal framework that any rational person could use when making personal decisions about risks.

The third chapter, "Risk assessment," represents an *epistemological* approach. We explore how non-epistemic values are involved in the assessment both of the probability and the severity of risk. The leading question is how the normative aspect of our experience of risk gets integrated with the scientific study of risk.

The fourth chapter, "Risk perception," represents a *psychological* approach where we discuss what influences our ordinary perception of risks, be it characteristics of the situation, the social-cultural context, or moral values. The leading question is, What does it mean to say that a perception can be wrong and/or needs to be corrected?

The fifth chapter, "Risk management," represents an *ethical* approach where we discuss three components of risk management: cost-benefit analysis, precautionary attitude, and risk communication. We describe how the cost-benefit methodology has traditionally been used and how the precautionary approach to risk management redefines the form and purpose of both cost-benefit analysis and risk communication. The leading question is whether and how the management of risk can respond to the variety of positions and concerns of different stakeholders and whether and how it can be attuned to those who are more exposed to societal risks.

The different chapters may be seen as standing for distinct moments in our relationship with risk: we start by learning, mostly through examples, what counts as risk at all, and we develop mostly implicit strategies for deciding what to do in face of personal risks. As a society, we formally, scientifically, assess them, through different means, depending on the kind of risk or the aim of the assessment. As social individuals, we form mostly unreflective opinions about the different risks we are exposed to or simply hear about. We manage them, at the individual or societal levels, by trying to reduce them, to keep them under control, or to eliminate them. And we try to make our decisions on the basis of principles that represent what it is to be a rational being.

In reality, these developmental stages are not independent of each other, or even entirely distinct. Those who conduct a formal *assessment* of a risk are among those who form individual *perceptions* of it. And the practice of risk *assessment* is not independent of or even prior to the process of risk *management*, because assessment can only take place within an already-existing management project whose goals are at least broadly defined. In return, the results from risk *assessment* can modify both the *perception* of risks and the way in which we go about *managing* them. Our models of *rational* decision-making shape the ways we go after *managing* risks, and the issues we encounter in this risk *management* endeavor highlight blind spots in the *rational* models and motivate subsequent efforts to refine them.

How risks are *identified* as such, in general and in particular, is not independent of how we *perceive* things, in general, what grabs our attention and concern. Nor is this process independent of how we *asses*s things, in general, what kind of measure we are able and willing to conduct and how we conduct them. Nor is it independent of how we *manage* risks, what we decide to see as "normal" or "acceptable."

And in reverse, our abilities and choices regarding how to *assess* and *manage* risks affect not only our *perception* of risks but also even our *conception* of what risk is: Is it something we need to continually endure, as a necessary casualty of an increase in overall well-being? Is it something always imposed on us simply by the way human life develops on earth, with its overbearing economic constraints? Or is it something we can decide, in some areas at least, to drastically reduce or even eliminate? On what basis should we decide, one way or another, who is it that does the deciding, and are these the ones who *should* be making the decisions?

Our different ways of relating to risk, through rational modeling, perception, assessment, management, are all communicating with each other, informing each other, and sometimes pressuring each other into changing form. Each way of relating takes "risk" as an object, but "risk," how we conceive of risk, is also the emergent result of all these perspectives and pressures combined, and the dynamic of their developments and interrelations.

Thus, what Wittgenstein said about length[1] is also true of risk: to better understand what it is for us, what it represents in our individual and societal lives, we need to learn the different ways in which we relate to it, through what kinds of practice, from rational modeling to perception to assessment to management, and what choices, goals, and values are shaping those relations with risk. We learn what "risk" means by learning what it is to deal with risk, with all its intermingling aspects.

Note

1 "What 'determining the length' means," says Wittgenstein (1953/1997), "is not learned by learning what *length* and *determining* are; the meaning of the word 'length' is learned by learning, among other things, what it is to determine length" (part II: 225).

Reference

Wittgenstein, L. (1997). *Philosophical investigations* (G. E. M. Anscombe, Trans.). Blackwell. (Original work published 1953). DOI: 10.1093/bjps/iv.15.258.

1 What is risk?

Contents

1.1 The many meanings of risk

The word "risk" appears frequently in everyday conversations as well as in technical contexts, and these appearances are so variable that it might be difficult to see how they could all belong to the same concept. A risk is something we can *do* ("She risked her life to save her son"), *take* ("He took

DOI: 10.4324/9780429023521-2

a risk when he invested in start-ups"), *run* ("He ran a risk when he put all his money on red"), or *manage* ("Hedging your bets cuts the risk involved"). Alternatively, a risk is something that might *happen to* us, such as incurring lung cancer or drowning.

Uniting these disparate appearances, however, are two common elements. When we use the word "risk," we are speaking of (1) something that involves uncertainty and of (2) exposure to the possibility of harm or unwanted consequences. As we will see, more is involved in the notion of risk, but we can take this much as our initial guide, our working concept. There is no risk where there is no uncertainty about an outcome. But uncertainty is not enough; the outcome must also be undesirable (Lee 1981). As philosopher Rana Ahmad explains, "indifferent events . . . are not risks since they lack the critical feature of harm, loss, danger or some other type of unwantedness" (2009: 93). A risk exists only where something of value is put at stake (Rosa 1998).

From these elements it is possible to construe risk as a particular kind of (unwanted) situation or outcome – like the embarrassment a comedian feels if their jokes fall flat. (Thus, we say that person who steps up to an open mike for the first time "risks embarrassment".) Others will see it as a measure, either of the uncertainty or of the combination between uncertainty and the magnitude of a possible loss.

The literature on risk presents a myriad of definitions that betray these differences in perspective by focusing, to differing degrees, on the uncertainty aspect, on the outcome, or on the situation that might lead to the (unwanted) outcome. Thus, risk can be characterized rather simply as "uncertainty of outcome . . . of actions and events" (Cabinet Office 2002) or, more precisely, as a "measure of the probability and severity of adverse effects" (Lowrance 1976). Alternately, it is the "consequence" of the adverse event or activity "with respect to something that humans value" (Aven & Renn 2009: 1) or is a "situation or event [itself] where something of human value (including humans themselves) is at stake and where the outcome is uncertain" (ibid.). Sometimes, risk simply is equated with "expected loss."

Our aim in Chapter 1 and throughout this book is not to select or propose a definition of *risk*; in fact, we do not assume any specific definition.[1] But we do, if only implicitly, show that some definitions are incomplete and, in some cases, simply not tenable. For instance, we will argue that risk implies exposure, by contrast to danger: rough-skinned newts are inherently dangerous (due to neurotoxins in their skin) but pose no risk to humans unless we lick or eat them.[2] So the risk lies in the activity that brings about the exposure. In fact, it is quite typical that risks are linked to activities in this way, especially when they are framed in terms of outcome. Producing nuclear energy exposes us to the risk of nuclear incident. Likewise, driving exposes us to the risk of a car crash, freestyle snowboarding to the risk of serious injury or death, hiking in the rain to the risk of being struck by lightning, living in South Florida to the risk of a hurricane, and so on. Exposure and activity are important to consider because they condition our experience of risk at the level of perception, assessment, and management. This is because the activities that create the exposure are also directed at achieving some goals, or satisfying some desires, and may be forced upon us or may be alternatives to other activities that we want to avoid.

Our discussion of risk assessment (Chapter 3) will show that the definition of risk as *simply* a measure of the probability or of the expected loss is inadequate. It is true that in some cases, a probability measure might be a good answer to the question "What is the risk of X?" (as in "What is the risk that the city of San Francisco will experience a large earthquake in the next ten years?"), but only because it is already agreed that there is exposure to X and that X is something undesirable. We will see that in some cases, it may be appropriate to assess a risk in terms of the expected loss, but the same risk might also be assessed while keeping the dimensions of uncertainty and severity (the extent of the loss) separate. For other risks, the calculation of an expected loss might not make much sense. For instance, suppose we ask how serious the risk is that a certain species will become extinct as a result of climate warming. The problem here is that the value of the loss may not be numerical, and even if we could put numbers to the loss, our values might differ depending on whether and to what extent we think we are responsible for this extinction.

While we are not aiming at one specific definition of risk, we are interested in clarifying the concept of risk as part of a larger effort to clarify how we experience risk at the individual or societal level, through our rationalization, perception, assessment, or management of risk. And even though we do not feel the need to adopt a certain definition of risk, we do take the three dimensions of uncertainty, unwantedness or undesirability, and exposure to be essential to the concept. Our goal for the rest of this chapter is to investigate these dimensions in detail and, furthermore, to use what we learn from this investigation to help show that the concept of risk has both objective and subjective components.

1.2 The three dimensions of risk

What does it take to identify something as a risk so that it becomes something that exists as if "out there," something that we may worry about, that we may want to avoid, that we may want to protect ourselves from, that may become an object of perception, assessment, or management? Most of the risks that we mentioned above concern the actions of an individual and the consequences for this individual; these we call *individual risks*. But a community or society may also be exposed to risks, namely, *societal risks*. These risks – which include inflation, climate change, lack of health care, smoking, terrorism, and many others – are faced and managed collectively even though the unwanted possibilities associated with them would affect individuals.

Scientific assessments are important for identifying societal risks, but these are only part of the process. For a societal risk to be identified as such, an agreement must be reached in the affected community or society as a whole. Reaching an agreement is an intersubjective process, hence affected by difficulties involving acceptance of evidence, which may be controversial, and difficulties in effective communication, which require trust.

Consider the case of the risk of lung cancer. It was first proposed in 1898 that tobacco dust, not smoke, might be causing elevated incidence of lung tumors (Proctor 2012: 87). By the 1920s, lung cancer was becoming more and more common. That smoking was related to this increase was one among several hypotheses. Only in the 1950s did systematic studies, from mortality statistics, animal testing, and chemical analysis, lead the American Cancer Society to announce that the evidence showed an "association between smoking, particularly cigarette smoking, and lung cancer" (quoted in Proctor 2012: 88). Finally, on January 11, 1964, the US Surgeon General issued a definitive report on the causal connection (United States Surgeon General's Advisory Committee on Smoking 1964).

This story makes it seem like all that was needed to finally recognize smoking as a health risk was strong evidence of the link between smoking and lung cancer – evidence strong enough, that is, to overcome the effort by the tobacco industry to deny it (Oreskes & Conway 2011). But what evidence is needed for something to be recognized as a risk is not always obvious.

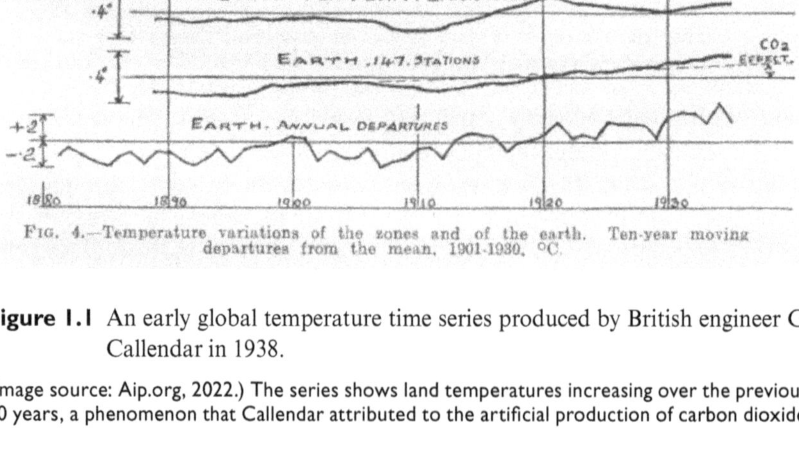

Figure 1.1 An early global temperature time series produced by British engineer Guy Callendar in 1938.

(Image source: Aip.org, 2022.) The series shows land temperatures increasing over the previous 50 years, a phenomenon that Callendar attributed to the artificial production of carbon dioxide.

Global temperature records suggesting a warming trend in the Earth's surface temperature began appearing in science journals nearly a century ago. Figure 1.1 shows one such record produced by G. S. Callendar in 1938. Like others produced around its time, Callendar's series relied on temperature, precipitation, and pressure data collected from hundreds of stations around the world, dating back to the early 1980s (Le Treut et al. 2007: 101). Many more global temperature time series were produced in the following decade.

Nevertheless, as such studies and evidence accumulated, there was still no consensus about the existence of global warming in the 1970s. By the 1990s, however, with ever more data and increasing computational capacity and speed, the great majority of scientists involved had become convinced that a serious global warming trend was underway (Boehmer-Christiansen 1993). June 23, 1988, marked the date when climate change became a national issue. In a landmark testimony before the US Senate Energy and Natural Resources Committee, James Hansen, then director of NASA's Institute for Space Studies, stated that:

> Global warming has reached a level such that we can ascribe with a high degree of confidence a cause-and-effect relationship between the greenhouse effect and observed warming. . . . In my opinion, the greenhouse effect has been detected, and it is changing our climate now.
>
> (Hansen Senate Testimony June 23, 1988)

The impact of Hansen's testimony was dramatic, capturing headlines in *The New York Times* and other major newspapers (Shabecoff 1988).

However, merely acknowledging the existence of something like climate change does not make the phenomenon, just by itself, a risk. For that judgment, we must know about the impacts and whether the impacts are regarded as harm or harm enough. And what is regarded as harm depends on what we value, what we really care about as a society.

Take the wave of recent reports on the risk faced by Black men of being killed in a police encounter (Edwards et al. 2020). If we reflect on our experience of how this risk gained prominence, we see that social media made it visible to millions of people and public outrage ensued, with people publicly expressing their opinion that this is not acceptable and that it has to change. (In Chapter 3, we will return to this risk and describe some studies that seek to measure it.)

Concern, outrage, and indignation are not the only reactions that can lead to the belief that something should not be happening. Fear can have a similar effect: fear of terrorism, immigration, nuclear or genetic technologies. In any case, a certain kind of subjective evaluation must always accompany the scientific data, explanations, and predictions so as to mark some possible consequences as unacceptable and worthy of response. As sociologist David

Garland writes, "[if] our orientation towards life's dangers were suddenly to shift from active concern to fatalistic acceptance, our world would be no less hazardous but the risk society would disappear" (2003: 52).[3]

To clarify what is involved in recognizing something as a risk, it is helpful to consider separately the three crucial factors that we distinguished earlier: *unwanted possible effects*, *uncertainty*, and *exposure*. We will see that each of these involves more than mere apprehension of facts.

1.2.1 Unwanted effect or harm

Sometimes the badness of an outcome is uncontroversial, as might be the case with failing a class or losing a limb. But this is not always the case. Take the well-rehearsed example of the risk of climate warming. More scientific data, better models, and spectacular simulations all help us better understand the extent and the effects of climate warming in the present and the future. But despite these many tools and their outputs, people disagree about whether the warming trend will result in significant harm.

Does it count as harm if only landscape and ecosystems are affected? If it would annihilate the conditions of existence of just some (but not our) species? The change in landscape in some areas, the threat to the balance of some ecosystems, and the survival of nonhuman species may not be an overwhelming concern for some people. Overall, though, it probably is more of a concern than it used to be as a result of the increased visibility and influence of ecological movements, some of which now have achieved the status of "green" political party. And what about creating new and worrisome conditions of life on the planet for future generations? This does not seem enough for many people either – though, again, it is probably more so than it used to be (Marris 2019).

Interestingly, concern for this issue seems partly a function of national identity. A majority of Europeans see global warming as one of the most serious problems facing the world (Lee et al. 2015). Whereas a poll conducted in the US in 2019 found that, although 67% of the American population believe that global warming is happening, only four in ten (38%) think that people in the US are being harmed "right now" (Leiserowitz et al. 2019). And despite evidence that some terrestrial and marine ecosystems are and will continue to be adversely affected by climate warming and that more and more species whose ecological niche is disappearing are going extinct, only 15% say they are "very worried" about it (Malcolm & Pitelka 2000).

What might it take for more Americans to become "very worried" about this phenomenon? An economic argument, perhaps? Recent research shows that unmitigated global warming (due to increased demand in energy and water and increased frequency in extreme weather events) could cost the US economy $14.5 trillion over the next 50 years (Philip et al. 2022). This figure is staggering, but it is unclear how the costs will be distributed, and many Americans do not have the privilege to be able to plan their finances far ahead. On the other hand, most realize that the implementation of serious governmental measures to address anthropogenic climate warming would affect them directly and immediately as individuals or business owners with the need to invest in energy efficiency and low-carbon technologies (Ackerman & Stanton 2010).

These impressions are not fixed, however, because our valuation of consequences is an ever-evolving task. What we perceive as unwanted or harmful depends not only on what we (dis)value but also on what we *learn* to (dis)value. Of course, this raises the reflective question of how we learn to (dis)value some consequences sufficiently to identify a new risk. How did it happen, for instance, that a near majority of Americans now see "illegal immigration" as a critical threat (Gallup 2022)?[4] And why is it, on the other hand, that they are less inclined to see lack of nationalized health care as a collective harm, by contrast with Canada and Germany?

Scientific descriptions and predictions alone cannot make climate warming or lack of health care a "risk." As suggested earlier, what's needed is an evaluative reaction to those descriptions and predictions: a reaction of deep concern or indignation and the belief that this is not acceptable, that something has to be done.

Evaluative reactions of this sort do not always form quickly, nor do the descriptions and predictions they attend. And because these developments never occur in social isolation, the process of identifying a risk is always much less straightforward than it may seem retrospectively. Indeed, assessing the possibility of harm as the outcome of our actions requires us to consider a range of scenarios. The outcome will, in each case, be a combination of some direct harm, some undesirable effects or side effects, some harm from the measures taken as precautions or remedies, and some undesirable results of those measures.

1.2.2 Uncertainty

Any behavior that could lead to harm is dangerous behavior. But even when this harm is unwanted, something more is required for us to call it risky behavior. An extreme example: swallowing a cyanide pill (as some Nazi war criminals did) leads to almost-instant death. We do not call that a risky action, because *risk* connotes a measure of uncertainty. On the other extreme, we do not normally think of watering a plant in our front yard as taking a risk of dying even though we may be fatally hit by a car passing by whose driver has suddenly lost consciousness. One explanation for this could be that we do not regard the probability of such an incident as steep enough for concern, especially when weighed against the ordinariness and convenience of the behavior.

Where and how this threshold of concern gets set, however, is not entirely clear. And it seems that, for us, the numbers aren't everything. One well-known study on the epidemiology of rock climbing accidents in Grand Teton National Park reported a fatality rate of 0.13 per 1,000 climber-hours, meaning, a climber dies approximately once in every 7,700 hours of climbing (Schussman et al. 1990). How concerning is this statistic, and what does it do for our sense of the sport's riskiness? Governments have passed legislation requiring helmets for motorcycle and, in some cases, even bicycle riding, but no such requirements have been imposed on rock climbing. This discrepancy may give the impression that motorcycle riding is riskier than rock climbing and that the mortality rates for motorcycling must therefore be comparably higher. But mortality rates can be expressed in a variety of units, making direct comparisons difficult. For instance, the fatality rate for motorcycling is typically expressed in deaths to miles instead of deaths to hours traveled. In the US, the motorcycle fatality rate is about 25 deaths per 100 million miles (National Center for Statistics and Analysis 2021).[5] If we assume an average speed of 50 mph, this figure converts to about one death in 80,000 hours. Surprisingly, this figure actually makes motorcycling look *less* risky than climbing (1 death / 80,000 hours versus 1 death / 7,700 hours). But it is easy to get different results by adjusting our assumption about how fast motorcyclists drive, which suggests there may be something dubious about an attempt to treat "death rate" as a univocal metric for comparison.

If we turn our attention to nonfatal injury rates, we can use the established parameter of injury rate per 1,000 hours of sport exposition (Schöffl et al. 2010). This measure makes sports like handball, at 50 injuries / 1,000 hours, or volleyball, at 6.7 injuries / 1,000 hours,[6] look considerably riskier than mountaineering and traditional climbing, which, according to one study by Schussman et al. (1990), produces just 0.56 injures in 1,000 hours. But this conclusion seems odd, given the popular judgment that mountaineering and climbing are high-risk sports whereas handball and volleyball are not. To explain this judgment, we might appeal to Kajtna and Tušak's (2004) definition of a "high-risk" sport as one where the possibility of severe injury or death is an inherent part of the activity. By this standard, activities like snowboarding, mountain biking, and surfing would also be categorized as high-risk despite their relatively low injury rates.[7] But this undermines the utility of injury rates for informing our relative impressions of the riskiness of different activities and conflicts with other proposed definitions of high-risk sports like that from Backx et al. (1991) – namely, those performed with a high jump or contact rate (e.g., basketball or volleyball).

Even if we could keep the units consistent and identify a standard minimum value for uncertainty beyond which something (outcome, activity) could be universally accepted as a significant risk (say, e.g., 40% chance of the unwanted outcome X from behavior Y), we would still have the practical problem of determining when that threshold gets met. This determination can be especially difficult in the case of sports because here a participant's real chances of injury or death will depend considerably on that individual's skill level, experience, and the details of their situation.

Figure 1.2 *Use at your own risk*. This sign, posted at the entrance to the famous Pinball terrain park at Northstar, CA, urges skiers and snowboarders to understand the risks associated with their sport. Like rock climbing, freestyle skiing and snowboarding are activities in which serious injury or death are potential outcomes, a fact which likely contributes to the popular impression of them as high-risk sports. By alerting riders to this risk, the sign applies a definition of *risk* as possible outcome: the "risk" is injury or death. No explicit reference to the likelihood of these outcomes is evidently necessary for people to appreciate and abide the warning; however, there may be an implicit admonition to know one's capabilities and limits and to ride accordingly, thereby reducing the chance of harm.

To see this, let's return to our earlier observation that there are no laws requiring the use of helmets for rock climbing. This does not mean that a climber who forgoes a helmet assumes no increased risk with this choice. But how much is the increase? It may be appreciable for a beginner or on loose terrain, where rockfall is a frequent threat. But it may be negligible for an experienced climber on a route with solid rock that they consider very easy, even though it might look significant to someone with less experience. Moreover, a helmet would seem useless for someone like Alex Honnold, who does much of his climbing without ropes or other safety gear on routes where a fall would certainly be fatal.[8]

If a beginner opts for a helmet, this might reduce their odds of serious injury. Regardless, their chance of accident is probably going to be considerably higher than general rates would suggest, because these rates report outcomes for climbers from a broad range of skill levels. Importantly, then, there can be huge variability within a given activity such that broad-stroke indicators like the existence of safety gear mandates or mean accident/mortality rates are poor measures of that activity's riskiness for any one individual – and thus, perhaps, poor determinants of our attitudes toward those risks.

FRAME 1: The risks of mountaineering

In "A Plea for Risk" (2013), Philip Ebert and Simon Robertson investigate disagreements about the riskiness of mountaineering between those who practice the sport and those who do not. They point out that the nonmountaineer will tend to see the activity as riskier and even regard it as reckless or irresponsible, whereas the mountaineer will tend to describe the risks as "acceptable" and may accuse the nonmountaineer of overestimating them. Likely, this disagreement stems partly from differing presumptions about the likelihood of bad outcomes. The uncertainty is more unquantifiable for the nonmountaineer, who looks at a rock face and can think only of how crazy it is that anyone should climb it, but to the eye of a trained mountaineer, the rock "present[s] a more specifiable and indeed lower risk" (50). However, the disagreement about risks is not just a disagreement about the presumed likelihood of a bad outcome. According to the authors, emotions also play an important role. If one feels an emotional attachment to the activity, as mountaineers do, they are more likely to judge the risks lower. Conversely, nonmountaineers, who have no such attachment, will judge the risks higher.

Thus, each party has both strengths and weaknesses concerning their ability to think accurately about the risks. The mountaineer is pulled by her affection for the activity to possibly underestimate the dangers, but her competency gives her the ability to make informed judgments about how a particular climb may go. The nonmountaineer is under no compulsion from affection, but his inexperience leaves him with an uncomfortable uncertainty that might prompt him to exaggerate the dangers.

What do you think? Which group, if either, is more likely to be "correct" in their risk judgment? What sort of evidence would be needed in order to settle this question? Would accident statistics be enough? If so, what kind?

1.2.3 Exposure

What counts as a risk in one set of circumstances may not be a risk in other circumstances. What counts as a risk for one person may not be a risk for another.

If, for example, a virus posed a danger only to people with a certain uncommon illness, it could be identified as a risk for that subpopulation, but not as a risk to public health. An example would be *general paresis*, which is due to damage to the brain from untreated syphilis. For an overwhelmingly large part of the population, there is little or no chance of exposure to syphilis bacteria. So although some are at risk, *general paresis* is not considered a risk to public health.

Whether a threat rises to the status of a public health risk might be a function of the number of people exposed to it and of the chance of exposure for that subpopulation. But the size of the exposed group isn't all that matters. Level of influence, visibility, and power of the exposed group are also major factors. This is one explanation that only 10% of global spending on health research is allocated to conditions or diseases that, however, "account for 90% of the global disease burden" (Morel 2003: 35). The bulk of the global disease burden is shouldered by nations and people groups with less influence, visibility, and power.

Some hazards disproportionately impact low-income and minority communities (Bolin & Kurtz 2018). Studies have found that higher rates of health issues, such as anemia, kidney disease, septicemia, tuberculosis, infant mortality, and low birth weight, are reported in communities located near large-scale animal farm facilities (Heederik et al. 2007). A 2018 study from North Carolina revealed that more African American and Native American residents live in zip codes with large hog farms (or CAFOs, concentrated animal feeding operations) compared to those living in areas without such facilities, and those who live near CAFOs have higher death rates from a variety of causes than comparable state residents who live farther away from such facilities (Kravchenko et al. 2018). Moreover, as the COVID-19 pandemic has made shockingly clear, some parts of the population are more exposed than others to social disruptions, in terms of health and economic status, and barriers to recovery (Gross et al. 2020). Thus, the judgment that something is a risk may intersect with questions about justice and social equity – a possibility we develop further in Chapter 5.

To summarize our findings in this section: the judgment of risk involves regard for relevant facts about uncertainty, unwanted consequences, and exposure. But in addition to those facts, there are also social, ethical, and political choices about the significance to be attached to them.

1.3 What is involved in the judgment of risk

1.3.1 Communication and its perils

One may be tempted to think that risks, because they have so much significance for our life and survival, will always be detectable and adequately perceived. Indeed, sometimes a risk is plainly such. Eating raw meat that has been sitting on the counter for days, drinking dirty water, dressing lightly for cold weather – these behaviors are obviously risky. But sometimes a risk goes largely unrecognized because those who are exposed may not have the voice to be heard or because the correlation between cause and effect is not obvious (as is the case between chemically contaminated drinking water and health problems such as cancer; see Paddock 2019).

Typically, a phenomenon X will first be identified as risk among a small circle of people, called "activists," who then spread the word to the larger population, urging them to recognize X as a risk. The activists may include the scientists who uncovered the phenomenon, or institutions in charge of public welfare, or civil rights or environment advocates. Or they may be individuals, laypersons who have personal experiences of some issues and who take up the challenge of making them public. Such figures include Erin Brockovich, who led the fight against the contamination of the groundwater of the Southern California town of Hinkley with hexavalent chromium,[9] or lawyer Robert Bilott, who brought to light the chemical manufacturer's responsibility for the contamination of the water supply around Parkersburg in West Virginia.[10]

Psychologists have developed a model of communication, called *the social amplification approach* (SARF), that explicates the process of public recognition of a risk as such by distinguishing different stages (Kasperson et al. 1988; Renn et al. 1992). The first stage is the reception of information, which depends on several social processes: the operation of channels that disseminate the information, the role of social institutions in modifying signals, and individual factors involved in the interpretation of the signals. In the second stage, risk messages "ripple out" through a widening range of social groupings from the individual to the society as a whole. The feedback between these processes results in either amplification or attenuation of risk signals.

Timelines for the COVID-19 pandemic that were published by the World Health Organization (2022) and news media provide nice illustrations of this feedback process. Because of the public scrutiny of "who knew what and when they did know it," the timelines show very clearly how the relevant information was disseminated in the various stages of our understanding of the virus, the channels through which this was done, and the social and national agencies and institutions involved. As the information was disseminated, the message about the risk was sometimes amplified, to encourage protective measures, or attenuated, to prevent panic or overreaction. These modifications of the message were not geographically or socially homogeneous, with the result that different parts of the public developed very different opinions about the gravity of the situation.

1.3.2 Justification

Statistical correlations are generally the first form of justification given to support a claim about the existence of a risk. The table we showed in Figure 1.1, constructed from a massive study that found significant temperature increase in the period between 1880 and 1935, was based on a statistical analysis of thousands of data points. Statisticians are required to go to extraordinary lengths to prevent bias in sampling, so that the data can be taken to be properly representative of the target conditions, and in the assumptions involved in that analysis.

But controversies can emerge from inquiries into the methods used to gather and interpret statistical data. For example, in the case of global warming, one early objection was that temperature data tended to be collected predominantly in regions surrounding centers with higher population density (the "urban heat island effect"). Methodological flaws like that one can be rectified. But as we will see in the chapters on risk assessment (Chapter 3) and risk management (Chapter 5), debates over what data should be collected to provide justification for a claim about risk will invariably surface to complicate the process. This is true about scientific study in general, but especially true about the science of risks, given the multidimensional character of its subject. Moreover, scientists assume a certain kind of risk whenever they interpret data. This "inductive risk," as it is called, is inherent to science. It can be managed, but not eliminated. As for any risk, managing inductive risk involves choices, particularly about how much evidence is evidence enough. Again, even though this is true for science in general, the choices are more likely to be controversial in risk studies because of the dimensions of uncertainty, unwantedness, and exposure. And also, because of those dimensions, the controversy may reach the public domain and from there create demand on scientists to produce more evidence or stronger explanation of the evidence.

Conclusions from the statistical data are typically challenged with the familiar caution that *correlation is not causation*: the fact that two phenomena vary with each other does not necessarily mean that one causes the other to occur. It's been shown, for instance, that in the aftermath of certain highly publicized suicides, the number of people who die in airline crashes increases by an alarming percentage, and the number of automobile fatalities skyrockets as well (Cialdini 2021: 168). This could suggest that the publicity surrounding the suicides somehow *causes* the increase in accidents, but it could also simply mean that the social conditions that make some people commit suicide cause others to die accidentally (Cialdini 2021: 168).[11]

To understand the import of this challenge, one must distinguish two forms of cause: *direct causes* and *common causes*. If I reset all the clocks in the house to daylight saving time, I am interfering with each of them and directly causing them to show a certain time at sunrise and sunset. That they all agree in the time they show, at any given moment, however, is not because they interfere with each other; it is due to the common cause, which is my action upon each of them. (Likewise, in the second explanation for the link between publicized suicide stories and crashes, social conditions appear as the common cause of both the suicides and the transportation accidents.)

When a correlation is found between two factors, models may differ in whether they attribute it to direct causation or to a common cause. In the case of the correlation between cigarette smoking and lung cancer, it was possible at the outset to suggest that this was due to a common cause – for example, a genetic disposition to both lung cancer and addiction to tobacco. In principle, there are empirical tests to distinguish the two. If effects A and B are correlated due to a common cause C, then manipulating A will not change B. In the case of my synchronized clocks, that is easily tested: adjusting one clock has no effect on what the other clock shows, while interfering with me when I am resetting the clocks may do so.

But it may not always be possible, for practical or ethical reasons, to manipulate the suspected cause directly. For instance, we don't want to manipulate people into doing things suspected to be unhealthy just to get evidence that the behaviors really are unhealthy. We would not want to increase publicity over suicides if we suspect, as many now do, that media reporting can trigger additional suicides (Niederkrotenthaler et al. 2020). We cannot erase industrialization to show that climate warming would not have happened without it. And we would not want to increase warming to show that it makes us worse off. It is true that scientists can use what has already happened in different conditions to identify possible causal factors and build causal models that can be used to make inferences about what will happen when these factors take different values. For instance, they may consult data from various historical cases about the impact of toxically contaminated water on the environment or on people. Still, they cannot conduct a systematic study of this impact that would consist in carefully varying the degree of contamination to measure the difference in the impact.

Scientists often attempt to rectify these limitations by experimenting on animals instead of humans. For instance, one of the earliest studies to suggest a link between e-cigarettes and lung cancer obtained their results by exposing a group of mice to nicotine-rich vapor that, after 12 weeks, showed DNA damage to their lungs, heart, and bladder (Tang et al. 2019). To obtain these results, scientists not only had to expose mice to an expected carcinogen but also had to kill their subjects to autopsy their tissues. Methodologies like this give us information that we could not gather from experiments on people. However, species differences between humans and animals (mice, in this case) confound efforts to translate such findings to humans, and experts disagree over the extent to which animal experiments provide a legitimate basis for generalizations to humans (Van der Worp et al. 2010; O'Connor & Sargeant 2014).

1.4 Risk: a thick concept

The philosopher Bernard Williams (1985) introduced the term *thick concept* to refer to terms that express an evaluation while also being substantially descriptive. Thin concepts, by contrast, can be evaluative without having any factual content of their own. For example, the term "good" is evaluative, but factual content comes only in its combination with other terms: a good woman may not be a good singer; a good artist may not be a good citizen. On the other hand, when we call an action cruel, for example, we are describing a certain kind of action, like using animals in fighting rings or saying certain words about someone, that inflicts pain in a specific manner, while also expressing the evaluative judgment that the action is morally wrong.

In this section, we develop reasons to construe the concept of risk as a thick concept that has both a descriptive objective component and an evaluative subjective component, which is itself comprised of multiple layers.[12]

1.4.1 Objective aspects of risk

Judgments about risk refer to facts – possible outcomes that we take to be essentially objective. Backcountry skiing is considered risky because it exposes one to the possibility of getting caught in an avalanche. Official announcements of the "risk of avalanche" are an estimation of the likelihood of such an event and refer to physical conditions that typically affect this likelihood, such as stability of the snowpack and the shape, direction, and degree of slope. The possible outcome of concern is for the skier to be caught in an avalanche, and that would be as much an event in nature as the avalanche's uprooting a tree.

Likewise, a diagnosis of the "risk of heart attack" refers to the chance or probability that a heart attack will occur as determined by factors such as age, obesity, blood pressure, and cholesterol level. The heart attack itself occurs when an artery supplying the heart with blood and oxygen becomes blocked, and the deprivation of blood causes damage to the heart muscle. This occurrence is just the sort of event, like blockage in a car's fuel pump, that we take to be objective. In other words, it is something that we can physically investigate and characterize through measurements and other descriptive devices.

This is not to deny that normative judgments are involved in the production of those physical characterizations. Indeed, in Chapter 3, we will introduce some important ways in which such normative judgments are involved in scientific risk assessment. Nor do we speak of objectivity here in the sense in which it appears in debates about the nature of science. "Objective" can be meant in many ways, and here we just mean it in the sense of something that we refer to through descriptive judgments (Lloyd 1995).

When we don't wear a face mask during a pandemic of an airborne disease, we assume the risk of contracting an illness that would manifest, say, in fever and exhaustion. When we ski, we risk falling and breaking a leg. When we say something very cruel to a friend, we risk losing them. The terms "fever," "exhaustion," "breaking a leg," and "losing someone" describe factual and commonly accessible states of affairs. They refer to something that can happen to different people, even if the experience of its happening will vary by person. And they refer to something that can, in some ways, be measured, even if the measurement is of a form that we, as a certain type of beings or as members of a certain type of society, have invented. Now, we can talk of the risk of being scared (say, by a horror film), and "being scared" does refer to an emotion that is a certain kind of subjective experience. But even in that case, what we are referring to is something that may happen, happen to us, in the way breaking a leg could happen to us; we are not referring immediately to our perceptions of being afraid.

So to be called risks, terms like "avalanche," "fever," and "losing someone" must describe objective possibilities. However, not just any such description can be used to refer to a risk. "Winning the lottery" is descriptive in the same way but generally does not refer to a risk. That is because risks only appear as such upon exposure to the possibility of something unwanted. The reason we do not want to be injured or killed in an avalanche is that we value our physical health and lives. Although this fact seems obvious, it needs to be said, lest we mistake a process that is free of controversial values for one that is free of any values (Hansson 2007: 22).

1.4.2 Subjective aspects of risk

1.4.2.1 Values

Identifying a risk is not a value-free process (Hansson 2007: 21–27). We identify states of affairs that are undesirable, and human desires reflect their values. Rana Ahmad has offered a thorough analysis of the value component of risk. She resolves the so-called "risk values" into three main categories: standard, aspirational, and moral.

Standard values (also called "primary goods") are the ones most associated with situations or events we describe as risky. They are connected to our "basic sense of well-being" (Ahmad 2009: 139). In addition to life and physical health, which were already mentioned, these values include protection from loss of something cherished or important, such as money, time, or other property. Despite exceptions, which should be respected, people tend to agree on the "fundamental" interests that are important to human well-being:

> Life, health, dignity, the physical integrity of the body, autonomy and freedom of movement, the interest in not experiencing severe pain, the interest

> in not experiencing severe mental or emotional distress, and certain kinds of property interest.
>
> (Perry 2007: 202)

Aspirational values are "those things that we aspire to in life such as our career or personal goals, or our hopes and dreams" (Ahmad 2009: 126). *Moral values* include "goodness, justice, honesty, etc." They can also include notions about human rights and vaguer intuitions about, say, what is "natural" versus "unnatural" (Hansson 2007: 25).

These values may all enter into how certain things are classified as risks or as risky. They are not aspects of the possible outcomes considered as events in nature but reflected in our evaluation of how those outcomes relate to what is wanted, desired, or desirable.

In the literature about risk, the potential for harm is often synonymous with risk, with both being (broadly) defined as whatever threatens what is of value to people. "A risky action," explains philosopher Stephen Perry, "[is] one that . . . gives rise to a morally significant risk of harm to [a] person" (Perry 2007: 198).

Thus, picking and eating wild mushrooms is a risky action because it exposes one to the possibility of harm by poison. Wild mushrooms are "harmful" insofar as they pose a threat to our life and health. In this example, harm does appear to be an inseparable component of risk. However, "harm" is a very general term with a broad range of technical and colloquial uses, including some where harm is not something unwanted. Pain from physical injury, which is perhaps the most common form of harm, can produce pleasure in some individuals rather than displeasure. Masochists are an obvious example, although such pleasure frequently occurs in mild form in athletes who "feel the burn" (of lactic acid) when working out or who achieve a "runner's high" through physical exhaustion. For these people, the prospect of at least some types of physical harm is desirable and therefore something to be pursued rather than avoided.

Other harms are wanted not for their own sake but are accepted as a means to prevent greater harms. Invasive surgical procedures, which compromise the integrity of the body, are a classic example. When a stage IIB melanoma is removed from someone's back, the surgeon may extract a remarkably large chunk of flesh, remove lymph nodes as well, and damage nerves in the process.[13] Patients may regard some of these outcomes for the sake of extending their life by many years. Indeed, the possibility of a painful path to recovery after a lifesaving surgery, however unwanted in itself, is not a risk, unless the pain interferes with the recovery itself.

1.4.2.2 Dependence on assessment

The concepts of risk and danger both have descriptive and evaluative components. But according to Garland, whereas *danger* is the potential for harm that inheres in some thing or situation, *risk* involves a measure of the likelihood and extent of that potential being realized. There may be unrecognized dangers, but risks "never exist outside of our knowledge of them," for they are "the product of future-oriented human calculations – assessments made by people in the face of an uncertain world and the possibilities that it holds for them" (2003: 52).

We may be able to assess the likelihood on the basis of fairly accurate measures of hazard frequency. The North American Avalanche Risk Scale, for example, is a quantitative measure of the potential for avalanches to cause harm or injury to backcountry travelers. It reports the likelihood, size, and distribution of avalanches (Statham et al. 2010). Yet Ahmad points out that for something to count as a risk, the assessment of likelihood need not be "expressed explicitly in terms of some estimated or measured probability" (2009: 92). The probabilistic predictions could be merely speculative, "impressionistic guesses, informed estimates," as with, say, the risk of getting poisoned by a wild mushroom that you picked out yourself (Garland 2003: 52).

Whatever the case, the core lesson is that risks depend for their existence, as part of the concept, on human knowledge and cognitions in ways that dangers do not. According to Thomas Nagel, "the appropriate form of a subjective attitude toward one's own future is expectation" (1986: 225). To grasp some aspect of your future "from within," "you must try to look *forward* to it – to see it as a *prospect*" (ibid.) It is risks, rather than dangers, that appear on the horizon of human expectation; it is only risks that are graspable "from within." An untold number of dangers exist "out there" in the world, many of which we are unaware. However, once they become an actual prospect for us, their potential for adverse consequences becomes part of a concrete vision for our future. We are encouraged to act on that vision because it is our future that is at stake. Thus, a risk is a call to action.

1.4.2.3 Dependence on exposure

An important difference between "risk" and "danger" is that risks exist only in relation to a subject exposed to them. Exposure to a danger, be it actual or potential, is crucial for identifying a risk as such.

This is reflected in differences in how we classify things as dangerous or as risky. We may say of the death cap fungus or whitewater rapids that they are dangerous,[14] and that is so whether or not we have any dealings with them. What is risky, on the other hand, is typically associated with an activity – foraging, whitewater kayaking – and the risk comes from our engaging in this activity (getting poisoned, being injured or killed in a rapid). A hazard is not classified as a risk until someone is or may be exposed to it.

Voluntary exposure

People often willingly expose themselves to hazards. When they do, they are taking voluntary risks. Mountaineering or backcountry skiing are relatively straightforward examples. Here, the volitional agent puts their own interests (for physical well-being, freedom from pain, etc.) on the line by directly exposing those interests to the possibility of harm. It is primarily from the perspective of the voluntary agents themselves that certain outcomes are evaluated negatively and judged undesirable.

Involuntary and unknowing exposure

Of course, willful exposure to danger is not the only way people get into situations where they face a significant risk of harm. Sometimes, people get into these situations on account of the risky actions of others, as when someone ignores warnings and sets off fireworks or lights a campfire in a fire hazard severity zone.[15] Thus, people "impose" risks on other people, often without their consent or even their knowledge. Given that, in such cases, a subject whose interests are at risk might not even know about the threat, it is harder to locate the evaluative component of the judgment that a risk has been imposed. One suggestion is to consider the subject's preferences in a *counterfactual* way – to ask, in other words, how they might feel if they did know about the danger to which they've been exposed. Suppose, as Stephen Perry (2007) imagines, that someone has buried a barrel of toxic waste underneath my house. Within the next ten years:

> There is a 30% chance that . . . this barrel will corrode and leak an extremely toxic substance into the groundwater. If such leakage occurs, it will pose, let us say, a 10% risk of death to me, the resident of the house. Taking these two risks together, there is a 3% risk that I might die as a result of having this noxious barrel stashed under my house.
>
> (200)

We can speculate along with Perry that living with this state of affairs would be most unwelcome, and this preference seems capable of warranting an ascription of risk, even if it is counterfactually dependent on knowledge of a hazard that I do actually possess. (Because, say, I am unaware of the presence of the barrel.)

Perry's buried waste example is a case of both involuntary and unknowing exposure to a hazard. To understand how such exposure could be judged a risk, it proved helpful to think counterfactually about what would be the case if the subject had been aware and (thus) capable of making this judgment themselves. But there are cases of imposed risk where this way of thinking is not so clear-cut, given the nature of the subjects who are exposed to the possible harm. Consider a dog left in a car on a hot day, a child left alone in the park or store, a fetus in a person who drinks or smokes. These are all circumstances in which it could plausibly be insisted that an "unknowing" subject is at risk. Because the subject is unknowing, we might try to justify the judgment using the previous counterfactual approach: perhaps, while we cannot attribute negative evaluations to the animal, child, or fetus, we can still imagine or suppose that if they were able to form the judgment, they would find the possible outcome (i.e., dying from overheating, getting abducted, being born with defects) undesirable.

The difficulty with this answer is that, in such cases, what we are asked to imagine is not just counterfactual but counter*possible*, since these creatures are cognitively incapable of forming judgments about undesirability. The problem isn't the subject's lack of knowledge but the lack of capacity. So in some cases, at least, it seems that evaluations by the subject who is exposed to the danger are not relevant for the ascription of risk. But then, whose judgment *is* relevant?

It may be tempting to attribute the relevant judgment to the dog's owner, the child's parents, or the pregnant person. But some owners do rather cavalierly leave their pets inside the car on a hot day, and some pregnant people do smoke or drink, leaving other people to reprimand their behavior and charge them with putting the dog or fetus at risk. So again, whose evaluation is relevant to the identification of those risks?

What this case of the dog left in a hot car suggests is that judgments about risk can sometimes be construed as expressing social-cultural norms about what counts as "unwanted" harm – norms that, in turn, reflect social-cultural values. We, as a society and as a culture, value the lives and health of our pets and children, so we deem risky any behaviors that jeopardize their safety and could lead to their suffering.

Interestingly, not all instances of possible suffering in animals get classified as risks. Ahmad writes of a place off the coast of South Africa called the "Ring of Death," where thousands of fur seals use one of the rocky islands to raise their young. "The area is known to attract the highest number of great white sharks in the world's oceans," she explains, "because the geographical features of the island make it a perfect hunting ground" (2009: 94). Ahmad suggests that these seals are "at great risk" or that they "take risks" whenever they enter the waters, looking for food.

But it may seem a bit stilted to describe the seals' circumstances and actions this way, even if we allow Ahmad's insight that we "ascribe our values onto the situation" by deeming getting eaten by a shark to be an "obvious harm" (2009: 75, 94). Humans tend to accept, at least as a practical principle, the predator-prey dynamics of the animal kingdom. We don't normally apply the term "risk" to every case of a gazelle stepping out from the bush, or the wildebeest lowering its head for a drink.[16] On the other hand, as mentioned, we certainly do speak of risks when it comes to leaving pets in hot cars or when a species is endangered as a result of human activity. For example, the polar bear is listed by the Northwest Territories as a "species at risk," largely due to threats to their environment caused by global warming – a problem attributed significantly to human behaviors (Species at Risk Committee 2021).

One plausible suggestion, then, is that when animal interests are threatened by exposure to possible harms, it matters whether the exposure is seen as natural or instead imposed on them as a consequence of human actions. We seem to be more inclined to talk of risks in the latter case.

1.4.2.4 Risk as prescription

As we saw, risk involves (negative) subjective evaluations. But value judgments do not appear to be the only kind of evaluation involved in a judgment of risk. The judgment that an activity or situation is risky seems also to imply that a certain action or situation should be avoided. For example, if you are planning a trip to the backcountry and a friend calls to tell you that there is a high risk of avalanche today, it may seem that she is not simply communicating that something undesirable could happen to you but also warning you not to go, or at least to be extracautious.

Understood this way, judgments about risk are *normative* (Ahmad 2009: 85–90). A *norm* is a standard for evaluating behavior or outcomes, and there are at least two main types: *norms for action* and *norms of being*. Norms of being imply that a certain state of affairs ought to obtain, i.e., is valuable or good in a certain sense. Norms for action, on the other hand, imply standards or evaluations for what ought to be done. Judgments of risk are normative in this second sense; they imply prescriptions for action. At the very least, it seems, if you have information that warrants a judgment that you are at risk, then, if you choose to ignore the implied prescription, you should have a reason for doing so.

It is not immediately obvious, though, that this prescriptive function really adds something to the extension of the concept of risk. After all, the idea that something should rather be avoided seems to be already implicit in the notion that it is undesirable or unwanted. And yet the fact that an action may have unwanted consequences does not automatically imply that we do not want to do it. A union worker might feel compelled to strike even though she dreads the consequences of this action. How can this be? Consider that there is a difference between what is desirable or undesirable *prima facie* ("on the face of it", "at first sight") and what is desirable or undesirable *all things considered*. We may have competing desires, with different priorities, and so to judge something unwanted *prima facie* cannot always immediately bring with it the prescription to avoid it. On the other hand, it would seem to be a paradigm of irrationality to expose ourselves to risks for no reason at all, *all things considered*, because there would be nothing left to counterbalance the disvalue attached to the risk.

Thus, we might expect the prescriptive dimension of the concept of risk to appear inessential in some cases. Suppose we call a friend and tell them there is a *risk* that we might arrive later than expected. This does convey that we find the prospect undesirable, whereas just saying that we might arrive later would not. And it does imply some prescriptions: they should not expect us on time, they should not start worrying if we are not on time, they should not plan something that requires us to be on time. But it isn't obvious that these prescriptions are any more strongly conveyed by using the word "risk" as opposed to simply admitting that we might arrive late.

However, in many cases, the prescriptive dimension of risk is strongly present. Official communication about the risk of climate warming or the risk of contamination by the coronavirus carries with it the prescription that we should recycle and reduce our consumption of water or should act in ways that protect us and others from contamination. Such might be the case in general for the communication of societal risks. And it may seem that this has only to do with the impact of our behavior on others. But we find similar pressures in communications about individual risks as well: announcements concerning the risk of lung cancer or the risk of sexually transmitted disease convey that we should not smoke or have unprotected casual sex. In all these communications, the word "risk" appears to function partly as an expression of social norms regarding certain behaviors.

When we tell a teenager who is smoking about the risk of lung cancer, or someone who uses a weedwhacker for the first time about the risk of cutting themselves, we are trying to inform them of something they may not know and, at the same time, are trying to give them reasons to act a certain way. The distinction between the motivating reason and the normative reason a person may have to act could be helpful for clarifying this intent. A *motivating reason* is internal to the agent, whereas a *normative reason* is independent of the agent's beliefs and is based on facts (Parfit & Broome 1997). Philosopher Derek Parfit gives an example of someone who jumps out of their hotel window because they believe, falsely, that the hotel is on fire (1997: 99). They have a motivating reason to jump out of the window because they do not want to die in the fire, but no normative reason to jump because, in fact, there is no fire. Telling the young smoker about the risk of lung cancer communicates that they have normative reasons to avoid the activity while implying that they may not know these reasons or take them seriously enough. This might be what my friend is doing when she calls me to tell me about the high risk of avalanche. It is also why we encourage people to "*know* the risks," e.g., of vaping, rideshare services, or unprotected sex. In some cases, discourse on risk can thus be thought of, at least in part, as an effort to reconcile motivating reasons with normative ones.

This type of prescriptive communication about risks probably assumes that the motivation to avoid possible harm has purchase or authority on an agent, in absence of any overriding desires or concerns, and therefore the only reason the agent would be insufficiently motivated to avoid a risk is that the normative reasons to do so are unknown to them. This assumption might turn out to be true in some cases, but results from studies in risk awareness and risk behavior suggest that it is far from being always the case. It sometimes seems that knowing more, increased awareness about a risk, does translate into more preparedness and mitigating behavior (Dryhurst et al. 2020; Floyd et al. 2000; Grima et al. 2021), and sometimes it seems not to (Wachinger et al. 2013).

So there are two forms of prescriptive messages associated with communications about risk: providing motivating reasons or providing normative reasons. But these two forms are not exclusive of each other. For example, a parent who describes unprotected sex as "risky" may be attempting to provide their child with normative reasons to avoid the behavior. But this attempt may be compounded (wittingly or not) with moral norms against extramarital sex, leading to potential confusion about the content of the communication.

FRAME 2: When is it "too risky"?

In a previous frame, we introduced "A Plea for Risk" and related the authors' insights about the disagreement between mountaineers and nonmountaineers regarding the risks associated with mountaineering. Late in the article, Ebert and Robertson present the idea that this disagreement is focused on something deeper than facts about accidents and potential consequences. They believe a denouncement of the sport as "too risky" expresses a normative judgment that the risks a mountaineer willingly takes are unjustified. In other words, the disagreement is over the question of whether mountaineering is a justifiable activity, and a nonmountaineer's various appeals to the riskiness are veiled substitutes for the claim that it is not. The authors present three possible positions regarding the normative status of mountaineering (56–57):

> [Risky] Mountaineering is not a justifiable activity, and that is because of the risks it involves.
> [Despite] Mountaineering endeavors can be justified; when they are justified, they are justified (a) *despite* the risks they involve and (b) by the further goods . . . they bring.
> [Because] Mountaineering endeavors can be justified (in part) *because* of the value that engaging with mountaineering risks has.

Which of these three positions best represents your own view of mountaineering? Why is this your view, and what are some of the influences that have led you to it?

1.5 Conclusion

Our efforts to clarify the conditions under which we refer to something as risk or to a situation or activity as risky, and what is implied in communicating to others that something is a risk or that a situation or activity is risky, revealed that the concept of risk is complex and multilayered. We have identified three main conditions for its application: uncertainty, exposure, and a negative evaluation that we could broadly describe as unwantedness.

To identify something as a risk requires identifying possible but uncertain outcomes of a situation that would count as harm, as loss, or more generally as unwanted. It also requires that someone who would be harmed be exposed to the uncertain outcome. We saw that the person exposed is not necessarily the one making or even able to make the judgment that the possible outcome is unwanted or would be harmful, since a child, a dog, or a fetus could be said to be exposed to a risk. It also requires the likelihood of effect to exceed a certain threshold, but this threshold will be different for different people or in different contexts and will depend on the severity of the possible outcomes.

With its criteria of application involving both factual and normative aspects, thus objective and subjective dimensions, risk is said to be a *thick concept.* Moreover, we saw that the subjective dimension is layered in that referring to risk may include different kinds of normative judgments (explicitly or not).

Note, finally, that people who study and write about risk sometimes make a distinction between "objective risk" and "subjective risk" – as if there were two separate concepts. This is not the distinction that we make when we speak of the objective and the subjective dimensions of risk. We maintain that there is just one concept of risk and that the concept has these two dimensions. This is evidenced by our discussion of the general conditions in which we use the concept, what those conditions require, and what they allow and disallow.

Review questions

1. A risk occurs when we confront a course of action that:
   A. Has possible, but not certain, negative consequences.
   B. Has uncertain consequences of any nature.
   C. Has certain negative consequences.
2. What is one reason people differ in their judgments about a risk?
   A. They cannot foresee any of its possible consequences.
   B. They disagree about how harmful its possible consequences are.
   C. They refuse to accept uncertainty.
3. The uncertainty associated with risky actions . . .
   A. Is reducible to a single numerical figure, which is the same for anyone who takes the action.

   B. Is reducible to a unique numerical figure, but that figure can change depending on who is taking the action and in what context.
   C. Is not reducible to a unique numerical figure, due to large variability regarding who is doing the activity and in what context.
4. What is one reason a risk can go largely unnoticed in the public sphere?
   A. No one has managed to uncover the phenomenon or sees that there's a threat.
   B. Those who are exposed to the possibility of harm are a marginal group whose voices are unheard.
   C. As a rule, the public generally pays little attention to governments and other social institutions when they speak up about societal threats.
5. Statistical correlations are commonly used to justify claims about the existence of a risk. But these correlations can incite controversy. This is partly because . . .
   A. Decisions about what data should be collected or how much evidence is enough cannot be made in a straightforward, value-free manner.
   B. Statistical correlations never point to causal relationships.
   C. Many statisticians use vague and unproven methodologies to collect their data.
6. What makes risk a *thick concept*?
   A. It has many different definitions and occurs frequently in everyday conversations as well as in technical contexts.
   B. It expresses an evaluation without referring to facts.
   C. It expresses an evaluation while also referring to facts.
7. In what sense can the concept of risk be said to be objective?
   A. It refers to facts about physical reality that we can describe and measure according to shared conventions.
   B. It can be applied without influence from emotions or prejudices.
   C. It derives its character and conditions of application from science.
8. In what sense can the concept of risk be said to be subjective?
   A. It does not refer to any facts that we can describe or measure.
   B. Its application is guided by human values and desires.
   C. There are no correct conditions for its use; anything can be called a risk, depending on who's making the judgment.
9. What is the main difference between risk and danger?
   A. There is danger only when there are possible dramatic consequences.
   B. There is risk only with exposure to possible negative consequences.
   C. There is risk only if negative consequences can be avoided.
10. Which of the following statements illustrates the prescriptive function of "risk"?
   A. Anyone who has a parent with Huntington's disease has a fifty-fifty chance of inheriting the gene that causes the disease and, thus, of developing the condition themselves.

B. Sports betters have two options for wagers: bet to risk or bet to win. When you bet to risk, you choose a specific amount to bet regardless of the odds. When you bet to win, you aim for a certain win amount and bet whatever is needed to win that amount based on the odds. Betting to risk gives you more control over your bet because you decide how much to risk rather than letting the odds determine this amount.

C. Drowsy driving is extremely risky. It significantly increases the chances of serious accident. All it takes is a few seconds of dozing off for your car to veer off the road or collide with another vehicle. If you're driving and you realize that you're feeling tired, pull over and nap or get someone else to drive. Stay alert. Stay alive.

Discussion topics

1. When is the last time you took a significant risk? What made the action risky in your mind? What are the worst outcomes that you considered, and how likely did you think these were to occur? What made you ultimately decide to take the risk? Did anyone else know about your decision, and if so, did they perceive it equally as risky?
2. In this chapter, we mentioned some controversies surrounding climate change and suggested that disagreements over the undesirability of its consequences can help explain why not everyone perceives the threat similarly. Physical "risks" that have been linked to climate change include extreme heat, drought, sea level rise, wildfires, hurricanes, and floods. The health and functioning of the greater biosphere are also threatened, as climate change may contribute to the degradation and fragmentation of ecosystems, and certain animal populations or species could become extinct. (Examples include polar bears; certain fish, frogs, and sea turtles; staghorn coral; koalas; monarch butterflies.) How undesirable are these potential outcomes to you? Are there some that you find more distressing than others? Which possibility, for you, is the most unwanted, and which is the least?
3. Recall the example of the pregnant woman who drinks and smokes without much regard for the fetus. Would you say that the fetus is at risk in this situation or that it is being subjected to a risk? How would you describe this "risk"? What would you say if the woman doing the drinking and smoking is not particularly concerned with outcomes and doesn't believe they're doing anything risky? Clearly, there may be some physiological consequences for the developing fetus that will manifest after birth, but how can we say these consequences are negative or bad if neither the fetus (due to lack of capacity) nor the woman (due to lack of concern) judges them to be so?

Notes

1 We take the fairly common view that word usage is subject to statistical variation and that, for this reason, we cannot always identify "the" meaning of a word. We accept the general strategy for definitions outlined by Irving Copi, Carl Cohen, and Kenneth McMahon in their *Introduction to Logic*, which is to "give an account of its various meanings, as determined by the uses it has in actual speech and writing" (2014: 85). But of course, we are also looking beyond common usage in efforts to identify theoretically adequate or scientifically useful descriptions of the things to which the term "risk" applies.

2 In the 1960s, three Oregon hunters died after drinking from a coffeepot that a rough-skinned newt had crawled into, presumably without their knowing (Zimmer 2019).

3 Garland is here alluding to Ulrich Beck's concept of a "risk society" (Beck 2004). According to Beck, modern societies have become mostly preoccupied with managing the risks, like ecological risks, technological risks, social risks, that were created by their own forms of social and technological development.

4 The Gallup polls referenced here asks, broadly, about "illegal immigration," which conflates different sorts of unauthorized immigration ("unauthorized" being the term used by the Department of Homeland Security – see, e.g. www.dhs.gov/immigration-statistics/population-estimates/unauthorized-resident). Unauthorized immigration may refer to certain applicants to legal permanent resident status and considered to be part of the resident unauthorized population until they have been granted lawful permanent residence even though they may be legally authorized to work. It may also refer to migrants having crossed the border without inspection at the border (a misdemeanor) or to those overstaying their visas (a civil violation). Asking about "illegal immigration" as this survey does may be taken to refer to a broader segment of the immigrant population, and that includes, for instance, migrants paroled as they are applying for asylum. It is possible, therefore, that "illegal immigration" is identified as a risk only under this vague characterization.

5 The fatality rate is relatively consistent from year 2010 to year 2019.

6 Both rates taken from Schöffl et al. 2010.

7 1 injury/1000 hrs., 1 injury/1000 hrs., and 0.41 injury/1000 hrs., respectively. Rates taken from Schöffl et al. 2010.

8 The 2018 documentary *Free Solo* (Chin & Vasarhelyi 2018) is, in many ways, a reflection of the profound risks associated with the activity of free soloing (i.e., climbing alone, without ropes or other safety gear), and most characters in the film address these risks explicitly. It is fitting to note that Alex's choice not to wear a helmet during his historic free solo of El Capitan's "Freerider" route isn't addressed by anyone at any time during the film.

9 The suit was settled in 2006 for $333 million for more than 600 residents.

10 The suit was settled in 2017 for $671 million for more than 3,500 plaintiffs.

11 In fact, the latter of these two explanations probably seems the more sensible. However, Robert Cialdini, reporting on the work of sociologist David Phillips, makes a compelling case for the former explanation in his popular book *Influence* (2021). The theory is that the car and plane wrecks are actually "hidden instances" of copycat suicide by people who do not want to appear to have killed themselves but would rather appear to have died accidentally. "So, purposively but furtively," Cialdini explains, "they cause the wreck of a car or plane they are operating or are simply riding in" (172). Combined with Phillips' data, this theory suggests that each front-page suicide story kills about 58 people who would otherwise go on living (170).

12 Like Möller (2009) points out, this means that the concept of risk is normative – i.e., includes nondescriptive, evaluative features – and that this normativity is irreducible, i.e., cannot be expressed using only nonnormative terms.

13 If this example seems oddly specific, it is because Christopher Wessels, one of the authors of this book, is citing personal experience.

14 Likewise, we could say that they are hazardous. Some find it important to distinguish between hazards and dangers. Hazards are often held to be more severe than dangers. Workplace safety manuals talk about hazards, like moving parts on equipment, as being manageable through control measures; the controls reduce the danger without removing the hazard. These distinctions are

relatively unimportant for our purposes, and we use "hazard" and "danger" relatively interchangeably to refer to an object or situation that has the possibility of causing harm (e.g., electricity, ladders, chemicals, etc.). Neither becomes a risk until exposure makes it possible to assess the likelihood (probability, chance, etc.) that a person will experience the possible harm.

15 Such behavior is, unfortunately, an all-too-common occurrence in many parts of California and is partly to blame for the state's ever-worsening problem with wildfires. The El Dorado Fire of September 2020, for instance, which burned more than 7,000 acres, was caused by a firework set off at a "gender-reveal party" in Yucaipa, despite ever-present warnings about the dry conditions and critical fire weather.

16 One of our referees, Philip Ebert, has suggested that this generalization may not hold up to scrutiny. Admittedly, it isn't hard to imagine David Attenborough speaking like this in one of his nature documentaries, and the suggestion that these animal behaviors are a form of risk-taking would be unlikely to turn many heads. Still, we believe there are evident dissimilarities in how people think about risk in the case of the dog locked in a hot car, for instance, versus the gazelle stepping from the bush. And we think that reflecting on these dissimilarities can yield insights regarding the nature of risk and its essential connection to human desires, decisions, and sense of responsibility.

References

Aip.org (2022). https://history.aip.org/climate/images/callendar.jpg.

Ackerman, F., & Stanton, E. A. (2007). "The cost of climate change: What we'll pay if global warming continues unchecked." Report commissioned by the Natural Resources Defence Council.

Ackerman, F., & Stanton, E. A. (2010). "The social cost of carbon." *Economics for Equity and Environment (E3 Network)*. http://static1.squarespace.com/static/5ad8 bb3336099 bd6ed7b022a/5b563fd4124f1c89fba029fe/5b564248124f1c89fba0862a/1532379720398/ SocialCostOfCarbon_SEI_20100401.pdf?format=original.

Ahmad, R. A. (2009). *A normative account of risk* (Doctoral dissertation, University of British Columbia).

Aven, T., & Renn, O. (2009). "On risk defined as an event where the outcome is uncertain." *Journal of Risk Research*, 12(1): 1–11. DOI: 10.1080/13669870802488883.

Backx, F. J., Beijer, H. J., Bol, E., & Erich, W. B. (1991). "Injuries in high-risk persons and high-risk sports: A longitudinal study of 1818 school children." *The American Journal of Sports Medicine*, 19(2): 124–130. DOI: 10.1177/036354659101900206.

Beck, U. (2004). *Ulrich Beck: A critical introduction to risk society*. London: Pluto Press. DOI: 10.2307/j.ctt18fs3c4.5.

Boehmer-Christiansen, S. (1993). "Scientific consensus and climate change: The codification of a global research agenda." *Energy & Environment*, 4(4): 362–407. DOI: 10.1177/0958305x9300400403.

Bolin, B., & Kurtz, L. C. (2018). "Race, class, ethnicity, and disaster vulnerability." *Handbook of Disaster Research*: 181–203. DOI: 10.1007/978-3-319-63254-4_10.

Callendar, G. S. (1938). "The artificial production of carbon dioxide and its influence on temperature." *Quarterly Journal of the Royal Meteorological Society*, 64(275): 223–240. DOI: 10.1002/qj.49706427503.

Chin, J., & Vasarhelyi, E. C. (Directors). (2018). *Free solo* [Film]. New York: Little Monster Films.

Cialdini, R. B. (2021). *Influence, new and expanded: The psychology of persuasion*. New York: HarperCollins Publishers.

Congressional testimony of dr. James Hansen, June 23, 1988. (n.d.). Hansen Senate Testimony, June 23, 1988. www.sealevel.info/1988_Hansen_Senate_Testimony.html.

Copi, I. M., Cohen, C., & McMahon, K. (2014). *Introduction to logic*. Harlow. DOI: 10.4324/9781315510897.

Dryhurst, et al. (2020). "Risk perceptions of COVID-19 around the world." *Journal of Risk Research*, 23(7–8): 994–1006. DOI: 10.1080/13669877.2020.1758193.

Ebert, P. A., & Robertson, S. (2013). "A plea for risk." *Royal Institute of Philosophy Supplements*, 73: 45–64. DOI: 10.1017/s1358246113000271.

Edwards, F., Lee, H., & Esposito, M. (2020). "Risk of being killed by police use-of-force in the US by age, race/ethnicity, and sex." *Proceedings of the National Academy of Sciences. Academy of Sciences*. DOI: 10.1073/pnas.1821204116.

Floyd, D. L., Prentice-Dunn, S., & Rogers, R. W. (2000). "A meta-analysis of research on protection motivation theory." *Journal of Applied Social Psychology*, 30(2): 407–429. DOI: 10.1111/j.1559–1816.2000.tb02323.x.

Gallup. (2022, April 11). "Immigration." *Gallup.com*. https://news.gallup.com/poll/1660/immigration.aspx.

Garland, D. (2003). "The rise of risk." In R. Ericson & A. Doyle (eds.), *Risk and morality* (pp. 48–86). Toronto: University of Toronto Press. DOI: 10.3138/9781442679382–005.

Grima, S., et al. (2021). "The relationship between risk perception and risk definition and risk-addressing behaviour during the early COVID-19 stages." *Journal of Risk and Financial Management*, 14: 272. DOI: 10.3390/jrfm14060272.

Gross, C., Essien, U., Pasha, S., Gross, J. R., Wang, S., & Nunez-Smith, M. (2020). "Racial and ethnic disparities in population-level COVID-19 mortality." *Journal of General Internal Medicine*, 35: 3097–3099. DOI: 10.1007/s11606–020–06081-w.

Hansson, S. O. (2007). "Risk and ethics: Three approaches." In T. Lewens (ed.), *Risk. Philosophical perspectives*. Routledge. DOI: 10.4324/9780203962596.

Heederik, D., Sigsgaard, T., Thorne, P. S., Kline, J. N., Avery, R., Bønløkke, J. H., Chrischilles, E. A., Dosman, J. A., Duchaine, C., Kirkhorn, S. R., Kulhankova, K., & Merchant, J. A. (2007). "Health effects of airborne exposures from concentrated animal feeding operations." *Environmental Health Perspectives*, 115(2): 298–302. DOI: 10.1289/ehp.8835.

Kajtna, T., & Tušak, M. (2004). "Some psychological studies of high risk sports." *Kinesiologia Slovenica*, 10(1): 96–105.

Kasperson, R. E., Renn, O., Slovic, P., Brown, H. S., Emel, J., Goble, R., Kasperson, J. X., & Ratick, S. (1988). "The social amplification of risk: A conceptual framework." *Risk Analysis*, 8(2): 177–187. DOI: 10.1111/j.1539–6924.1988.tb01168.x.

Kravchenko, J., Rhew, S. H., Akushevich, I., Agarwal, P., & Lyerly, H. K. (2018). "Mortality and health outcomes in North Carolina communities located in close proximity to hog concentrated animal feeding operations." *North Carolina Medical Journal*, 79(5): 278–288. DOI: 10.18043/ncm.79.5.278.

Le Treut, H., Somerville, R., Cubasch, U., Ding, Y., Mauritzen, C., Mokssit, A., Peterson, T., & Prather, M. (2007). "Historical overview of climate change." In S. Solomon, D. Qin, M. Manning, Z. Chen, M. Marquis, K. B. Averyt, M. Tignor, & H. L. Miller (eds.), *Climate change 2007: The physical science basis. Contribution of working group I to the fourth assessment report of the intergovernmental panel on climate change*. Cambridge and New York: Cambridge University Press.

Lee, T. M., Markowitz, E. M., Howe, P. D., Ko, C. Y., & Leiserowitz, A. A. (2015). "Predictors of public climate change awareness and risk perception around the world." *Nature Climate Change*, 5(11): 1014–1020. DOI: 10.1038/nclimate2728.

Lee, T. R. (1981). "Perception of risk-The public's perception of risk and the question of irrationality." *Proceedings of the Royal Society of London. A. Mathematical and Physical Sciences*, 376(1764): 5–16. DOI: 10.1098/rspa.1981.0072.

Leiserowitz, A., Maibach, E. W., Rosenthal, S., Kotcher, J., Bergquist, P., Ballew, M., . . . Gustafson, A. (2019). "Climate change in the American mind: April 2019." In *Yale University and George Mason University*. New Haven, CT: Yale Program on Climate Change Communication. DOI: 10.31219/osf.io/3bwj8.

Lloyd, L. (1995). "Objectivity and the double standard for feminist epistemologies." *Synthese*, 104(3): 351–381. DOI: 10.1007/bf01064505.

Lowrance, W. W. (1976). "Of acceptable risk: Science and the determination of safety." DOI: 10.1149/1.2132690.

Malcolm, J. R., & Pitelka, L. (2000). *Ecosystems & global climate change: A review of potential impacts on US terrestrial ecosystems and biodiversity*. Arlington: Pew Center on Global Climate Change.

Marris, E. (2019, September 18). "Why young climate activists have captured the world's attention." *Nature News*, Nature Publishing Group. www.nature.com/articles/d41586-019-02696-0. DOI: 10.1038/d41586-019-02696-0.

Möller, N. (2009). *Thick concepts in practice: Normative aspects of risk and safety* (Doctoral thesis, Stockholm: Royal Institute of Technology).

Morel, C. M. (2003). "Neglected diseases: Under-funded research and inadequate health interventions. Can we change this reality?" *EMBO Reports*, 4 Spec No. (Suppl 1): 35–38. DOI: 10.1038/sj.embor.embor851.

Nagel, T. (1986). *The view from nowhere*. New York: Oxford University Press. DOI: 10.21825/philosophica.82423.

National Center for Statistics and Analysis. (2021, April). *Motorcycles: 2019 data* (Traffic Safety Facts. Report No. DOT HS 813 112). National Highway Traffic Safety Administration.

Niederkrotenthaler, T., Braun, M., Pirkis, J., Till, B., Stack, S., Sinyor, M., . . . Spittal, M. J. (2020). Association between suicide reporting in the media and suicide: Systematic review and meta-analysis. *BMJ*, *368*. DOI: 10.1136/bmj.m575.

O'Connor, A. M., & Sargeant, J. M. (2014). "Critical appraisal of studies using laboratory animal models." *ILAR Journal*, 55(3): 405–417. DOI: 10.1093/ilar/ilu038.

Office, C. (2002). "Risk: Improving government's capability to handle risk and uncertainty." Strategy Unit Report.

Oreskes, N., & Conway, E. M. (2011). *Merchants of doubt: How a handful of scientists obscured the truth on issues from tobacco smoke to global warming*. Bloomsbury Publishing. DOI: 10.1086/663066.

Paddock, C. (2019, September 23). "Scientists evaluate cancer risk of drinking water." *Medical News Today*. www.medicalnewstoday.com/articles/326423.

Parfit, D., & Broome, J. (1997). "Reasons and motivation." *Proceedings of the Aristotelian Society, Supplementary Volumes*, 71: 99–146.

Perry, S. (2007). "Risk, harm, interests, and rights." In T. Lewens (ed.), *Risk: Philosophical perspectives* (pp. 190–209). London: Routledge.

Philip, P., Ibrahim, C., & Hodges, C. (2022). *The tuning point: A new economic climate in the United States*. London: Deloitte.

Proctor, R. N. (2012). "The history of the discovery of the cigarette – lung cancer link: Evidentiary traditions, corporate denial, global toll." *Tobacco Control*, 21(2): 87–91. DOI: 10.1136/tobaccocontrol-2011–050338.

Renn, O., Burns, W., Kasperson, J., Kasperson, R., & Slovic, P. (1992). "The social amplification of risk: Theoretical foundations and empirical applications." *Journal of Social Issues*, 48(4): 137–60. DOI: 10.1111/j.1540–4560.1992.tb01949.x.

Rosa, E. A. (1998). "Metatheoretical foundations for post-normal risk." *Journal of Risk Research*, 1(1): 15–44. DOI: 10.1080/136698798377303.

Schöffl, V., Morrison, A., Schwarz, U., Schöffl, I., & Küpper, T. (2010). "Evaluation of injury and fatality risk in rock and ice climbing." *Sports Medicine*, 40(8): 657–679. DOI: 10.2165/11533690–000000000–00000.

Schussman, L. C., Lutz, L. J., Shaw, R. R., & Bohnn, C. R. (1990). The epidemiology of mountaineering and rock climbing accidents. *Journal of Wilderness Medicine*, 1(4): 235–248. DOI: 10.1580/0953–9859–1.4.235.

Shabecoff, P. (1988, June 24). "Global warming has begun, expert tells senate." *The New York Times*. www.nytimes.com/1988/06/24/us/global-warming-has-begun-expert-tells-senate.html.

Species at Risk Committee. (2021). *Species status report for polar bear (Ursus maritimus) in the Northwest territories*. Yellowknife, NT: Species at Risk Committee. www.nwtspeciesatrisk.ca/sites/enr-species-at-risk/files/polar_bear_status_and_reassessment_report_final_april2021.pdf.

Statham, G., Haegeli, P., Birkeland, K. W., Greene, E., Israelson, C., Tremper, B., . . . Kelly, J. (2010). "The North American public avalanche danger scale." *2010 International Snow Science Workshop*: 117–123.

Tang, M. S., Wu, X. R., Lee, H. W., Xia, Y., Deng, F. M., Moreira, A. L., . . . Lepor, H. (2019). "Electronic-cigarette smoke induces lung adenocarcinoma and bladder urothelial hyperplasia in mice." *Proceedings of the National Academy of Sciences*, 116(43): 21727–21731. DOI: 10.1073/pnas.1911321116.

United States. Surgeon General's Advisory Committee on Smoking. (1964). "Smoking and health: Report of the advisory committee to the surgeon general of the public health service (No. 1103)." US Department of Health, Education, and Welfare, Public Health Service.

Van der Worp, H. B., Howells, D. W., Sena, E. S., Porritt, M. J., Rewell, S., O'Collins, V., & Macleod, M. R. (2010). "Can animal models of disease reliably inform human studies?" *PLOS Medicine*, 7(3): e1000245. DOI: 10.1371/journal.pmed.1000245.

Wachinger, G., Renn, O., Begg, C., & Kuhlicke, C. (2013). "The risk perception paradox – implications for governance and communication of natural hazards." *Risk Analysis*, 33: 1049–1065. DOI: 10.1111/j.1539–6924.2012.01942.x.

Williams, B. (1985). *Ethics and the limits of philosophy*. Harvard University Press. DOI: 10.1080/00455091.1989.10716481.

World Health Organization. (2022). *Timeline: Who's covid-19 response*. www.who.int/emergencies/diseases/novel-coronavirus-2019/interactive-timeline.

Zimmer, C. (2019, October 7). "A beautiful web of poison extends a new Strand." *Discover Magazine*. www.discovermagazine.com/planet-earth/a-beautiful-web-of-poison-extends-a-new-strand#.U6t9mfldWRI.

2 Decision-making under risk

Contents

DOI: 10.4324/9780429023521-3

We make decisions, small and large, every day. There is always something at stake: our own safety, benefits to others, benefits and dangers to society, if we are involved in government. If there is a possibility, and some uncertainty, of unwanted consequences, then the decision is made under risk. How should we go about making such a decision?

We will begin with an example from daily life, of a situation that is not too difficult to imagine as one that could be our own. The questions it raises have been addressed in *decision theory*, an interdisciplinary field that is not free of controversy.

Decision theory usually involves an agent, that is, someone who is capable of action and deliberation. An agent may be an ideal agent, a rational-thinking entity that always acts optimally, or an imperfect person, whose choices and actions are affected by their emotions, false beliefs, and incomplete information. To discuss decision theory under risk, and to see how it could help guide actual decision-making, we ask you to consider decisions you could plausibly make in the real world, from the agent's point of view. Let us then consider a scenario you could have conceivably experienced.

2.1 A questionable decision, after rational(?) deliberation

It's 10:15 at night, it's Friday, and you're on Ocean Beach at the end of San Francisco's Sunset District. Today is your friend's birthday and you've had a few drinks. It's now time to go home, and even though you didn't have that much to drink, it was enough to wonder whether you should drive or walk back home. You lost your phone in the sand, so calling a Lyft or an Uber is not an option. Home is only about two miles away, so it's not that far. It's late and you're tired and a bit tipsy, and if you walk, you'll have to walk by cars driving very fast on Lincoln Avenue – nobody there seems to care about the 25 mph limit. So what should you do?

Either option seems risky: you can either make yourself vulnerable to dangerous cars or break the law and risk harming others and yourself at high speed.

It's perhaps not morally commendable, but maybe you'll think about your own safety, first and foremost. There's probably no chance you'll get caught driving under the influence. That simplifies the problem: all you need to consider is just how *likely* you are to be harmed, and how severely, in either case.

So how likely is it? It would be good to have some information, such as statistical records about car and pedestrian casualties. But you lost your phone, so you can't Google that. However, as it happens, you just spent an hour talking to this Google employee who works on solving world poverty by developing algorithms and hopes to replace all political deliberations with automated decision-making. She had been inspired, she told you, by the book *Freakonomics*. And she told you about the chapter where they compare the risk of drunk driving and drunk walking (Huynh 2011). Your memory is bit hazy; all you remember is that a mile walked drunk turns out to be eight times more dangerous than the mile driven drunk. You have two miles to go, so your choice is easy: you'll drunk-drive!

It does not turn out so well. You are arrested for speeding through a red light on Geary Avenue and test positive for illegally high blood alcohol content. A few weeks later, you find yourself in front of a judge and have to explain your choice. You tell the judge exactly how you had reasoned: you cared about your safety, and you were eight times more likely to be safe, under those conditions, if you drove rather than walked.

The judge wouldn't hear any of it: "A five-minute ride is not worth a lifetime of guilt." That's not how you had reasoned at all. How do you compare the two? A two-mile drive was eight times safer than a two-mile walk; you knew that. You could have hurt someone, so maybe you should feel guilty indeed. But how could you put a number on "a lifetime of guilt"?

Where did it go wrong? The calculation seemed reasonable: given the little information you had about the risk of driving, given how much you care about your own safety, you chose right, did you not? By just comparing the two options coldly, mathematically, and preferring the option that minimizes risk, the choice to drive was the better one. But the judge's reaction puts the entire reasoning into doubt.

What can we learn from this? Is there a general framework of decision-making under risk that would allow you to identify better decisions, that would help you see either what the judge wants you to see or why she's wrong?

2.2 What does it mean to choose between two risky options?

What does it mean to choose between driving home and walking home? Maybe the judge and you were talking about different risks: you were concerned about your safety and risks to your own health, and she was concerned about the risks to you and others, about not only health outcomes but also such things as feelings of guilt. And she focused on a longer time frame than the time it would take you to get back home.

The judge and you shared a common understanding about the evaluation of risks: identifying risks involves identifying people who are at risk, how much risk they are exposed to, how much harm and benefit could result from a risk taken or avoided, and how likely are the harm or benefit. But you identified different people as relevantly at risk and took into account different harms and benefits.

Both the judge and you engaged in a sort of calculus. On your part, you even used what you took to be quantitative data: that under the circumstances, walking was eight times more dangerous than driving. The judge probably had some rough idea of the statistics about drunk driving in mind as well, but the harm she envisaged, a lifetime of guilt, was so severe that the numbers hardly mattered.

Could you have taken into account the same factors as the judge and reached a different decision? That depends on your values and how different they could be from the judge's. How much do you care about guilt over harm to other? If you did not care very much, your reasoning could look like this:

> Driving back home is very likely to ensure my safety, which I care very much about.
>
> Walking back home is very unlikely to protect me from guilt, which I don't very much care about, and is also less likely to ensure my safety than if I drive.

So the decision would have been the same.

If you had some idea of how to quantify the comparisons, the decision could still have been the same, based on how you weighed the different harms involved. Something like this:

> Driving back home is very likely (say, with a 95% chance) to result in something I very much value, getting back home safe.
>
> Or walking back home is not very likely (say, 3%) to guarantee a lack of guilt (which I value only 1/100th of getting back home safe) but is less likely (say, with a 90% chance) to get me back home safely.

Again, the pattern of reasoning is not different; its result depends on the input we supply. So decision theory begins with several informal notions: to seek to minimize the risk, to minimize the overall expected utility of a negative outcome, to maximize the overall expected utility of a wanted outcome.

The fundamental idea behind one of the main frameworks of decision-making under risk, *expected utility theory*, is this:

> When facing a choice between uncertain options, this theory of decision-making states that you should *choose the option with the highest expected utility*.

To understand this, each of these notions needs to be made precise.

2.3 Expected utility theory

The two basic concepts in this theory are *utility* and *expectation*. The concept of utility was introduced because when it comes to assigning values to possible outcomes, we often run into the problem of comparing oranges and apples. In our example, the defendant, you, asks yourself, "How could I put a number on 'a lifetime of guilt'?" In the end, we saw the defendant saying, "A lack of guilt (which I value only 1/100th of getting back home safe)." After reflection, you did have a quantitative comparison. But what was the unit of comparison? In simpler cases, it might have been a matter of money, and the unit could have been dollars or francs or pounds. In this case, it is hard to say what value it is that is 100 times greater for getting back home safe.

Expected utility theory starts with the assumption that all such quantitative comparisons make sense and can be expressed with a simple unit: the *utile*. That is, it always makes sense to say of two outcomes that the utility of one equals X times the utility of the other. This is admittedly an abstraction, but for so general a theory, abstraction is inevitable.

Expected utility theory can be conceived, on the one hand, as a descriptive/predictive theory – a theory whose goal is to describe what decisions people make or will make, and the reasons behind these decisions – or it can be conceived, on the other hand, as a normative theory – a theory of what decisions we *ought* to make. In this chapter, we alternate between the two conceptions of expected utility theory, sometimes to reveal preferences, other times to find what one ought to do. We will see later in §2.6 and later that either view of EUT is faced with challenges.

In the second step, the possible outcomes of a decision are to be evaluated on the basis of their *expected utility*. This is itself a complex concept, for it involves the further notion of *probability*. It is not sufficient to take into account the utility of an outcome. Its probability, how likely it is to be the actual outcome, matters as well. Let's use very simple examples to show how this works (Briggs 2019).

2.3.1 Utilities and the decision matrix

Imagine you are about to walk outside of your home and you don't know if it will rain or not. Should you take an umbrella? This is a relatively simple choice because we can agree about the kind of utility to consider (not looking any further just now, we don't see any moral ramifications of the choice). We can draw a diagram, a "decision matrix," and it will look like this:

Table 2.1 Decision matrix for the choice to take an umbrella or not depending on whether or not it rains displaying the possible outcomes.

	It Rains	*It Doesn't Rain*
Take umbrella	Encumbered, dry	Encumbered, dry
Don't take umbrella	Unencumbered, wet	Unencumbered, dry

In this matrix, the utility of either action is expressed in terms of how encumbered and wet or dry you will be (the different possible *outcomes*), depending on the *state of affairs*. That state of affairs (whether or not it will rain) is not currently known: we have the uncertainty that typifies a risk.

But what is the utility, to you, of each outcome? You need to indicate how you value them. Maybe you could choose to express these different outcomes with a particular value unit (i.e., a utile). For instance, maybe you can put a dollar value on each of them, or some kind of grade. Most simply, you could use just two values, with 😐 the greater and ☹ the lesser and 😐 halfway between the two.[1]

Maybe you would pick different ratings, but we may still agree that this is a reasonable one. In any case here, let's assume that these outcomes are easily comparable with a scale of this kind.

This is not enough for you to reach a decision: now you need to take into account just how likely it is that it will rain.

Sometimes the situation is made very simple, because the probability is either so high or so low that we can afford not to bother with a comparison. Indeed, this decision will be very different if you are in Las Vegas or London. If you're in Las Vegas, the state of affairs "it rains" will be very, very unlikely, and your choice is reduced to the following, very easy decision matrix.

Table 2.2 Decision matrix for the choice to take an umbrella or not depending on whether or not it rains where the outcomes are expressed on a ☹-😐-☺ scale.

	It Rains	*It Doesn't Rain*
Take umbrella	😐	😐
Don't take umbrella	☹	☺

Table 2.3 Decision matrix for the choice to take an umbrella or not if it doesn't rain and where the outcomes are expressed on a ☹-😐-☺ scale.

	It Doesn't Rain
Take umbrella	😐
Don't take umbrella	☺

Table 2.4 Decision matrix for the choice to take an umbrella or not if it rains and where the outcomes are expressed on a ☹-😐-☺ scale.

	It Rains
Take umbrella	😐
Don't take umbrella	☹

But if you're in London and you're quite sure it is going to rain, the decision matrix will be different but equally simple.

If you're in London, you should take an umbrella, and if you're in Las Vegas, you should not.

But now, what if you live in the northwestern side of San Francisco? The climate in the San Francisco Peninsula is notoriously capricious, and such a decision there will be trickier. We need to figure in the probabilities and somehow mesh them with the utilities to reach a decision.

(By the way, where do we get those probabilities?)

FRAME 1: Whence probability?

The nature of probability is itself a contentious topic. Broadly speaking, a probability is a measure of uncertainty. What's the uncertainty, and where does it come from? For example, if you say that there's an 80% chance that it will rain, what does it mean? There are broadly two sides to the interpretation of probability:

1. A *frequentist* interpretation. On that view, probabilities are just statistics. They reflect the frequency of an event to occur or not. They can be observed frequencies, actual unknown frequencies, or hypothetical frequencies in an imagined, infinite "long run."
2. A *subjective* interpretation. On that view, probabilities are a measure of *our* uncertainty. They reflect not what the world is but what we know (or don't) about it or how confident we are in our knowledge.

On the frequentist view, if we say that there is an 80% chance that it will rain tomorrow, we have in mind a *reference class*, such as the class of days in July in our century in the San Francisco Bay Area. And we will be right if in 80% of those, it rains.

On the subjectivist view, what we meant instead is that it seems to us four times as likely as not that it will rain tomorrow. There is no similar simple criterion of rightness or wrongness, but there certainly are objective criteria to be met. We can score a weather forecaster by logging his predictions and the outcomes over a given time. If it rained on 80% of the days on which he said there was an 80% chance of rain (and similarly for the other numbers), we say that in that period, he was *perfectly calibrated*. And we would prefer to listen to weather forecasters who are known to be highly calibrated.

Among philosophers and statisticians, those who hold the subjectivist view are *probabilists*, and most are *Bayesians* – we will learn more about them in the following passages – who have a special view of rational updating of probabilities. Although Bayesian statisticians have developed their own methods, they solve the same problems, with more or less the same results, as "orthodox" statisticians, who are in the main frequentists. For the problems we discuss about risk, the differences between the frequentist and subjectivist views are good to keep in mind but do not make a practical difference for our calculations.

2.3.2 Calculating the expected utility of each choice

> [I]n order to judge of what we ought to do in order to obtain a good and to avoid an evil, it is necessary to consider not only the good and evil in themselves, but also the probability of their happening and not happening, and to regard geometrically the proportion which all these things have, taken together.
>
> (Arnauld & Nicole 1662)

This seventeenth-century textbook rule applies equally well to our examples: to compare the value of the choices (taking an umbrella or not), you need to compare the utilities of the possible outcomes, *weighted* by their probabilities.[2] The result we call their *expected utility*.

For example, if there are two possible outcomes P and Q, then you have to compare:

Expected utility of outcome P:	(utility of P × probability of P)
Expected utility of outcome Q:	(utility of Q × probability of Q)

Let's say that, in our example, you use the probability that your weather app gives you. Your app tells you that for the next two hours or so, the probability of rain is 30%. You now have the following decision matrix.

Table 2.5 Decision matrix for the choice to take an umbrella or not depending on the weather (expressed as a probabilistic forecast) and where the outcomes are expressed on a ☹-😐-☺ scale.

	It Rains (30% Chance)	*It Doesn't Rain (70% Chance)*
Take umbrella	😐	😐
Don't take umbrella	☹	☺

You can now calculate the expected utility of taking your umbrella and then compare it with that of not taking your umbrella:

1. Expected utility of taking your umbrella:
   0.30 × 😐 + 0.70 × 😐 = 100% 😐 = 😐
2. Expected utility of not taking your umbrella: 0.30 × ☹ + 0.70 × ☺

Admittedly, this rating system with frowny and smiley faces is pretty crude. But remember that 😐 is *halfway between* ☹ and ☺. In line 2, we see a combination in which the happy face gets more than half the weight. So that combination is *better than halfway between* ☹ and ☺. So line 2 describes the better option overall. You can now decide: the option without umbrella is to be preferred.[3]

That's decided: you're not taking your umbrella!

It is time now to see how this theory fares when we get into some more complex, more realistic decision scenarios.

2.3.3 Choices with multiple outcomes

If the decision is whether or not to take an umbrella, then, depending on rain, each choice has one definite outcome. But the situation is not always that simple.

Suppose you have some extra dollars to spend in a convenience store and you are trying to choose between buying a chocolate bar and a lottery ticket. The choice to buy chocolate has one definite outcome: you'll have the pleasure of eating chocolate. But the choice to buy a lottery ticket has more than one possible outcome, and they are not under your control.

Let's say that the lottery has just two sorts of prizes, a single $1 million grand prize and ten $100 consolation prizes. Two million and one tickets have been sold. You figure that the probability that you will win the grand prize is, for all practical purposes, one in two million, and the probability that you will get a consolation prize is ten in two million. The chocolate bar you value at $5.

What does, or should, your deliberation look like now? Because getting a chocolate bar if you choose to buy one is certain, probability 1, the expected utility of this choice is 5.

If you choose to buy the lottery ticket, there are three possible outcomes: that you will get $1 million or get $100 or get 0. The probabilities of these outcomes are 1 / 2 million, 10 / 2 million, (2 million minus 11) / 2 million, respectively. What is your expected utility?

The answer, in expected utility theory, is that it is the sum of the expected utilities of each of these outcomes:

(probability of grand prize × 1 million) + (probability of consolation prize × $100) + (probability of no prize × 0)

Notice that the three probabilities add up to 1 – that is because it is certain that one of these outcomes will come about if you buy the ticket. A quick calculation shows that this expected value is approximately 1,001/2,000, about 0.5, so ten times less than the expected value of buying a chocolate bar.

FRAME 2: Probability theory

When working with specific probabilities, the most important first step is to describe the exact possibilities to take into account. So if the question is, "What is the probability that it will rain or snow tomorrow?" we have to notice that we are dealing with four distinct, mutually exclusive possibilities. Let's write A for "It will rain tomorrow" and B for "It will snow tomorrow." Then we have to look at:

(A & ~B): it will rain but not snow.
(A & B): it will both rain and snow.
(~A & B): it will not rain but snow.
(~A & ~B): it will neither rain nor snow.

Each of these must have a probability, and since they exhaust what is possible, those probabilities have to add up to 1 (or 100%). It is useful to adapt the Venn diagrams used in logic:

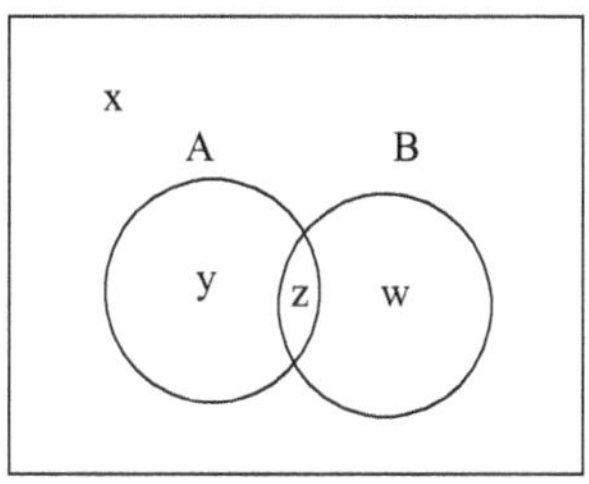

Figure 2.1 Venn diagram representing propositions A ("It will rain tomorrow") and B ("It will snow tomorrow") and their intersection A & B.

The proposition A & B, "It will both rain and snow tomorrow," corresponds to the overlap of the two circles. The letters refer to the probabilities (here left indefinite): A & B has probability z, while A & ~B has probability y.

Using *P* for probability, we write: P (A & ~B) = y, P (A & B) = x.

These two parts make up A, and so A (the whole circle on the left) has probability y + z. This illustrates at once the basic law:

If X and Y are mutually exclusive, then P (X or Y) = P(X) + P(Y)

EXERCISE: Looking at this diagram, verify that:

$$P(A \text{ or } B) + P(A \,\&\, B) = P(A) + P(B)$$

Now we can sum up the two basic principles of normative expected utility theory:

- The expected utility of a choice is the sum of the utilities of its possible outcomes, weighted by their probabilities.
- The maxim for rational choice is to maximize your expected utility.

In the rain example, we maximized our expected utility by not taking an umbrella, and in the convenience store by buying a chocolate bar.

2.4 Should the police officer have arrested you? Conditional probabilities and Bayes' theorem

In our initial example, you went through a red light and the officer who stopped you gave you a Breathalyzer test. It showed your blood alcohol content to be well above the legal limit, so he arrested you for driving under the influence. Could you have protested?

Tests are not 100% accurate. There is some percentage of false positives as well as of false negatives. So yes, you could have mentioned that. Unfortunately, your case was pretty clear. The test result was well above the legal limit, so well outside the margin of probable error. And you knew you had been drinking, so you wouldn't have welcomed repetition of the test.

In principle, though, the probability of a false positive is not something to be neglected. But we have to be careful about how we take account of this. Suppose your test result is positive and the probability of a false positive is 1%; does that mean that you are in fact positive with a probability of 99%? Let's see.

2.4.1 Understanding conditional probability

It would be easy to think so, for we could have presented the facts as follows: the probability that your result was a false positive, ***given that*** the test result was positive, equals 1%. The words "given that" are important here; this phrase is often replaced by "on the assumption that" or "conditional on the fact that." Whichever words we use, they indicate that the probability in question is a *conditional probability.*

We often rely on conditional probabilities, together with new evidence, to revise or update our opinions. As an example, consider two propositions: the proposition that you will spend a great weekend and the proposition that you will go on a hike in the Sierra. You don't know if either is true, and unfortunately, let's assume, both seem unlikely to you. The chance that you'll have a great weekend, *given that* you will be hiking in the Sierra, is very, very high (almost 100%). The chance that you will be hiking the Sierra *on the assumption that* (another way to say "given that") you're having a great weekend, then, is not small but not as high (assuming that there are other things that could make you happy).

Finally, you met with a friend on Friday and you told her all this. Now, imagine either scenario:

1. You text her on Monday that you went to the Sierra; she's probably surprised (because you didn't expect it).
2. She meets you on Monday and you look like you had a great weekend; she is surprised (because it didn't seem like it was going to happen).

In case 1, because of the first conditional probability, she is practically certain that you had a great weekend. In case 2, because of the second conditional probability, she thinks it is quite likely (but far from certain) that you went to the Sierra.

FRAME 3: Conditional probability

We can use the muddy Venn diagram again to see how conditional probability works. Remember the mud heaped on the parts to represent the probability of each proposition depicted. Now let us ask the question:

What is the probability that it will snow tomorrow, ***given that*** it will rain tomorrow?

In symbols, that is the question "What is P (B | A)?"

The way to answer this is to wipe away all the mud that is outside A. The assumption A, that it will rain tomorrow, eliminates all possibilities contrary to A. When we do that, the only numbers really left are y and z. The others have become 0.

Having done that, what is the new probability of B? It is the same as the new probability of A & B. That is represented by the proportion of mud on that intersection of the circles, after our wiping operation. So it is the proportion of y in the total amount (y + z), that is, y / (y + z).

This illustrates the basic law:

P (X | Y) = P (X & Y) / P(Y), provided P(Y) is not zero.

EXERCISE: Let's insert some real numbers in this example.

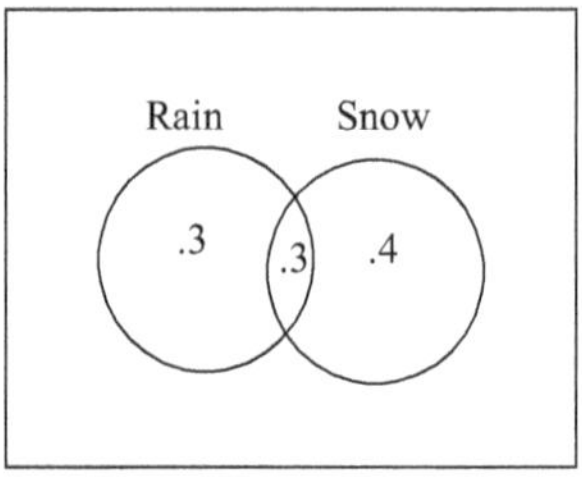

Figure 2.2 Venn diagram representing propositions "It will rain tomorrow" and "It will snow tomorrow" and their intersection and respective probabilities. Think of the letters *x*, *y*, *z*, and *w* as standing for amounts of mud, heaped on this diagram, to represent the *proportion* of probability on each part. We call this the muddy Venn diagram, and it is very useful for calculating intuitively with probabilities

Given this, what happens if you wipe the mud that lies outside A? All that is left is 0.3 on A & B and 0.3 on A & ~B. The amount of mud on A is 0.6, just as it was. Now look at the mud left on B: how much is that of what is left on A?

The answer will be P (B |A) when those numbers are the real probabilities.

There are, however, many examples to show that conditional probabilities do not easily lead to unconditional probabilities. A standard example going back to 1960 was this (Hempel 1960):

> Petersen is a Swede. Less than 2% of Swedes are Catholic. So, almost certainly Petersen is not Roman Catholic.
>
> Petersen made a pilgrimage to Lourdes. Less than 2% of pilgrims to Lourdes are not Catholic. So, almost certainly Petersen is Catholic.

How is that going to matter in practice? Let's go back to the policeman who arrested you, but change the example, for clarity. Let's take it that the policeman and you both had some more ignorance and some more knowledge. You did not get caught going through a red light, let's say, but were just stopped randomly in a nightly police stakeout. The policeman administered the Breathalyzer test, and you tested positive.

2.4.2 Helping the policeman: Bayes' theorem

To keep this amended example simple enough, we'll make some assumptions. The test is not 100% reliable. In general, there are false positives and false negatives. Let's be generous with the police and assume that their test is 98% accurate in this sense: 98% of positive results are true positives, and 98% of negative results are true negatives. Let's further assume that the police officer knows that at any given time, 1% of drivers are under the influence; there are perhaps some times of the day when that probability is higher, but let's say that the statistics available aren't more specific than this.

You tested positive, and the test is 98% accurate, so should we conclude that you are 98% certain to be drunk? Not so fast! We should not ignore that as a randomly stopped motorist, you were unlikely to be positive in the first place. Ignoring this would be committing what is called the prosecutor's fallacy.

To see this, let's do a thought experiment. Suppose that the total number of randomly stopped motorists was 10,000 and that they were all tested. What will be the result?

> 1%, namely, 100, are really positive; 98 of these test positive, and 2 test negative (the false negatives).
> 99%, namely, 9,900, are negative; of these 2%, namely 198, test positive (false positives), and the rest test negative.
> Total who test positive: 98 + 198 = 296. Of these, 98 are actually positive.
> So among the ones who test positive, 98/296 are really positive, which is about 33%.

That is the answer to the question!

The policeman should raise the probability that you are drunk from 1% to 33%. That is indeed a 33-fold increase but is certainly not damning as the quite-unwarranted conclusion that you are 98% certain to be under the influence.

In practice, of course, the policeman is not going to let you go so easily. If you protest, he can retest you or ask you to walk a straight line or to stand on one foot, and so forth. But the example is still very important for us because it brings out the importance of thinking about conditional probability.

The conditional probability of being under the influence, given that you are a driver, was 1%. The conditional probability of being under the influence given that you tested positive was 98%. Neither warrants us to conclude to an unconditional probability in any simple or straightforward way.

The argument that we went through here is an example of a famous procedure, updating opinion in accordance with *Bayes' theorem*, named after the eighteenth-century British clergyman and probabilist Thomas Bayes.

To explain this in general, there are two notions we need to make precise.

The first is conditional probability itself. Looking back to the example of Petersen, we can see that it involved the conditional probability of Petersen being Catholic, given that Petersen was a Swede. The implicit evaluation, in the example, was clearly that this conditional probability equaled the percentage or *proportion of Catholic Swedes among Swedes*. The generalization of this example,

> the probability of A given B = the probability of A & B divided by the probability of B

is the standard technical definition of conditional probability.

The second important notion is that of *updating* a probability judgment. In the example where the policeman administers the Breathalyzer test, he has as his initial or prior probability that the driver is over the limit, namely, 1%. Then he gets new evidence: the driver fails the test, and the test is 98% accurate. In view of this new evidence, he needs to update his probability, from 1% to a new number.

Expected utility theory takes it for granted that rational updating of our opinion about a proposition A, upon new evidence E, takes this form:

> new probability of A = old conditional probability of A given evidence E

Rather than "new" and "old," it is customary to say "posterior" and "prior." This procedure is also called *Bayesian updating*.

Writing P^* for the posterior probability and P for the prior probability with "|" for "|" the formula is therefore:

$$\begin{aligned} P^*(A) &= P(A \mid E) \\ &= P(A \,\&\, E) / P(E) \end{aligned}$$

In general, it is not easy to see at once what P (A & E) will be. Bayes' theorem shows how this formula can be put into a user-friendly, calculation-friendly form.

FRAME 4: Bayes' theorem and Bayesian updating

Bayes' theorem follows directly from the way probabilities and conditional probabilities are calculated, but it is of great practical use. As we saw in the frame on conditional probability, for two propositions X and Y, provided the probability of Y P(Y) is not zero, the probability of X given Y is

$$P(X \mid Y) = P(X \,\&\, Y) / P(Y).$$

It may not be at once obvious, but the following is true for the same reason:

$$P(X \,\&\, Y) = P(X) \cdot P(Y \mid X).$$

Substituting for P (X & Y) in the first equation, we then get:

Bayes' Theorem: $P(X \mid Y) = P(Y \mid X) \cdot (P(X)/P(Y))$

A common way to use Bayes' theorem is to express the degree of support (or confirmation) for a *hypothesis* by another proposition offered as *evidence*. Suppose we have a hypothesis H ("There are extraterrestrials") and are offered some evidence E ("Some people were abducted in a flying saucer"). We have our doubts about both H and E but do have some subjective probability for them. Let's say $P(H) = 0.1$ and $P(E) = 0.2$ – a bit larger, because flying saucers could have been made by terrestrials.

What would be the probability that H is true if the putative evidence E were actually true? That is the conditional probability $P(H \mid E)$. On the face of it, that is hard to answer. There are so many possibilities: maybe extraterrestrials don't abduct or flying saucers are made by human kidnappers.

But you may have a definite opinion about how likely extraterrestrials, if they are here, would abduct people. Suppose you think they would very likely do that: $P(E \mid H) = 0.6$. The question just how much E would support H can then be calculated. Bayes' theorem tells us:

$$\begin{aligned} P(H \mid E) &= P(E \mid H) \cdot P(H)/P(E) \\ &= 0.6 \times (0.1 / 0.2) = 0.3 \end{aligned}$$

The *Bayesian updating rule* now prescribes a change in our opinion if we learn that E is true: change your probability that there are extraterrestrials here from 0.1 to 0.3.

EXERCISE: If a coin is fair and is tossed fairly, the chance of getting ten heads in a row is (1/2)^10, which is approximately 1/1,000. You have found a coin with a little note that says, "This coin is fair." You take that as a hypothesis, and your initial probability that it is true is just 1/2. Before you toss the coin, you are asked, "How likely is it that this coin will come up heads ten times in a row?" You realize that it could either be fair or biased in any number of ways. After some deliberation, you answer, "About one in a hundred." Now you toss it, and the evidence you obtain is that it just landed heads ten times in a row. If you follow the Bayesian updating rule, what will be your new (posterior) probability that the hypothesis is true, that the coin is fair?

There is also an easily remembered, user-friendly form of the updating procedure, but it is written in the way bettors at the racetrack talk. Instead of talking about the probability that a horse will win, they talk about the *odds*. The two ways of talking are equivalent: that the odds of winning are 2/1 ("two to one"), for example, means that the probability of winning is 2/3. Similarly, that the probability of the police arresting you for drunk driving equals 4/5 is the same as the odds being 4/1, and in general, if the odds of A (as against not-A) are 4/9, then the probability of A equals 4/13.

In general:

> The odds of A (against ~A) are x/y if and only if the probability of A equals x / (x + y).

Returning now to the intuitive calculation that led us to the conclusion that the probability of someone being drunk is conditional on his having failed the Breathalyzer test, let us see how we can replay that. You remember that in the calculation we had to take into account both the true positives and the false positives. That is:

P (fail | drunk), the probability that the test is failed, given that the person is drunk.
P (fail |not drunk), the probability that the test is failed, given that the person is not drunk.

The ratio of these two conditional probabilities, the first **divided** by the second, is called the *Bayes factor*. And the formula for Bayesian updating can be written like this:

> (*) the posterior odds = the Bayes factor **times** the prior odds

In our example, the prior probability of your being drunk was 1%; equivalently, the prior odds are 1/99. The Bayes factor here was 0.98 divided by 0.02, which is 49. Thus, we get:

> the posterior odds that you are drunk = 49 times 1/99 = 49/99

This we translate into: the posterior probability that you are drunk = 49 / (49 +99) = 49/148 = 0.331 – exactly the same answer as we found, by intuitive reasoning, in the preceding passages.

EXERCISE: John is a college student and learns that the incidence of STD among college students is 1 in 500. His prior probability for being STD-positive is 1/500 = 0.2%. He takes a test and tests positive for an STD. The test is 99% accurate (1% false positives, 1% false negatives). What is his posterior probability that he is STD-positive?

To do this exercise, follow either the intuitive procedure using imagined statistics or the Bayesian updating procedure formulated in terms of odds.

2.5 Expected utility theory and Bayesian probability as a general framework of decision-making under risk?

What we've seen so far sounds promising: if you can assign expected values to different options, then making decisions or assessing and comparing risky options could maybe just come down to a calculus.

For deciding whether or not you should take an umbrella, you compare the expected utility of different value and choose that with the highest expected utility. If the decision is more complex and if the probability is conditional on other knowledge or events you don't know happened or not, you can use Bayes' theorem.

This framework made of simple ingredients allows you to both assess and compare risky options. And as we've seen, it protects us against intuitive but misleading judgments. This result alone is enough to make this a valuable framework of decision-making.

2.5.1 *Avoiding the base rate fallacy*

To see this, consider another example: if you are a medical doctor and a test for one of your patients comes back positive, is that enough to think that they are affected by the disease they were just tested for? How likely is it that they are affected? Bayes' theorem reminds us that we should take into account the *base rate* (how large are the pool of people affected versus the number of false positives) to avoid what is called the *base rate fallacy.*

Indeed, a study published in 1982 revealed that 95% of physicians conflated a chance of being affected by a disease with the chance of a test coming positive. That is, if patients affected by a disease tested positive to a test 80% of the time, the overwhelming majority of medical providers surveyed thought

Table 2.6 False and true positives, and false and true negatives, for 1,000 patients if only 2% of them are infected and assuming a 5% false positive rate and a 0% false negative rate.

Number of People	*Infected*	*Uninfected*	*Total*
Test Positive	20 (true positive)	49 (false positive)	69
Test Negative	0 (false negative)	931 (true negative)	931
Total	20	980	1,000

that a positive test meant that there was an 80% chance of being affected by that disease. This fallacy in risk assessment led to serious health-care decisions, such as unnecessary mastectomies.[4]

Ignoring the base rate may especially lead to underestimating the proportion of false positives. In the following example of 1,000 patients tested for a certain infection, with only 2% infected and a false positive rate of just 5%, we actually see that the false positive are actually more than twice the true positives.

It appears, then, that decision-making in accordance with EUT can be very advantageous and help to avoid common and typical errors.

But however simple and powerful this framework is, it is also limited. The restriction to its short list of ingredients (expectations, utilities, and a preference for the highest expected utility) may only apply under limited circumstances. The problems we will examine now include difficulties in measuring utility and difficulties about reconciling decisions based on maximum expected utility with our intuitive judgments about rational decisions.

2.5.2 *Defining and measuring utilities*

Using expected utility theory as a framework for decision-making implies that we have a well-defined utility measure. Yet there might be situations where different situations or choice outcomes can't easily be compared with a ☹-😐-☺ scale. Consider the judge in the initial example: she had a choice in deciding whether or not you were guilty, but also in what sentence to issue. In doing so, she had to consider the value attached to each outcome – for you, for the community, and for the law. Can such a decision reasonably be expected to be expressed in terms of a ☹-☺ scale?

We often use money as a universal yardstick for a lot of decisions. It can serve as a convenient utility scale (i.e., as a utile). For instance, should you buy this safety feature on your new car or not? There is a way to interpret this decision strictly in monetary terms: the state-of-the-art braking system costs $1,000 more, but it will reduce your insurance monthly rate by $5. Based on this information alone, the extra investment is probably not worth it unless you decide to keep your new car longer than 200 months, which is unlikely. Of course, saving on insurance is not the main reason you would purchase an extra safety feature: you could do it for the added safety benefits. But it is common to express such considerations in dollar terms too.

For instance, to put a value on safety benefits, we can estimate the money we can expect to save on health-care expenses: if buying some safety car feature improves by 1% your chance of a costly hospitalization that would have cost $100,000, then you can estimate the value of this safety feature, its expected utility, at $1,000. With that calculus, and if safety is indeed all you care about, then you shouldn't need the insurance rebate to convince you to buy this safety feature.[5]

The United States Environmental Protection Agency (EPA) offers a prime example of how a value can be placed on harm. Here is how it comments on its Mortality Risk Valuation:

> The EPA does not place a dollar value on individual lives. Rather, when conducting a benefit-cost analysis of new environmental policies, the Agency uses estimates of how much people are willing to pay for small reductions in their risks of dying from adverse health conditions that may be caused by environmental pollution.
>
> (United States Environmental Protection Agency n.d.)

The EPA routinely assesses risks, harms, the value of safety measures, etc. It does so with dollars as a utility unit, even when assessing risks to human health. To do so, it relies on the *value of a statistical life* (VSL), which depends on the *willingness to pay* (WTP) for small reductions in mortality risks. This mortality risk is often calculated on a short-term basis, such as the risk of dying over the next year, and for an average person among a large group. If on average in a group of 100 people each person is willing to pay $50 for a risk reduction of 1% over the next year, then the saving of 1 statistical life (1% of 100 people = 1 prevented fatality) is worth $50 × 100 = $5,000.[6] [7]

As one can imagine, the willingness to pay for a small decrease in mortality risk is not set in stone. Even if we put inflation aside, it will depend on a number of factors:

- The country of residence of population considered. The richer the people, the higher their VSL. The value of a prevented fatality in the UK will be worth less than one in the US, and more generally, it will be less for people from low-income countries.[8]
- The age and health of the population considered. A survey-based study by Krupnick and collaborators (Krupnick et al. 2002) showed that WTP is constant with age up to 70 years and is about 30% lower for persons aged 70 and older and that WTP is unaffected by physical health status but is affected by mental health.
- Whether the willingness to pay is self-reported, as in a survey, or revealed by observing actual consumer behavior. People can declare to be more risk averse (and so more willing to pay for a risk reduction) than they

actually are; conversely, consumers may underestimate their WTP for a hypothetical safety measure if they are unfamiliar with the harm it would protect them from.[9]

It's not clear that we have gained a sufficient perspective on your judge's decision yet, but you have a hard time imagining that this is the sort of calculus she engaged in. Hopefully, her decision to sentence you, and what sentence to issue, didn't depend on whether you were speeding in a rich or a poor neighborhood, whether there were tourists from the UK or Indonesia (with different VSLs), or whether you drove by a retirement home (with a relatively lower VSL). More generally, it doesn't seem just that her sentence would depend on such an arbitrary or psychologically driven assessment of expected utility.

Even though this may not be how your judge reasoned, the use of money as a single metric by which to assess harms, risks, and benefits reveals what we should expect from a utility unit in general and also, at the same time, what challenges it faces.

2.5.3 *Can money provide the universal utility unit?*

Money is a convenient utility unit because it is versatile: many dimensions of human life are monetized. We spend or make money for our sustenance, to get an education, for our health care, to define our social status, or to find love. We can also use money to measure social justice: if we care about reducing inequality, we will look at wealth or income distribution; if we care about alleviating poverty, we will be concerned about how many people live with less than a certain amount; a country's economic wealth can be measured by its citizens' median wage; and so on.

FRAME 5: Money as utility unit and preference order

Money is not just bills and coins in our pockets. The more abstract concept of money, which covers also what is in bank accounts and makes no distinction between currencies, is this: it is a medium of exchange, a store of value, and a unit for accounting. Money has some properties that we would expect of a utility unit. Assuming that for a given choice we can give all alternatives a monetary value, then:

- Any two options can be compared, and we can express a preference between them (completeness).
- We can rank them all unambiguously (transitivity).
- For any option, there's a combination of lesser options, which, as a whole, is preferable to it (continuity or Archimedean condition).

- Our preferences will be unchanged by the presence of an irrelevant alternative: if you prefer an offer worth $10 to one worth $9, then adding $1 to both alternatives won't change your choice. (See also the frame on independence of irrelevant alternatives.)

John von Neumann and Oskar Morgenstern (1944) showed that these properties allow us to define a utility function, that is, a function that allows us to express and compare complex choices among possible combinations of options.[10]

We can also use money to measure both an individual's and a country's preference; the same unit can be used at different scales. To be sure, the same amount of money is not always equally meaningful in our assessments of expected utility. For instance, imagine that the judge had given you a choice between the following sentences:

- Pay a $1,000 fine in two settlements: $500 now and $500 in three months.
- Pay a $1,200 fine in three months.

Depending on how much you have on your bank account now, it's possible that you could prefer the second sentence even though it's more expensive overall. In this case, using money as a unique, simple scale for expected utility assumes that timing doesn't matter.

But this faces a problem: variation in the *marginal utility* of money. Put bluntly, a dollar bill does not have the same value for a billionaire as for a houseless person!

Let's explain this with an example. Assume that you have an average-paying job in an average community in America in 2019 and that you are a worker with average qualification and experience. The median yearly salary for such a job would be about $47,000, or $23.50 per hour (assuming 40 hours per week and 50 working weeks per year).

Now, how much more would you ask your employer in exchange for working 1 extra hour per week: $23.50? More? Less? And how much of a raise would you ask in exchange for working 10 extra hours per week? If so, that would mean a $235 weekly increase, or a yearly salary of $58,750 instead. If you think that a 25% increase in working hours should correspond to a 25% increase in salary, would you agree to another 10 hours of work per week – we're now at 60 hours per week – for another $235 per week (for a total yearly salary of $70,500)? What about 10 more hours per week? What about 10 more still? Wherever it is, there will be a point when you will ask for much more than $23.50 to work 1 extra hour.

What this thought experiment illustrates is that money has *diminishing marginal utility*. You have probably heard that "money doesn't buy happiness." Whether or not this is true, there are studies of emotional well-being which report that at least, at some point, "more money doesn't buy more happiness" (Kahneman & Deaton 2010).

But there certainly is a practical, if limited, use of money as utility unit (i.e., as a utile). If we take into account human psychology, money isn't a linear utility unit, and it is not easily scalable. But there is an intuitive sense in which it can be useful as a utility unit: if you're willing to pay for *A* more than for *B*, then it's reasonable to say that you prefer *A* to *B*. Allowing us to express preference relationships is something we want in a utility unit.

Moreover, we can express an ordered series of preference such that if you're willing to pay more for *A* than *B* and more for *B* than *C*, then you won't be willing to pay more for *C* than *A*. This seems obvious, but that's something that money as a utility unit provides us that we might otherwise not get.

Assume, for instance, that you don't want to use money as your utility scale but instead want to use your favorite vacation destinations. Let's assume a very simple scale with only a few degrees: going to Venice, visiting New York, or hiking in Yosemite. We can imagine that, given the choice, one would rather go to New York than hike in Yosemite and would rather hike in Yosemite than visit Venice but also would rather visit Venice than go to New York. Now, we can't necessarily translate these travel options into a value such that one can rank them unequivocally – that is, because these preferences aren't *transitive* – and so we can't use them to define a utility unit. But it's easy to conceive of money as a *transitive scale* (assuming that more money is always better).

These few considerations show us why money can be used as a utility unit, if only at limited scales: it allows us to express and compare complex choices among possible combinations of options.

2.5.4 Risk and cost-benefit analysis

Now, it doesn't seem like this was how your judge, in our earlier example, reasoned. She surely didn't bring everything back to money, and she probably wouldn't want you to do that either. Similarly, making decisions based on a monetary evaluation of policies, as the EPA does, seems to be wrong or at least committing a category mistake.

This is in fact a common objection to using money as the only unit, for instance, in a risk and cost-benefit analysis. Using money as *the* yardstick by which to express all our preferences seems overly simplistic.

A *cost-benefit analysis* is an economic evaluation in which all costs and consequences of a certain decision are expressed in the same units, usually money. Kristine Shrader-Frechette (1985) reviewed different philosophical objections to cost-benefit analysis. These objections include metaphysical and ethical objections. Dollar value ignores finer nuances between different options, but also nuances in how we express our preferences; it ignores human intuitions and moral values that we can't monetize.[11]

For instance, if the EPA reduces all policy alternatives to dollar amounts and made policy choices based on the sum of all benefits (in $) minus all costs (in $), how would it take into account distributive justice? Intuitively, justice demands constraints on how harms and gains are distributed among the general population. Such moral considerations may escape a crude valuation of our preferences in dollar terms. Shrader-Frechette thus summarizes objections to weighing all risks in dollar terms:

> Moral commitments, rights, and basic goods are inviolable and incommensurable, and hence cannot be "bargained away" in a utilitarian scheme like Risk Cost-Benefit Analysis, which is unable to take adequate account of them and of values like distributive justice.
>
> (Shrader-Frechette 1985: 404)

Like the EPA, regulatory agencies might try to reduce every attribute to a dollar amount. As we saw earlier, such an approach is commonly criticized as comparing incomparable attributes (Dorman 1996). Can someone's well-being that comes from being healthy truly be expressed in terms of a dollar amount? Expressing the value of one's health in monetary terms might feel arbitrary and specious; no one, for instance, would sell their life in exchange for the (monetary) value of a statistical life we saw earlier.

But as Shrader-Frechette argued, these ethical objections are not unsurmountable. It's not simply because we are weighing our preference in dollar terms that we are making a venal, morally vacuous calculus. Value judgments are already made when we choose what alternatives to consider, which alternatives to give a rank at a discount, or to which we assign an arrestingly high price.

One might wonder, however, if instead of complicating the idea of a single value unit, we shouldn't simply use a different system of values.

2.5.5 Multivalued risk assessment?

A *multivalued risk assessment* would allow us to make explicitly more complex and perhaps more nuanced evaluations. Maybe the EPA doesn't have to reduce the value of species or human lives to dollars. Perhaps EUT can model the sort of decision your judge made when she considered such factors as potential harm to bystanders, the duty to follow traffic regulations, and whether jail time or a fine would constitute an adequate sanction.

Consider the decision matrix we saw earlier: you had to choose between taking your umbrella or not depending on different possible outcomes.

These outcomes were given with two types of units: dry or not, encumbered or not. With only two possible values for two possible units, there are four possible outcomes: encumbered and dry, unencumbered and wet, unencumbered and dry, and encumbered and wet.[12] The single unit you used to make a decision in these tables showed how you ranked three of these outcomes, namely, dry and unencumbered > dry and encumbered > wet and unencumbered. The table above doesn't tell us how to rank the fourth outcome, wet and encumbered, but it's clear in this scenario that you would strictly rank it the worst of all four outcomes; as such, you prefer being dry to wet, and unencumbered to encumbered. It's also clear from the ☹-☺ scale that being dry or not has more weight overall for you than being encumbered or not.[13]

Now, even though there are two independent value units (dry or not and encumbered or not), it's not clear how you could continue this multivalued assessment as soon as you introduce minor but realistic nuances. And we can see that this is the case even though you have defined the relative worth of these two value units. Consider, for instance, the following decision matrix.

You knew how to rank different outcomes of taking your umbrella in the event of rain or not. But what if instead of raining, it only drizzled? Just the kind of very light rain that we sometimes get when there's a dense fog. Would you try to avoid it? Would your answer depend on how heavy your umbrella is? That shouldn't be a difficult decision; you have clearly identified value units and distinct outcomes, which you can all express in function of these

Table 2.7 Decision matrix for the choice to take an umbrella or not depending on whether or not it rains, displaying the possible outcomes, which are also expressed on a ☹-😐-☺ scale.

	It Rains	*It Doesn't Rain*
Take umbrella	Encumbered, dry = 😐	Encumbered, dry = 😐
Don't take umbrella	Unencumbered, wet = ☹	Unencumbered, dry = ☺

Table 2.8 Decision matrix for the choice to take an umbrella or not depending on whether or not it rains, but also on whether it drizzles, displaying the possible outcomes, which are also expressed on a ☹-😐-☺ scale

	It Rains	*It Drizzles*	*It Doesn't Rain*
Take umbrella	Encumbered, dry = 😐	**Encumbered, lightly wet = ?**	Encumbered, dry = 😐
Don't take umbrella	Unencumbered, wet = ☹	**Unencumbered, lightly wet = ?**	Unencumbered, dry = ☺

two value units. We have now merely introduced an additional value, lightly wet, preferable to wet but not to dry.

If multivalued risk assessment is possible, surely, it could decide this. Yet nothing in what you have said so far about your preferences about being dry or not or encumbered or not implies that you would know for certain how these two new possible outcomes would rank. To do that, you would need to continue defining what is, in fact, a third, *single*-value unit, which combines the other two units, expressed on a ☹-☺ scale, or an equivalent scale, such as a dollar-valued one.

Multivalued risk analysis (MVRA) aims to address this arbitrariness and what can be seen as a manufactured equivalence between money and other utility units. Expected utility theory assumes that we can express our preference ranking with a utility unit, and a common way to establish an equivalence between choices expressed with one or several utility units is to see how we would trade between them; we consider that these options have equal utility value if we are indifferent between them. For instance, a statistical life is worth $10,000,000 if that's the price you're willing to pay for it; your very fast BMW is worth $35,000 if you're indifferent between being offered $35,000 and a similar BMW model.

It is assumed in EUT that we can define a utility function, which models our preference over a defined set of alternative options, by establishing a series of lotteries that we would agree to enter in. MVRA starts from a criticism of that tenet of EUT by contending that indifference between options expressed in different units is not enough to claim that they have equal value; instead, MVRA proponents argue, this indifference may reveal that the two alternatives are truly incomparable.

In other words, to find a common metric to assess options, their relative risk and expected utility, we could, following EUT, play a long game of comparing options and finding the "right price" (in whatever unit we pick as our common yardstick) for all of them. MVRA proponents claim that finding this right price by determining when we're indifferent between alternatives is as meaningful as playing "would you rather?"; sometimes, alternatives in a game of "would you rather?" are comparable – for instance, "Would you rather be covered in fur or covered in scales?" – but sometimes not – "Would you rather know the history of every object you touched or be able to talk to animals?"

Martin Peterson objects to the MVRA approach that, even though the criticism of arbitrariness and artificialness of lotteries required by EUT may be sound, any decision afforded by a multivalued assessment will seem equally reductive and arbitrary (Peterson 2007). Indeed, even though the EPA, for instance, aimed at taking into account very different, *incomparable* set of values – species conservation, economic cost, harm to human health, etc. – to decide whether or not to implement an uncertain, risky policy, it would still need to *compare* them, force a choice, and thus assume a common unit.[14]

A set of rules on how to weigh different value units at different thresholds would in fact define a new, single-value unit; this single-value unit – this utile – doesn't need to be a dollar amount, but it needs to be simple enough to enable decision-making between alternatives. This reduction would occur whether we explicitly conduct a single- or multivalue risk assessment, and therefore, for Peterson, MVRA cannot, in principle, solve the arbitrariness issues it purports to do.

But what could do so? There have been serious clashes in the United States between cultural values honored by Native Americans and material advantages proposed for the common good. The controversial construction of the Dakota Access Pipeline gained national and international attention when the US Army Corps of Engineers accepted an application filed by Energy Transfer Partners, a Texas-based developer behind the project. The Standing Rock Sioux tribe, operating as a sovereign nation, passed a resolution regarding the pipeline stating that "the Dakota Access Pipeline poses a serious risk to the very survival of [their] Tribe and . . . would destroy valuable cultural resources." Could there be, in principle, a rationally compelled choice of a unit of comparison to weigh the two values involved against each other?

2.6 Limitations of expected utility theory

Does the judge expect you to be an expected utility theorist? Is that how you should define, assess, and compare all decisions that involve risk or uncertainty? Maybe that could be the lesson to draw from this ordeal; if it's good enough for the EPA, it's probably good enough for you. We have seen that criticisms about EUT as a framework for decision-making could be overcome, or at least remain problems for alternatives like the MVRA.

But when we match decisions made in accordance with EUT with our intuitions about rational decision-making, we run into real problems. In fact, even if we assume a definable, well-behaved utility unit, the EUT framework doesn't seem psychologically sound.

2.6.1 *The Allais paradox*

Indeed, consider the following choice between two options:

CHOICE I

Option A: win $1 million with 100% chance.
Option B: win $1 million with 89% chance, nothing with 1% chance, or $5 million with 10% chance.

EUT allows you to compare these two options: the expected utility of option A is $1 million, and that of option B is $1.39 million. EUT is unambiguous in this case: option B is clearly preferable to option A.

FRAME 6: EUT: lotteries, choices, and irrelevant alternatives

An advantage of EUT is that it allows us to express preferences between scenarios – or their likelihoods – that we don't know with certainty; this is what we express with a lottery (or bets) or a series of lotteries. We can sometimes elicit a preference straightforwardly: if you are willing to exchange a chocolate bar for six gummy drops, and vice versa, then the utility of chocolate bar for you is six times that of a gummy drop. But in general, it is not so straightforward.

A more sensitive way to probe preference orderings is to ask a subject to express a choice between two different lotteries. Since the alternatives can be "weighted" by the chances involved, they can elicit less simple orderings.

What is important for the theory is that there are general principles which must hold if the preference ordering is to be consistent. One is that preference must be *transitive*: if choice A is preferred to choice B, and choice B to choice C, then A is preferred to C.

Also important is the *principle of irrelevant alternatives.* That is, if certain alternatives are the same regardless of the choice made, then the choice would have had to be the same without that alternative. As a simple example, let's ask which you would prefer:

A. A 90% chance to win a chocolate bar, and 10% chance to win a gummy drop.
B. A 90% chance to win a chocolate bar, and 10% chance to win a toffee.

In this case, we would immediately conclude from your choice of A that you value a gummy drop more than a toffee. In concluding that, we would be implicitly ignoring the alternative of winning a chocolate bar with 90% chance, because it is the same in both choices: it is an *irrelevant alternative.*

Well, is it? How realistic is that? You can try to ask yourself, or ask around you: would you really turn away a guaranteed $1 million for a less-than-certain chance to win the same $1 million, a much smaller chance to win $5 million, but also a nonzero chance to win nothing at all? If you have the choice between option A and option B, option B sure looks like the risk to lose a sure gain of $1 million, doesn't it? Only if you already have millions in the bank, so that the marginal utility of $1 million would not be high, would it make sense to pick B.

To illustrate what this shows, consider this other choice between two alternative lunch options:

CHOICE II

Option A': a precooked bowl of mac and cheese from a box.
Option B': a lunch at this new place that has a good health grade and only ten reviews on Yelp, where two reviews say, "Barely food but still edible," and eight reviews that contain the phrase "The most amazing meal of my life."

If we try to compare these options as an expected utility theorist, we can say that the first option has a 100% certainty of being a mediocre meal, and the second option has a small likelihood of being worse than a homemade mac and cheese lunch and a high likelihood of being much, much better than that. The expected utility of the second option seems to be higher than the first, but would it not also be reasonable (although not automatic) to prefer the safe comfort food over a risk, however small, to eat something bad?

The key factor in this decision is not how much more you value mac and cheese over a bad meal but rather the fact that the first option is a *sure thing*: there's no risk with it, you don't have to guess, and you know what you'll get! You will never pay for a bowl of mac and cheese ten or a thousand times more than a really uninteresting dish at a restaurant. So the reason you might want to pick the homemade comfort food over the risky restaurant dinner isn't that you should redefine your utility unit but just the fact that *one menu is risky and the other isn't*. And EUT can't account for this preference for a sure thing ("risk aversion") that we sometimes have.

The problem is then that EUT cannot account for our preference for a sure gain (whether in value or in utility). That already seems like quite a challenge to how realistic EUT is. But let's go back to options A and B seen earlier. Assume that you are either a good expected utility theorist and pick option A or very rich and don't care about the risk of losing a sure $1 million and pick option B.

Now, consider the following related choice between two options:

CHOICE III

Option C: win $1 million with 11% chance, or nothing with 89% chance.
Option D: win nothing with 90% chance, or $5 million with 10% chance.

A choice between C and D is similar to one between A and B, except that the chances are different. You would probably choose option D over option C.

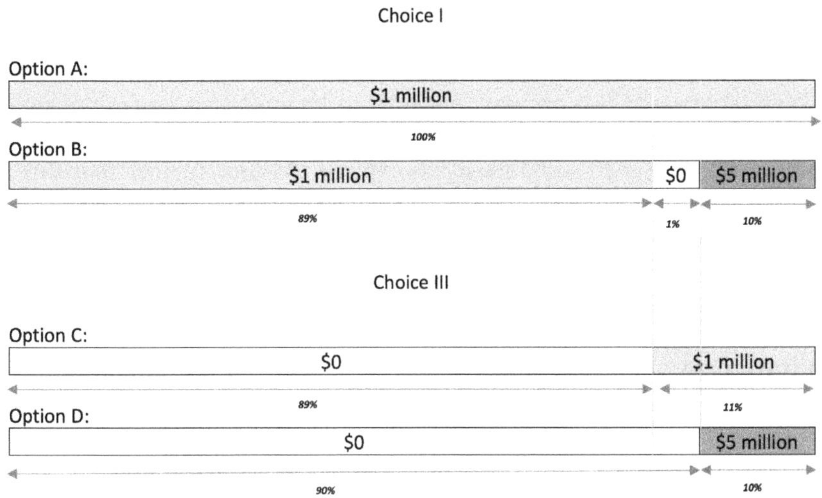

Figure 2.3 Expected utility of each option for Choice I and Choice III to illustrate the Allais paradox.

In fact, it is what EUT would prescribe: the expected utility of C is $110,000, and that of option D is $500,000.

But here is the problem: notice the difference in our reactions to Choice I and Choice III and ask yourself what accounts for the difference.

Picking D over C seems obvious, doesn't it? It seems much easier than choosing between A and B. Or at least, even though it's conceivable that someone could choose either A or B, it's hard to imagine why anyone wouldn't choose D over C.

Yet for EUT, a choice between C and D is *the same* as one between A and B. In both cases, one expected utility is higher than the other, and so that's it; the choice should be entirely determined.

This is a challenge for expected utility theory as a realistic theory of decision-making. If it can't account for choices many people would make and find natural, there is a clear distance between theory and practice. Indeed, most people would choose A over B, and D over C.[15] Yet only the latter choice is the right one according to EUT.

The challenge is about what we should expect from EUT or, more generally, a theory of decision-making. According to EUT, the choice between A and B is *exactly the same* as one between C and D. It is not debatable that D is preferable to C, but it's not unreasonable to prefer A to B or even B to A. But you may recall from the independence of irrelevant alternatives (see Frame 6 prior), which EUT entails, that adding an 89% chance of $0 win to both A and B to get a choice between C and D is *irrelevant* and *should not* affect our decision-making.

To illustrate this issue in another way, consider again the choice we saw earlier between a guaranteed meal of mac and cheese at home or a lunch at a restaurant with some uncertainty about the quality of the food you could get.

Take these same two options, but instead imagine that you're not quite sure whether your box of precooked mac and cheese has expired or not. You would say there's a 30% chance it has expired. Assume further that this is all you have to eat at home. Now, imagine that you're not entirely sure if the restaurant is open today; let's say you're 70% confident it's open. Now, you only have so much time for lunch before you have to go back to work, and so you have to decide between the following two options. Which do you choose?

CHOICE IV

Option C': eat at home with a 70% chance of precooked bowl of mac and cheese from a box and a 30% chance of no lunch at all.

Option D': go to this new place that has a good health grade and only ten reviews on Yelp, where one review says, "Barely food but still edible," and nine reviews that contain the phrase "The most amazing meal of my life," but a 30% chance that this restaurant is closed today, and so you would miss lunch entirely.

Based on expected utility theory, if earlier you chose the mac and cheese option, then you *have* to choose it again: the choice hasn't changed, because for each option you added the *same* 30% chance of no lunch at all. But that doesn't seem right, does it? If in both cases you risk skipping lunch altogether, then you might be willing to risk going to the new restaurant because you could get a great meal; the risk of a bad restaurant lunch doesn't seem so terrible now, does it?

The problem appears to be this: EUT only requires two ingredients as a theory of decision-making – your preferences about different outcomes (for instance here, if you prefer this dish or another dish) and the likelihood of each dish to occur. For EUT, your preference for one dish or another is to be defined independently of its likelihood. But contrary to what EUT asks us to do, we don't always define utilities independently of their likelihoods.

This problem is called the Allais paradox (Allais 1953). It challenges EUT in two ways: first, if you agree that A is preferable to B (or A' to B'), then you will agree that EUT fails to adequately predict your preference. Second, whether or not you prefer A to B, you will probably agree that EUT is wrong to consider that choosing D over C is the *same* as choosing B over A.

Here is how we can state the problem we have with EUT. Is it meant to be a descriptive theory, about decision-making, or a prescriptive theory, about rational decision-making? If we expect it to be a descriptive theory, one that models how people make decisions, then we just saw that it seems inadequate. It fails as a descriptive theory of how most people would choose. If, on the other hand, we expect EUT to be a theory of how *rational* people should think, i.e., a normative theory of rational decision-making, then we saw that it lacks nuance (see Heukelom 2015).

2.6.2 The Ellsberg paradox

Daniel Ellsberg[16] showed that in realistic scenarios with incomplete knowledge, EUT breaks down as it may yield inconsistent results. Here is such a scenario:

> Imagine an urn containing 90 balls: 30 red, and the rest either blue or green (maybe 30 green and 30 blue, or maybe 10 blue and 50 green – we don't know). Someone draws one of the 90 balls. Now, according to EUT, which of these two bets should you prefer?

CHOICE V

Option E: You win \$100 if a red ball is drawn, nothing otherwise.
Option F: You win \$100 if a blue ball is drawn, nothing otherwise.

We don't know how many blue balls there are, so in option F, the expected payoff could be either \$0 or \$60. EUT doesn't tell us anything about how to choose between E and F. Either you prefer to *maximize the minimal gain* and go with option E, where you *know* that you have a 30% chance of winning something, or you prefer to *maximize the maximal gain* and go with option F, where at most you have a 60% chance of winning \$100. EUT is of no help here.

The Allais paradox already showed that a realistic theory of decision-making has to take into account our attitudes toward risk – i.e., whether we are risk-seeking or risk-avoiding – and in particular our attitude toward loss.[17] But now consider the following additional choice between two bets:

CHOICE VI

Option G: You win \$100 if a red ball is drawn, nothing if blue, \$100 if green.
Option H: You win \$100 if a blue ball is drawn, nothing if red, \$100 if green.

Option H can be rewritten as follows: you win nothing if a red ball is drawn, \$100 otherwise, but the previous formulation shows that G and H are the same as E and F, respectively, except for the same modification in both cases – the possibility to win \$100 if a green ball is drawn.

Table 2.9 Decision matrix for the Ellsberg paradox presenting 4 options (E, F, G, H) with different payoffs for different balls drawn, with a known number of red balls (30) but an unknown number of blue and green balls (between 0 and 60 and between 60 and 0, respectively).

	Red (30)	*Blue (Between 0 and 60)*	*Green (Between 60 and 0)*
E	$100	0	0
F	0	$100	0
G	$100	0	$100
H	0	$100	$100

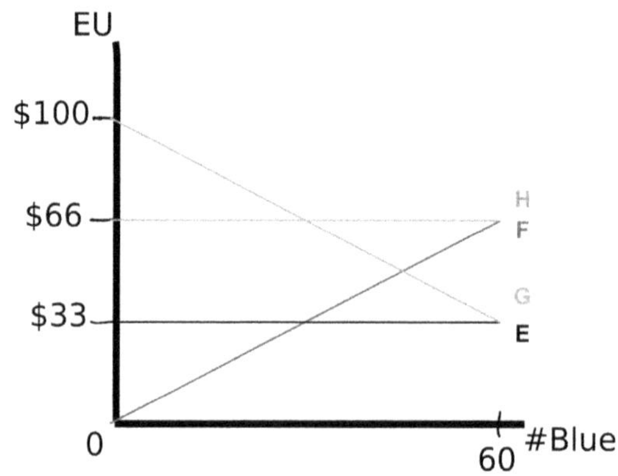

Figure 2.4 Expected utility of each option for Choice V and Choice VI to illustrate the Ellsberg paradox: depending on the (unknown) number of blue balls, the choice with the highest expected utility varies.

We can sum up these two choices as follows:

We already saw with the Allais paradox that the addition of an irrelevant alternative – irrelevant because it's added equally to both options E and F to give us options G and H, respectively – shouldn't affect our ranking between these options: according to EUT, if you prefer E to F, then you should also prefer G to H.

As with the Allais paradox, this is not realistic; most people would prefer E to F, but H to G. Contrary to the Allais paradox, EUT can't tell us how to choose; there is no set expected utility for bets F and G because the number of blue balls is unknown.

One way to see it is to represent the expected utility of each bet as a function of the number of blue balls:

We saw that to choose between E and F under such uncertainty, we should know if we prefer to maximize our *minimal* gain (and go with E) or maximize our *maximal* gain (and go with F) – attitudes that EUT can't account for. Assume that we choose F; this implies that the probability of drawing a blue ball is greater than that of drawing a green ball,[18] yet under that assumption H is preferable to G, which is consistent with EUT but inconsistent with the preference for maximizing the maximal gain.

Therefore, to decide in either of these two choices (between E and F or between G and H), EUT can't tell us how to choose without knowing something about our attitudes toward possible loss and gain, but these attitudes can't dictate our choices without violating EUT.

This paradox isn't just, as was the case with the Allais paradox, an illustration of how unrealistic EUT is but in addition a challenge to the applicability of EUT and its ability to prescribe choices, even taking into account our attitudes toward loss and gain.

As a matter of fact, as mentioned earlier, most people would prefer bet E and bet H, and this is observed regardless of payoff and of attitudes toward loss and gain. This is why such a series of bets is taken to reveal *ambiguity aversion*; indeed, only bets E and H have well-defined expected utilities.

2.7 Psychological alternatives to expected utility theory

The two previous paradoxes are quite a challenge for EUT: it's a theory of decision-making that isn't realistic and lacks nuance, and in some simple cases of incomplete information – which is something we're likely to encounter! –EUT may make inconsistent prescriptions even if we try to take into account attitudes about minimum and maximum expected outcome. What is it good for, then, except in very simple scenarios?

Because of the paradoxes we saw above (the Allais paradox in particular), economists have sought to amend EUT so as to model *actual* decision-making behavior. A key contribution by Daniel Kahneman and Amos Tversky was to take into account attitudes about loss and gain (Kahneman & Tversky 1979). We saw with the Allais paradox that the possibility of a sure loss or sure gain will affect our decision-making psychologically, which EUT doesn't account for.

2.7.1 Prospect theory

In order to capture the actual behavior of actual human beings, Kahneman and Tversky argued that we needed to consider not just expected gains and losses (i.e., expected utility) but these expected utilities *compared* to what a decision maker will consider to be a status quo as well. That is, agents assess not just utilities but *prospects* relative to a reference point.

Recall the following choice in the Allais paradox:

CHOICE I

Option A: win $1 million with 100% chance.
Option B: win $1 million with 89% chance, nothing with 1% chance, or $5 million with 10% chance.

EUT dictates that option B is the better choice (it has a higher expected utility), but many people would choose A. However, the same person could choose either A or B if their circumstances (their reference points) change. If you are wealthy, then you won't mind losing $1 million but will very much value the possible gain of a better expected payoff. But if $1 million could be life-changing to you, then you will very much see option B as a loss of a sure $1 million gain. The same bet, option B, could represent either a possible loss of $1 million or an expected gain of $1.39 million, depending on your reference point.

Prospect theory builds from some key empirical findings about the psychology of decision-making:

- People hate losing much more than they like winning,[19] or in EUT terms, the disutility of a loss is greater than the utility of a similar gain.

Think of when you throw a 50th quarter in a slot machine after 49 failures, telling yourself that if you didn't play that 50th quarter, "all that would have been for nothing!" even though the chance of success for each quarter is completely independent from the previous attempts; all this "sunk cost fallacy" does is make you pay just to avoid acknowledging a loss!

- People tend to overestimate the risk of small probability events (especially potential losses) but treat near certainty as certainty (especially for potential gains).

A 1% difference in chance is perceived as having much more importance for decision-making if it's between a 5% chance and a 6% chance gain than if it's between a 95% and a 96% chance gain.[20]

These observations motivated Kahneman and Tversky's prospect theory, according to which decision-making under risk proceeds in several stages:

> People reframe a choice as a prospect, according to a reference point (i.e., interpret it as a potential loss or a potential gain), and give a value to each possible outcome as they would in EUT, but by overvaluing losses and undervaluing large gains, and then by weighting the events' probabilities. This weighting would overemphasize small probability events and underemphasize large probability events.

To illustrate this idea of "reference point," consider the following scenario:

> If at the end of a month's work you gain your normal salary, you would perceive it as a reference point.
>
> If you earn less because you damaged some of the company's equipment and your boss deducted their value from your salary, your salary will feel like a loss.
>
> If you have a bonus, it will feel like a gain compared to that reference point.

What is considered to be a loss or a gain is a matter of perspective, a *prospect*.

Kahneman and Tversky's two key insights result in a model of decision-making in which small-probability losses are greatly overvalued, and large-probability gains undervalued.

This approach predicts the following general shape for a utility function.

The x axis shows actual (objective) losses and gains, the y axis how they are valued (subjectively) according to some utility unit. The faint dotted line shows

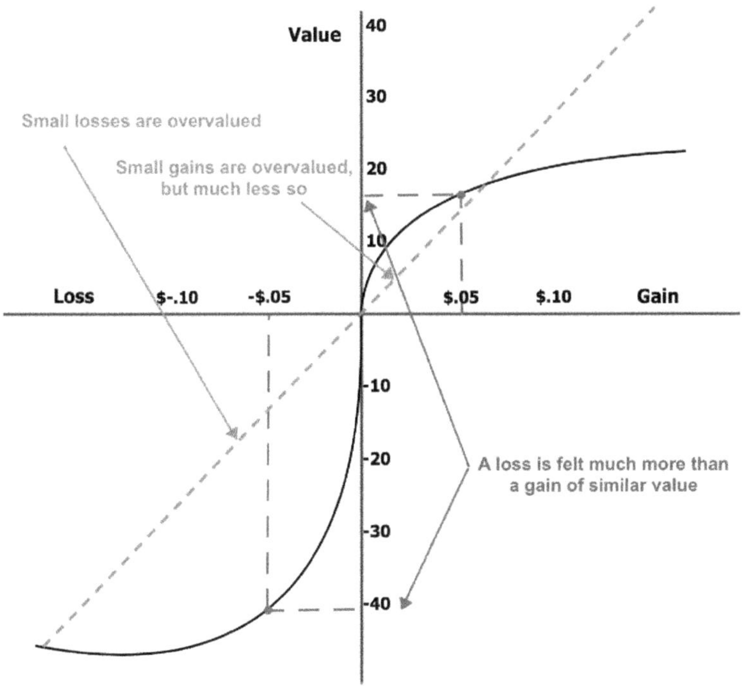

Figure 2.5 General shape, according to prospect theory, of a utility function that overemphasizes small gains over large gains and overemphasizes small losses over large losses but that generally overvalues losses much more than it does gains.

a linear correspondence between actual and subjective value; the solid line is a utility curve.

This black S-shaped utility curve is asymmetric, and this asymmetry depends on what is taken as the reference point: the curve is steeper when we consider losses (on the lower left-hand side) than when we consider gains (on the upper right-hand side). It shows that people overvalue small losses compared to large losses but also that they overreact to small losses more than they overreact to small gains (the area between the red dotted line and the utility curve is much larger on the negative side than on the positive side). The plateau on the positive side also accounts for diminishing returns.

FRAME 7: Prospect theory: how utility is modified

This nonlinear utility function *u* for events *x* each having a probability *P(x)* is then weighted by a modifier *w* that overemphasizes small probabilities and underemphasizes large ones. On this account, when evaluating choices, people would then calculate an expected value, but not quite as they would with EUT.

Table F2.1 Comparison between expected utility and prospect theory.

	EUT	*Prospect Theory*
Utility	A (possibly subjective) utility function *u* that is complete (defined for all possible outcomes under consideration), transitive, continuous, and independent from irrelevant alternative and that doesn't depend on a reference point that separates losses and gains.	A subjective, nonlinear, asymmetric utility function u_o centered on a reference point *o* that overvalues losses, and especially small losses, but with diminishing gains for higher gains.
Expectation	The probability *P(x)* of each event *x*. The probability can be subjective or objective but should be known for each outcome; otherwise, EUT may break down under incomplete information (Ellsberg's paradox).	The weighted probability of each events *w.P(x)*, with an overemphasis on small probabilities and an underemphasis on small probabilities. The expectation is not a probability function but a psychological reinterpretation of how probabilities (whether objective or subjective) are perceived.

	EUT	Prospect Theory
Expected utility of a lottery (i.e., a series of possible outcomes in a bet)	The sum over i for all x_i of $P(x_i).u(x_i)$.	The sum over i for all x_i of $w.P(x_i) \bullet u_0(x_i)$.

This allows us to reconsider the Allais paradox: someone facing both options A and B could take a $1 million gain as a reference point (the status quo), then reframe option B in terms of losses and gains as follows: a $0 gain over option A with 89% chance, a 1% chance of a $1 million loss, or a $4 million gain with 10% chance. Assuming option A's outcome as the status quo, option B's expected utility could still be higher than A's ($4 million is much greater than $1 million), but scaled back, by giving more importance to losses. One would further reassess these prospects by weighting small and large probabilities differently (i.e., by overvaluing small probabilities). Based on the realistic, observed principles of decision-making we just saw, this weighting would tweak our overall expected utility of option B by over-emphasizing small-probability losses over large-probability gains, thereby accounting for the common preference for option A over B.

2.7.2 *Merits of the prospect theory*

This utility curve and probability weighting accounts for many biases and framing effects that psychologists observe:

1. We make different choices if alternatives are presented as a potential loss or a potential gain.
   Consider the following framing effect.[21] A group of people is asked to choose between two treatments for a disease that is expected to kill 600 people:

   a. Treatment α. 200 people are certain to be saved.
   b. Treatment β: either all 600 are saved with probability 1/3 or there's a 2/3 probability that no one is saved.

   α and β have the same expected utility and EUT can't decide between them, but as with the Allais scenarios, most people would prefer α's certain outcome. Now, imagine that the same or another group faces instead the same choice but phrased differently:

c. Treatment γ: 400 people are certain to die.
d. Treatment δ: either all 600 die with probability 2/3 or there's a 1/3 probability that no one dies.

Even though this is just a rephrasing of the previous choice, most people's preferences would be reversed (i.e., most would prefer δ to γ), illustrating that we are *risk averse about gains* but *risk seeking about losses.*

2. We make different choices when the reference point (what you consider to be the *status quo*) changes. For instance, we are likelier to buy a car while sitting in it (since not buying it would be perceived as "losing" it) than if we're not in the car (where not having the car would be perceived as the reference point, i.e., the status quo). This is called an "endowment effect."
3. We overvalue small-probability events perceived as a potential loss. For instance, we are willing to overpay for insurance against unlikely events or are inclined to dread very intensely such small-probability events as a nuclear plant accident.
4. More money doesn't always mean more happiness (this is the effect of diminishing return we saw earlier).
5. We overthink small changes (particularly small losses). Think, for instance, about how we feel when it comes to incurring some losses in comfort in order to preserve a lifestyle that's otherwise more or less the one we have now: the loss of our resource-intensive and CO_2-emitting meat, cars, and air travel is felt much more strongly than a potential gain of getting to keep the climate we are used to.

This framework of decision-making has been corroborated empirically many times since it was first proposed in 1979, for all these effects and more, across different cultures (Ruggeri et al. 2020). It has helped economists, psychologists, and political scientists understand human behavior, how car salespersons make a sale, scientists communicate about climate change risks (Holden & Quiggin 2017), politicians sell policies or manage risks,[22] law enforcement punishes rather than rewards, and countries sign treaties.[23]

2.7.3 Limitations of prospect theory

All that is well, but . . . what about you? What do you care if you have a convex utility function for losses and a concave one for gains? How does that help you learn anything from your arrest and your confrontation with the judge?

For one thing, this approach shows us that, instead of just comparing outcomes for different decisions, you can envisage an action in terms of what you might gain or lose from it. And it shows that your reaction to different outcomes and actions depends on what you consider to be the status quo. Think of the decision you made to speed and run through a red light: when you did so, you probably took as a reference point (the status quo) an anticipated state of maximal short-term comfort, your being back home as fast as possible; not speeding meant a loss of comfort, which you wanted to avoid as much as possible. Maybe you could have had a different utility function, one that places more value on public safety, or maybe you could have adopted a different reference point – such as the amount of guilt you feel either now or at the end of your trip back home – in order to assess different prospects.

This descriptive framework of decision-making also pushes us to acknowledge some biases and psychological shortcuts we have: we resent our losses more than we count our blessings, we don't like ambiguity and will round up large probabilities as certainties, yet we overvalue small risks, etc. And very importantly, it shows that our decisions are greatly affected by how they're framed: what we consider to be status quo, from your perspective or someone else's, now or later. This can certainly help you get a handle on the way you reason and help you incorporate feedback and change.

But prospect theory is a *descriptive* approach to decision-making under risk, not a *normative* one. It doesn't aim to tell you what you *should* do and how you *should* think. Learning and growing is hard and tedious, unfortunately, and prospect theory can't be the ready-made theory of decision-making you were looking for.

So does prospect theory describe rational or irrational decision-making?[24] One thing we expect from a utility measure is *transitivity*, that all choices could be ranked unambiguously and unchangeably. If a preference rule is transitive for, say, alternatives A, B, and C, then necessarily, if A is preferred to B and B to C, then A is preferred to C. If your ranking is not transitive, what would happen? Suppose you prefer one chocolate over two licorices, one licorice over two gummy drops, and one gummy drop over two chocolates. One may trade you a gummy drop for two chocolates, then one chocolate for two licorices, and finally, one licorice for two gummy drops. Each trade was in accordance with your preference ranking, but the result was not so good for you!

A related notion is that of *dominance*: the rule of dominance requires that if choice A yields at least as much (and at times more) of a good outcome as choice B – or if A yields at most as much (and at times less) of a bad outcome as B – under all circumstances, then you should prefer A to B. Psychological studies have shown evidence of typical violations of this rule in pricing decisions (Mellers et al. 1992).

Both transitivity and dominance seem to be requirements of rational decision-making, and a good expected utility theorist would meet these principles. However, prospect theory cannot account for some violations of dominance.[25] A modification of the theory to avoid these then led to violations of transitivity.

Even though prospect theory aims to be a descriptive theory of decision-making, it would be more useful if it could help us model or explain *acceptable* decision-making: the decisions many would make in the Allais scenarios may not be those of an ideal, rational decision maker, but they seem acceptable nonetheless. In contrast, dominance or transitivity are difficult to renounce.

To avoid this, John Quiggin proposed to modify prospect theory (Quiggin 1982). He proposed that the weighting of different outcomes' probabilities be partially determined by the ranking of these outcomes, i.e., by how good or bad each outcome is relative to other outcomes. And add some constraints to the possible weighting of events' probability.

Quiggin's approach, called "rank-dependent expected utility," was then incorporated into prospect theory to form cumulative prospect theory. A considerable advantage in revising prospect theory according to Quiggin's insight was to avoid problems of dominance and transitivity.

Such an insight – that we don't just overemphasize small probabilities generally but that we do so depending on *how relatively good* or bad the outcome is and depending on our *disposition* toward good or bad outcomes – more readily explains some behaviors than prospect theory. For instance, the fact that we can be *risk seeking* and optimistic for unlikely gains (when we gamble our money away playing the lotto) and risk avoiding and pessimistic for unlikely losses (when we insure ourselves against such unlikely events as a car crash or an earthquake) is easy to model as an acceptable (i.e., not completely incoherent) behavior with that approach.

2.8 Conclusions: constraints, uses, and limitations of formal theories of decision-making

We were first hoping to find a framework to help us learn from our mistakes and make better decisions when we face risks. Or maybe you just wanted to get away from a speeding ticket and a DUI and you wanted to appeal the judge's decision with an ironclad defense and prove to her that your actions were the most reasonable possible. In either case, we were hoping to find some sort of mechanism, some sort of "decision calculus" that would make decisions for us and tell what's the best option when we face uncertain and possibly dangerous situations.

Along the way we learned a few things:

- If you want to treat decision about potential harms and rewards as a calculus, then you can express different options with a utility measure that has to meet some criteria (completeness, continuity, and transitivity); otherwise, it could lead to inconsistent decisions.
- If your decisions are multifactorial, you still need to simplify them and find a way to express them as a unique utility measure, which leaves a lot of room for interpretation, discussion, value judgments, etc.

Think, for instance, of expressing your choice to speed or not in terms of public safety (and not in terms of the time you could save, your comfort, how fun it is to speed, etc.). Even if that's your approach, do you frame it as a fatality risk per mile or per minute, as a potential cost to taxpayers who would have to pay someone's hospital bill? We saw the conclusion could be very different! Ideally, you should be able to express alternative risk options with a unique value unit, one that we all agree on, and such that equivalent units won't yield different results.

- That such a system may break down when you have incomplete information (that was Ellsberg's paradox), which happens a lot.
- That in simple situations where you can quantify harms or rewards and their probability, the Bayesian updating rule is a useful tool.
- That your assessments of risks and decisions depend not only on how you value the outcomes and probabilities (which may not be shared by everyone) but also on your own state of mind (i.e., what you consider to be the status quo as opposed to what you might lose or gain) when you do such an assessment and how different choices are phrased.
- That you can't have a framework of decision-making that is both rational (i.e., completely consistent) and psychologically realistic.

Moreover, since there's no universal and psychologically realistic way to present a problem (because we can't all be in the same state of mind or material situation in front of the same choice), you can't improve either aspect (consistency or psychological realism) without a cost.

- That even a system that aims only at consistency and not descriptive accuracy requires as input a choice of preferences about different outcomes, as well as things like your general attitude about risk or your optimism about some events, which will hardly apply to more than one person at a time and only at a given time.

And so what do you make of the judge's proposed calculus: saving a few minutes of driving versus a lifetime of guilt? Was that just a rhetorical point? It probably wasn't; she could have offered you a different calculus, one about your safety and comfort against that of others.

Maybe her point was that even if you just think about yourself, when you make decisions that you know could be risky, you can add a bit more perspective in a calculus entirely focused on your own comfort. You can be selfish, and even then, speeding is not worth it, if you're capable of guilt.

Her framing of the decision you were facing that night, much like any of the aforementioned steps, assumes many normative choices, many value judgments about what you look for in a decision, who makes that decision, for whom, and under what circumstances.

There goes our hope for a clean, one-size-fits-all, and automatized framework of decision-making under risk. There is no avoiding our responsibility for the choices we make.

Review questions

1. Which of these choices have the greatest expected utility?
   A. I gain \$1 if a coin toss results in heads, and I lose \$3 if it rains tomorrow (there's a 1/3 chance that it will rain).
   B. I gain \$10 no matter what, and I gain \$100 if I roll a 6 with a die throw with one single throw (and if I roll any other number, I lose \$100).
   C. I gain \$1 if a coin toss results in heads and lose \$1 if it results in tails.
2. Some general rules of probabilities, otherwise known as the Kolmogorov axioms, dictate that (1) if Ω represents the totality of all possibilities, the probability of Ω is $P(\Omega) = 1$ (normativity); (2) for any possibility p in Ω (and which is not Ω itself), the probability of p is strictly greater than zero and strictly smaller than 1: $0<P(p)<1$ (non-negativity); (3) if p and q are two mutually exclusive possibilities (for instance, "It rains" and "It doesn't rain"), then the probability of "p or q" is the sum of the probability of each of them: $P(p \text{ or } q) = P(p) + P(q)$ (additivity).
   - From these axioms, show that the following theorem obtains, for any possibilities a and b, $P(a \text{ or } b) = P(a) + P(b) - P(a \,\&\, b)$.

     We also saw the formula for conditionalization, for two possibilities p and q: $P(p \mid q) = P(p \,\&\, q) / P(q)$, provided $P(q) \neq 0$.
   - Using Kolmogorov's axioms and conditionalization, show that the following version of Bayes' theorem obtains (the other version of Bayes' theorem we saw is a simpler version) $P(X \mid Y) = (P(Y \mid X) \cdot P(X)) / (P(Y \mid X) \cdot P(X) + P(Y \mid {\sim}X) \cdot P({\sim}X))$, provided the denominator is not equal to zero and where ~X means "not X."
3. Consider the following information (adapted from Tversky & Kahneman 1983):

   Linda is 31 years old, single, outspoken and very bright. She majored in philosophy. As a student, she was deeply concerned with issues of discrimination and social justice, and also participated in anti-nuclear demonstrations.

   Knowing only this, which of the following two arguments is correct? Could you phrase it with conditional probabilities? (Hint: conjunction fallacy.)
   A. Linda is more likely to be a bank teller than a feminist bank teller because all feminist bank tellers are feminists, and Linda could possibly be a nonfeminist bank teller.
   B. Linda is more likely to be a feminist bank teller than she is likely to be a bank teller because she fits the profile of a feminist, and if any bank teller is going to be a feminist, then it will be Linda.

4. Most people would choose a 100% chance to win \$950,000 over a 98% chance to win \$1,000,000. Why is that a challenge for expected utility theory?
   A. As a normative theory of decision-making, expected utility theory should describe how many people should act, and if it can't account for a common response to such a simple choice, then it can't be a good theory.
   B. This fact is a reminder that most people are irrational, and hoping that they would follow the rules of expected utility theory – let alone learn basic math – is a lost cause.
   C. If expected utility theory aims to guide actual decision-making, then it should be able to accommodate such a common human behavior as risk aversion; otherwise, it is a theory that treats most people as irrational even when they are making a very sensible decision.
5. In what way do the Ellsberg and the Allais paradoxes represent different types of challenges to expected utility theory?
   A. The Allais paradox only applies when all options are well-defined and possible, when the probability of each event is known with certainty, whereas the Ellsberg paradox only applies in cases when options are uncertain; taken together, both paradoxes challenge EUT in all possible cases.
   B. The Allais paradox is a challenge to the applicability of EUT as a theory of actual decision-making, whereas the Ellsberg paradox is a challenge to the very consistency of EUT under some simple circumstances of uncertainty.
   C. The Allais paradox is only a paradox for a normative conception of a theory of decision-making, whereas the Ellsberg paradox is only a paradox for a descriptive conception of a theory of decision-making.
6. Prospect theory differs from expected utility theory in that:
   A. Because it takes into account psychological attitudes toward gain and loss and the perspective from which we assess them, it is a more psychologically realistic account of expected utility.
   B. It better takes into account future choices.
   C. Although both are normative theories of decision-making, prospect theory was designed to avoid the Allais paradox.

Discussion topics

Remember that the night of your arrest for drunk driving, you had been speaking with a friend who worked at Google? She was telling you about her new AI project. She mentioned working on ethics and algorithms. It's all about the math, she claimed, and sounded a lot like an application of EUT principles.

But it could save the world, preserve humankind for all of eternity, and solve poverty on Earth. Her great ambition was to confront *existential risks.*

Some risks are extremely unlikely but have the potential to destroy all of humankind: Earth-shattering asteroids, nuclear carnage, pandemics that depopulate whole continents, but also the rise of malevolent artificial intelligence that would take over the Earth. Nick Bostrom asked, Shouldn't we then reallocate all our funds, now devoted to solving relatively minor problems (such as famine, disparity in education, resource-intensive urban sprawl), to solving these existential risks? (Bostrom 2013).

The probability for an existential risk may be small, but as small as it is, since the harm is existential – infinite, one might argue, or at least as large as the value of our survival as a species – the risks are immense. So Bostrom argues that we should prioritize such existential risks because the harm they would do is much larger, for potentially many, many more people (those alive now but also all those that could be in the future) than any problem we currently face.

Even if we dismiss the threat of a malevolent AI, we can still be concerned about the prospect of existential risks. If so, then this looks like a good case study for EUT. Indeed, the nature of this conundrum doesn't depend much on how we describe and measure the potential harm. As long as the risk is possible, the harm is, for all practical purposes, as good as infinite! It is impervious to framing effects (for instance, the loss of all humankind is not a psychological effect; it's not the sort of loss aversion that prospect theory would try to account for). In short, this could be a simple decision-making problem involving risks that is not affected by any of the problems we discussed for EUT.

Yet it makes the normative, value-laden aspect of any decision under risk obvious. The particular choice of utility unit might seem irrelevant: the argument stands whether we talk about lives lost, pain suffered, dollars lost, etc. But we are asked to compare actual lives against future lives – isn't that debatable? Well, governments do this when devising long-term policies, and isn't that what we do when we advocate sustainable lifestyles that could curb climate change? But what is the cost if it means abandoning efforts aimed at those "relatively minor" problems of famine, housing, urban sprawl, or local poverty?

Aren't there different versions of EUT that could minimize the importance of existential risks? For instance, an *average utilitarianism* that is concerned with maximizing *average* expected utility among all humankind wouldn't be so concerned about humanity's early ending but rather about the quality of the few that will live; on the other hand, *maximal utilitarianism* will be concerned about the sum total of all utiles, which will greatly depend on how much humans there will ever be. If we don't think that we should attach so much importance to existential but highly unlikely risks, does it mean we're just average utilitarians who might even welcome humankind's early demise if it means preventing future suffering?

***

When we discuss decision-making and the reasons behind choices between alternatives, we assume that it makes sense to compare or merely contemplate these different options. Consider the choice of driving versus walking back home under the influence in this chapter's scenario; the judge admonished you to consider the lifetime of guilt that you may experience if you had injured someone with your car. But when making a decision about whether or not to drive, can you reasonably be expected to consider what such a transformative experience as that of killing a pedestrian would be like? Does it make sense to expect from a framework of decision-making to account for such profound changes in the decision-making agent?

In her book, L. A. Paul (2014) questions the soundness of such assumptions. It is difficult – meaningless, perhaps – to value (or disvalue) an outcome if it is something that we have not experienced. Many of the risks we face have outcomes that we have not experienced, or indeed cannot experience, because the loss occurs in other species (e.g., biodiversity loss) or on too grand a scale (e.g., climate change). To what extent does it undermine the project, discussed in this chapter, to find a framework for decision-making?

Notes

1 Rephrased in terms of a utile, this could be, for instance, -1 utile for ☹, 0 utile for 😐, and +1 utile for ☺.
2 See the frame on the axioms and rules of probability on page 45 (frame "Probability theory").
3 Could you see this intuitively? You can check it by giving some numbers to those emoticons: say, 10 to the happy one, 2 to the unhappy one, and 6 to the in-between. Then the expected utility of taking your umbrella is 6, while the expected utility of not taking it is (0.3)(2) + (0.7)(10) = 7.6.
4 See Eddy 1982. The mistake here is to conflate the probability of being ill given a positive test, P(ill|+), with that of a test being positive in case of an illness, P(+|ill). For a more recent example, on inferences about racial disparities in police violence, see, for instance, Knox and Mummolo (2020).
5 In practice, you do need nudges: you are human, and as such, you value short-term gains (like an immediate rebate on your premium) relatively much more than you value long-term gains (such as an overall reduction in your hospital bills). The insurance company, which also saves a lot of money each time a customer purchases this safety bias, knows about this *availability bias*, and that's why it makes sense for them to offer the premium rebate.
6 In fact, the US EPA relies on much higher estimates over larger populations. These estimates currently range between one and several dozen million dollars: see, for instance, a ten-million-dollar estimate in United States Environmental Protection Agency 2014.
7 For further discussion on VSL and a case study, see Chapter 5 on cost-benefit analysis.
8 See León & Miguel 2017, a customer preference study in Sierra Leone that found that the VSL of an African traveler ($577,000 per statistical life) was far lower than that of a non-African traveler ($924,000 per statistical life).
9 See, for instance, Cohen and Zilberman (1997) for a criticism of a stated WTP study. WTP studies can be conducted to assess consumer preference, e.g., of organic over genetically modified produced; there again, stated WTP may differ from observed WTP. See, for instance, Knight et al. (2005).
10 For a historical and conceptual introduction to this notion, see Moscati (2018).
11 For instance, if the EPA reduces all policy alternatives to dollar amounts and made policy choices based on the sum of all benefits (in $) minus all costs (in $), it's not clear how they would take into

account distributional concerns (how harms and gains are distributed among the general population). Such moral considerations may escape a crude valuation.

12 Only the last of these four outcomes was not included in Table 2.1; it would correspond to what would happen if, in case of rain, you had taken a hammer or a spoon instead of an umbrella.

13 Otherwise, you wouldn't have ranked "wet and unencumbered" lower than "dry and encumbered."

14 Here we are overlooking the difference between additive and nonadditive (e.g., categorical) units. If we want to have a metric to use in an EUT calculus, as we have seen earlier, then we need a metric (additive, by definition). That doesn't change the point here that MVRA, in principle, can't claim to avoid the arbitrariness and possibly convoluted aspect of reducing several attributes to just one value unit. Moreover, Shrader-Frechette (see 1985) responded to the "category mistake" criticism against risk / cost-benefit analysis conducted in dollars; if we object to combining and reducing complex sets of attributes to one scale, then we object to much of economics as a field.

15 There is, in fact, little evidence to support this claim according to Lara Buchak (2013: fn. 34), who cites two studies published decades apart: MacCrimmon and Larsson (1979), in support of this claim, and Oliver (2003), where gambles are over health outcomes rather than monetary outcomes and where only 14 out of the 38 subjects showed such preferences. You should try to ask around you to get more data!

16 Yes, the same Daniel Ellsberg played by Matthews Rhys in the 2017 movie *The Post* alongside Tom Hanks and Meryl Streep.

17 Indeed, preferring A to B is usually taken to reveal loss aversion.

18 This paradox was, in fact, introduced as a challenge to EUT even under a subjective interpretation of probabilities (Ellsberg 1961).

19 You can probably think of elections where, if you were somewhat undecided, "My opponent hates you, don't let her win because it would make you a loser!" was a more powerful incentive than the mere prospect of helping win a political team you could join.

20 You might think, for instance, of how surprised people were that a candidate with a 95% chance of winning an election didn't win, and you probably wouldn't fly a plane if told there's a 5% chance it could crash!

21 Example from Fischhoff and Kadvany (2011: 76).

22 See, for instance, Mercer (2005) reminding us that politicians would rather sell an economic reform as yielding 90% employment (i.e., framed as a gain) rather than 10% unemployment (framed as a loss).

23 See, for instance, Hager et al. (2019). More generally, for a discussion of possible applications of prospect theory in describing the psychology of decision-making but the difficulties in applying it (e.g., because it's not a prescriptive theory and because it was developed as an individual rather than collective theory of decision-making), see, e.g., Barberis (2013).

24 Indeed, what makes the S shape of the utility curve valuable and the insights behind prospect theory (namely, that very high-probability events will be treated as certain ones and small-probability events either discarded for large gains or greatly exaggerated for small losses) places a limit on the *continuity* of such a utility function. As Kahneman and Tversky, referring to a "quantal effect," put it, "there is a limit to how small a decision weight can be attached to an event, if it is given any weight at all" (1979: 280).

25 This example is taken from Tversky and Kahneman (1986); see problems 7 and 8, pp. 263–265.

References

Allais, M. (1953). "Le comportement de l'homme rationnel devant le risque: Critique des postulats et axiomes de l'école américaine." *Econometrica*, 21(4): 503. https://doi.org/10.2307/1907921.

Arnauld, A., & Nicole, P. (1662). *La logique ou l'art de penser (Logique de Port-Royal)* (J. V. Buroker, Trans.). Logic or the Art of Thinking.

Barberis, N. C. (2013). "Thirty years of prospect theory in economics: A review and assessment." *Journal of Economic Perspectives*, 27(1): 173–196. https://doi.org/10.1257/jep.27.1.173.

Bostrom, N. (2013). "Existential risk prevention as global priority." *Global Policy*, 4(1): 15–31. https://doi.org/10.1111/1758-5899.12002.

Briggs, R. A. (2019). "Normative theories of rational choice: Expected utility." Retrieved September 11, 2021, from https://plato.stanford.edu/entries/rationality-normative-utility/.

Buchak, L. (2013). *Risk and rationality*. Oxford University Press. https://doi.org/10.1093/acprof:oso/9780199672165.001.0001.

Cohen, D. R., & Zilberman, D. (1997). "Actual versus stated willingness to pay: A comment." *Journal of Agricultural and Resource Economics*. https://doi.org/10.22004/ag.econ.30849.

Dorman, P. (1996). *Markets and mortality: Economics, dangerous work, and the value of human life*. Cambridge University Press. https://doi.org/10.1017/CBO9780511628382.

Eddy, D. M. (1982). "Probabilistic reasoning in clinical medicine: Problems and opportunities." In D. Kahneman, P. Slovic, & A. Tversky (eds.), *Judgment under Uncertainty: Heuristics and Biases* (pp. 249–267). Cambridge University Press. https://doi.org/10.1017/cbo9780511809477.019.

Ellsberg, D. (1961). "Risk, ambiguity, and the Savage axioms." *Quarterly Journal of Economics*, 75(4): 643–669. https://doi.org/10.2307/1884324.

Fischhoff, B., & Kadvany, J. (2011). *Risk: A very short introduction*. Oxford University Press. https://doi.org/10.1093/ACTRADE/9780199576203.001.0001.

Hager, L., Roy, O., Hancock, L. E., & Ensley, M. J. (2019). Selling the iran nuclear agreement: Prospect theory and the campaign to frame the joint comprehensive plan of action." *Congress & the Presidency*, 46(3): 417–445. https://doi.org/10.1080/07343469.2019.1600172.

Hempel, C. G. (1960). "Inductive inconsistencies." *Synthese*, 12, 439–469. https://doi.org/10.1007/BF00485428.

Heukelom, F. (2015). "A history of the Allais paradox." *British Journal for the History of Science*, 48(1): 147–169. https://doi.org/10.1017/S0007087414000570.

Holden, S. T., & Quiggin, J. (2017). "Climate risk and state-contingent technology adoption: Shocks, drought tolerance and preferences." *European Review of Agricultural Economics*, 44(2): 285–308. https://doi.org/10.1093/ERAE/JBW016.

Huynh, D. (2011). "The perils of drunk walking (Ep. 55) – Freakonomics freakonomics." Retrieved September 11, 2021, from https://freakonomics.com/2011/12/28/the-perils-of-drunk-walking/.

Kahneman, D., & Deaton, A. (2010). "High income improves evaluation of life but not emotional well-being." *Proceedings of the National Academy of Sciences of the United States of America*, 107(38): 16489–16493. https://doi.org/10.1073/pnas.1011492107.

Kahneman, D., & Tversky, A. (1979). "Prospect theory: An analysis of decision under risk." *Econometrica*, 47(2): 263–292. https://doi.org/10.2307/1914185.

Knight, J. G., Mather, D. W., & Holdsworth, D. K. (2005). "Consumer benefits and acceptance of genetically modified food." *Journal of Public Affairs*, 5(3–4): 226–235. https://doi.org/10.1002/pa.24.

Knox, D., & Mummolo, J. (2020). "Making inferences about racial disparities in police violence." *Proceedings of the National Academy of Sciences*, 117(3): 1261–1262. https://doi.org/10.1073/pnas.1919418117.

Krupnick, A., Alberini, A., Cropper, M., Simon, N., O'Brien, B., Goeree, R., & Heintzelman, M. (2002). "Age, health and the willingness to pay for mortality risk reductions: A contingent valuation survey of Ontario residents." *Journal of Risk and Uncertainty*. https://doi.org/10.1023/A:1014020027011.

León, G., & Miguel, E. (2017). "Risky transportation choices and the value of a statistical life." *American Economic Journal: Applied Economics*, 9(1): 202–228. https://doi.org/10.1257/app.20160140.

MacCrimmon, K. R., & Larsson, S. (1979). "Utility theory: Axioms versus 'paradoxes'." *Expected Utility Hypotheses and the Allais Paradox*: 333–409. https://doi.org/10.1007/978-94-015-7629-1_15.

Mellers, B., Weiss, R., & Birnbaum, M. (1992). "Violations of dominance in pricing judgments." *Journal of Risk and Uncertainty*, 5(1): 73–90. https://doi.org/10.1007/BF00208788.

Mercer, J. (2005). "Prospect theory and political science." *Annual Review of Political Science*, 8, 1–21. https://doi.org/10.1146/ANNUREV.POLISCI.8.082103.104911.

Moscati, I. (2018). *Measuring utility: From the marginal revolution to behavioral economics*. Oxford University Press. https://doi.org/10.1093/oso/9780199372768.001.0001.

Oliver, A. (2003). "A quantitative and qualitative test of the Allais paradox using health outcomes." *Journal of Economic Psychology*, 24(1): 35–48. https://doi.org/10.1016/S0167-4870(02)00153-8.

Paul, L. A. (2014). *Transformative experience*. Oxford University Press. https://doi.org/10.1093/acprof:oso/9780198717959.001.0001.

Peterson, M. (2007). "On multi-attribute risk analysis." In T. Lewens (ed.), *Risk: Philosophical perspectives* (pp. 78–93). Routledge. https://doi.org/10.4324/9780203962596-10.

Quiggin, J. (1982). "A theory of anticipated utility." *Journal of Economic Behavior & Organization*, 3(4): 323–343. https://doi.org/10.1016/0167-2681(82)90008-7.

Ruggeri, K., Alí, S., Berge, M. L., Bertoldo, G., Bjørndal, L. D., Cortijos-Bernabeu, A., . . . Folke, T. (2020). "Replicating patterns of prospect theory for decision under risk." *Nature Human Behaviour*, 4(6): 622–633. https://doi.org/10.1038/s41562-020-0886-x.

Shrader-Frechette, K. (1985). The real risks of risk-cost-benefit analysis. *Technology in Society*, 7(4): 399–409. https://doi.org/10.1016/0160-791X(85)90007-7.

Tversky, A., & Kahneman, D. (1983). "Extensional versus intuitive reasoning: The conjunction fallacy in probability judgment." *Psychological Review*, 90(4): 293.

Tversky, A., & Kahneman, D. (1986). "Rational choice and the framing of decisions." *The Journal of Business*, 59(4): S251–S278. https://doi.org/10.1080/03057240802227486.

United States Environmental Protection Agency. (n.d.). "Mortality risk valuation | US EPA." Retrieved September 11, 2021, from www.epa.gov/environmental-economics/mortality-risk-valuation.

United States Environmental Protection Agency. (2014). *Regulatory impact analysis of the proposed revisions to the national ambient air quality standards for ground-level ozone*. Research Triangle Park, NC: Office of Air Quality Planning and Standards Air Quality Strategies and Standards Division. Publication No. EPA-452/R-07-008 July 2007. https://www.epa.gov/sites/default/files/2020-07/documents/naaqs-o3_ria_proposal_2007-07.pdf.

von Neumann, J., & Morgenstern, O. (1944). *Theory of games and economic behavior. Theory of Games and Economic Behavior*. Princeton: Princeton University Press.

3 Risk assessment

Contents

DOI: 10.4324/9780429023521-4

3.1 Risk assessment and normativity

When the hurricane season starts, or when a virus begins to spread in the population, we want to know how much is at risk for us, both as individuals and as a society. Scientific risk assessment is based on prior knowledge of the danger (how hurricanes develop, how viruses spread in the population) and hard data on the current situation. Government policies which rely on scientific risk assessment can pride themselves on being data-driven and science-driven and are right to do so.

But what does that mean exactly to be "data-driven" or "science-driven"? Does that mean that the assessment is a mere description of what things are with no influence of what we value, what our interests or aims are? Is it what science does for us, a description of things, phenomena, around us from the perspective of someone who has no interest or preference whatsoever? Descriptive judgments are typically contrasted with normative judgments. In general, normative judgments are the expression of what we think something should be, and so the expression of what we value and disvalue. In the context of this chapter, we take norms to the expression of values: "You should be kind" is the expression of our judgment that being kind is better than not being kind, and so that we value being kind.

The norms can be ethical, expressing, for instance, what kind of behavior we value or disvalue, as in "We should take better care of the environment." Or they can be social and express what kind of society we value or disvalue, as in "There should not be so much economic disparity in the distribution of wealth and income." Our leading question throughout this chapter is whether and how normative judgments are involved in scientific risk assessment.

Whether normative judgment is involved in scientific risk assessment is a special case of a more general question: "Does the production of scientific knowledge involve normative judgments?" And happily, this question has been the object of a great amount of academic work in the past decades (Brown 2020; Kincaid et al. 2007). Philosophy of science studies have made it clear that, indeed, it does, and necessarily so: some of the norms or values involved are referred to as "epistemic values" and include empirical adequacy or predictive power, internal consistency, consistency with other theories, explanatory scope, simplicity. Epistemic norms are regarded as promoting the formation of better beliefs, just as ethical norms are regarded as promoting the formation of better behaviors, and social norms the formation of better societies, even though, of course, what "better" means in each of those cases is very different. But it has also been shown that epistemic norms are not the only kind of norms involved in science, and it is in those other kinds of norms that we will be especially interested in this chapter.

We will discuss how risk is formally, scientifically assessed, with a focus on how some normative judgments are involved. As we now know, there is risk where there is exposure to the possibility of unwanted effects. Formal assessment of risk uses scientific methods to study the probability, the mechanisms of occurrence, and the extent of those effects. So much of what can be said in general about science regarding the role of normative judgments will apply to the study of risk. But because risk involves exposure and effects that are unwanted, there are particular issues, regarding the role of normative judgments, which arise in the study of risk that do not arise, or not in the same way, in other forms of scientific activity.

3.1.1 Epistemic normative judgments

That normative judgments are playing an ineliminable role in science may come as a surprise. We think of the aim and result of science as the explanation of natural phenomena; it produces descriptions and explanations for what we observe. And we think of these explanations as descriptive, as describing the way things work in the world independently of whatever human beings think about it, and independently of whatever human beings think about what the world or anything else should be like.

But some kinds of normative judgments are absolutely crucial to the production of scientific knowledge, and that it is so has become part of our understanding of scientific practice. And after all, we are well aware that not just anything will count as scientific explanation of a phenomenon and that some explanations will be better than others, in the same way as we see some behaviors as morally better than others (sharing is better than stealing), or some political systems as socially better than others (a democracy is better than a dictatorship).

There is a group of norms involved in scientific practice that comprises what is referred to as epistemic norms because they are regarded as promoting knowledge, such as features that make a scientific explanation a good one or better than another one. Some of these norms will be at play in some kinds of scientific practices and not in others, or they will play a more important role in some than in others. So there is not a rigid, finite set of norms that could mechanically be applied in just any case of scientific activity (Kuhn 1962; Laudan 1984). What epistemic norms will be favored in a particular case and how they will be applied do not follow mechanical rules, and in fact, it is even intrinsic to what they are and how they are involved in scientific activity that they are not and cannot be applied mechanically, no more than norms that are at play in other domains. For instance, typical epistemic norms are predictive accuracy and simplicity, but it is clear that predictive accuracy is of little relevance to string theories, since they are not physically applied, and simplicity will only have comparative relevance in the case of theories of climate change that have to account for the interactions between several complex systems and the result of this interaction turned into a computer simulation. So if it plays a role at all, it will be under an understanding of simplicity very different from the one at play in the study of simpler phenomena.

3.1.2 Non-epistemic normative judgments

As we just explained, scientific practice involves, at its core, the use of epistemic normative judgments. But philosophical and social science studies have also shown that there are norms often involved in scientific practice that are not among those recognized as epistemic, that is, non-epistemic norms and normative judgments.[1]

Philosophers have made the distinction between three moments of scientific research: choice of a research program, scientific research, application of the results. They have argued that non-epistemic values are necessarily playing a role in the first and third of those three moments: in determining what domain of research should be developed and in determining how the results of the research should be applied. And it used to be generally accepted that they should not play a role in the scientific reasoning that leads to the acceptance of a theory, that theory acceptance should only be based on epistemic values or epistemic criteria (Douglas 2009).

But what has actually been shown is that non-epistemic normative judgments are also playing a role in the scientific research itself, in the part of science that is producing scientific results. This is because scientific research includes much more than deciding whether or not to accept a theory. In particular, there is the choice of methodology used to gather evidence and the choice of what constitutes enough evidence to accept the theory. Non-epistemic values are inevitably involved in these two steps. It is not allowed to experiment on human beings in the way it is allowed to experiment on other animals, and that is the clear expression of values that we have no reason to think are conducive to the truth that we are generally seeking, which is about human beings. And as we will discuss later in this chapter, different strengths of evidence supporting a theory will generally be required, depending on what kind and extent of consequences would follow from accepting and acting on this theory if it is false.

The extent of the role played by non-epistemic norms is not as easy to bring to light as that of epistemic norms. It requires to look closely and carefully at the way the study of a certain phenomenon has developed, and often these norms will have been silently involved in the development of the concept of the phenomenon itself, the development of the method to investigate the phenomenon, the determination of what counts as evidence for the phenomenon (Peschard & van Fraassen 2014). Often, these non-epistemic norms have been androcentric or anthropocentric (Longino 2001; Anderson 2004).

Does that mean that non-epistemic values do play a role in what theory is accepted, since it plays a role in what data are produced and how much evidence is required to accept the theory? Even if the ethical norms may contribute to the choice of the methodology ("experiments on all animals but humans are allowed"), it seems that acceptance itself of a claim, a hypothesis, could and should only be based on epistemic norms, especially whether it is supported by empirical evidence. Of course, ethical norms will have an influence on what evidence is available at all to confirm the theory, and so it has an influence on what theory can be supported at all by the evidence; for instance, results about the effect of a drug on other animals do not provide evidence for a claim about the effect of the drug on humans. But that does not mean that ethical or social values, in what is regarded as good science, play a direct role in evaluating and selecting claims about the world.

However, the line between the choice of a methodology, on the one hand, and what claims are selected on the basis of evidence, on the other hand, is actually not as clear as it may seem. Brigandt (2015) illustrates this point with the example of drug trials sponsored by the company producing the drug. The results of the study are more likely to be positive for the company than do results from independent studies, but the drug company results are produced in scientific journals and so can be assumed to follow scientific norms. The explanation is in how the trials are set up and what questions exactly are tested by the study.

> The explanation for the bias is that industry-sponsored trials know to "ask the right questions" . . ., e.g., having the trial drug run against too low a dose of a competitor drug (making the trial drug seem more effective) or against too high a dose of a competitor drug (making the trial drug's side-effects appear relatively minor).
>
> (Brigandt 2015)

The choice of one methodology rather than another, the kind of evidence that is produced rather than another, the kind of questions asked, the kind of claims that are allowed to receive evidential support – all that combine to produce a certain conception of the world around us. If that were not the case, drug companies would not take the pain to conduct their own studies. In the case of drugs, some independent testings are there to counterbalance this effect. But there might be cases where there is no such "independent" testing, and it is difficult or made difficult to see that a specific methodology or kind of methodology has been selected at the expense of any other.

And it may also be that there is never "independent" testing but only testing from a particular standpoint that includes a certain type of methodology, a certain type of question, and channeling all the choices that are made, specific aims. When that becomes clear, it looks like non-epistemic values are involved in all the moments of science. It does not mean that the different ways in which different values are involved is irrelevant; it is not the same at all to accept a theory because it is politically convenient or because it is supported by evidence. But it means that a claim about a phenomenon can be both supported by evidence and biased in some ways – biased by the specific choices that were made at many steps of the process that ended with the supporting evidence. And it means that it is extremely important to scrutinize also the aspects of research other than whether there is evidential support, and how much (cf. Kourany 2010), to become aware of how many choices shape our conception of the phenomena around us and become able to critically consider this influence, and maybe try other choices:

> [N]ot every set of true statements about a given phenomenon constitutes an acceptable theory of that phenomenon. Some sets offer a distorted,

> biased representation of the whole. This can make them unworthy representations of a phenomenon even if they contain no falsehoods. But what constitutes an adequate, unbiased representation of the whole is relative to our values, interests, and aims, some of which have moral and political import.
>
> (Anderson 1995: 37)

As we will see in the chapter on risk management, the alternatives assessment approach to risk management argues that traditional forms of risk management rely on a form of assessment whose specific aim is to check whether a certain source of potential harm, like emission of toxic substance, is not "too" harmful (O'Brien 2000). And it is based on some "research questions," looking at specific effects, that may not represent the variety of interests of the population exposed to the risk. By contrast, the alternatives assessment approach advocates the search of alternative courses of action, including some that are *not* harmful and for giving a voice in the process to the population exposed.

In this chapter on risk assessment, we are looking into whether and how some non-epistemic normative judgments are involved in risk assessment. Of course, there is an obvious way in which non-epistemic normative judgments are involved in any study of a risk: when something is identified as "unwanted" effect. But what we are interested in is, more specifically, whether and how some non-epistemic normative judgments are involved in the evaluation of the likeliness (probability), extent of the unwanted effects (severity), and acceptability (or unacceptability) of the risk.

3.2 Risk assessment: probability and severity

Very often, the assessment of risk is given simply as a measure of a probability, as we saw in Chapter 2. For instance, if one asks how serious the risk of rain or the risk of losing at a game is, the answer that is expected is generally a probability. It does not mean that risk, even in this context, is the same as probability. Talking about risk implies that there is a possibility of something unwanted happening, whereas we can talk just as well about the probability of something very desirable to happen. But sometimes, when we ask about a measure of a risk, an appropriate answer is in terms of probability. This is, however, not always the case.[2]

When an insurance company is assessing the risk of your vehicle being stolen or your home suffering in an earthquake in order to determine what premium they will ask you to pay, they take into account the chance, that is, the probability that your vehicle will be stolen or that your home will suffer in an earthquake. But they also take into account, in their assessment of the risk, the severity of the damage in terms of the value of the vehicle or the value of the house and the belongings in it.

Similarly, if you were considering playing a game of chance, you would be wise, before you enter the game, to make an assessment of the risk, knowing the game with the lowest probability of losing is not always the least risky; it also depends on the amount of the possible loss. So risk assessment will include not only an evaluation of the uncertainty of losing but also of the severity of the loss.

What will be a good answer to the question of what the risk of X is will depend very much on the context of the question. For instance, if we ask about the risk of dying from being struck by lightning or getting lung cancer, what we are asking for is a probability. But if we are asking about the risk of a nuclear war with North Korea or about the risk of an increase in the global average surface temperature of 3° Fahrenheit by the end of the twenty-first century, what we probably want to know is not just the probability but also the extent of the consequences, that is, the severity. Whereas if the purpose of the question about the risk of a nuclear war with North Korea is to compare the risk under the Trump presidency with the same risk under the Biden presidency, what we are interested in might just be the probability. More generally, when we ask about the risk of X with already a shared understanding of what the severity of the risk is, especially if the unwanted consequence of X is simply death, what we are asking about is usually the probability. It is important to remember, though, that even when the expected answer to the question "What is the risk of X?" is a probability, it is only because we already have a tacit understanding of the evaluation of the severity of the risk.

In the detailed discussion that follows, we will focus specifically on four main ways in which normativity enters in risk assessment:

- **Probability.** The probability assessed may not be unique: different reference classes may be relevant, and their choice significant.
- **Severity.** Effects are rarely as well-defined as a loss in a game. What is an unwanted effect? Unwanted by whom? Are distinct economic or health effects impacting different populations differently?
- **Risk of error.** In making an assessment, there is a possibility of error either on the side of overestimation or underestimation. A scientist may be more concerned to avoid the former, and a policy adviser more intent on avoiding the latter.
- **Acceptability.** An assessment will show the level of risk, but it is a further question at what level a risk is acceptable or unacceptable, either to the individual or to society. Emotion plays a role in determining such a threshold.

3.3 Expected value as a model

One typical way, as we saw, to measure the seriousness of a risk is to calculate the *risk expected value*, the expected value of the loss.[3] In the simplest case, that is just the probability of the loss times the value of the loss. The best illustration of the concept of *risk expected value* is with a game of chance.

Suppose that the game has just two possible outcomes, one with a gain, one with a loss. The risk expected value of the game is simply the product of the probability of the loss outcome by the value of the loss. Suppose you are tossing a fair coin and the gain is $5 on heads while the loss is $3 on tails. Since the coin is fair, the probability of the coin falling on tails is 0.5, so the risk expected value of the game is 0.5×3. If it is a game that has several possible outcomes, the expected value of the risk of entering this game, or risk expected value of the game, would be the sum of the risk expected values of all the possible negative outcomes.

For another example, suppose you throw a fair die and the gain is $5 if it falls on 1, 2, or 3, while the loss is $3 if it falls on 4, 5, or 6. The probability of falling on either side is the same for each side and is 1/6. There are three possible outcomes associated with a loss, each has probability 1/6 to occur, and for each of them the loss is $3. So the expected value of the loss would be $(1/6) \times 3 + (1/6) \times 3 + (1/6) \times 3 = 1.5$.[4]

Calculating the expected value looks like an easy way to calculate and compare different risks, but it is not as easy in real life as it is in a game of chance. Regarding the measure of probability, life events are never as similar as two tosses of a coin, so we need to decide what similarities are required for two events to count as instances of the same phenomenon.

For instance, if we ask about the risk of getting lung cancer, we could calculate the probability based on the total number of cases of lung cancer within a year in the overall population. But it might be more informative to distinguish the probability of getting lung cancer for a smoker versus for a nonsmoker, since we know that smoking makes a difference. We may also want to distinguish between the probability of getting lung cancer for a smoker who exercises and for a smoker who does not exercise, because exercising might make a difference. In those different cases, we are taking different populations as reference, general population versus population of smokers, to calculate the probability, and which population we should take as reference will be a normative judgment, a value judgment, a judgment based on what we think is *most valuable given our purpose*, which in turn is an expression of our interests and values. This idea will be developed further in the next sections.

Regarding the measure of severity, the unwanted effects of the activity or technology that we regard as risky are rarely as well-defined as a loss in a game. For instance, if we try to estimate the risk of entering a war, we could consider only the national casualties or the overall casualties, we could count the harm done to citizens in the same way as the harm done to soldiers or differently, among citizens we could count the harm done to children in the same way as the harm done to adults or differently, we could count cultural harm in addition to economic harm or not, count harm for the future generations, born during or after the war, or only to present generations, etc. All these choices will take the form of a normative judgment, a value judgment, a judgment based on what we think is *most appropriate based on our interests and values*.

And finally, one of the biggest differences between risk in real life and risk in a game of chance is that the unwanted consequences in real life are not always immediately expressed in monetary value. For example, regarding the cost of degrading a place that has historical or cultural significance: should it depend on whose history or culture it is? An estimate of the severity of such kinds of consequence will be based on our interests and values.

The risk expected value is useful when the aim is to insure against a loss and *might* be useful when one wants to compare two risky options that can be modeled as a game of chance. But this kind of assessment is opaque in that it provides little information about the risk itself and so may not be of great use when the assessment is directed at managing the risk that is assessed.

For most of the risks that we are facing, especially societal risks, the calculation of the expected value cannot be done, and if it somehow could be done, it may not be very useful. This is because most often risk assessment is part of a risk management project, and in such cases, we generally need to know about what is happening and how it is happening. We also want to know about the process that is creating the risk, whether we are talking about an epidemic, a nuclear facility, or climate warming. For instance, in the case of an epidemic, we could calculate the expected value of the risk that a certain number of people will die within a certain period of time, using some monetary value of a statistical life. But it would not help to address the epidemic as it is unfolding. For that, we want to have access to the statistics of the contamination and how it evolves. Or we want to have models that represent the different factors that have an effect on how the epidemic may propagate and are able to show not the expected value of one possible outcome but the distribution of probabilities of different possible outcomes depending on the value of some of the factors that we may be able to intervene on.[5] Both the statistics and the models are important components of a management project because they can provide guidance for action.[6]

3.4 Approaches to risk assessment

Before we explore the details in how probability and severity assessments are reached in scientific risk assessment, we will distinguish different approaches to risk assessment in general and discuss the role of expert judgment and the need for a calibrated judgment.

3.4.1 Three approaches to risk assessment

We can distinguish three distinct forms of risk assessment: *insurantial*, *epidemiological*,[7] and *social-structural*. Examples of each will be familiar. The insurantial approach is exemplified in the common forms of insurance many people have in our society: medical insurance, home insurance (against fire and weather damage), auto insurance (against loss and liability in crashes), and life insurance. This approach to risk assessment represents the assessment of risk in terms of expected value, with the task of assigning a value to the probability and the severity of the risk that is to be insured against and to combine them.

The second approach is evidenced in the announcements by medical experts and government spokespersons in the course of an epidemic. The assessment here focuses on assessing the probability and is seemingly directed, in its use, at individuals. For instance, we estimate the seriousness of COVID-19 in terms of the proportion of persons contaminated at a given time, and it gives to individuals an estimate of the probability to be contaminated. This approach applies also to the estimate of the risks of exposure to chemical contaminants. The severity of the risk, that is, that it is "bad" to be contaminated and how "bad" it is, is kept as a different dimension. It is assessed on the basis of previous cases of exposure or extrapolation from results of experiments on animals.

The third approach may be illustrated with the use of integrated assessment models for climate change which integrate both physical considerations (about the climate system) and social considerations (about emission regulation or population growth). The result of this kind of assessment is not reducible to a number; it is an exploration of possibilities.[8] It is not directed, in its use, at individuals but at institutions, including the government, to help in deciding whether to implement new policies.

- **Insurantial risk assessment**

We need to think about insurance here both from the client's point of view and from the insurance company's. The client who takes out an insurance policy for a house or for health does so in order not to eliminate but to reduce risk through reducing not the probability but the impact. The policy could be taken out for anything of value that could be lost; for example, home insurance guarantees the cost of rebuilding if the house is lost to fire. The risk is not eliminated, because the person can still lose their home and all their belongings, and it will still be a tragic incident. But the insurance is a way to get through what may happen if it happens. The company that sells the policy, of course, has a different aim.

For the client, this is not typically a matter of calculating an expected value. We typically expect that we can pay for all the small mishaps that we think are at all likely to happen. So in effect, our expected value for the act of buying the policy is negative. But we recognize the extremely unlikely possibility of disastrous incidents. While we do not expect any such disaster, we realize that without insurance, it would lead to ruin; the insurance eliminates that possibility, and this is what we take to be worth the cost.

FRAME 1: Is the policy worth it?

Adam has taken out pet insurance for his cat Violet. The monthly fees are $80, and the insurance will refund 80% of medical costs for illness or accidents.

Adam calculates that after any and all refunds, he will still be paying much out of pocket: the total of the fees paid plus 20% of the medical costs. The expected monetary value of buying the policy is negative, whatever be the probabilities of illness or accidents. (In gambler terminology, this is a "Dutch book.")

So why did Adam buy the policy nevertheless? What risk did that eliminate?

By buying the policy, Adam guaranteed that the medical expenses for Violet would always be at a relatively low level. He eliminated the possibility of *disastrous loss*, of expenses that at any given time could be in the thousands of dollars rather than hundreds. The real value of the policy for Adam is not the calculated monetary expected value but the value he places on this level of security.

For the company, the approach is different, but it must itself guard against the risk it takes in issuing those policies. It does not expect to pay for a disaster for any given client, but it has to face the possibility that the unlikely will occur for some clients, if there are many. The insurance company has a special problem: under certain conditions, the same unlikely event will happen to many clients simultaneously. For example, the loss of a house to fire is unlikely, but wildfires may result in many houses, across an area or even the country, being lost to fire at the same time.

The insurance company's assessment is an expected value calculation with the probability based on statistics and causal modeling. Causal modeling, which we will discuss further in the following passages, consists in isolating relevant factors for the mishap in question, with reference to the set of clients as a population. How many are in an area exposed to hurricanes, and how severe is hurricane damage in that area? What are the statistics for the past so many years, and do these statistics show any trend upward or downward when it comes to damage?

With the salient assignment of values to the insured goods or activities, the assessment may properly be called *normative*; the assessment of the risk aims to determine what the entity taking the insurance should pay for it and should be entitled to receive. Different insurance companies will end up with different numbers without it being seen as evidence of a mistake. In fact, it is expected that we will get different numbers precisely because we understand that this assessment is normative, with no "truth of the matter" to be found anywhere. Our reaction rather would be one of indignation at some numbers being too high; we may even find it immoral.

- **Epidemiological risk assessment**

A virus may spread so as to create an epidemic, but other processes, such as toxic contamination, can similarly create an unwanted effect spreading both geographically and over time. In this case, the scientific assessment focuses on the statistical distribution and its change over time. During the COVID-19 pandemic, the government and news media published statistics daily showing the number of new cases and the number of deaths, in a specific country or in the world, with the percentage of increase for both numbers over a certain period of time.

The unwantedness of the consequences, sickness with possible death, is somewhat taken for granted and is assessed separately: what the symptoms are and how long they last, what the recovery looks like and whether it is total.

This approach is also the one that is used to arrive at tables showing the risk of death as a consequence of various activities, like shown in the following table:

Activity	**Rate**
Plague in London in 1665	15,000
Rock climbing while on rock face	4,000
Fireman in London air raids, 1940	1,000
Travel by helicopter	500
Civilian in London air raids, 1940	200
Jack-up platform in winter at UK code limit	200
Policeman in Northern Ireland, average	70
Construction, high-rise erectors	70
"Tolerable" limit of 1 in 1,000 per year at work	*50*
Smoking, average	40
Travel by air	40
Travel by car	30
Oil and gas extraction	15
Average man in 30s from accident	8
Average man in 30s from disease	8
Radon gas natural radiation "action level"	6
Construction, average	5
Traveling by train	5

Figure 3.1 Number of deaths in the UK per 10^8 hours, from Warner (1992: 81).

Activity	**Rate**
Factory work, average	4
Accident at home, all ages	4
Accident at home, able-bodied	1
All manufacturing industries	1
"Tolerable" limit 1 in 10,000 per year near major hazard	*1*
"Tolerable" limit 1 in 100,000 per year near nuclear plant	*0.1*
Terrorist bomb in London area	0.01
Target risk for fire in public building	0.005
Building falling down	0.002

Figure 3.1 Continued

This type of approach to risk is *descriptive*, but not in the sense that it is simply based on a descriptive use of statistics, where statistics are used to describe aspects of a population. It is also generally based on inferential use of statistics, where statistics are used to make inferences about a population on the basis of results obtained on a different population. For instance, the effects of exposure to chemical contaminants will, typically, be inferred from experimental results of laboratory animals' exposure to the contaminants – with the issues of reliability that this type of inference can raise (Ram 2019; Rom et al. 2013).

The epidemiological approach to risk assessment is descriptive in that it purports to describe some facts, like facts about the current rate of the contamination and the rate of propagation. We can see the result of the assessment is descriptive in how we react if two institutes provide different numbers: either they did not really measure the same thing or one of them is wrong. And this reaction is very different from our reaction when two insurance companies provide different quotes for the same risk.

- **Social-structural risk assessment**

This is an approach to risks that typically views them as pertaining to a society taken as a whole, emerging from some parts of the social structure and threatening the stability of the social structure, with consequences that are seen as not simply the sum of the consequences for affected individuals.

A large-scale famine, for example, would not just result in death for many; it would have cascading social effects, diminishing the workforce for industry as well as the consumption of every kind of goods, increasing the number of orphans. In the 1840s, Northern and Western Europe faced a food crisis when a fungus-like organism, the potato blight, spread through the region.

In Ireland, where the British Parliament's response was inadequate, this resulted in the death of roughly one million Irish from starvation and related causes, while another million were left as refugees. In Scotland, the social response was considerably more effective and prevented large-scale starvation even though the form of that response nevertheless led to the emigration of approximately one-third of the Highlands population.

Though such lessons are not easily learned, the next century saw increasingly more social programs designed to forestall such large-scale disasters by putting resources for adequate response in place. Examples are unemployment benefits and national pension plans of various sorts.

More contemporary examples in Western societies of risks that are objects of this kind of approach are crime, health care, terrorism, climate change, immigration, economic crash, and homelessness, to name just a few.

The risks are seen as emerging from a social structure, and the response to the risk is a modification of some elements of this structure. The risk is object of a causal model that includes the social factors thought to contribute to the possible unwanted effects and thereby suggests forms of intervention to mitigate the risk. As we can see with terrorism, immigration, climate change, war, crime, and health care, a causal-social assessment of those risk can be used to define a political platform with "original" proposals as to how to address the risks.

This approach is *prospective*: the aim is to explore the synergic effect of different factors that are regarded as relevant and to get a sense of the different ways in which a problem could be addressed. Like with the normative approach, we expect that different institutions will produce different assessments of the same risks, but like with the epidemiological approach, we expect it to be answerable to the world and reliable as a basis for action, political action, regarding, for instance, health care or the climate.

It is important to note that these approaches are not exclusive and are not generally determined by the kind of risk that is assessed. The assessment of same risks can be done in different ways. For instance, an epidemic can be object of an epidemiological approach and also of a modeling approach: instead of describing the state of the contamination, this approach uses models that integrate different physical (for instance, about how the virus spreads) and social dimensions (for instance, about the traffic of people given the geographical location of the country or the period of the year). And at the same time, individuals may turn to insurance to mitigate their personal risk of being contaminated.

3.4.2 The role of expert judgment

As risk assessment has increasingly involved highly advanced technology and sophisticated statistical, modeling, and simulation methods, it may seem that expert judgment is playing ever less a role. We can point here especially at the development of *probabilistic risk assessment* (PRA) as the methodology developed and adopted in the aeronautics and nuclear industry. As things stand, however, and as we shall see, expert judgment is ineliminable and plays an essential role as input in addition to "hard data."[9]

3.4.2.1 How PRA developed in the nuclear industry

In the United States, the Atomic Energy Commission (AEC) was established in 1946 to oversee the development of atomic (nuclear) energy both for the military and for industry. Its form for risk assessment was "maximum credible accent" (MCA) identification. The MCA is meant to be the greatest accident possible under realistic conditions that reactors are designed to withstand. The method has four main steps:

> Screen all applicable events to determine which ones are credible for the reactor design.
>
> Group the credible events together into event categories based on similar phenomenology of challenge to safety.
>
> Identify and analyze the bounding events in each category. Review this set of bounding events to determine whether the bounding event in one category is also bounded by the bounding event in another category to develop a final set of overarching bounding events
>
> Identify the most challenging event to the safety of the plant based on the worst single failure or worst single cause of common cause failures, which is then designated the MCA.
>
> (OKLO 2021)

A first study of this sort, published by the AEC in 1957, examined three scenarios of radioactive release from a nuclear power plant and reported a consensus, among more than 40 experts, that the chances of major accident "are exceedingly small" (Atomic Energy Report WASH-740: vii). But the experts' judgments were mainly qualitative, and among those who "ventured to express their opinions in numerical terms," the estimates ranged from 1/100,000 to 1/1,000,000,000 (ibid.: viii). To be frank, the report states at the outset that "no one knows now or will ever know the exact magnitude of this low probability" (ibid.: 3).

In 1974, the AEC was replaced by the US Nuclear Regulatory Commission. Design improvements were introduced to reduce the probability of catastrophic release, and probabilistic risk assessment (PRA) was introduced, with what is now regarded as the first clear statement of the method, "The Reactor Safety Study" (RSS).[10] When this was reviewed in the physics community (by the American Physical Society in 1975, and the Union of Concerned Scientists in 1977), the reception was very – indeed extremely – critical: the calculations and probability estimates were not well based, and not all relevant physical processes were taken into account in the analysis. The US Congress created a special review panel led by Prof. Harold Lewis.

What was especially important in the Lewis report was that it highlighted the involvement of the experts' subjective probabilities and declared it inevitable, while raising the question of how its validity was to be investigated:

> It is our view that the use of subjective probabilities is necessary and appropriate, and provides a reasonable input to the RSS probability calculations. But their use must be clearly identified, and their limits of validity must be defined.
>
> (United States Nuclear Regulatory Commission 1978; NUREG/CR-400)

3.4.2.2 Learning from the Challenger *disaster at NASA*

The National Aeronautics and Space Administration (NASA) publishes a manual for PRA, and it begins with a rueful note speaking about the agency's early history:

> Over the years, NASA has been a leader in most of the technologies it has employed in its programs. One would think that PRA should be no exception. . . .
>
> Methods to perform risk and reliability assessment in the early 1960s originated in U.S. aerospace and missile programs. . . . It would have been a reasonable extrapolation to expect that NASA would also become the world leader in the application of PRA. That was, however, not to happen.
>
> (National Aeronautics and Space Administration 2011: NASA/SP-2011–3421)

What did happen, however, is that NASA took heed and switched to PRA after the *Challenger* shuttle disaster in 1986.

During its 30-year lifetime, the Space Shuttle flew 135 missions to low Earth orbit (LEO). Two of those missions resulted in catastrophic events (i.e., *Challenger* 1986 and *Columbia* 2003 accidents).

The space shuttle *Challenger* disaster was a fatal accident in the United States space program that occurred on January 28, 1986, when the space shuttle *Challenger* (OV-099, on its tenth flight) broke apart 73 seconds into its flight. All seven crew members aboard were killed, including two female astronauts, Judith Resnik, an engineer, and Christa McAuliffe, a schoolteacher.

The disaster was due to the failure of the two humble O-ring seals in a joint in the space shuttle's right solid rocket booster (SRB). The record-low temperatures of the launch reduced the elasticity of the rubber O-rings, reducing their ability to seal the joints. The broken seals caused a breach into the joint shortly after liftoff, which allowed pressurized gas from within the SRB to leak and burn through the wall to the adjacent external fuel tank.

What happened at NASA before the disaster?

There were many reviews of what had led to the disaster, including a Presidential Commission (the Rogers Commission) and an investigation by the US House Committee on Science and Technology, as well as discussions in engineering technical literature.

The special report by the editors of *IEEE Spectrum* begins with the assertion that culture and policy in NASA resisted probabilistic risk analysis for 20 years and so failed to even collect statistical data (Bell & Esch 1989). They cite Will Willoughby, NASA director during the earlier Apollo program, as arguing that "statistics don't count for anything" and "have no place in engineering." The reliance at NASA at that time was instead on the expertise in the manufacture of the parts and design of the vehicle. The methodology favored was FMEA (failure modes and effects analysis), carried out by the contractor building each shuttle element or subsystem. Items that did not meet reliability and safety requirements were placed on the CIL (critical items list). A subsequent hazards analysis took into account the FMEA/CIL data as well as other threats posed by mission objectives, crew-machine interfaces, and environment. NASA engineers and managers then engaged in triage: eliminate the cause of the hazard, control the cause if it could not be eliminated, or accept the hazard if it could not be controlled.

Safety was certainly a paramount concern at the agency, but there was a troubling history of what happened with safety reviews (Boyer et al. 2019). These were not PRAs. One study was conducted by J. H. Wiggins Co., between 1979 and 1982. It put the overall risk of losing a shuttle with payload during launch at between 1/500 and 1/5,000, with the greatest risk coming from the solid fuel rocket booster. A new study in 1983, the Weatherwax analysis, which reviewed the Wiggins study, put the overall risk of losing a shuttle at 1/35. Then a further study was done in 1983 by Teledyne Energy Systems Inc., which concluded that past data suggested a failure rate of 1/100. But NASA's own safety analysis at the Johnson Space Center in 1985 examined fractures similar to what was to happen in the *Challenger* accident and assigned these a chance of 1/100,000.

What happened at NASA after *Challenger*?

The Rogers Commission, which examined the *Challenger* accident in 1986, recommended that NASA use PRA to evaluate the shuttle design and operation. This became the accepted methodology.

The PRA manual, which we cited previously, specifies that the assessments must focus on three questions:

- What kinds of events or scenarios can occur (i.e., what can go wrong)?
- What are the likelihoods and associated uncertainties of the events or scenarios?
- What consequences could result from these events or scenarios?

It gives a detailed example to show what such an assessment must yield: an analysis of a spacecraft propellant distribution module.

The analysis lists scenarios leading to loss of vehicle as a result of a hydrazine leak and, for each of them, estimates of their permission probabilities. But how are such probabilities determined? Is there input from expert judgment as well as from statistical data?

3.4.2.3 Expert judgment, ineliminable

The text of the NASA manual addresses the question of how to determine the probability, though in very guarded phrases. In Section 3.3.5, "Uncertainties: A Probabilistic Perspective," it is admitted that in many cases, "there is substantial epistemic uncertainty regarding basic event probability" (ibid. 3–21). Although there are methods to generate relevant statistics (e.g., Monte Carlo sampling), "in many cases, a useful assessment of uncertainty cannot be obtained from existing performance data" (ibid. 3–22). And it concludes, "In these cases, it is necessary to do the best one can, integrating such information as is available into a state-of-knowledge probability distribution." While written in neutral, third-person style, this is a directive to the members of the team of experts that conduct the assessment and thus refers to input from expert judgment.

The evaluation of expert judgment is therefore a crucial supplement to probabilistic risk assessment in its practical applications. The Canadian Department of Defense report on expert judgment in risk assessment begins with:

> Decision and risk analysis models often require both qualitative and quantitative assessments of uncertain events; in many cases, expert knowledge is essentially the only source of good information. Over the last decade, uncertainty analysis has become an increasingly important part of operations research models.
>
> The use of expert judgements has provoked questions related to the practice of utilizing experts' opinions and to the accuracy of the obtained results. (Leung & Verga 2007)

Research and development accordingly need specific procedures not only for experts to assess risk but also for assessing the quality and limits of validity of expert judgment.

3.4.3 Assessing expertise: the challenge of calibration

There is a saying attributed (though perhaps apocryphally) to the famous rock climber Lynn Hill: "There are three things I need to think of when I climb: the probability of a fall, the consequences of a fall, and my own ability to judge the first two."

Lynn Hill is a climbing expert and right to rely on her judgment of probability and severity, but this statement recognizes that expert judgments themselves must (as the Lewis report to the Nuclear Regulatory Commission urged) have their limits of validity evaluated.

What we want, first of all, is *accuracy*, that the experts' probabilities track the statistics correctly, that is, that their judgment is *well calibrated*. So one main task is to understand what *accuracy* or *calibration* means in this case.

But we want more than accuracy. If accuracy were all that was required, very vague experts would be good experts. A person who just utters tautologies, like "Whatever will be will be," always speaks the truth. If a weather forecaster were to just announce every day, say, in San Francisco, that the next day's temperature would be between 0 and 100, his accuracy would be perfect. Similarly, if an event is known to be rare, a forecaster would likely have near-perfect accuracy if simply declaring, each day, that it won't happen (Ebert & Milne 2022).

What is required of experts in addition to accuracy is to be *informative*. The challenge is that to be too definite and precise in their pronouncements may lead them to be overconfident (McKenzie et al. 2008).

3.4.3.1 Calibration

In the evening, a weather forecaster says that the probability of rain the next day is 80%. Then the next day, either it rains or it doesn't. Was that a good forecast?

That is the wrong way to ask the question. Forecasters are following a forecast policy that relies on weather data and weather models (we will look at those in some detail in the succeeding paragraphs), and it is this on which they base their judgment each day. For the forecaster to be a good forecaster, this procedure has to give good results over time. To be precise, for the forecaster to be *perfectly calibrated*, it has to rain on precisely 80% of the days for which his forecast was that there was an 80% probability of rain, and similarly for other numbers.

Perfection is not usually attainable, so there are specific measures used to determine the degree of calibration, that is, the degree to which the assessed probabilities agree with observed statistics.

It helps to imagine how a forecaster could, in principle, be perfectly calibrated and how her actual performance can be compared to this. No model, no forecasting policy, makes infinitely fine distinctions. So each forecast occasion, characterized by the data, falls into one of a finite number of classes B(1), . . . B(n), the classification cells. There are many days for which data have been gathered, and there is, in these data, a definite proportion percent (**rain**/B[j]) of rainy days among the days in class B(j). What would happen if, *on each day*, the forecaster correctly classifies the day as belonging to one of these classes, say, B(k), and then announces as probability of rain that very number of percentage (**rain**/B[k])?

The answer is, as you will have guessed, that the forecaster is perfectly calibrated: the proportion of rain among the days on which she presents her forecast probability is precisely that probability. And if her announcements are on the average, say, 10% different from the proportions in those classification cells, her distance from perfect calibration is that as well.

3.4.3.2 How well calibrated are experts in actual situations?

There are systematic studies that compare the accuracy of expert and lay judgment; the results vary, and the methods used by different investigators have been mutually criticized.

A series of studies by Bolger, Wright, and Rowe focused on two salient differences in tasks that can be set to experts and laypersons to compare their performance (Bolger & Wright 1994; Wright et al. 2002). First, to what extent do the questions in the experts' domain of professional experience require answers in metrics familiar to the experts? They call this the question of *ecological validity*. This is obviously important to the results; there is no reason to expect experts to perform differently from laypersons if the questions are not within their professional domain. Second, to what degree is it possible, in the relevant task domain, for good judgment to be learned? This is the question of *learnability*. Again, this is relevant for the significance of the results: in the absence of usable feedback, for example, there is no learnability, and thus no difference between experts and laypersons except for the experts' initial education: "expert performance will be largely a function of the interaction between . . . ecological validity and learnability – if both are high then good performance will be manifest, but if one or both are low then performance will be poor" (Wright et al. 2002: 1109). Weather forecasting is a task domain that has both high ecological validity and high learnability.

Wright and colleagues (2002) designed an experiment to compare performance of life insurance underwriters to that of business school students on a series of assessments concerning the lethality of certain events. They verified that all the assessments were within the underwriters' domain of professional experience, to guarantee a (very) high degree of ecological validity. There were two main sorts of assessments given as tasks:

- Marginal assessments. Questions such as, "What is the death rate per 100,000 from asthma?"
- Conditional assessments. Questions such as, "What is the probability of death from stomach cancer *given that* an individual is diagnosed with that condition?"

In both groups, marginal probabilities were, on the whole, significantly higher than the true marginals. There was no systematic overestimation of conditional probabilities, but the estimates varied widely in both groups, between over- and underestimation.

The important result was this: the experts were "generally, a little better in their risk judgments than the lay persons" but "the differences in performance between experts and lay persons were small in magnitude, and the nature of biases . . . were common to both groups" (Wright, Bolger, and Rowe, op. cit. 1118).

Given that the task had great ecological validity, the study concluded that the culprit was the low degree of learnability. The life insurance underwriters received no feedback from actual frequencies since most clients will not die till many years after the policy is issued.

There is also an actual example to explore in the Reactor Safety Study, which we discussed prior, which gave some evidence about actual calibration of expert probability assessments. There was an ongoing project at the Oak Ridge National Laboratory to evaluate operating experience at nuclear installations.[11] There were no complete nuclear meltdowns, but there were less-severe incidents whose frequencies were estimated in the Reactor Safety Study. In the 1984 report, the observed frequencies were reported for such incidents as these:

Pressurized Water Reactor:

Small loss of coolant accident
Auxiliary feedwater system (failure/demand)
High-pressure injection (failure/demand)
Long-term core cooling (failure/demand)

Boiling Water Reactor:

Small loss of coolant accident
Automatic depressurization system (failure/demand)
High-pressure coolant injection (failure/demand)

For each of these, the values from operating experience were outside the Reactor Safety Study confidence bounds (Cooke op. cit. 36–38). (That was not all bad news for the nuclear industry – some of the incidents were much less frequent than expected.)

Later studies showed much more satisfactory calibration. But there is another factor to be considered: how confident are the experts about the accuracy of their probability judgments? They can indicate their confidence by specifying a smaller or larger interval for the assessed probability. And as noted prior, we want probability assessments to be *informative*: the larger the interval, the less informative the assessment. But at the same time, there can be drawbacks to relying on highly confident forecasts.

To give a simple example, two weather forecasters making the same predictions might, on the average, be within three degrees of the actual temperature. But that average might hide individual differences that were, for the most part, either more than three degrees above or more than three degrees below. If one of the two forecasters always announces probabilities "plus or minus two degrees" and the other always says "plus or minus six degrees," we call the first one the more confident. But given the actual divergences from the average, we'll have to say that the first forecaster was overconfident. In this case, relying too strictly on those forecasts when deciding whether to take one's umbrella would likely not have had the better result.

In one study, which showed quite satisfactory accuracy for risk assessments for two American nuclear power plants, this question of confidence was also investigated (Mosleh et al. 1987). The experts' assessments were, on the whole, overconfident. This is not atypical (cf. Christensen-Szalanski & Bushyhead 1981). Studies of various professions have typically shown prevalence of overconfidence, but also that calibration and accuracy in self-assessment can improve remarkably when there is constant feedback on performance (Cooke 1991; Hora 2004). Learnability matters.

3.4.3.3 Risk expert as scientist

The role of the risk expert that has been discussed prior focused on making judgments about risk. As we saw, the risk experts' judgment about risk is especially salient when the source of risk (activity in a nuclear facility, the launch of a shuttle) is something new or when the possible unwanted consequences have been extremely rare.

But the experts' judgment is required even when there are data and theories that make it possible to produce statistics or construct models.

First, the risk experts, with their knowledge, explicit and tacit, and their experience, are needed to interpret the statistics-based or model-based results. They interpret those results by taking into account, in particular, the conditions in which the results were produced and specific aspects of the situation to which the results are to be applied.

We will be looking at the following specific example: a randomized control trial (RCT) in Tennessee with results that turned out not to be applicable in California. In many cases, data are gathered under specific conditions, and it is a question whether the sample is representative of the general population or of a subpopulation. This question we will encounter in another detailed example that follows: statistical studies of the risks in an encounter with the police. These are examples for statistics-based results. But in the case of model-based results, the questions about whether specific conditions or aspects of the situation match the model assumptions arise as well. For example, engineers rely, for the design and construction of airplanes and bridges, on classical mechanics, with no need to worry about the theory of relativity.

But this has changed; in the design of GPS satellites, relativistic corrections must be applied. Models from classical physics would, in this case, fail to take certain specific, relevant aspects of the situation into account.

Secondly, risk experts are generally scientists involved in the very enterprise in which they have to assess the risks. To give one dramatic example, the scientists involved in the Manhattan Project, which developed the first atomic bomb, had to assess the risks involved in the first test, risks to both environment and personnel. But this is only a special example of a common process; in every stage of a new construction or new product, and in every stage of a new scientific inquiry, there are calls for judgment: *unforced choices* that need to be made.

This is a general pattern in scientific inquiry, as has been argued by Matthew J. Brown (2020). Any scientific inquiry begins in doubt or perplexity, which is followed by recognizable stages of inquiry, and "concludes when a clear sense of the problem and a solution grounded in evidence are brought together in judgment" (op. cit., 30). The stages (not necessarily in this order, distinguished not by time order but by function, and not entirely separable from each other) are:

- Observation. Gathering of data, finding out the "facts," what is "fixed" in the situation. Special problem: what is relevant as data? *Relevance* is not written on the events' sleeves
- Problem framing. Clarifying and formulating the problem in such a way that the direction of inquiry becomes clear, as well as the distinction between relevant and irrelevant.
- Suggestion. Generation of hypotheses. A creative process, not rule-governed.
- Reasoning. Drawing out the implications of the hypotheses so as to make it possible to evaluate them.
- Experimental testing. It is one thing to ask how the hypotheses are in accord with the data, and another thing to design procedures that will create new relevant phenomena that will also have to be accommodated.

The explanations here attached to each phase highlight the unforced choices along the way in each phase of the inquiry that result in a theory or model. Each such choice is made with deliberation; this is where the expert's knowledge, both explicit and tacit, comes into play. The history of modern optics furnishes some dramatic illustrations, beginning with the discovery that the speed of light is infinite. Galileo discussed this, conceding that our everyday experiences are in line with the idea that illumination is instantaneous. But he argued that the evidence showed only that light is faster than what we can compare it with: when a cannon is fired at a great distance from us, we see the flash well before we hear the sound. But Galileo had no idea of how to measure the speed of light. It was an astronomer late in the seventeenth century, Ole Roemer, who noticed that differences in the observed eclipses of a satellite of Jupiter meant that light took some time to travel from there to the earthly observer. Sometimes the choices of data erupt into controversy. Goethe described how color is perceived in a wide variety of situations and regarded Newton's observations as special cases. Physicists did not deny the observations but hotly contested their relevance and significance.

Similarly, experimental testing is not an algorithmic procedure, and there, too, we see controversies that highlight the choice points. Early in the nineteenth century, the greatest mathematical physicists of the day, such as Poisson and Laplace, held the Newtonian corpuscular theory of light; Huygens's wave theory had not managed to replace it. Then, in 1819, the Paris Academy of Sciences received a prize essay from an obscure provincial engineer, Auguste Fresnel of the Corps des Ponts et Chaussées, who presented an impressive and well-supported wave theory of light. Poisson, who wanted to show it up, deduced what he called an absurd consequence of Fresnel's theory: there would be a spot of light in the middle of the shadow cast by an opaque object. The experimentalist Arago tested this, and lo, the spot of light was there, just as predicted.

But Brown's theme, the prevalence of the need for choices, applies well beyond theoretical physics. If a vaccine has been tested on a sample representative of the population as a whole, what does prudence require by way of more tests on specific subpopulations: children, the aged, diabetics, recovering surgery patients, etc.?

To take a more salient example, what judgment calls would have prevented the 2016 polls from suggesting that Hillary Clinton would win the US presidency? There were certainly a number of reasons, but some can be attributed to unforced choices in the statistical modeling of the population. Polling is not a matter of just extrapolating straight from the data. *Weighting*, a standard polling practice, gives more statistical value to groups that pollsters know are being underrepresented in surveys, in an attempt to ensure that the inference from the sample more accurately reflects the characteristics of the population from which it was drawn. Pollsters habitually weight for characteristics such as age, race, or gender to make sure that their polling sample matches up with census data for those groups in that area. But some 2016 polls, and particularly those polling at state level, were not weighted by education (a choice now regretted) and failed to adjust for an overrepresentation of college graduates, although there are significant differences in how changes in the economy impact different education levels (American Association for Public Opinion Research 2017: 3.4).

In what follows, we will look specifically at one of the important choices that need to be made when calculating probabilities, the choice of a reference class, and also at one of the choices that need to be made when building a model, the choice of the relevant attributes.

3.5 Assessing probability

When the severity of possible consequences is recognized and generally agreed upon, risk assessment focuses mainly on the probabilities of the harm. How those probabilities are determined, however, is itself an important question.

3.5.1 Statistics-based vs. model-based assessment

When we are discussing the assessment of risk, it is helpful to distinguish between two kinds of risk: risks that can be assessed on the basis of statistics alone, and risks that have to be assessed on the basis of causal modeling. Only risks that have a history of exposure can be assessed on the basis of statistics, like breast cancer, epidemics, car crashes . . .

Risks that do not have a history of exposure, because they are new or rare, have to be assessed on the basis of a causal model. The risk of a nuclear reactor accident provides a good example: when these were first constructed, there were, of course, no historical data for such accidents.

This distinction between these two forms of risk assessment is not sharp. As we shall see, the use of statistics to generate probabilities of harm involves choices that amount to an elementary form of modeling. On the other hand, causal models cannot generate forecast probabilities without an input that includes statistical data.

Our detailed examples will focus on relatively clear cases of each: risk assessment for danger in police encounters, based on statistical analysis of public records, and risk assessment for natural danger in weather events and wildfires, based on advanced modeling techniques.

3.5.2 Statistics-based probability

We are treated to statistical news every day, whether in newspapers or in the magazines and journals that report on our own special interests. As an example, let's take an article on injury rates in popular sports, published in *Wilderness and Environmental Medicine* (Flores et al. 2008). This study analyzed 212,708 people who were treated for injuries sustained in outdoor activities in American emergency departments during 2004 and 2005. The study found that 72.1 injuries occurred among every 100,000 Americans, with 68.2% of injuries to males and 31.8% to females. Snowboarding accounted for 25.5% of all injuries, and most of those to young men. The next two highest are sledding, with 10.8% of injuries, and hiking, with 6.3%. Climbing, including both rock and mountain climbing, accounted for 4.9% of outdoor injuries.

Should we conclude from this that the risk of injury is highest in snowboarding and much less in rock climbing than in sledding or hiking?

Clearly not. Among the patients treated for injuries, the numbers of hikers, sledders, and climbers were surely not equal. If there were few climbers in the total sampled population, one would expect the percentage of injured climbers among those 200,000 or so patients to be small as well.

A comparative study of sport injuries appeared in the journal *Sports Medicine* (Schoeffl et al. 2010). They scored injuries in terms of severity (1, 2: no acute intervention needed; 7: death). Then they compared the total score per 100 hours of sport activity, calculated from the available statistics: ice hockey, 83; rock climbing ca. 1980, 37.5; basketball, 9.8; rock climbing, recent, 0.56; and surfing, 0.41.

The reason the second study is more informative about which sports are the more dangerous is that the statistics refer to a more relevant classification. Even if we extrapolate our probabilities directly from the statistics, we cannot count the probability that a random patient with a sports injury is a climber as very useful when it comes to comparing levels of risk in different sports.

To calculate the probability of an event on the basis of statistics, that is, on the basis of recorded past occurrences of similar events, we need to select a *reference class*.

3.5.2.1 Reference class

Consider Mr. Jason James, who has applied for a life insurance policy that pays his beneficiaries $100,000 upon his death. What should the insurance company set as his yearly premium? That clearly depends on how long the company expects him to live: its profit will be the total of the premiums collected minus the payoff.

Mr. James has to answer certain questions: where does he live, what are his current age, occupation, and leisure activities? These answers select a class of people similar to Mr. James in this respect. The company bases its decision on the mortality statistics it has for the class determined by these factors. It is the *reference class* in which it places Mr. James. The assumption involved in the company's pricing of the policy is that the probability that Mr. James will die before age 80, for example, equals the proportion of deaths in the reference class of before age 80.

This seems straightforward, but the choice of reference class itself involves far-reaching assumptions. The company knows very well that other factors, not in its questionnaire, affect longevity: diet, both current and the one on which the person grew up, being a main example. Under what conditions is it warranted for the company to omit questions about that? Only with the assumption that the reference class is more or less homogeneous in that respect. That means there is no statistically significant subdivision of this class, in terms of diet, in which the mortality rate is very different from that of the class as a whole. The company might have some statistics bearing on this, in the specific case of diet, but obviously, it cannot have comprehensive knowledge about all the factors absent from its questionnaire.

The company's reasoning is suited to its purpose, and its choice of reference class for Mr. James is meant to be the right one for that purpose. That purpose is to make a profit overall, from selling many policies, on the basis of classification of the clients in a finite family of reference classes.

The role of normative judgments in the selection of a reference class

Since the choice of reference class involves assumptions, risk assessment is, to some extent, subjective and may be affected by personal factors. Suppose that a company is looking to hire a new CEO and views the female candidate as less likely to be successful than the male candidate despite equal or better competence and experience. What could be the basis for this?

We would regard this as a sexist bias if they base this estimate, if only intuitively, on a different reference class depending on the gender. This would be so if they estimate the probability that the woman will not be successful by taking as reference class, if only implicitly, the general population of women, while for the man they take as reference class the population of active people with similar competence and experience.

The choice of a reference class is a necessary step when we calculate the probability that a certain event will occur or not occur given a certain *condition*. Examples include the event of not being successful as CEO given the condition of being a woman, the event of getting COVID-19 given the condition of being an elderly person, the event of having lung cancer given the condition of being an American adult, the event of a nuclear accident given the condition of a specific nuclear facility. In all cases, the estimate of the probability requires to determine what count as *relevantly similar conditions*, conditions of exposure to the risk.

Each time, a choice has to be made based on the purpose of the estimate, some beliefs we have about the situation. But it will also depend on certain values that make us regard some aspects of the situation as more relevant than others.

3.5.2.2 Is exposure to risk a harm in itself?

FRAME 2: An imposed risk that does not materialize

Let's imagine an extreme case where there is a risk but no unwanted consequence at all:

> Marshall Jones (evil twin of Indiana Jones) is walking along a quite-deserted, sunny beach when he comes upon a lone sleeper at rest on the warm sand. Just for fun, Jones takes out his revolver,

> loads it with one bullet, and decides to play Russian roulette with this unwitting sleeper. He spins the cylinder, points the gun, and pulls the trigger.
>
> Now, there are two scenarios. In the first, the gun fires, the sleeper dies, and Jones is most certainly, both morally and legally, guilty of murder.
>
> In the second scenario, the gun does not fire, Jones smiles sardonically, and he walks on. The sleeper does not wake up (it is a well-oiled gun, and pulling the trigger makes practically no noise), and when she does wake up later on, she feels relaxed and happy to have had such a restful afternoon.
>
> Jones most certainly imposed a risk on the sleeper, a risk of death. But as it happened, there was no physical harm. Nor was there emotional stress or mental agony, since the sleeper was entirely unaware of Jones's action. Did the sleeper suffer a harm nevertheless? Was the imposed risk itself a harm?

The problem of whether being exposed to a risk is, just by itself, a harm done to the person exposed illustrates the philosophical relevance of a reference class.

Suppose that, in fact, Jones is with a friend of his and they both play Russian roulette on a sleeper. They use the same kind of gun, with the same number of bullets in them. And they both spin the cylinder, point the gun, and pull the trigger. The friend's gun shots a bullet. One sleeper is dead; the other one is not. But is it fair that Jones would walk away as if he had done nothing wrong just because he was lucky? Wasn't something really bad done to the sleeper, even if she was not physically or psychologically harmed, just by exposing her to the risk of harm or even death?

> It has sometimes been claimed that when one person A acts in such a way as to subject another person B to the risk of, say, physical harm, the fact that B has been subjected to such a risk is itself a form of harm to B, and that is so whether or not any physical harm ultimately occurs to B.
>
> (Perry 2007: 193)

When the sleeper wakes up and learns about what happened to her, she may well feel that the way she was treated was not right and that both perpetrators should somehow pay for what they did. According to McCarthy (1997), "we each have a right that other people not impose risks of harm upon us" (p. 208), and "other things being equal, if one person infringes the right of another, then, very roughly, the infringer is under a duty to compensate the bearer of the right" (p. 219; see further Handfield 2005).

An illustration, perhaps, of this belief in a duty to compensate for risk exposure is "The Great Toyota Panic" of 2010. There were some allegations that Toyota vehicles had a defect causing sudden unintended acceleration. Even though government studies concluded that driver error was the most common cause of the incidents, Toyota owners filed more than 200 cases against Toyota (Scheuerman 2003). This kind of lawsuit, a no-injury lawsuit, against a company by customers who have not experienced any incidents, is not extraordinary:

> Typically the plaintiffs purchased a product; the product malfunctioned for other consumers; the plaintiffs' products have not yet malfunctioned in any way; and the plaintiffs have not suffered any personal injury or property damage, nor do they claim any emotional harm or fear of injury.

Under tort theories, most of the suits are dismissed as lacking evidence of injury. For instance, in 2017, in *Berry et al., v. The City of Chicago*,[12] plaintiffs filed a suit on the basis of increased lead in their drinking water resulting from construction performed by the city of Chicago. The Illinois Supreme Court concluded that an *increased risk of future harm* is not an injury and that the city of Chicago cannot be found negligent without an injury.

Using a different approach, some plaintiffs have started to argue that "the product's 'propensity to fail' renders the product less valuable than represented by the manufacturer" (Scheuerman 2003: 694) and that the injury was this loss in value. But the success of this approach is far from common and depends on the cases and the courts.

It may not seem surprising that someone who bought a product that works fine will generally not be seen as being harmed. But what about the industry emitting air or water contaminants that could have a toxic impact on some people, thereby increasing the risk for all those living in proximity to get sick, or the bus driver driving under the influence of alcohol and thereby increasing the risk for all the passengers to be harmed in a car accident? Shouldn't the industry or the bus driver be liable for the risk they impose on those people, even if their conduct, by luck, does not result in an accident?

> It is commonly accepted that punishment is deserved if persons are at fault, and that fault depends on their choice to do the wrongful action, not on what is beyond their control. . . . Would the Russian Roulette player deserve less punishment if the bullet happened to be in another chamber?
>
> (Sanford Kadish (1994) quoted in Finkelstein (2003: 988))

As we saw, in tort law, injury is treated as a necessary condition for liability. But that risk exposure is not recognized as an injury in court does not show that it is not harm.

Tort law also typically does not compensate for emotional impact. In a lawsuit against the railroad *Metro-North Commuter RR. v. Buckley*, the plaintiff, an employee, claimed that he had been subjected to increased risk of cancer because of his being exposed to substantial amounts of asbestos dust through his employment. The court rejected his argument on the basis that it was a claim for emotional distress. That the court does not find liability for imposed emotional distress obviously does not mean that emotional distress does not exist. "Similarly, the fact that the law does not normally compensate those who wrongfully suffer risk harm does not imply that no such harm exists, or even that the law presumes such harms do not exist" (Finkelstein 2003: 977).

Exposure to risk is not harm

Stephen Perry (2007) has argued that exposure to risk itself is not a form of harm. His argument starts with a discussion of how we would assess the risk to which someone is exposed. Suppose that Mr. Smith is exposed to the risk of getting a disease. In order to determine the seriousness of the risk, we would have to calculate the probability of Mr. Smith getting the disease. Suppose we know that for the general population, the risk is 10%, that is, 10 out of 100 people in the general population who are exposed do get the disease. If we do not know anything about Mr. Smith, 10% will be our assessment of the probability of Mr. Smith getting the disease. This assessment is obtained by using a certain reference class, members of the general population who have been exposed to the same conditions as Mr. Smith.

But suppose we also know that for someone with a certain factor X, say, age above 70, the probability is 25%. Then, if we know that Mr. Smith is older than 70, 25% will be our assessment of the probability of Mr. Smith getting the disease. Here, the reference class that we are using is that of members of the general population who are older than 70 and who have been exposed to the same conditions as Mr. Smith.

Now, suppose we also know that for someone who is older than 70 and also a smoker, the risk of getting the disease in 60%. Then, if we know that Mr. Smith is both older than 70 and a smoker, we know that Mr. Smith belongs to this reference class for which the probability of getting the disease is 60%. As we learn more about Mr. Smith, we are able to place him in a different reference class, even though he still, of course, belongs to the other ones, and we get a different probability, and each time we change our probability, we also change our assessment of the risk.

Perry, then, says:

> It is surely very odd to claim that the 25 per cent risk is a harm in itself, given that our assessment of the risk would be quite different if the state

> of our knowledge were different. . . . It is, surely, a very strange form of harm that varies in this way with our state of knowledge.
>
> (p. 195)

Perry concludes, then, that exposure to risk itself is not a harm.

The immediate response might be: the assessment of the risk depends on what we know. But what about the risk itself? After all, even if what harm is done, if any, does not depend on our knowledge, the assessment of the harm might – in fact, must inevitably – depend on our knowledge: our physiological, medical, psychological, and moral knowledge. And even our characterization of the harm as being physical, psychological, or moral will depend on our knowledge. We generally don't think that the fact that our assessments depend on what we know prevents us from getting it right. So isn't there something like "the correct" reference class, which is what it is, independently of what we know?[13]

The right reference class?

We do have a strong intuition that the more causally relevant factors are included in the reference class, given what we know about, say, the disease and the physiology of the exposed, the more reliable is the evaluation of the probability. Suppose we wonder about the probability of getting lung cancer. We Google it and find some general statistics about the risk of cancer for someone in the general population, with no defining features. It does not tell us much about the chances for ourselves. We would want a reference class that at least specifies the age (and limited to age about the same as ours), when people started to smoke (only people who started about the same age), how much they were smoking (only people with consumption similar to ours). And it would seem even better if it could also specify the kind of tobacco, the weight of the persons, whether they exercise and how much, their diet. And maybe also the family history of cancer, the level of air pollution of where they live, how long they've been living there, whether they are exposed to secondhand smoke. It seems that there is a list of factors that are causally relevant to the disease, as enablers (e.g., secondhand smoke) or defeaters (e.g., exercise), and we are looking for the reference class that includes all those factors.

But suppose that we look at a class of people who have all exactly the same values for all the causally relevant factors (same age, same degree of exercise, have been smoking for the same amount of time, smoke the same kinds of cigarette, same family history, etc.). Could we find out that some of them got the disease and the other ones did not get the disease? No. If that were the case, we would have to conclude that there are some causally relevant factors that were not included in the list and that they explain why some got the disease and some did not.

The presupposition here is that there is a set of causally relevant factors such that if we look at a class of people who have all exactly the same values for all the causal factors, then either everyone in this reference class has the disease or no one has it. If we were to use this "complete" (ideally complete) reference class for ourselves, we would find either that all people in this class have it or that none do. No more uncertainty, no more risk. If we are using this reference class, the question of exposure to risk does not even make sense.

And there is another reason the idea of a complete reference class cannot help.

Epistemic perspectives

On what basis would we say of the class that includes all the causally relevant factors that it is "the right" one? Perry introduces the notion of *epistemic perspective.*

An epistemic perspective is characterized in terms of a network of background knowledge, beliefs, assumptions. There is an epistemic perspective that includes all the currently available scientific knowledge, there are some that include the currently available knowledge only of some sciences, there are epistemic perspectives that don't include scientific knowledge at all, and everything in between. And there are some epistemic perspectives that are constructed, like the omniscient epistemic perspective, where everything that there is to know is known, or the reasonable person perspective that includes the knowledge and beliefs of a so-called reasonable person. The epistemic perspective of a reasonable person is a normative notion that is used in a legal context to determine what a person in the defendant's situation should have known, can be expected to have known.

In any given case, the omniscient epistemic perspective includes the complete reference class, whereas the reasonable person epistemic perspective may not. But both are epistemic perspectives. One is not more "right" than the other in and by itself. There is no right reference class independently of a purpose which determines what epistemic perspective is appropriate.

The assessment of risk cancer will be different dependent on whether the one exposed to the risk is seen as part of the general population or as a 20-year-long smoker. But for the purpose of broad comparison or the basis of societal action, the first one is more appropriate, whereas for the purpose of individual action, the second is more appropriate. That may be why some have said that there is no risk independently of our assessment of it (Garland 2003). There is only risk where there is uncertainty, and there is uncertainty only relative to a certain reference class that is appropriate based on some purpose we have.

Imposition

The discussion so far showed that the exposure to risk cannot be harm by itself. But we actually already knew that exposure to risk just by itself is not harm, since we don't take voluntary exposure to be harm (although, in some cases, it might come to be interpreted as doing some harm to oneself). What we are concerned with, though, is not mere exposure to risk but *imposed* exposure.

To be exposed, be subjected to risk, is to be placed in a position where something *unwanted* could happen. It is like being reduced to a pawn that is moved, without consent, from one place to another one, where it would not want to be. Being acted upon in that way can be seen as a violation or deprivation of one's autonomy, and one could say, *that* is the harm done to the exposed, like Mr. Smith.

Within the constraints of living in a functioning society, John Oberdiek (2017) says, we demand autonomy, the ability to determine the course of our life. Adriana Placani (2017) views the harm done as a violation of *dignity* which strikes the core of an individual's moral worth (p. 88). One may argue that autonomy and dignity do not have degrees and their deprivation is due to the act of exposing someone to risk without their permission or agreement. In Kantian terms, it is a violation of the categorical demand that others should be treated as ends in themselves and never merely as means.[14]

According to Claire Finkelstein (2003), minimizing one's risk exposure is an element of an agent's basic welfare; it is a basic interest. Subjecting someone to the possibility of harm is harm in that "[a] person who inflicts a risk of harm on another damages that interest [in avoiding unwanted risks]" (p. 966). And it is a form of harm that is, seemingly, independent of the outcome of the exposure and so does not depend on how we assess the risk to which the person was exposed.

But from the omniscient perspective, all that we would see is that Mr. Smith was put in a position where either something bad happens to him or nothing happens to him. He was never "exposed to a risk." On the other hand, the question of whether risk of harm is harm assumes that there is a risk of harm, a *possibility* to be hurt. That means that the question already assumes a certain epistemic perspective that is not the omniscient one, or, simply, that does not include the complete reference class. But which one? Is it the epistemic perspective of Mr. Smith? The epistemic perspective of our best science? The epistemic perspective of whoever is exposing Smith to the disease?

Suppose a company is adding a component to some of their food products and it is discovered a few weeks later that this component is toxic. Suppose also that the company had investigated the toxicity of this component very rigorously and had found that it was not toxic (maybe because the techniques that existed at that time were not able to reveal this toxicity). Did the company impose a risk on you?

Or imagine that you served some of those food products to some friends before anything was known about the toxicity. Would you say that you imposed that risk on them? That you did some harm to your friends? They may have been exposed to a risk by being served this food product, but it is not clear that it was imposed on them any more than if they go for a walk and a storm suddenly and unexpectedly breaks out and they find themselves exposed to the risk of being struck by lightning. We would not think of this risk as being *imposed* on them, probably because there is no one to do this imposition. Maybe the same goes for risks to which one is exposed as a result of the actions of others. But as Perry might say, it would be a strange form of harm that would depend for its existence on the knowledge of whoever is creating the risk.

Another problem here is whether imposition could really be all that is relevant. Are we not inclined to think that if being subjected to risk is being harmed, how much harm is done will depend on the severity of the possible unwanted consequences? For example, it seems very different to have Jones playing Russian roulette on a sleeper, and thereby exposing them to the risk of death, and to have Jones pulling the curtains in their bedroom while they are asleep, exposing them, thereby, to the risk of waking up much earlier than they intended. We may agree that autonomy or interests are violated in both cases and, also, that those cases are very different in terms of the harm done, if any. Maybe violation of autonomy or dignity comes in degrees, after all. In any case, if the harm done depends not just on the violation of autonomy but also on the seriousness of the risk to which one was subjected, then we are back to the need to choose a reference class to determine how much harm was done. Again, which one should that be? From the epistemic point of view of Mr. Smith? From the epistemic point of view of our best science? From the epistemic point of view of whoever is exposing Smith to the disease? In any case, it would make how much harm is done dependent on the choice of an epistemic perspective.

Admittedly, we are not offering here an answer to the question of whether exposure to a risk by itself is a harm. There are many studies in the legal literature and philosophy of law, with diverse points of view.[15] But the discussion shows well the philosophical importance of the selection of reference class in risk assessment and highlights how its relevance depends on normative factors.

3.5.2.3 The risk of being shot by the police: a case study

In some cases of risk assessment, it may be not only challenging but also controversial to determine what reference class is the relevant one and thus what probability is the relevant one. As we saw, the selection of a reference class as the relevant one will be based on beliefs that we have about the situation, the data that are available, and the purpose of estimating the probability. The purpose of assessing the risk, which entails assessing the probability, is generally part of a *risk management* project: what particular effects do we regard as unwanted, what conditions of exposure are we particularly interested in, why do we regard those as unwanted?

The example we are going to present here shows that there may be a back-and-forth between defining the risk that we want to assess and gathering the data needed for this assessment. That is similar to the back-and-forth in science in general, between defining a scientific concept (for example, what we mean by *consciousness*) and determining the experimental context in which it can be investigated, that is, what kind of data will be a measure of that concept (cf. Peschard & van Fraassen 2014). But in addition, as we shall see, it is not, in general, possible to avoid normative questions in this process.

What is the risk of being shot by the police?

We do not aim here to answer the question of what the risk is to be shot by the police. Our interest is in the *methodology* of studies which address that question. Our focus is on the difficulties which any such study may encounter, as exemplified in this particular case.

Let us see how scientific studies could answer the following question: *Is there a greater risk of being shot by the police if you are Black than if you are White?*

How can we assess this risk, what should we measure to obtain evidence that there is or not a greater risk, and how can we measure it?

What we'll see is that:

1. There is a debate about what data are needed to assess the risk, that is, what the relevant reference class is.
2. What data are needed depend on our purpose in assessing this risk, that is, what the risk management project is that motivates the risk assessment.

For instance, do we want to assess the risk of being shot by the police because we, as a society, have the risk management project of reducing the risk of fatalities during encounters with the police? Or is it because we, as a society, have the risk management project of reducing the risk for anyone to be a victim of racial bias? Or something else?

Reported statistics and their interpretation

The great variety of reported statistics about fatalities in encounters with the police seems to leave little doubt that there is an appreciable risk, in our society, of being shot in such an encounter. They also appear to show that the risk is unevenly distributed along ethnic, racial, or social lines (Edwards et al. 2019; Ross 2015; Schwartz & Jahn 2020). Recent analyses of independently validated data collected by the citizen science initiative *Fatal Encounters* showed police accounted for more than 1 in 12 of all homicides of adult men between 2012 and 2018. It showed as well that 26% of civilians killed by police shootings in 2015 were Black, even though Black civilians comprise only 12% of the US population.[16] For some, this disparity in proportion tends to show the existence of racial bias in policing.

But does it? There are arguments which concede the disparity but claim that it is accounted for by two other factors: differences in crime rates and in frequency of encounters with the police. These arguments point to such statistics as the rate of arrests for violent crime in the US in 2018 being 3.6 times higher for Blacks as for Whites. Instead, then, of attributing the disproportion in rates of shooting to racial bias, this kind of argument suggests that different rates of police shooting could be instead related to differences in reported crimes across different groups. But it could also point to a bias, this time in decisions to arrest, or in the classification of behavior as violent or not violent.

If the police are called to the scene of, for instance, a reported robbery in progress, do they consciously or unconsciously apply different standards when they classify behavior as threatening or violent? Or on a more basic level, does racial profiling shift the balance by raising not just the probability of a shooting during an encounter with the police but the probability of police encounters, of any sort, as well for certain racial groups?[17]

This glimpse into the debates and controversies around how to interpret data about police shooting already shows some of the difficulties. What do we need to measure exactly, and what data do we need for this measurement? These are not questions whose answers are clear or settled beforehand. We need to have a closer look at the process of data collection and interpretation to get clearer on what is at issue in these debates and the different ways of interpreting these data.

Why assess the risk?

That risk management project that informs the judgment of significance of the data (what the data mean, what conclusion they support) and the judgment of relevance of the data (which data are needed and why) is not always formulated explicitly in the debate. This may be because risk assessment is seen as a process that should be kept independent of risk management so as to keep it unbiased. Risk assessment would consist simply in gathering the data (even if it is rarely simple), and then risk management would decide what to do about it. But the data are not somewhere waiting to be gathered. They have to be produced, and many different kinds of data can be produced about the same facts, like police shootings. What kinds of data we want depends on the motivation we have to produce these data, what kind of risk we are interested in managing, or in mitigating, if needed (O'Brien 2000).

Apart from the assessment of risk for the individual in an encounter with the police, the motivations for the statistical analysis of data about racial disparities in police shootings could be:

- To gather potential evidence for or against hypotheses about racial bias or discrimination (e.g., whether to protect the general public, populations more at risk of police bias, or police officers against possibly unsubstantiated allegations).

- To identify and measure the factors that affect the chance that a given police encounter will devolve into fatal violence.
- To identify policies or programs that may lessen the chances of violent police encounters.

Of course, this list is not exhaustive, and these different goals don't have to be exclusive of one another.

What can the statistics be evidence for?

It is important, especially when we discuss this kind of studies, to be clear on the distinction among the terms "bias," "discrimination," and "disparity." Disparities are differences observed in comparable set of data. Disparities can be shown *directly* by a statistical analysis of the data.

Typical definitions of bias characterize it as an inclination of the mind, prejudice, or preconceived opinion, with selective revealing or suppression of information as associated behavior. Similarly, typical definitions of discrimination list a prejudiced or prejudicial outlook or judgment, with unequal treatment as associated behavior. Thus, bias and discrimination are among the factors that may lead to, or explain, the disparities in treatment. Conversely, such disparities may be evidence for bias and discrimination. But bias or discrimination are not directly observed in the data. They are interpretations of the data.

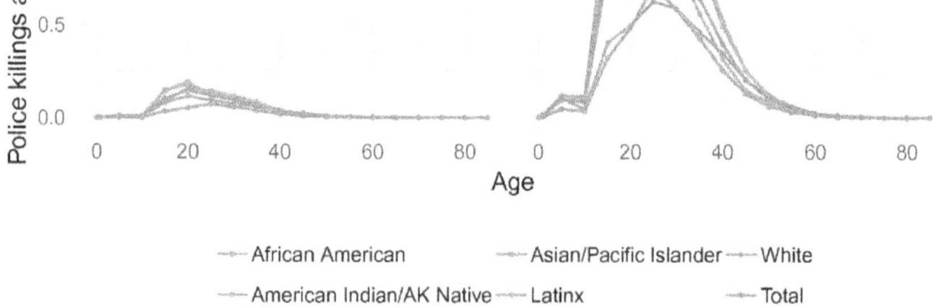

Figure 3.2 Deaths caused by police use of force (median model–based prediction) as a percentage of all deaths by age, race, and sex. Life tables were calculated using model simulations from 2013 to 2018 Fatal Encounters data and 2017 National Vital Statistics System.

The question is, Which data exactly are relevant to reveal possible disparity that would have to be explained or would be best explained by racial bias or discrimination? For instance, in this graph based on reported results of actual statistical analyses and published in *The Proceedings of the National Academy of Sciences*, the initial disparities for boys and men of different ethnic groups are certainly clear (Edwards et al. 2019).

But as clear as the disparity is, without more data it cannot be taken as confirmation of a racial bias. This graph shows clearly, for example, that among boys and men in the age range 15–30, the proportion of deaths caused by police use of force in the Black population is considerably higher than in the White population. One possible reason for this is differences in police behavior toward the different racial groupings (for example, racial profiling). But one could argue that the reason, instead, is differences in the kinds of situations encountered by the police.

To look into this question, of what accounts for the disparities shown in the diagram, other data or other features of the data need to be taken into account.

Different questions addressed in these studies

The first question addressed in much of the literature concerns *the risk a Black man or boy has of dying in an* <u>encounter</u> *with the police* and *how that risk compares* to the risk faced by men and boys in other ethnic and racial groups in the society, especially White men and boys.

To calculate the risk of dying in a police encounter, we need to calculate the probability that an encounter would be a fatal one, and for that we need data both about all the encounters and about the fatal ones. But there is actually no systematic official or government projects to collect data about encounters.

Nonofficial projects were started to collect data about *fatal* encounters. One example, typical in form, is the *Deadspin Police-Shooting Database*, which was started in 2014 to collate news reports on shootings. Every entry in this database details a reported police encounter, including the race of the person who was shot. Another nonofficial database that is often used is *Fatal Encounters*, which was started by a journalist and has more than 28,000 entries for incidents from 2000 to mid-2020.

According to one source, in the years 2017 to mid-2020, the number of White people shot to death by the police in the USA was 1,430, and the number of Black people in those same years was 772. But those numbers do not show that a White person is almost twice as likely to be fatally shot by police as is a Black person.

First of all, there are many more White people in the US population than Black people. In fact, statistics from the USA Census Bureau Population Estimates (July 1, 2019) about the whole population shows that the ratio of

Whites to Blacks is almost 6 to 1. If the probability of being fatally shot were the same for Whites as for Blacks, then the ratio of Whites shot to Blacks shot would also be almost 6 to 1, whereas it is actually just less than 2 to 1. So it seems that the probability of being fatally shot for a White person in general is less than a third of what it is for a Black person in general.

But that the probability of being fatally shot for a White person is much less than that for a Black person is not by itself uncontroversial evidence that bias is the explanation of it. If the probability of *being in a police encounter* were different for a Black person, then it may not be surprising that the probability of a fatal encounter would be different too if the differences between the two kinds of probability are comparable. Or maybe we would find that actually there is a strong discrepancy between the two kinds of probability. To get further, we need to have the probabilities for Blacks and for Whites of being in a police encounter.

Unfortunately, as mentioned already, official data about police encounters are not available, and they are impossible to gather in a nonofficial manner. This is a real impasse.

Some researchers have compared the number of Blacks who were fatally shot in a given area (which could be the whole country or a smaller area) to data about the population of Blacks in this area. They will arrive at, for instance, the following result: "Over the life course, about 1 in every 1,000 Black men [or boys] can expect to be killed by police" (Edwards et al. 2019).

But the problem remains: not every boy or man in the Black population or White population has the same chance of being shot during an encounter with the police in their lifetime. Some people, based on their age, where they live, what they or their parents or relatives or friends do for a living, have a very low chance of encountering the police. Others have a very high chance of encountering the police. Those in the former group have a lower chance of being killed during an encounter than those in the latter group, simply because there are fewer encounters.

That is not to say that there is any certainty about whether given people will or will not encounter the police. Philando Castile was shot with a baby in his car,[18] and a baby would, in most cases, be considered as having a low or very low chance of encountering the police. And yet this baby did not only encounter the police but also could well have been shot in the process. Nevertheless, it is uncontroversial that not everybody has the same chance of encountering the police and that this chance is not distributed at random.

So calculating probabilities with the whole population as reference class does not serve well the purpose of investigating whether the existence and extent of a racial bias explains discrepancies in rates of fatal encounters with the police.

The effect of a change in reference class

Differences in geographic distribution

As we said, data about the population of encounters are not available, and using the overall population of Blacks or Whites is not very informative. So researchers have tried to get some insight by using other reference classes. In particular, the *Fatal Encounters* database was utilized for a study that subdivides fatal police encounters by geographic and demographic factors, focusing on US metropolitan areas (Schwartz & Jahn 2020). The study estimated the ratios comparing rates of fatal police violence experienced by Black people relative to those experienced by White people in different areas of the US.

And the results show that the value of this ratio, and so the value of the discrepancy, is strongly dependent on the geographic area. One explanation that appears possible is that racial bias exists in some areas more than in others, or maybe the explanation is another difference between some areas and others.

Are there other factors which may be important or which, if added, would change the apparent results for the different geographic areas? And are there data that could explain the differences in the discrepancy?

The effect of refining a reference class

If other factors that may be important are taken into account, the statistical analysis is refined, and perhaps refined again, step-by-step. And refining a question may lead to surprising results.

There is a simple example to illustrate this effect. In a certain (imagined) university, it was noticed that the admission ratio for women to graduate school was much less than that for men.

The question asked, of course, was whether that was due to some bias in the admission procedure. So the next step in the inquiry was to ask each department for the ratio of female to male in the admission of applicants to their graduate program. Surprisingly, it was found that the admission ratio for women was about the same as that for men in each department considered separately.

How was that possible? It sounds paradoxical, and in fact it is often referred to as *Simpson's paradox*, after the statistician who first discussed that sort of case. But there is no real paradox. The explanation was that a much larger proportion of the women applicants were applying to very popular departments, where the overall admission ratio was low.

So a positive correlation that shows up at one level of statistical analysis, for a certain reference class (e.g., general admission level, the whole population of the country) may disappear in the next step of inquiry, when the

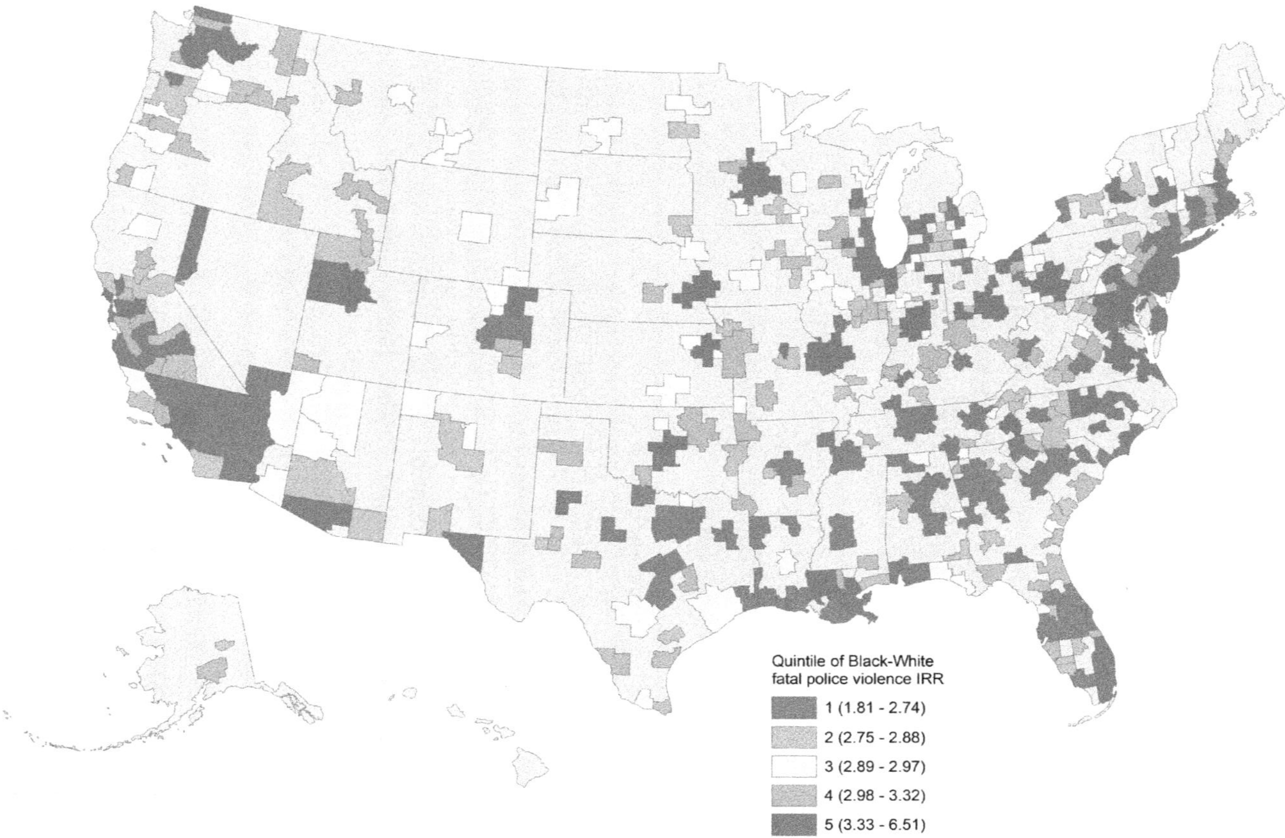

Figure 3.3 Estimated Black-White incidence rate ratios (annual) for fatal police violence, by Metropolitan Statistical Area. Source: Fig. 2 from (Schwartz & Jahn 2020).

reference class is refined (e.g., department admission level, population of a specific US metropolitan area).

Disparities in reference classes based on crime rates

There are factors other than the geographic area which, when taken into account, modify the apparent results, and they are at the center of disputes about what the data show. Instead of using the overall Black versus White populations, or the Black versus White populations, of encounters, the probability of being in a fatal encounter could be calculated by reference to the population of those apprehended as criminals. The comparison of interest would be between (a) the ratio of White to Black among people who were in a fatal encounter and (b) the ratio of White to Black among people who are apprehended as criminals.

Someone might wonder whether the disproportion of Blacks who were in a fatal encounter is due not to racial bias but to the disproportion of Blacks who are apprehended as criminals. Such an explanation, though, would raise a new question: why is there a disproportion of Blacks who are apprehended as criminals? Is there racial bias at that level, if not at the level of the shooting?

And if data about all encounters were available, it is possible that taking this population as reference class would reveal another instance of Simpson's effect. For there the proportion among Blacks of people being fatally shot by the police might or might not be larger than the proportion among Whites of people being shot. The disparity found at one level, the level of the population, could have disappeared at the level of the encounters. The explanation for the disparity found at the level of the whole populations of Black and Whites would then be that Blacks find themselves much more often in police encounters. But here again, such an explanation would raise a new question: why is there a disproportion of Blacks in police encounters? Is there a racial bias at that level, if not at the level of the shooting?

The probability of being in a fatal encounter could also be calculated in reference to the population of violent encounters. There are no data about all encounters, but there might be data about encounters in which a violent crime was committed, or threatened, or perceived as imminent. But it is doubtful that a decrease in the disparity in this kind of data would be telling. The reason is that if it is a case in which a suspect shoots a civilian or a policeman, or is armed and threatens to do so, or is perceived to be armed and in a dangerous state of mind, the probability of the police shooting the suspect if able to do so is near or at 100%, regardless of any other characteristics of the situation.

The point would also apply to lesser violence. For example, if the suspect is armed, that by itself might outweigh any tendency to withhold fire, regardless of other factors, though we can expect that the counterweight will be correlated with the type of weapon, less for a golf club or baseball bat, more for a chainsaw or gun.

So reducing the reference class to encounters in which a violent crime was committed, or threatened, or perceived as imminent, may change the results about disparity. But it might do so because the conditions of the encounter could outweigh the effect of a racial bias even if it existed.[19] The results would be informative about what affects the existence of the disparity, but not conclusive regarding the existence of a racial bias.

What about data about shootings in encounters where the apprehended crimes are nonviolent? For example, during the July 4 weekend in 2020 at Langston University in Del City, Oklahoma, a policeman shot a suspected shoplifter.[20] Happily, the shoplifter was not seriously injured, but this could have been an impromptu death sentence.

Shoplifting is generally a misdemeanor rather than a felony, in view of the value of what can be taken. The law distinguishes between infractions (the least serious), misdemeanors, and felonies. If we had the statistics for police shootings in police encounters where the suspected, apprehended, or putative offense was not a felony, would we see equal proportions for Blacks and Whites that were shot?

If not, if for example the proportion was higher for Blacks than for Whites, would that indicate a significant difference in the apparent value placed on Black lives?

Our discussion points to a general feature of statistical studies: when certain proportions are unknown, others are used which are taken to be indicative of, or correlated with, the former ("proxies"). But that they are indeed indicative is another question that could, in principle, only be answered by a further statistical analysis.

And there are many other methodological limitations that challenge the validity of such inquiries. As Nix (2020) pointed out, analyses such as that of Schwartz and Jahn (2020) or Ross and colleagues (2015, 2021) are limited in that they rely on the reporting of fatal shootings of the police that may be incomplete, but also on the fact that they try to assess police bias in *shooting* from reports of *fatal shootings*; thus, they draw from a nonrandom sample of victims of shootings who *died* from that shooting. This sample may be more biased toward Blacks, e.g., because they are more likely to have worse access to health-care facilities, or less biased toward Blacks if, for instance, Black victims of police shootings are likelier to be younger and healthier and therefore better able to recover from a gunshot wound. In a subsequent study, Nix and Shjarback (2021) observed the latter and found that racial and age disparities in police shootings are likely more pronounced than previous estimates suggest (notwithstanding substantial uncertainties about the completeness and validity of the underlying data).

Conclusions from this discussion

What sorts of proportional disparities should be measured to arrive at results that would be clearly telling with respect to racial bias or discrimination?

The case of police shooting shows the need to select a reference class when we are using statistics to try to obtain a "description" of a situation, like the situation of people being shot by the police. It also shows the difficulties that arise in the process of doing so and the controversies that may come up regarding which reference class is appropriate.

As we saw, what reference will be seen as appropriate will depend on:

- The purpose of the description. Do we want to know about the risk of being shot by the police in general, about the conditions in which it is most likely to happen in general, about whether there is some racial bias involved, etc.?
- What data are available. Since official data about encounters with the police are not available, are there other data that could provide equivalent information?
- Beliefs that we have about the situation and some elements of the situation. Beliefs that there might be some racial bias, that racial bias could be present not just after one is apprehended but also in deciding to arrest someone, and that if data using apprehended criminals as reference class did not show a discrepancy between Black and White probability of being shot, that would not yet show that there is no racial bias.
- Our values. If we look for data that show whether or not the probability of being in a fatal encounter with the police is influenced by racial bias, it is that we care about it; if we think that data based on the reference class of apprehended criminal cannot show that there is no bias, it is because we also think there might be such a thing as racial profiling and we think it is wrong.

3.5.2.4 Inference and reference population

There is another way in which statistics are used: it is to make inference from one population to another. Statistics obtained on the basis of a sample of a certain population are used to make predictions about individuals of a different population. For instance, a study of the mail-in voting behavior of a sample of voters in California could be used to make inference about the mail-in voting behavior of voters in Oregon; the reaction to a drug injected to rats could be used to make inference about the reaction to the drug if injected to humans. Here, also, the issue arises of whether the class that is used as reference is appropriate to make inferences about individuals of the new class.

A statistical study conducted on the Tennessee population concluded that a class size reduction program implemented in Tennessee had been successful in improving a number of educational outcomes, including reading scores (Cartwright 2009). When the class size reduction program was implemented in California, however, reading scores did not improve (Bohrnstedt & Stecher 2002). The statistical results did not travel well from one population to another.

When a statistical study is conducted to measure the effect of a given treatment, which could be a program, a new policy, or a drug, the effect of interest is defined as a variable that can be measured. If the drug is supposed to cure diabetes, the variable will be the glycemia; if the treatment is an educational program, the variable will be a measure of some educational outcomes, like reading scores. During the study, the efficacy of the treatment will be evaluated by comparing the evolution of this variable in the group that received the treatment, the study group, and in the group that did not receive the treatment, the control group. The study group and the control group are supposed to be identical in all respects except for receiving and not receiving the treatment. If the two groups can be considered identical in all respects except for receiving versus not receiving the treatment, and if the evolution of the variable in each group is correctly evaluated, then the difference in the evolution of the variable between the two groups can be reliably attributed to the causal effect of the treatment given to one of them.

When the success of the educational program in Tennessee is taken for a reason to think that the program will be successful in California, an assumption is made about the population in Tennessee and the population in California: that they are similar in the respects that are relevant to the success of the program. That is, the study population in Tennessee is used as an equivalent of a reference class for the members of the study population in California. The expectation of a successful implementation of the policy in California is based on the assumption that a situation in California where the policy is implemented is similar enough to the situation in Tennessee to see it as a member of the set of situations in Tennessee.

But when the program was implemented in California, it was implemented state-wise and in a short period of time, which created the need for new teachers and rooms, which the state had difficulty to meet. In a hurry, less-experienced teachers were hired and rooms were taken that were used for supportive learning activities. Reduction in the quality of the teaching and in the offering of supportive learning activities worked against the improvement in educational outcomes that the reduction in class size was supposed to produce.

Another relevant example of the same issue is the use of animal testing to predict the effect of a treatment on humans (Shanks et al. 2009). Some drugs can be used in animals to test their efficiency on animals, with the prospect, if it is successful, of testing it on humans. This is an exploratory use of experiments on animals. But results of studies on animals are not predictive of results on humans: "Currently, nine out of ten experimental drugs fail in clinical studies because we cannot accurately predict how they will behave in people based on laboratory and animal studies."[21]

The reason that animal testing is not predictive of the efficacy on humans is the same as the reason success of the educational program in Tennessee was not predictive of its success in California. What the comparison between study and control populations in the original statistical experiment, like the one conducted in Tennessee or the one conducted on animals, shows is that *in the specific conditions* of the implementation of the policy or administration of the drug, such and such result, positive or negative, was obtained. It shows that in *these conditions*, the implementation makes a difference. But it says little about the difference it might make in a new population. The reason is that the "treatment" population, that which received the treatment, and the control population, which did not receive it, are made of individuals that are all different in some respects from one another.

Randomization ensures that the two populations can be regarded as identical to the extent that they are diverse "in the same way." That suffices to guarantee there is no feature that can just, by itself, independently of the treatment, account for the difference in results between the treatment and the control populations. But it is still very likely that the treatment only has an effect on some people in the treatment population, in virtue of some features that they have and others don't have: "If there is a higher average effect in the treatment group than in the control group, we are assured that the treatment helped at least someone in the study population" (Cartwright 2018). We do not know who these people that the treatment helped are and what all the features that made the treatment work are. So we don't know exactly what features need to be present for the treatment to be successful or what features may prevent the treatment to be successful.

If the implementation is successful, there probably are several factors that are contributing, in addition to the treatment itself, be it a policy or a drug, to the success of the production of the outcome targeted by the treatment. In a new situation/population, some of these factors may not be present, whereas other factors may be present that could hamper the production of the outcome.

One more complication is that the success of the treatment may result from a combination of different factors, physiological, social, environmental, and there might be different combinations that will produce similar effects:

> We know that two populations can have the same prevalence of exposure, but different causal effects, if the distribution of component causes differs across these populations. Further, two populations can have the same causal effect, but different distributions of the prevalence of causes, which has direct implications for how we intervene on those causes.
>
> (Keyes & Galea 2017)

The focus on identifying isolated factors that contribute to the production of the effect in experimental conditions is useful to understand how the effect is produced in these conditions. But it may not have great value when it comes to applying the treatment on a new population in different conditions.

When we use the statistical result about a study population to make inference about a new population, we choose to see the new population as relevantly similar to the study population, in the same way as when we use a certain reference class to make probabilistic inference about a subject (be it a person, an animal, or a certain situation): we choose to see this subject as sharing the characteristics that define the members of the reference class (as just member of the general population, as a smoker, as a woman, as a Black person, etc.). In both cases, this choice is a normative judgment to the effect that this population should be seen as similar to this one or that one or this subject should be seen as belonging to this or that class. In both cases, this choice is the expression of a value judgment.

In the case of the probabilistic inference about a subject, we do have to select a reference class. That we have to, though, does not free us from the responsibility of what choice we are making and what goals and values are motivating this choice. In the case of the statistical inference to a new population, some authors have been arguing, insistently, that instead of using results that were obtained for a different population, we should rather use a causal model that represents the factors that are characteristic of the new population and suspected to be relevant to the implementation of the new treatment, a new policy, a new drug.

3.5.3 Model-based probability: selection of model attributes

In the preceding passages, we examined the case study concerning education strategy in Tennessee and California with regard to the choice of reference class. A statistical study in Tennessee concluded that class size reduction had been successful at improving a number of educational outcomes, including reading scores (Cartwright 2009). But when the class size reduction program was implemented in California, the reading scores did not improve (Bohrnstedt & Stecher 2002).

The teachers' level of experience, the quality of teaching, and the availability of supportive learning activities were all cited as relevant causal factors that were not taken into account in the original statistical study and counteracted the benefit of class size reduction.

The statistical study in Tennessee was a randomized controlled trial (RCT), and RCTs are generally taken as the gold standard for statistical investigation, as a basis for effective strategies and policies. They are prevalent, for example, in determining efficacy of medicines, side effects of cosmetics, preservatives in food, fertilizers in agriculture, and as here, benefits of changes to school curricula. But the Tennessee-California example shows that the relevance of their results is sensitive to factors not included in what is systematically varied or controlled in such a trial.

Accordingly, Nancy Cartwright argues that, as a preliminary to any such statistical study or RCT, a *purpose-built causal model* must be constructed beforehand (Cartwright 2018). In its simplest form, a causal model can be a directed graph, with arrows indicating which factors have, or may have, an influence on other factors. A result, such as reading score, may be a function of several factors, and their combined effect is not just a sum of their individual effects. In the study in Tennessee, data were gathered to investigate the supposed causal link to educational outcomes, but only one factor (class size) was manipulated.

The causal model to be constructed before the statistical study needs to involve all the causally relevant factors but needs also to be flexible enough to apply if those factors change during the implementation of the policy under study.

Can the model itself provide us with the right probabilities for what will happen? Certainly not by itself. Probabilities can be built into a model, but then actual trials are needed to check whether those are right in a particular case. However, the actual trials are to be designed on the basis of the model, in which all the relevant factors are present as model attributes, so as to make the trial itself truly relevant.

Then, the modeling can be taken one step further: actual statistics can be among its inputs, and the model can be updated as more data arrive.

3.5.3.1 Models and model evaluation: the example of weather forecasting

The points just made about purpose-built models are well illustrated with the reliance on models in today's weather forecasting. If we go to the National Weather Service (NWS) for our local forecast and turn to the Area Forecast Discussion, we quickly find information of this sort: "Most high-resolution models are showing the strongest winds to be right now . . ." and "The same models are showing another uptick in offshore winds tonight . . ."

The models in question are purpose-built for a particular area. They are based on equations taken from fluid dynamics, characterizing air movement and the interaction of heat and moisture in the atmosphere. The data are observations of pressure, wind speed, temperature, and moisture at weather stations, ground sensors, and weather satellites. The model utilizes a geographic representation of the forecast area, divided into a three-dimensional grid. Each point in the grid is assigned the data (the initial conditions). Then the equations are applied and stepped forward in time to predict the future weather at each grid point.

The NWS publishes details on the models it uses (www.weather.gov/hnx/models). In some cases, when the models relied on are not all in agreement, the forecasters discuss the differences and explain how much weight they give to each. Then they post the results, such as the probability or the expectation value of precipitation.

Where does this probability come from? Statistics based on earlier data were used to construct the model. But these models themselves are not static: their performance is constantly evaluated, and they are modified in response to new statistical data about their results.

FRAME 3: How models are evaluated

There are programs that evaluate weather forecasting models in practice, and their results are public. They set specific standards for each predicted outcome; for example, temperature forecasts may be counted as correct if they are within three degrees of the actual temperature.

Task 1. Find one such program and investigate the reliability of weather forecasting in your own area. Which forecasting services were the most accurate?

For example, as of this writing, you can go to the Forecast Advisor (www.forecastadvisor.com) and enter your zip code. There you will see the scorecard for the modeling relied on by the major weather forecast providers, such as the Weather Channel, including the NWS itself, for the preceding month and the preceding year. They are not perfect but still quite high. For example, the accuracy for predicted high temperatures for Pinole, in California, ranged from 64.38% to 75.87% in the year 2020.

Task 2. Investigate how forecast success is measured for a number of weather features. There are explanations published by the NWS, but also elsewhere. For example, on the "frequently asked questions" page of Forecast Advisor, and in the associated Forecast Watch page (www.forecastwatch.com/), there is precise information about how forecast success is measured for wind, precipitation, sky cover, and the like.[22]

It is the constant interaction of feedback in the form of statistical data, relating model results to actual events, with the models on which the predictions rely that provides an adequate basis for accurate prediction and effective strategies.

3.5.3.2 Stages in model construction: the example of wildfire forecasting

How precisely are such models constructed in the first place? The preliminary causal model for forecasting of weather, wildfires, avalanches, fish populations, crops, and the like relies, first of all, on equations drawn from classical physics. As noted prior, numerical weather prediction relies on the equations of fluid dynamics and thermodynamics that extrapolate the state of a fluid over time. The relevant physical quantities that characterize the fluid, in this case atmosphere or water, are temperature, density, moisture content, and pressure.

Modeling wildfire occurrence and intensity is similar in outline. Construction of such a model begins with the adaption of general modeling programs, first by selection of a set of relevant parameters (topographic, vegetation, and climate) on which data are gathered (today largely by satellite remote sensing), a GIS (geographic information system) in which the spatial

Input Type	*Landscape (GIS Layers)*	*Fuel*	*Climatic*	*Ignition Probability*	*Misc.*	*Ignition Point*
Input	- Latitude - Elevation map - Slope map - Aspect map - Fuel map - Vegetation map - Cover map	- Adjustment - Fuel moisture	- Wind speed and direction - Relative humidity - Temperature	- Road probability map - Random percentage - Number of simulations	- Burn period	- Ignition point for fire point

Figure 3.4 Input parameters used for FARSITE software.

data on these parameters are aggregated and organized, and a simulation program to generate fire occurrence scenarios in the modeled region (Scott 2013). The following chart (Table 1 in Kanga et al. 2014) illustrates what goes into such a simulation.

3.5.3.3 Normative judgments in causal modeling

It might seem that there is no room for normative judgments in causal modeling. The statistics used as input and as control come straightforwardly from the data. The model must, it is insisted, include all relevant causal factors, and that means factors which affect the outcomes regardless of our knowledge or ignorance about them.

But models are built with a purpose, to address a problem that we have formulated for ourselves in a specific way ("Is the global surface temperature changing?"), from which we derived some questions that we deem worth answering ("What will be the temperature in 2050 if this and that conditions remain the same?"), on the basis of previous observations that we have deemed reliable and assumptions that we have deemed acceptable. The judgment of what count as relevant causal factors is embedded in a network of judgments, decisions, choices that we have made and that we may decide to revise in the course of the modeling process.

When models are constructed to provide a basis for effective policies, the success of the policy will be evaluated in terms of stated criteria which will determine which causal factors are the *relevant* ones to be included in the model. In the Tennessee-California example, those criteria were desired educational outcomes, such as improvement in reading scores. But in the choice of those criteria, there are always different options. Is it improvement of average reading scores across the state or improvement of reading scores gauged separately for each school year? Or in the interest of diversity, gauged separately for a partition into subpopulations: Latino, Black, etc.? What is counted as relevant depends on what is viewed as to be taken into account, and that is a normative judgment. If differences in results for different subpopulations are not included in what is to be evaluated, the purpose-built model will not include causal factors differentiating between those subpopulations (see further Cartwright & Marcellesi 2016). This has been a salient concern in wildfire events and their aftermath (Anderson, S. 2020).

That is one way in which normative judgments enter purpose-built causal modeling.

We can see another way value judgments enter into model construction in the Department of Agriculture / Forest Service framework for wildfire risk assessment and management (United States Department of Agriculture 2013, RMRS-GTR-315). It begins with the assertion that to develop cost-effective mitigation strategies, information is required, not just the frequency and intensity with which they might occur, but also "with what impacts to highly valued resources and assets (HVRAs; that is, the things we care about)."

In the section on HVRA identification, a certain hierarchy is recognized, distinguishing primary HRVAs from a series of sub-HRVAs:

> For instance, habitat can be the primary HVRA, with sub-HVRAs defined as the habitat for various individual species or species groups. Critical infrastructure is another example, with sub-HVRAs of telecommunication sites, power lines, fire lookouts, etc. Often primary HVRAs will include the wildland urban interface (WUI), other built structures, and municipal watersheds. HVRAs may also be more ecologically oriented and relate to vegetation structure and assemblage.
>
> (op. cit. p. 29)

What counts as HVRA, but also what is designated as primary, are choices, and clearly value-based, and those choices play a major role in the modeling within this framework.

3.6 Assessing severity

When a danger is known and well-defined, we may measure the risk just by the probability of encountering that danger. But the possible impacts of the possible unwanted outcomes contribute to the seriousness of the risk as well. One may decline playing a game of chance where the probability to lose is very low but the possible loss is very high.

Scientific risk assessment aims at quantifying risks. Quantification makes possible comparison, clear criteria of acceptability, prioritization. So typically, risk assessment focuses on unwanted effects that have a physical impact, in terms of monetary loss, or a health impact, which, too, can easily be converted into monetary loss for the society. COVID-19 was a case in point. The effects that were emphasized were quantifiable: the medical condition it caused, the pressure on medical resources and health workers, and the harm to the economy with workers calling in sick or customers avoiding usual forms of consumption to avoid being contaminated.

An advantage of the quantification of the possible unwanted effects is that it creates an objective measure of the severity – objective in the sense that the method can be evaluated and criticized and that the result is reported in the form of a number which can easily be added or compared to other numbers. Thus, the assessment of severity looks like a measure akin to the measure of any physical quantity.

This may be deceptive. It may give the impression that assessing risk is just a matter of gathering some data waiting somewhere to be gathered. Taking the neat and shiny appearance of numbers, the assessment wears no trace of subjectivity; it does not appear to be from a certain perspective, to have any personal involvement, or to involve any value judgment. But that the method produces a number does not preclude that the design of the method involves value judgments.

To examine this, we will look at examples that are important because they exemplify issues of risk assessment crucial to risk management. We will pay attention specifically to aspects of assessment that concern the issue of distributive justice in risk management. These aspects are, first, the selection of the effects that will be counted as unwanted effects and, second, who bears the risk and how that may influence the selection or omission of certain effects as unwanted.

3.6.1 What kinds of "unwanted" consequences?

Scientific risk assessment focuses on possible effects that can be quantified. As we will see in the chapter on risk perception, however, people's informal evaluation of risks is sensitive to aspects of the possible impacts that are not easily quantifiable. Risk perception is sensitive to whether the impact has a human cause or a natural cause and whether it is perceived as a result of tampering with nature. It is sensitive to the perception of controllability and whether the effects are immediate or delayed.

Risk perception may even be seen as irrational, because such aspects as whether the effect has a human or a natural cause may seem unlikely to make a substantial difference to the physical impact on things or on people. It is then assumed that what we care about, or rather, what we should care about, is precisely this physical impact and how much it would cost. To know how much it would cost is regarded as crucial information because it plays a major role in deciding how much it is rational to invest in order to mitigate the risk. It would seem irrational to invest $100 in mitigating a risk that could only create $1 in damages. It would if all that matters to the impact and the mitigation is their monetary cost.

But "All we should care about is . . ." is a *normative judgment*, a judgment not about what things are, which would be descriptive judgment, but a judgment that expresses a norm, about how things should be. And a normative judgment is a value judgment, a judgment that expresses some values which motivate and support the selection of a certain norm rather than another. But what other norms could there be?

FRAME 4: Is disagreement with scientific assessment of risk based on ignorance?

This question was studied in connection with the general public's reaction to GMO technology (Marris 2001). Claire Marris argues, on the basis of interviews and debates with focus group participants, that the view that the general public simply needs better knowledge of the technology and its benefits to become more rational in their evaluation and come to agree with experts' evaluation of the risk is a myth.

It is true that they may not indeed understand the technology very well. But people's suspicious, reluctant attitude toward GMO is not essentially based on lack of knowledge of the technology. Their reaction is not so much to a specific technology as it is to the institutional context in which it is developed. They do not trust that the companies and agencies in charge of developing and controlling the technology have the public's interest as their top priority. For instance, they are aware that GMO technology could perhaps be used to reduce hunger in some developing countries, if there were a sufficient motivation to do so, but they believe it is mostly a hypocritical argument by companies primarily interested in profit.

The study also found that people are aware that the technology has medical applications but make a clear distinction between the medical and the agricultural application in terms of voluntariness of exposure and the context of the exposure. Someone who decides to use a medicine chooses to do it and can discuss this decision in a personal discussion with their physician, who does not have a personal interest in the decision. They also think that, in the case of medical application, there is a better control because the drug will go through testing and its effects will keep being monitored after it is on the market. By contrast, when the technology is applied to food production, it becomes hidden and forgotten. People perceive GMO technology as unnatural, but so as well pesticides and animal-derived animal feed, and in all cases, it is related to the feeling that "such developments were driven by the need or desire for increased productivity, regardless of health and environmental considerations thus leading to uniform and tasteless food."

Source: Marris, C. (2001).

What the public concerns show through this kind of interviews and debates are norms, norms other than the ones that are normally used in scientific assessment. For instance, how much individual control there will be over the conditions of exposure, how much monitoring there will be after conditions of exposure are created, what the reliability, the trustworthiness, is of the institutional context in which the new technology will be developed and monitored. People may also be concerned with new technologies producing goods or practices that will replace things in their life that they value, like social media changing the ways we form friendship or the ways we interact.

These kinds of impact, that are not physical harms, that are not easily quantifiable, that do not come with a monetary tag on them, have been called "soft" impacts by contrast to the "hard" impacts that are normally considered by scientific risk assessment (Swierstra & te Molder 2012). One example of a soft impact is the perception of unnaturalness, for instance, regarding food production or preservatives or animal-based animal feed. It is easy to dismiss this concern as spurring from a naive and unclear understanding of what is or is not natural. But the dismissal is not based on a descriptive judgment about the absence of a distinction between what is natural and what is not natural. We all, after all, sometimes make this distinction even if we are not able to formulate a general explication of the distinction. Rather, it is a normative judgment about the lack of relevance of this concern when it comes to evaluating the severity of a risk. A nondismissive attitude might, instead, aim at a clarification of this concern and a deliberation involving members of the public on whether and how this concern should be taken into account in the assessment of the severity of a risk.

Similarly, to dismiss the lack of control over one's exposure to a risk as something irrelevant to the assessment of severity is a value judgment. It might well be that life in society necessarily generates risks that people will be exposed to without having control over the exposure. For instance, we need forms of transportation, and to satisfy this need, we create hazards both for those who are using them and for those who are not using them: a car may hurt a pedestrian, and a plane could crash on a house. It may well be that people will conceive of lack of control in different ways in different contexts. And there is no easy way to quantify this aspect of a risk. But none of these considerations make it less of a value judgment to dismiss this aspect rather than to try to integrate it to the evaluation of the severity of a risk.

3.6.2 "Unwanted" consequences for whom?

Another way in which value judgments are involved in assessing severity is with respect to who is exposed to the risk. For instance, the fact that electronic cigarettes were extremely popular among teenagers played a large part in the uproar that resulted in bans or restriction of the sale of vaping products: "Just as back in the Joe Camel days, we proved tobacco companies were targeting young people to smoke and get them addicted to their products; fast forward to Juul, we have the same thing happening."[23]

But in other cases, that it is a specific subpart of the population that is most exposed to a risk makes it more likely that it will be treated as acceptable. One reason is that the probability, if the reference class is the whole population, will be low. Another reason is that if the subpart of the population is socially and/or economically disadvantaged, people with precarious jobs or are part of a racial, ethnic, or sexual and gender minority, they may not have the resources to make themselves heard about their situation.

For instance, studies have found that in the US, Black and Latino adolescents are more likely to be exposed to violence, more likely to have health issues, more likely to be neither enrolled at school nor working (Cauce et al. 2011). Environmental risks also are not uniformly distributed across different parts of the population. The level of exposure to industrial air pollution, hazardous chemicals, and more generally, hazardous air is much higher for racial and ethnic minorities than for the general population (Tabuchi & Popovich 2021). And the difference in exposure to chemicals has been hypothesized to contribute to racial disparities in rates of some diseases, such as diabetes, cardiovascular diseases, and cancer (Vy Kim Nguyen et al. 2020; Ruiz et al. 2018; United States Department of Health and Human Services 2010).

It could be said that the factors that create those increased risks for minorities are social, related to income, education, neighborhood, rather than to race and ethnicity, per se. But the fact is that there is a disproportionate representation of racial and ethnic minorities among people with low income and education or living near industrial sites or power sites and that "race and ethnicity are extremely salient factors when examining health inequity" (Baciu et al. 2017).

The typical rationale to justify the increased risk coming from living in proximity to industrial sites is that it provides the benefit of increased employment opportunities for those same people who are suffering the effects of the environmental pollution. A study examined the top 1,000 polluting facility of the US and found that for Blacks and Hispanics, "the exposure shares of both population subgroups generally exceeded their employment shares, often by a substantial margin" (Ash & Boyce 2018).

In addition, studies have shown that residential segregation not only is associated with a higher exposure to ambient hazards but also that the experience of segregation itself generates an experience of stress that also contributes to an increased risk of cardiovascular disease and cancer among racial and ethnic minority adults. So the differential exposure of racial and ethnic minorities to higher environmental pollution contributes to higher health risks because of the greater exposure to hazards. And in addition, it is a source of individual stressors that increase further the health risks that were already higher than for the general population (Gee et al. 2004; Williams & Mohammed 2009). The same effect from stressors can probably be said of other cases of differential exposure to risks that come from a social, cultural, or economical form of segregation.

A traditional form of risk assessment that focuses on the probability and the physical or monetary impact would only consider the social conditions of the exposure (e.g., proximity to industrial site) as a risk factor – a factor that may contribute to an increase of the risk. But when approaching health risks not as individual risks but as social risks, it would make sense to consider the social conditions as risk impacts. That is, the fact that a certain part of the population is under greater exposure could be viewed as contributing to the severity of the risk. After all, that was the case for teenagers' exposure to vaping. That teenagers were especially exposed was not taken into account in a formal way, but it certainly contributed to the public reaction to the risk as unacceptable. One could imagine that who is exposed to a risk, what part of the population, would become one formal dimension of risk assessment through the evaluation of its severity.

Regarding health-related risk, there are indeed different possible strategies to improve public health.[24] For instance, regarding obesity, one strategy could be to shift the entire distribution of risk to a lower level, without targeting the difference in exposure for different parts of the population. Those who are most at risk remain so, as well as those who are least at risk. But all parts of the population are less at risk. Another approach would be to aim at reducing the risk of those in the highest-risk category with no change of the mean level, which would be akin to a "redistribution of some good (e.g., income, education, housing, or health care) [that] reduces inequality without necessarily changing the mean of the distribution of that good."

These strategies seem to pertain to risk management more than risk assessment. But as noted in the discussion of the police shooting case study, the two are not independent. How we assess risk depends on the purpose of the assessment, what we are trying to understand, to evaluate, and on the management project that we have. If part of our management project is to reduce the impact of inequality, we need a form of assessment that makes inequality and its impact visible, and that means making visible the differences in exposure for different parts of the population. If our management project is, by contrast, to reduce the mean level of risk, to create the most cost-efficient form of intervention, to create the greatest good for the largest number of people, the specific level of exposure of minorities may not be a very relevant information.

What should be clear is that whether or not we do take into consideration who is exposed when assessing social risks, and how we take it into account, is the expression of a value judgment. That remains the case whatever the reasons are to take it or not to take it into account. No justification, such as cost-effectiveness, can change that (Harvard et al. 2021).

The consideration of who is exposed could be extended beyond traditional subparts of the population. For instance, the fact that future generations will be exposed to risks that we are creating could be a component in risk assessment that increases the severity of the risk. The rationale could be that we are imposing the risk on them and that that should make the risk appear less acceptable. The link between the two statements, of course, will be a normative judgment: that we should not impose a risk on those who have no say in the matter. And this normative judgment is the expression of values, such as, say, respect for autonomy.

We could also adopt a similar attitude toward risk that human society is imposing on other animals or even ecosystems. Instead of denouncing the deleterious effect of pesticides on bees on the basis that a threat to bee population is a threat to the well-being of human beings, we could imagine a form of assessment that takes into account, in the calculation of its severity, the fact that we impose it on the bees. Domesticated animals are considered as properties, and except for acts of extreme cruelty, the harm done to an animal is, in the law, only harm done to the owner whose property is damaged. Not to recognize the harm done to other animals for itself is not an attitude based on some descriptive judgment regarding animals' capacity or incapacity to have their life, their health, mental or physical, affected by the impact of pollution and urban or industrial developments. It is based on value judgments regarding the value of their life and well-being.

More generally, whether and how we take into consideration, when evaluating the seriousness of a risk, the fact that it is imposed on others who have no say in the matter and may not even be aware of it is the expression of values regarding the importance of taking responsibility and the respect of others' interests.

3.6.3 Availability of information

An assessment of a risk must be based on data, and data are available only if they are collected and preserved. Data collection and analysis is meant to be professional, and increasing demands for transparency in government, business, and industry require them to be made public. The role of normative judgments becomes evident when we look into the question of availability or unavailability of information.

In some cases, the unavailability of information is due to value judgments included in a political program or platform. The United States Environmental Protection Agency (EPA) normally has a website with a page providing public information on climate change, including the EPA's *Inventory of US Greenhouse Gas Emissions and Sinks*.[25] The *Scientific American*, on January 10, 2018, reported that thousands of webpages with climate change information had been removed from the EPA, the Interior and Energy Departments, and elsewhere across the government. Much of this was restored after a new administration took office.

More often, that information is unavailable is due to the fact that data were not collected, or not in a systematic way. As we saw in the case study on police shootings, statistical analysis was hindered or hamstrung because no data were available. In some cases, private efforts filled in by setting up databases to make up for what official sources did not supply. But data on police encounters in general, as opposed to arrest records, do not even exist, and there is no systematic effort to collect them.

It is reasonable to observe that neither the police nor other public agencies have the resources for all the large-scale data collection and analysis that such studies would wish to draw on. But when the decisions, say, about how to allocate available resources, are made, value judgments inevitably play a role. Which sorts of data are worthwhile, important, or necessary to collect, preserve, collate, or compile? When private efforts set up new databases, collecting information on police shootings, the reason was not that certain kinds of bookkeeping were incomplete – the reason was that certain kinds of information ought to be available.

Another example is the case of "forever chemicals."[26] Those chemicals owe their surname to the fact that they do not break down naturally. Once they are released in the environment, they stay there. They are used in many things, like firefighting foams on military bases, cosmetics, nonstick cookware, or water-repellent fabrics.

Over the decades, they have turned up in the water supplies of communities across the country and soil, food, blood.[27] Exposure to those chemicals at certain levels can lead to infertility risks, thyroid disease, certain types of cancers, and developmental problems in children. *The Washington Post* announced in October 2021: "Biden administration moves to curtail toxic 'forever chemicals.'" And the EPA administrator applauded: "This is a really bold set of actions for a big problem." The good news is that the EPA will "require manufacturers to provide detailed data about entire classes of compounds they produce, and plans to designate some of them as hazardous chemicals." The not-so-good news is that it was not done before. Data are not available to assess the extent of the contamination. And the assessment will take years: "The Defense Department announced Monday that it will finish initial assessments of possible PFAS contamination stemming from nearly 700 of its installations by 2023."

Not too good either is that similar promise was done under both the Obama and Trump administrations, in 2009 and in 2019: "But little meaningful change has resulted, as the chemicals have continued to surface across the country and remain unregulated by the federal government in the nation's water systems."

3.7 Risk of error

A risk assessment may be in error. While errors can be matters of accident or chance, the process of assessment may also be subject to error due to choices that fall well within the constraints of rationality.

3.7.1 Data, hypotheses, and underdetermination

To study risk often means either to try to anticipate the effects that may follow from a current or imagined situation ("What would be the effect on the global average temperature of an increase in greenhouse gas (GHG) emission?" "Is the economic upheaval created by the COVID-19 pandemic going to translate into a recession?") or to identify the cause of some effects that have been observed (some people are showing similar symptoms; the frequency and intensity of some type of natural catastrophe has been increasing). We are aiming at formulating general hypothetical statements that fit our data and can be extrapolated to new conditions. For instance, we want models of climate warming that are able to retrodict past temperatures and to predict temperatures for a new domain of conditions. Unfortunately, theories are infamously underdetermined by the data, meaning, that there are always, at least in principle, different ways to explain a set of data.

FRAME 5: Underdetermination and curve fitting

The easiest way to understand the idea of underdetermination of a theory by the data is to imagine a set of three aligned points. One way to explain the relation between these three points is as linear, that is, as three points on a straight line, the line being the "explanation" of the data. But there are many different kinds of lines that could just as well join the same three points, for instance, an oscillatory one.

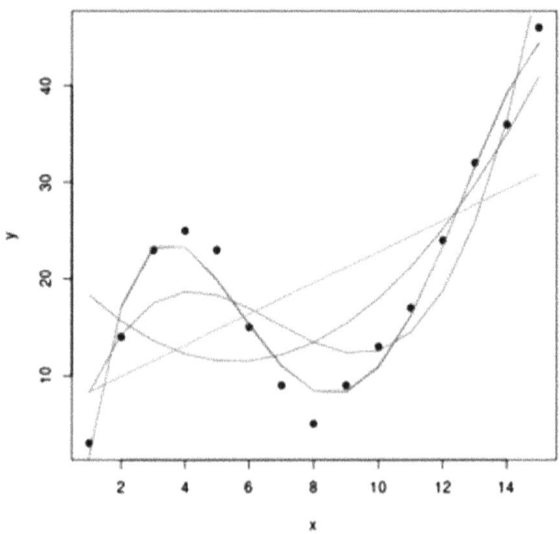

Figure 3.5 Illustration of the idea of underdetermination of a theory by the data.

More generally, with many data, what is asked for is a curve that "best" fits the data, and what is requested is not just any sort of curve but one that can be described by a manageable equation and hence can be extrapolated to a projection into the future.

In the diagram presented, the straight line is a linear approximation to the data, while the other lines are polynomial functions that fit the data much more closely.

Actually, there is a danger that the brown line fits the data too closely! There is in curve fitting a tempting error called "overfitting." That is the name for an analysis that corresponds too closely or exactly to a set of data and, for that very reason, may fail to fit additional data that may appear. It could even happen that, in the long run, the linear approximation fits better, because the irregularity in the initial data points, represented by the dots, turns out to have been atypical.[28]

Question: what kind of error is overfitting? Is it a case of hasty generalization, or is it instead a failure to generalize?

In general, we may find several answers that satisfy our desiderata. Consequently, when we claim that we have found an explanation for our data, we are selecting one hypothesis among other possible ones, and we always run the risk of being wrong, even if we estimate the risk as very low.

This risk is known as *inductive risk*: the risk of error in accepting or rejecting a hypothesis. But this sort of error takes two forms.

3.7.2 Two types of error

There are two types of error that we and scientists alike can make when we are trying to explain some data. Let's use the example of climate science to illustrate them. On the basis of collected data, scientists try to determine whether the climate is warming. One type of error they could make is to claim, by looking at the data, that the climate is indeed warming when, in fact, it is not warming. Another mistake they could make is to claim that the climate is not warming when, in fact, it is warming. Or once the warming trend has become uncontroversial, one type of error could be to claim that the source of the warming is anthropogenic when it is not. Another type of error would be to claim that the source of warming is not anthropogenic when, in fact, it is.

The first type of error, known as **type-1 error**, consists in claiming that something is happening ("The climate is warming," "The drug is having an effect") when nothing is happening ("The climate is actually not warming," "The drug is not actually having an effect"). We may call this *epistemic* *hallucination*. The second type of error, **type-2 error**, consists in claiming that nothing is happening ("There is no climate warming," "The drug is having no effect") when in fact something is happening. This we may give the mnemonic name *epistemic blindness*.

FRAME 6: Type-1 error and type-2 error in hypothesis testing

Interesting, disturbing, or challenging hypotheses about food supplements are often in the news, especially if they are disputed. The simplest case, perhaps, that of a person brought to trial for murder. It is a principle of justice that the defendant is presumed innocent, that is, the *null hypothesis*. The prosecution argues for the *alternative hypothesis*, that the defendant is guilty. The jury must make a fateful decision: it will make a type-1 error if it convicts an innocent person. But it will make a type-2 error if it lets a guilty person go free.

	Verdict: Convict!	*Verdict: Acquit!*
defendant guilty	correct	type-2 error
defendant innocent ("null hypothesis")	type-1 error	correct

Less dramatic but just as important for the possible impact on large numbers of people are hypotheses about food supplements and drugs. In the USA, the Food and Drug Administration (FDA) has to evaluate the scientific data to determine whether such hypotheses are true.

For example, in December 2021, the FDA reported multiple reports of patients who needed medical intervention after self-medicating with *ivermectin*. The hypothesis on which these patients apparently acted was that ivermectin was effective for prevention or treatment of COVID-19. Ivermectin, though mainly used in veterinary medicine, is available for humans for treatment of certain parasitic worms, head lice, and certain skin conditions. At that time, already a number of federally funded as well as independent clinical studies on ivermectin related to COVID-19 were ongoing to test that hypothesis; the studies concluded that the ivermectin treatment of COVID-19 did not work.[29]

In such a case, the test will be statistical: is there a statistically significant difference, with respect to COVID-19 treatment, between subjects who take the drug and subjects who do not take it?

In any particular case, say, of a single patient, the test result could be misleading: there could be a *false positive* result if the patient recovers quickly although the drug has no efficacy, or a *false negative* result if the patient does not recover quickly although the drug is efficacious. Tests are not perfect; there is generally no way to guarantee that there will not be any false positives or false negatives. So the statistical analysis needs to be designed to attain *a high probability* that the level of error will be *acceptably low*. Randomized control trials are designed for this. The methodology involves a judgment call for what will count as a sufficiently high probability of a certain level of error to be acceptably low.

Researchers in natural sciences in general are especially wary of type-1 error. Such an error would amount to claim they have discovered something when there was nothing to be discovered. They may feel they would be seen as being too hasty, insufficiently careful, maybe presumptuous. They may feel that they would be seen as doing a disservice to science for the sake of personal ambition. Or it may just be for the sake of a professional ethic that they have assimilated in the course of their training.

In other contexts, one may be more wary of type-2 error. Imagine a drug is being developed and a few patients had a stroke shortly after starting to take the drug. It may be that the drug does have the potential to generate deadly side effects. Or there may be a confounding factor, something that all those people who took the drug also had in common and that was the real cause of the effect. Not to make a claim about the existence of side effects on the basis of the limited available evidence would prevent one to make a type-1 error, that is, to claim, erroneously, that there is something going on.

To make a claim about the side effects of the drug, on the other hand, would prevent one to make a type-2 error, that is, to claim, erroneously, that there is nothing going on, that the drug is safe. What error would a policy maker be more wary of making? If they intervene to withdraw the drug from the market and the drug turns out to be safe, they may irritate the pharma companies, but for the public, they will appear as prudent and vigilant. If the drug turns out not to be safe and they did not intervene, they will be seen as negligent and be held responsible. So they would probably rather err on the side of caution and prefer making a type-1 error than a type-2 error.

3.7.3 Risk experts in the face of inductive risk

But what kind of error should risk experts be most wary of?

Risk assessment is a scientific activity, and as scientists, we expect that risk experts may be inclined toward avoiding type-1 error. But as Heather Douglas (2008) explains, risk experts have a social function that is different from scientists'. On the one hand, they do investigate some phenomena using scientific methods. But on the other hand, they often have a role of social policy counsel. They inform policy makers of the risks attached to a certain situation, a nuclear facility, an epidemic, the climate, the state of the economy, a drug that is to be marketed. So on the one hand, as scientists, they are in an investigative relationship with the world and aims at making accurate claims about the world on the basis of empirical data. On the other hand, as policy counsel, they are those we turn to as a society for counsel, and when doing so, we expect them to put their expertise in the service of our safety.

Scientists are regularly confronted with having to choose between different possible explanations, different possible hypotheses, and they use a set of values said to be epistemic because they are believed to promote knowledge, like the value of predictive accuracy or explanatory power or consistency with other domain-related theories. But risk experts generally investigate phenomena that have or may have social impact: earthquakes, climate warming, substances suspected to be toxic, etc. And because the phenomenon under investigation is known or suspected to have a social impact, which hypothesis is selected to account for it can also be expected to have social consequences.

Suppose we accept the hypothesis that climate warming is anthropogenic and we are wrong. Then the society will have wasted lots of money to implement some costly measures to reduce emission of GHG from human activity. Suppose we accept, instead, the hypothesis that it is not anthropogenic and we are wrong. Then we will have continued to increase GHG emission from human activity, thereby contributing to accelerating the rate of warming, and with it the rate at which sea levels is raising and threatening coastal cities, the rate of depletion of species who are losing their habitat to warming; we will have created conditions under which droughts in some parts of the world become more severe, water more scarce, natural catastrophes more intense and frequent.

So the selection of a hypothesis has epistemic consequences in that it affects what we believe about the world. And sometimes, especially when the object of study is identified as a risk, it can also have non-epistemic consequences that have a direct effect on life in society and thereby are relevant to policy making. According to Douglas (2000), who has written extensively on the subject, when the choice between hypotheses is expected to have non-epistemic consequences, to use only epistemic value to make the choice is not sufficient: "where the weighing of inductive risk requires the consideration of non-epistemic consequences, non-epistemic values have a legitimate role to play" (2000: 565). That non-epistemic values have a role to play is not to say that epistemic values do not have a role to play as well. The selection of a hypothesis should still include weighing evidence and considering the predictive accuracy or explanatory power of the hypothesis, but this is not enough. The consideration and evaluation of the practical consequences of being wrong should have a role in the selection as well in determining how much evidence is evidence enough to accept or reject a hypothesis.[30]

3.7.4 Normative judgments involved in risk assessment and error avoidance

How we weigh the different non-epistemic consequences of making an erroneous choice will depend on goals and values: "Values are needed to weigh the consequences of the possible errors one makes in accepting or rejecting a hypothesis, i.e., the consequences that follow from the inductive risk" (Douglas 2000: 562). For instance, in the examples about climate warming being or not being anthropogenic, the most serious consequence of being wrong in saying that it is anthropogenic would be economic; the most serious consequence of being wrong in saying that it is not anthropogenic would be harm to people, other animals, and future generations. Part of the decision of selecting one hypothesis, again in addition to closely evaluating the evidence for each hypothesis, is to make a value judgment about what kind of consequences would be worst, what kind of consequences we want most to avoid.

We asked earlier what kind of error risk experts should be most wary of, and we can see now that it will depend on what kind of hypothesis is under discussion and, more specifically, what kind of action, and with what consequences, would follow from accepting a hypothesis that is false or rejecting one that is true. Non-epistemic values are not supposed to promote our understanding of the world, so when the choice between the hypotheses under consideration only affect our understanding of the world, non-epistemic values have no role to play. But when the choice between the hypotheses may affect, through policy making, what course of action we are taking or not taking, with this choice potentially affecting the life and well-beings of individuals and what they value, then non-epistemic values, related to how we think of a good life or our well-being, have a role to play: "Where non-epistemic consequences follow from error, non-epistemic values are essential for deciding which inductive risks we should accept, or which choice we should make" (2000: 565).

So according to the view just presented, when risk experts are considering hypotheses that have non-epistemic consequences, they should go through the work of weighing the risk of making an error. One may agree that such value judgments should be part of the choice between hypotheses but argue that it is not the role of the scientists to take into account values that are not epistemic. Maybe then the scientist should present the different hypotheses and the public or a chosen committee would make the choice between them. But one may reply that scientists are those who are in the best position to make the choice. They are the ones who best understand the implications of the different hypotheses and the practical impact of accepting one that is not correct.

In addition, risk experts are always already, as pointed out earlier, in a social role that is different from the role scientists in general have. They are relied upon for decisions by people, be it policy makers or the public, who do not understand the risk they are assessing as well as they do. To be concerned by truth only would fail to fulfill this expectation we have toward experts: their social responsibility, their responsibility as those whose view will influence the shaping of social policy:

> [E]xperts must be responsible in the claims that they make, responsible to the epistemic authority they wield. . . . Experts must be responsible to the public in how they handle the uncertainties and weighty judgments that are part of their expertise.
>
> (Douglas 2008: 3).

The shaping of social policy is not just a matter of getting things right, not just a matter of answering to the world; it is a matter of helping to keep people safe. So risk experts who are assessing a risk that could have non-epistemic consequence should evaluate the consequences, the impacts of the risk of being wrong. And this evaluation will require non-epistemic values, values expressing how much we care about avoiding those possible impacts.

FRAME 7: Risk assessment example: the dose-response relationship

A typical situation where risk experts have to make a choice between two hypotheses that have non-epistemic consequences is with respect to what is called the *dose-response relationship.* The dose-response relationship is the relationship between exposure to an increasing dose of a toxic product and the response. The study of this relationship is important to determine what are the levels of exposure that are safe versus toxic so it will have implication for the public policies regulating the use of the product.

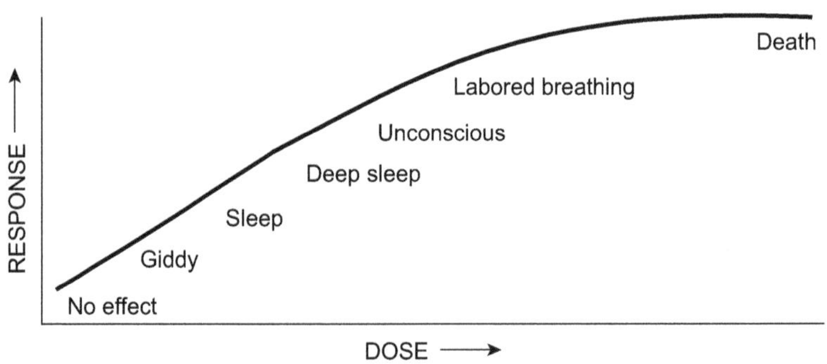

Figure 3.6a The diagram on the left illustrates a dose-response curve for toxicity of alcohol.

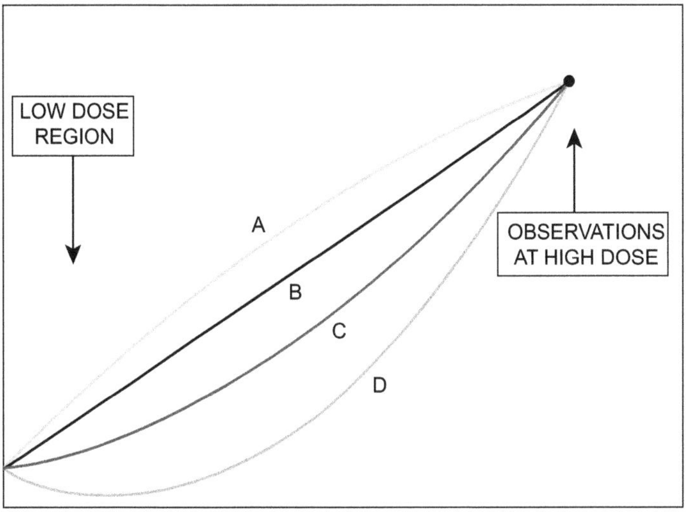

Figure 3.6b The diagram on the right illustrates how different equations that fit equally well in normal or high range may differ on the response relationship at low doses.

The issue here concerns the representation of the response for low doses. In general, there are different mathematical functions that can be used to fit the empirical data that characterize the observed responses to different doses. But they need to be extrapolated to the region of very low doses, and in this region, these different functions will predict different results. (See, for example, "Hazard Characterization for Pathogens in Food and Water," *Microbiological Risk Assessment* Series 3, WHO/FOA, 2003.)

A traditional assumption about the dose-response relationship is that there is a threshold level of the dose, referred to as the "minimal infectious dose," that is needed to provoke a response from the organism. The alternative assumption is that, however small the dose, there is always the possibility of a response, with the probability of a response increasing as the dose increases. There will be different non-epistemic consequences of making an error with the two kinds of extrapolation. With the threshold type of extrapolation, an error in the threshold dose could mean that the "safe" dose is set too high, with not enough protection of public health. With the linear type of extrapolation, an error could lead to regulations stricter than necessary. Both the impacts on public safety and on the level of regulations are non-epistemic impacts of a choice that is made during the scientific process of determining the dose-response relationship. Epistemic values are not sufficient for deciding between the two models: social ethical values have a role to play in the decision in the weighing, from one case to another, the social-ethical concerns for safety on the one hand and overregulation on the other hand.

3.8 Conclusion: normativity in scientific risk assessment

The question of the role of normative judgments in scientific risk assessment is intimately linked to the question of whether there is such a thing as objective risk, measured by science and dependent only on objective/empirical facts.

Slovic and Weber write that, for some traditions in social sciences, "risk is seen as inherently subjective."

> *[R]isk* is seen as a concept that human beings have invented to help them understand and cope with the dangers and uncertainties of life. Although these dangers are real, there is no such thing as "real risk" or "objective risk."
>
> (Slovic & Weber 2002: 4)

But as we saw in Chapter 1, if we draw the relevant distinctions, we can see how objectivity and subjectivity are intimately related and do not exclude each other.

Risk can be an object of scientific assessment because the phenomenon that comes to be identified as source of risk, and its possible consequences, exists in a way that is largely independent of whether we identify them as such or not. Only largely independent because to identify a phenomenon or a situation as risk will generally generate a change in our attitude toward the phenomenon that may affect the phenomenon itself and its possible consequences.

For instance, as more people become aware of the risk of getting COVID-19, more people start wearing masks and washing their hands more often; as more people wear masks and wash their hands more often, the spread of viruses decrease. Similarly, the seat belt modifies the possible consequences of a being in a car crash. But this kind of dependency does not add a subjective dimension to risk; it adds a social dimension that makes risk an "interactive phenomenon" and makes the assessment of the risk in time more challenging (Adams 1995).

Scientific risk assessment relies on hard data, known facts and scientifically evaluated theories, statistical analysis, and quantitative measures of damage. But as we have now seen, normative judgments enter at every stage of scientific inquiry, with scientific risk assessment being no exception to this.

To begin with, the first stage of data collection already involves choices expressed in normative judgments. Which data are to be collected, recorded, compiled, analyzed? In our example of studies of police shootings, we saw that they were hampered at every turn by the fact that no data were available for certain questions and that, for a long time, no resources had been allocated to the construction of national databases relevant to the study. Which data ought to be collected can be controversial. In 2017, for example, the Department of Justice requested the Census Bureau to incorporate a question on citizenship status. The controversy over this continued throughout the next four years.

A statistical analysis of the data is designed, in each case, to serve a certain purpose. Studies of police shootings do not analyze the data to find out whether red-haired people are more likely to be shot than blondes are. The required probability judgments concern what is deemed relevant, which is determined by the purpose of the inquiry, and which factors are deemed relevant determines the reference class in which the statistics will form the basis for those probability judgments.

In addition to the relevant probabilities, risk assessment must involve an evaluation of the unwanted consequences in the risk. How severe will such consequences be, and by what criteria of severity? The Forest Service's framework for wildfire risk assessment and management begins with the classification of highly valued resources and assets (HVRAs). Mitigation and containment of wildfires gives priority to those which are designated as HVRAs. Here there have been controversies between official policies and environmentalists.

Finally, a scientific assessment will offer a quantitative evaluation of conditional probabilities and severity of consequences but does not answer the question that will be crucial to decision-making: at what level is the risk acceptable? Acceptable to whom, with costs borne by whom, and benefits reaped where? This is a question for risk management.

Reading questions

1. **Normativity**

   Q1

   What has been controversial in the philosophy of science regarding the role of values is:

   A. That epistemic values are involved in scientific evaluation of a hypothesis.
   B. That non-epistemic values are involved in the choice of the research program.
   C. That non-epistemic values are involved in scientific research.

Q2

What explains that the results of drug trials sponsored by pharmaceutical companies, even when peer-reviewed, are more likely to be in favor of the drug than trials conducted by independent researchers?

A. The drug trials sponsored by the company do not follow the norms of scientific research.
B. The conclusion of the research can be influenced by the methods used for conducting the drug trials.
C. The results of the drug trials sponsored by the company are systematically misinterpreted.

2. **Probability and Severity**

Q3

Sometimes, when we ask about the risk of something (e.g., risk of rain or risk of war), we are expecting an answer in terms of probability. What does that show?

A. That risk sometimes is reducible to the likelihood of an outcome.
B. That we are confused about what is meant by "risk."
C. That we are processing the severity of the risk separately.

3. **Expected value as a model**

Q4

Why is it not as straightforward to calculate the risk expected value for life events as it is for a game of chance?

A. Because to calculate the probability, we need to decide what will count as similar events.
B. Because we can never put a number on a loss in ordinary life.
C. Because different events in real life are never sufficiently similar.

Q5

What is limiting the usefulness of the risk expected value in risk management?

A. It does not give a specific estimate of the risk.
B. It clumps together the evaluation of probability and of severity.
C. It is complicated to calculate.

4. **Approaches to risk assessment**

Q6

In what sense is the risk assessment approach based on expected value *normative*?

A. It aims at telling how the risk should be managed.
B. It provides norms for assessing the risk.
C. It tells us how much the risk coverage should be.

Q7

In what sense is the risk assessment based on modeling *prospective*?

A. It shows the possible benefits of taking a given risk.

B. It provides a tool for exploring the impact of different courses of action.
C. It produces prescriptions to reduce the risk.

Q8

What does that take for a risk expert to be well calibrated?

A. The risk expert must have a thorough understanding of the mechanism that creates the risk.
B. The risk expert must be capable of updating their opinion on the basis of new information.
C. The risk expert must receive feedback on the accuracy of their assessment.

Q9

According to Wright and colleagues' 2002 study, why are life insurance experts not better than the public at assessing risk?

A. The experts do not have enough knowledge of their field.
B. The experts don't receive enough feedback on their assessments.
C. The field of experience of the experts is too narrow.

5. **Assessing probabilities**

Q10

In his argument, Stephen Perry starts by saying that our estimate of the risk one is exposed to will depend on what we know. Why?

A. Because it will depend on a choice of reference class.
B. Because it will depend on the cultural context.
C. Because what counts as exposure is purely subjective.

Q11

Stephen Perry argues that being exposed to risk is not by itself harm because:

A. If mere exposure to risk were harm, harm would have to depend on what we know.
B. If mere exposure to risk were harm, it would make harm subjective.
C. If mere exposure to risk were harm, exposure to greater risk would imply greater harm.

6. **Error**

Q12

The controversial argument that Heather Douglas makes regarding the role of non-epistemic value judgments is that they play a role in . . .

A. The selection of a scientific research topic.
B. The selection of an explanation for the observations / the data.
C. How scientific results are applied.

Q13

What does it mean that an explanation is underdetermined by the data?

A. The same data can be fitted/explained in different ways.
B. There is only one possible theoretical interpretation.
C. Scientific theories are always wrong.

Q14

Suppose you claim that there is evidence for telepathic communication with animals and it turns out to be a misinterpretation of the evidence. What kind of error did you make?

A. False positive.
B. False negative.

Q15

What does it mean that being wrong about a risk, like climate change, can have non-epistemic consequences?

A. It means that how we act toward the risk, based on what we believe, can have some effect outside science, on people, the society, or the environment.
B. It means that the conclusions made by the experts about this risk could be a setback for science.
C. It means that there are still lots of uncertainties about the subject.

Discussion topics

Topic 1

What are the most distinctive characteristics of scientific understanding of phenomena around us, like the climate or the COVID-19 epidemic, that make it different from other forms of understanding, like ones based on intuition or experience? Think of the kinds of activities that comprise scientific research, of the norms that govern the publication of scientific results and the kind of social organization that form the scientific community. What is it that gives to the scientific study of risks, like climate warming or epidemics, a kind of social significance that other types of science, like the science of cellular physiology or some research in geology or archeology, may not have, even though they may have a different kind of social significance?

Topic 2

We have shown in this chapter that the scientific assessment of risk requires making some choices, at different moments of the process of assessment, that are not determined by scientific knowledge or scientific norms. In particular, we have discussed at length the required choice of a class of reference to calculate the probability associated with a risk. And we have also discussed the required choice of a level of evidence that will be regarded as "evidence enough" for the existence of a certain phenomenon or, more generally, of some possible consequences of an activity, like the consequence of climate warming in response to anthropogenic activities.

Do you think that scientists should consider the social consequences of the choices that they are making in the course of their research and let this consideration influence those choices? Try to think of specific examples of scientific research topics that may have some social impacts, like diseases, epidemics, or new technologies. Discuss whether there is a risk that science could become politicized if the consideration of social consequences openly influences the conduct of scientific research. What would it mean that science becomes politicized? In what sense could that be called a "risk"? What could be done to mitigate this risk?

Notes

1 The extensive literature includes Longino 1990; Rooney1992; Dorato 2004; Kincaid et al. 2007; Brown 2013; Douglas 2016.
2 For an argument that a measure with different formal properties than probability may be called for, see Philip A. Ebert et al. (2020).
3 The use of expected value as a model for decision-making and the shortcomings of this model are addressed in Chapter 2.
4 Note again that the expected value is an average and not the same as the most likely value. Here the expected value of the loss, $1.5, is not the same as the number of what a possible loss could be. Similarly, if a fair die is tossed, the expected value of the outcome is (1/6) (1 + 2 + 3 + 4 + 5 + 6) = 3.5, which does not equal the number of points on any face of the die.
5 For an accessible and illuminating defense of the use of distribution of probabilities and Monte Carlo simulations in risk assessment and risk management, see Hubbard (2009).
6 For a discussion of different metrics used to measure risks depending on the purpose, see Aven (2016).
7 The distinction between insurantial and epidemiological approaches to risk assessment is inspired by the distinction made by Dean (1997) between three types of risk strategies: insurantial, epidemiological, and clinical, discussed in Lupton (1999/2013).
8 See, for instance, Fenton & Neil 2018; Kouser et al. 2021; Cheng et al. 2020; Suter 1999.
9 For a thorough study of this subject, see Cooke 1991.
10 AEC WASH-1400, "Reactor Safety Study" NUREG 75/014). This has been successively revised and improved; the 2016 version is available as NUREG/KM-0010. www.nrc.gov/docs/ML1622/ML16225A002.pdf.
11 The reports were titled "Precursors to Potential Severe Core Damage Accidents: [year] Status Report" and were issued for the years 1969–1989. www.nrc.gov/reading-rm/doc-collections/gen-comm/info-notices/1990/in90074.html.
12 www.courthousenews.com/wp-content/uploads/2020/09/LeadinWater.pdf.
13 We note that the problem of determining the right reference class (also called the problem of the single case) was the main difficulty for the frequency interpretation of probability from the beginning. Its discussion began with Reichenbach (1949: 366–378), continued with Hempel (1968), Salmon (1971, 1977), and Fetzer (1977), and was taken up in different ways by Cartwright (1979) and van Fraassen (1983).
14 This is how Immanuel Kant codified the categorical imperative in his *Groundwork of the Metaphysics of Morals*.
15 In addition to the studies already referred to, see also Lewis (1989) and McCarthy (2000).
16 "2015 Washington Post database of police shootings." *The Washington Post*. www.washingtonpost.com/graphics/investigations/police-shootings-database/. Accessed 5 March 2022.
17 While we know of no direct answers to these questions, there are related data to consider. For New York City, in which there was a stop-and-frisk program, the data for the years 2002–2019 appear to show a substantial disparity of stops for different racial groups, while 90% of the persons stopped were not convicted of any crime. [A, N].
18 www.npr.org/2016/07/07/485049343/minn-man-shot-by-police-while-inside-a-car-with-a-woman-and-child;www.nbcnews.com/news/us-news/philando-castile-case-ex-officer-involved-fatal-shooting-gets-48-n781636.

19 An analysis of whether racial disparities in fatal shootings by police could be explained by different rates of violent crime based on where these fatal shootings occurred discounted that hypothesis (Ross et al. 2021).
20 *KOKO News*, Oklahoma City, July 6, 2020. "Off-duty Langston University officer opens fire on alleged shoplifting suspect outside Del City Walmart."
21 "FDA Issues Advice to Make Earliest Stages of Clinical Drug Development More Efficient." www.fda.gov/bbs/topics/news/2006/NEW01296.htm.l.
22 www.forecastwatch.com/wp-content/uploads/2018/09/ForecastWatch_Overview_H2-2018.pdf.
23 Former San Francisco City Attorney Louise Renne interviewed for SF Chronicle, "Juul Lawsuit: San Francisco unified, other Bay Area districts join," by Catherine Ho, December 17, 2019.
24 Institute of Medicine (US) Committee on Assuring the Health of the Public in the 21st Century. "The Future of the Public's Health in the 21st Century. 2, Understanding Population Health and Its Determinants," 2002, Washington (DC): National Academies Press (US).
25 www.epa.gov/ghgemissions.
26 *The Washington Post*, October 18, 2021, "Biden administration moves to curtail 'forever chemicals.'"
27 See the powerful movie *Dark Waters* for the effects of the contamination of drinking waters with "forever chemicals."
28 For a philosophical exploration of overfitting (and how to correct for it), see Forbes, M., and E. Sober (1994), "How to tell when simpler, more unified, or less ad hoc theories will provide more accurate predictions." *The British Journal for the Philosophy of Science*, 45: 1–35.
29 See ClinicalTrials.gov: www.clinicaltrials.gov/ct2/show/results/NCT04646109?term=ivermectin&cond=-COVID-19&draw=2&rank=2 and https://academic.oup.com/cid/article/74/6/1022/6310839?login=true.
30 For an analysis of the social dimension of inductive risk mitigation, see Gabriele Contessa (2021).

References

Adams, J. (1995). *Risk*. New York: Routledge.

American Association for Public Opinion Research. (2017). "An evaluation of 2016 election polls in the U. S." www.aapor.org/Education-Resources/Reports/An-Evaluation-of-2016-Election-Polls-in-the-U-S.aspx#INTRODUCTION.

Anderson, E. (1995). "Knowledge, human interests, and objectivity in Feminist Epistemology." *Philosophical Topics*, 23(2): 27–58.

Anderson, E. (2004). "Uses of value judgments in science: A general argument, with lessons from a case study of feminist research on divorce." *Hypatia*, 19(1): 1–24. DOI: 10.1111/j.1527-2001.2004.tb01266.x.

Anderson, S., et al. (2020). "Inequality in agency responsiveness: Evidence from salient wildfire events." Working Paper 20–22, Resources for the Future. www.rff.org/publications/working-papers/inequality-agency-responsiveness-evidence-salient-wildfire-events/.

Ash, M., & Boyce, J. K. (2018). "Racial disparities in pollution exposure and employment at US industrial facilities." *Proceedings of the National Academy of Sciences*, 115(42): 10636–10641. https://doi.org/10.1073/pnas.1721640115.

Aven, T. (2016). "Risk assessment and risk management: Review of recent advances on their foundation." *European Journal of Operational Research*, 253: 1–13. DOI: 10.1016/j.ejor.

Baciu, A., Negussie, Y., Geller, A., et al. (eds.). (2017). "The state of health disparities in the United States." In *Communities in action: Pathways to health equity*. Washington, DC: National Academies Press. DOI: 10.17226/24624. www.ncbi.nlm.nih.gov/books/NBK425844/.

Bell, T. E., & Esch, K. (1989). "The space shuttle: A case of subjective engineering." *IEEE Spectrum*, 26(6): 42–46. DOI: 10.1109/6.29339.

Bohrnstedt, G. W., & Stecher, B. M. (eds.). (2002). *What we have learned about class size reduction in California*. Sacramento, CA: California Department of Education.

Bolger, F., & Wright, G. (1994). "Assessing the quality of expert judgment: Issues and analysis." *Decision Support Systems*, II: 1–24.

Boyer, R. L., et al. (2019). "'Making Safety Happen' through probabilistic risk assessment at NASA." NASA Document ID 20200001592. https://ntrs.nasa.gov/citations/20200001592.

Brigandt, I. (2015). "Social values influence the adequacy conditions of scientific theories: Beyond inductive risk." *Canadian Journal of Philosophy*, 45(3): 326–356. DOI: 10.1080/00455091.2015.1079004.

Brown, M. J. (2013). "The source and status of values for socially responsible science." *Philosophical Studies*, 163(1): 67–76.

Brown, M. J. (2020). *Science and moral imagination: A new ideal for values in science*. Pittsburgh: University of Pittsburgh Press.

Cartwright, N. (1979). "Causal laws and effective strategies." *Noûs*, 13: 419–437.

Cartwright, N. (2009). "Evidence-based policy: What's to be done about relevance?" *Philosophical Studies*, 143(1): 127–136. https://doi.org/10.1007/s11098-008-9311-4.

Cartwright, N. (2018). "Will your policy work? Experiments versus models." In I. Peschard & B. van Fraassen (eds.), *The experimental side of modeling* (pp. 148–167). Minneapolis: University of Minnesota Press.

Cartwright, N., & Marcellesi, A. (2016). "Deliberating policy: Where morals and methods mix." In M. Couch & J. Pfeifer (eds.), *The philosophy of Philip Kitcher* (pp. 229–252). New York: Oxford University Press.

Cauce, A. M., et al. (2011). "The face of the future: Risk and resilience in minority youth." *Nebraska Symposium on Motivation. Nebraska Symposium on Motivation*, 57: 13–32. DOI: 10.1007/978-1-4419-7092-3_2.

Cheng, S. H., McKinnon, M. C., Masuda, Y. J., Garside, R., Jones, K. W., Miller, D. C., et al. (2020). "Strengthen causal models for better conservation outcomes for human well-being." *PLOS ONE*, 15(3): e0230495. https://doi.org/10.1371/journal.pone.0230495.

Christensen-Szalanski, J. J., & Bushyhead, J. B. (1981). "Physicians' use of probabilistic information in a real clinical setting." *Journal of Experimental Psychology: Human Perception and Performance*, 7: 928–935.

Contessa, G. (2021). "On the mitigation of inductive risk." *European Journal for Philosophy of Science*, 11(3). https://doi.org/10.1007/s13194-021-00381-6.

Cooke, R. (1991). *Experts in uncertainty: Opinion and subjective probability in science*. Oxford: Oxford University Press.

Dean, M. (1997). "Sociology after society." In D. Owen (ed.), *Sociology after post-modernism* (pp. 205–228). London: Sage.

Dorato, M. (2004). "Epistemic and non-epistemic values in science." In P. Machamer & G. Wolters (eds.), *Science, values, and objectivity* (pp. 52–77). Pittsburgh: University of Pittsburgh Press.

Douglas, H. (2000). "Inductive risk and values in science." *Philosophy of Science*, 67: 559–579. https://doi.org/10.1086/392855.

Douglas, H. (2008). "The role of values in expert reasoning." *Public Affairs Quarterly*, 22(1): 1–18. www.jstor.org/stable/40441475.

Douglas, H. (2009). *Science, policy, and the value-free ideal*. Pittsburgh: University of Pittsburgh Press.

Douglas, H. (2016). "Values in science." In P. Humphreys (ed.), *Oxford handbook of philosophy of science* (pp. 609–630). New York: Oxford University Press.

Ebert, P. A., et al. (2020). "Varieties of risk." *Philosophy and Phenomenological Research*, 101: 432–455.

Ebert, P. A., & Milne, P. (2022). "Methodological and conceptual challenges in rare and severe event forecast verification." *Natural Hazards and Earth System Sciences*, 22: 539–557. https://doi.org/10.5194/nhess-22-539-2022.

Edwards, F., Lee, H., & Esposito, M. (2019, August 20). "Risk of being killed by police use of force in the United States by age, race-ethnicity, and sex." *The Proceedings of the National Academy of Sciences*, 116 #34: 16793–16798. https://doi.org/10.1073/pnas.1821204116.

Fenton, N., & Neil, M. (2018). "The need for causal, explanatory models in risk assessment." In *Risk assessment and decision analysis with Bayesian networks*. New York: Chapman and Hall/CRC.

Fetzer, J. (1977). "Reichenbach, reference classes, and single case 'probabilities'." In W. Salmon (ed.), *Hans Reichenbach: Logical empiricist* (pp. 187–219). Dordrecht: Reidel.

Finkelstein, C. (2003). "Is risk a harm?" *University of Pennsylvania Law Review*, 151: 963–1001.

Flores, A. H., et al. (2008). "National estimates of outdoor recreational injuries treated in emergency departments, United States, 2004–2005." *Wilderness and Environmental Medicine*, 19: 91–98. DOI: 10.1580/07-WEME-OR-152.1.

Garland, D. (2003). "The rise of risk." In R. Ericson & A. Doyle (eds.), *Risk and morality* (pp. 48–86). Toronto: University of Toronto Press. DOI: 10.3138/9781442679382–005.

Gee, G. C., & Payne-Sturges, D. C. (2004). "Environmental health disparities: A framework integrating psychosocial and environmental concepts." *Environmental Health Perspectives*, 112(17): 1645–1653. DOI: 10.1289/ehp.7074.

Handfield, T. (2005). "Is the risk-liability theory compatible with negligence law." *Legal Theory*, 11: 387–404. DOI: 10.1017/S1352325205050202.

Harvard, S., Winsberg, E., Symonds, J., & Adibi, A. (2021). "Value judgments in a COVID-19 vaccination model: A case study in the need for public involvement in health-oriented modeling." *Social Science & Medicine*, 286: 114323.

Hempel, C. G. (1968). "Lawlikeness and maximal specificity in probabilistic explanation." *Philosophy of Science*, 35: 116–133.

Hora, S. C. (2004). "Probability judgements for continuous quantities: Linear combinations and calibration." *Management Science*, 50: 597–604.

Hubbard, D. (2009). *The failure of risk management*. Hoboken, NJ: Wiley.

Kadish, S. (1994). "The criminal law and the luck of the draw." *The Journal of Criminal law and Criminology*, 84(4): 679–702.

Kanga, S., et al. (2014). "GIS modeling approach for forest fire risk assessment and management." *International Journal of Advancement in Remote Sensing, GIS and Geography*, 2: 30–44.

Keyes, K., & Galea, S. (2017). "The limits of risk factors revisited: Is it time for a causal architecture approach?" *Epidemiology*, 28(1): 1–5. DOI: 10.1097/EDE.0000000000000578.

Kincaid, H., Dupré, J., & Wylie, A. (ed.). (2007). *Value-free science? Ideals and illusions*. Oxford: Oxford University Press.

Kourany, J. A. (2010). *Philosophy of science after feminism*. Oxford: Oxford University Press.

Kouser, H. N., Barnard-Mayers, R., & Murray, E. (2021). "Complex systems models for causal inference in social epidemiology." *The Journal of Epidemiology and Community Health*, 75: 702–708.

Kuhn, T. (1962). *The structure of scientific revolutions*. Chicago: University of Chicago Press.

Laudan, L. (1984). *Science and values: The aims of science and their role in scientific debates*. University of California Press.

Leung, K., & Verga, S. (2007). "Expert judgement in risk assessment." Defence R& D Canada Technical Memorandum DRDC CORA TM 2007–57.
Lewis, D. K. (1989). "The punishment that leaves something to chance." *Philosophy Public Affairs*, 18(1): 53–67.
Longino, H. (1990). *Science as social knowledge: Values and objectivity in scientific inquiry*. Princeton: Princeton University Press.
Longino, H. (2001). *The fate of knowledge*. Princeton: Princeton University Press.
Lupton, D. (1999/2013). *Risk*. New York: Routledge.
Marris, C. (2001). "Public views on GMOs: Deconstructing the myths." *EMBO Reports*, 2(7): 545–548.
McCarthy, D. (1997). "Rights, explanation, and risks." *Ethics*, 107(2): 205–225.
McCarthy, D. (2000). "Harming and allowing harm." *Ethics*, 110(4): 749–779. https://doi.org/10.1086/233372.
McKenzie, C., Liersch, M., & Yaniv, I. (2008). "Overconfidence in interval estimates: What does expertise buy you?" *Organizational Behavior and Human Decision Processes*, 107(2): 179–191.
Mosleh, A., et al. (1987). "Methods for the elicitation and use of expert opinion in risk assessment." NUREG/CR-462. www.nrc.gov/docs/ML2023/ML20238A589.pdf.
National Aeronautics and Space Administration. (2011). "Probabilistic risk assessment procedures guide for NASA managers and practitioners." NASA/SP-2011–3421. Second Edition.
Nix, J. (2020). "On the challenges associated with the study of police use of deadly force in the United States: A response to Schwartz & Jahn." *PLOS ONE*, 15(7): e0236158. https://doi.org/10.1371/journal.pone.0236158.
Nix, J., & Shjarback, J. A. (2021). "Factors associated with police shooting mortality: A focus on race and a plea for more comprehensive data." *PLOS ONE*, 16(11): e0259024. https://doi.org/10.1371/journal.pone.0259024.
Oberdiek, J. (2017). *Imposing risk: A normative framework*. Oxford: Oxford University Press.
O'Brien, M. (2000, 2001). *Making better environmental decisions: An alternative to risk assessment*. Cambridge, MA: MIT Press.
OKLO. (2021). "Maximum credible accident methodology." Oklo-2021-R-19-NP.
Perry, S. (2007). "Risk, harm, interests, and rights." In T. Lewens (ed.), *Risk: Philosophical perspectives* (pp. 190–209). London: Routledge.
Peschard, I., & van Fraassen, B. (2014). "Making the abstract concrete: The role of norms and values in experimental modeling." *Studies in History and Philosophy of Science*, 46: 3–10.
Placani, A. (2017). "When the risk of harm harms." *Law and Philosophy*, 36: 77–100. https://doi.org/10.1007/s10982-016-9277-x.
Ram, R. (2019). "Extrapolation of animal research data to humans: An analysis of the evidence." In *Animal experimentation: Working towards a paradigm change* (pp. 341–375). Leiden: Brill.
Reichenbach, H. (1949). *The theory of probability*. Los Angeles: University of California Press.
Rom, W. N., Boushey, H., & Caplan, A. (2013). "Experimental human exposure to air pollutants is essential to understand adverse health effects." *American Journal of Respiratory Cell and Molecular Biology*, 49(5): 691–696. https://doi.org/10.1165/rcmb.2013-0253PS.
Rooney, P. (1992). "On values in science: Is the epistemic/non-epistemic distinction useful?" *Philosophy of Science*, 1: 13–22.

Ross, C. T. (2015). "A multi-level Bayesian analysis of racial bias in police shootings at the county-level in the United States, 2011–2014." *PLOS ONE*, 10(11): e0141854. https://doi.org/10.1371/journal.pone.0141854.

Ross, C. T., Winterhalder, B., & McElreath, R. (2021). "Racial disparities in police use of deadly force against unarmed individuals persist after appropriately benchmarking shooting data on violent crime rates." *Social Psychological and Personality Science*, 12(3): 323–332. https://doi.org/10.1177/1948550620916071.

Ruiz, D., Becerra, M., Jagai, J. S., Ard, K., & Sargis, R. M. (2018). "Disparities in environmental exposures to endocrine-disrupting chemicals and diabetes risk in vulnerable populations." *Diabetes Care*, 41(1): 193–205. DOI: 10.2337/dc16–2765.

Salmon, W. (1971). *Statistical explanation and statistical relevance*. Pittsburg: University of Pittsburg Press.

Salmon, W. (1977). "The philosophy of Hans Reichenbach." In W. Salmon (ed.), *Hans Reichenbach: Logical empiricist* (pp. 1–84). Dordrecht: Reidel.

Scheuerman, S. B. (2003). "Against liability for private risk exposure." *Harvard Journal of Law and Public Policy*, 35(2).

Schoeffl, V., et al. (2010). "Evaluation of injury and fatality risk in rock and ice climbing." *Sports Medicine*, 40: 657–679.

Schwartz, G. L., & Jahn, J. L. (2020). "Mapping fatal police violence across U.S. Metropolitan areas: Overall rates and racial/ethnic inequities, 2013–2017." *PLOS ONE*, 15(6): e0229686. https://doi.org/10.1371/journal.pone.0229686.

Scott, J. H., et al. (2013). "A wildfire risk assessment framework for land and resource management." USDA General Technical Report RMRS-GTR-315.

Shanks, N., Greek, R., & Greek, J. (2009). "Are animal models predictive for humans?" *Philosophy, Ethics, and Humanities in Medicine*, 4: 2. Published 2009 January 15. DOI: 10.1186/1747-5341-4-2.

Slovic, P., & Weber, E. U. (2002, April 12–13). "Perception of risk posed by extreme events." Paper prepared for discussion at the conference "Risk management strategies in an Uncertain World," Palisades, New York.

Suter, G. W. (1999). "II Developing conceptual models for complex ecological risk assessments." *Human and Ecological Risk Assessment*, 5(2): 375–396.

Swierstra, T., & te Molder, H. (2012). "Risk and soft impacts." In S. Roeser, R. Hillerbrand, M. Peterson, & P. Sandin (eds.), *Handbook of risk theory: Epistemology, decision theory, ethics, and social implications of risk* (pp. 1049–1066). Dordrecht: Springer.

Tabuchi, H., & Popovich, N. (2021, April 28). "People of color breathe more hazardous air: The sources are everywhere." *New York Times*.

United States Department of Agriculture. (2013). "A wildfire risk assessment framework for land and resource management." General Technical Report RMRS-GTR-315, October 2013.

United States Department of Health and Human Services. (2010). *Healthy People 2010*. 2nd ed. Washington, DC: U.S. Available DHHS 2000. www.healthypeople.gov/publications/.

United States Nuclear Regulatory Commission. (1978). "Risk assessment review group report to the U. S. Nuclear regulatory commission." NUREG/CR-0400.

Van Fraassen, B. C. (1983). "Calibration: A frequency justification for personal probability." In R. S. Cohen & L. Laudan (eds.), *Physics, philosophy, and psychoanalysis* (pp. 295–319). Dordrecht: Reidel.

Vy Kim Nguyen, et al. (2020). "A comprehensive analysis of racial disparities in chemical biomarker concentrations in United States women, 1999–2014." *Environment International*, 137: 105496. https://doi.org/10.1016/j.envint.2020.105496.

Warner, F. (1992). *Risk: Analysis, perception and management*. United Kingdom: Royal Society.

Williams, D. R., & Mohammed, S. A. (2009). "Discrimination and racial disparities in health: Evidence and needed research." *Journal of Behavioral Medicine*, 32(1): 20–47. DOI: 10.1007/s10865-008-9185-0.

Wright, G., Bolger, F., & Rowe, G. (2002). "An empirical test of the relative validity of expert and lay judgments of risk." *Risk Analysis*, 22: 1107–1122. https://doi.org/10.1111/risa.13539.

4 Risk perception

Contents

DOI: 10.4324/9780429023521-5

> Risk perceptions refer to people's intuitive evaluations of hazards that they are or might be exposed to.
>
> Cori et al. (2020)

4.1 Introduction

The quotation from Cori et al. may be read as a definition of what risk perception is, and it correctly emphasizes three aspects: **one**, risk perception is individual and so, at least in some way, subjective, and **two**, it is intuitive – meaning, it does not follow an explicit method and it is often unconscious – but **three**, it is not passive, for it results in a form of evaluation and a belief about how serious a risk is. These aspects raise questions about the value of risk perception that will be explored in this chapter. If it is subjective, does that mean it is arbitrary? If it does not follow a method, does that mean it is meaningless?

Recent debates in the news concerning such topics as the COVID-19 pandemic and climate change make it easy to understand why risk perception is regarded as an important subject of study.

Why are some people so reluctant to adopt measures that are presented as essential to the reduction of the risk of climate change (like reducing the consumption of fossil fuel, water, and animal products) or the risk of COVID-19 contamination (like wearing a mask in public)? Why do some people need to be threatened with a fine in order not to drive under the influence of alcohol or not to write text messages while driving?

In 2009, there was an influenza pandemic, and studies of that period have shown that the adoption of protective measures and the perception of risk go hand in hand. People are more willing to adopt protective measures against influenza when they perceive the risk as serious (Van der Weerd et al. 2011; Ibuka et al. 2010). Similarly, there are studies indicating that risk perception is an important predictor of public willingness to help reduce climate change.[1]

All this means that whether the public perceives a risk as serious enough might be an important condition for the successful implementation of protective measures.

A conflict between scientific analysis and risk perception?

When the scientific study of risk perception started in the 1970s, it was motivated by the public's opposition to the development of new technologies, such as the development of nuclear energy and genetically modified organisms (Sjöberg 1999). Such opposition is sometimes simply regarded as "completely out of touch with the results of scientific risk analysis" (Cohen 1998: 101). Here, of course, *out of touch* does not just mean "different"; it means different and also irrelevant, irrelevant to policy decision-making. The implication is that policy decision-making should be based on scientific risk assessment and ignore risk perception.

The motivating question of this chapter is precisely whether the public's perception of risk should be regarded as relevant or irrelevant to policy decision-making. Whether risk perception should be taken into account, together with scientific risk assessment, for policy making has become one of the main questions in scholarly discussions of risk perception (Okrent & Pidgeon 1998). But why should there be a question at all about whether risk perception should be taken into account for policy making? Should not the government, especially in a democracy, take seriously and try to mitigate the risks that people take seriously and adjust its effort to mitigate risks in general so that it reflects the concerns of the population? Some authors, especially social scientists, do argue that risk perception should be considered for policy making, but others argue the opposite, that risk perception has little place in policy making.

This debate reflects a tension between two aspects of democratic governance. On the one hand, an idea at the core of democratic governance is that it is in the service of the people. On the other hand, not everyone will have the same perception of a given risk. Listening to the people might just mean listening to the louder voices, possibly at the expense of other parts of the population that have difficulty to be heard and who may be exposed to risks that are of no concern to those with the louder voices.

And even if there was a unanimous opinion about a given risk, what if it is nevertheless one that is mistaken, irrational, or biased in ways that do not reflect democratic ideals of inclusiveness? Democratic governance is supposed to be in the interest of the people. To act on the basis of an opinion that is unreliable is not much in the interest of the people, even if it is people's opinion and it may provide people with the immediate satisfaction of being heard.

The issue of how to take into account, if that is what we want to do, public opinion about risk and how to do it without taking into account just the louder voices would be an issue for risk management. But the issue of whether risk perception is indeed mistaken, irrational, or biased is one for this chapter. For this should be discussed on the basis of an understanding of what risk perception is, in what sense it is subjective, and how people come to perceive some risks as more or less serious. As we will see, one main goal of studies of risk perception is precisely to "measure" how seriously people perceive some risks to be and what factors influence their perception (Slovic et al. 1982).

Risk perception: the process and the result

Let's notice that the proposed definition of *risk perception* is ambiguous, for the terms "evaluation" and "perception" are ambiguous in the same way. In one usage, "perception of risk" or "risk perception" refers to a *cognitive process*, a process of evaluation of risk that is happening at the individual level, in a way that is unreflective and, for a large part, unconscious. But the same terms are also used to refer to the *results* of this process. For example, to say that people perceive the risk of dying in a train accident as greater than the risk of dying in a car crash is to describe a judgment that is the *result* of the corresponding cognitive process. The studies on risk perception that will be discussed in this chapter are studies of the *process* of risk perception, trying to understand what personal or social factors are influencing the result of the process. But when people talk about the conflict or tension between risk perception and expert assessment of risk, they are referring to the result of this process, put in the form of a judgment about the riskiness of an activity or a technology.

Because the cognitive process of risk perception is subjective, it might be tempting, in case of conflict, to think that laypersons and experts are simply talking past one another and that the best resolution is to dismiss risk perception. We will discuss the relation between risk perception and expert assessment in the chapter on risk management. But we mention it here because a better understanding of risk perception as a process will help us have a more constructive discussion of the relation between risk perception, as a result of this process, and expert assessment, as well as how to address conflicts between the two.

What informs our perception of risk?

Many of our ordinary choices are, for a large part, based on our perception of risks. Just think of our choices for transportation, where to go on vacation, what kind of food we chose to eat, how much we care about whether food is organic or genetically modified, whether we put sunscreen on our skin, whether we get ourselves screened for cancer, whom we vote for.

What is informing or influencing our perception of risk in general? On what basis do we perceive some risks as negligible, some as serious but acceptable, and some as so serious they must be avoided? A few decades of scientific research on risk perception have shown that many different elements, and of different kinds, are involved in how we perceive risks.

From the following list of factors, which do you think has the least influence on our perception of the risk associated with hazards to which we are or could be exposed?

How well the effects of the hazard can be controlled
Social media reporting on the hazard
Possible benefits from the exposure
Political ideology
Scientific knowledge of the hazard
Sociocultural environment
Moral values

The surprising answer is scientific knowledge of the hazard. Each of the other factors has a greater impact on how most people perceive risk. Some studies have found that there is a correlation between more knowledge of a risk and lower risk perception of it (Johnson 1993). But the correlation is small so that "very little of the variance in risk perception can be explained by variation in knowledge" (Sjöberg 1999: 2).

The following diagram, Figure 4.1, used with kind permission from the author, nicely depicts the many interactions in the process which lead from appraisal to action.

As we can see on Figure 4.1, there are two main groups of conditions that influence the perception of risk:

- The individual context, which includes age and gender; level of education; perceived characteristics of the hazard, for instance, regarding its catastrophic potential or whether its impacts are delayed or immediate; belief that one has control over the situation of exposure and its impacts (for instance, one believes that they are a good driver and so has very low risk of car accident, or that jogging regularly keeps the impact of smoking under control); and also personal experience (maybe one has been exposed and impacted or knows someone or has heard of someone who has been exposed and impacted by this or a similar hazard).
- The sociocultural context, which includes attitudes toward technology and safety and what is called a "worldview" to refer to sets of beliefs and values about nature or social organization and could include political ideology (for instance, the belief that a first political priority should be a strong economy or reducing differences in levels of individual wealth) and moral judgments (for instance, that the depletion of natural resources is unethical).

In general, knowledge and information are not irrelevant to risk perception, but the effect appears as muted in studies of popular attitudes. Thus,

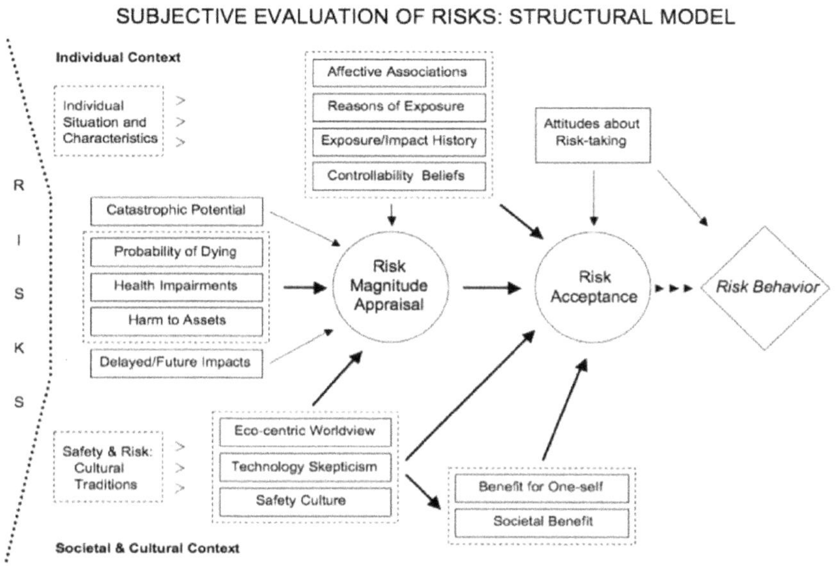

Figure 4.1 The different kinds of factors that influence risk perception (Rohrmann 2008).

one study, drawing on data from the United Kingdom concerning climate change risk perception, concluded that experiential and sociocultural factors play a greater role in explaining variance in risk perception than either cognitive or sociodemographic characteristics and suggested that "that general knowledge about climate change may not readily map onto a personalized sense of risk" (van der Linden 2015: 121), even though other studies have concluded that the perception of the existence of scientific consensus about a certain risk has an influence on how this risk is perceived (Kerr & Wilson 2018).

Can risk perception and scientific analysis complement each other?

Studies have shown that our perception of risks is influenced by our personal experiences as well as our perception of specific characteristics of the risky activity or technology, how we feel about them, what kind of emotions they trigger, as well as some sociocultural background, trust in institutions, and social interactions. So the process of risk perception is a complex and highly individualized psychological phenomenon. It is to be expected, then, that people will have different risk perceptions. In this sense, our perception of risk is an expression of who we are, and as such, it cannot be mistaken.

On the other hand, the existence of risks is grounded in widely shared, most often empirically based, beliefs about the world. Someone who would believe that they can continue their life normally during the COVID-19 pandemic without being susceptible to getting COVID-19 would be seen as having unrealistic beliefs. That risk perception can take the form of beliefs which may be unrealistic, and therefore corrigible, shows that it is not subjective in the way one's preference for rap over country music is subjective. And yet if risk perception is subjective and personal, it is not clear in what sense it could be said to be right or wrong. But if risk perception clashes with experts' opinion and experts' opinion is right, then does not risk perception have to be wrong? One way out would be that expert risk assessment and risk perception offer two perspectives on a situation so that a conflict would not imply that one is wrong. But it would not imply that they are both necessarily valid and relevant input to policy decision-making. The aim of this chapter is to clarify the process of risk perception, in terms of what kinds of factors have an influence on this process, so as to be in a better position to determine what could make risk perception a valid or invalid input to the process of policy decision-making.

4.2 Case study: how is risk of COVID-19 perceived?

The methods used to measure risk perception have been applied recently to try to clarify the way in which the risk of COVID-19 was perceived around the world. Data show how the perception of the risk of COVID-19 has evolved over time and has been correlated with different factors, such as political affiliation, gender, education level, and social class.

Let's have a quick look at the results of one particular study before looking into more general theories and studies of risk perception that were developed in the last decades and the results that have informed and guided such studies as the one on the risk perception of COVID-19.

4.2.1 Citizens' reaction to protective measures

In reaction to the spread of the coronavirus in spring 2020, hundreds of different protective measures have been implemented worldwide, from floor stickers in stores that mark a six-foot distance to wearing face masks to school and indoor restaurant closure. The efficacy of the different types of governmental response has been an object of intense interest for journalists and researchers (Calsyn et al. 2020).

A team of researchers at the London School of Hygiene and Tropical Medicine developed a platform able to aggregate data collected by several teams of researchers and volunteers (Dryhurst et al. 2020). The data were about what measures different countries had implemented, like school closures, public event cancellations, public information campaigns, and fiscal and monetary measures and emergency investment in health care, how soon they had implemented them, and with what results in terms of death from COVID-19 per capita. The aim of this project was to analyze the effect of introducing or removing protective measures on the transmission rates and infection numbers.

However, the transmission rate and infection numbers are not solely or mostly dependent on what measures are implemented by the governments. They are also, and even more so, directly dependent on whether, and to what extent, people respect the measures that are implemented.

Risk perception was found to be an important determinant of the public's willingness to cooperate and adopt health-protective behaviors during pandemics, including frequent handwashing, physical distancing, avoiding public places, and wearing face masks (Rudisil 2012; Dryhurst et al. 2020). A better understanding of what influences risk perception could then help understand the variety of attitudes toward adopting protective measures.

4.2.2 How is risk perception studied?

Studies of risk perception often use questionnaires that have two parts, to measure the *dependent measure* and the *predictors*.

For the dependent measure, the questionnaire has a set of questions that aim to measure how serious people perceive a given risk to be. For the predictors, the questions aim to gather different kinds of information about people, their gender, their level of education, their experience with the risk, their perception of some characteristics of the situation or the hazard, and some social or political values they hold.

Then, the task of the study is to try to find correlations between how people answer the first kind of questions and how they answer the second kind of questions so as to determine what factors are influencing risk perception.

4.2.2.1 Risk perceptions of COVID-19 around the world

The study initiated in April 2020 by the London School of Hygiene and Tropical Medicine mentioned prior aimed at assessing the public risk perception of COVID-19 around the world.

The study measured the perception of the seriousness of the risk with questions that aim to cover the cognitive (likelihood), emotional (worry), and temporal-spatial dimensions:

- How worried are you personally about the following issues at present? (Coronavirus/COVID-19.)
- How likely do you think it is that you will be directly and personally affected by the following in the next six months? (Catching the coronavirus/COVID-19.)

- How likely do you think it is that your friends and family in the country you are currently living in will be directly affected by the following in the next six months? (Catching the coronavirus/COVID-19.)
- How much do you agree or disagree with the following statement: "I will probably get sick with the coronavirus/ COVID-19"?
- How much do you agree or disagree with the following statement: "Getting sick with the coronavirus/COVID-19 can be serious"?

The search for predictors covered demographic variables, gender (binary: male, female), age, political ideology (liberal, conservative), and education (ranging from "no formal education above 16" to "PhD"), as well as personal experience with COVID-19, trust in institutions, social values, political ideology, and feeling about efficacy as well as personal and social knowledge. Interestingly, and surprisingly, the personal knowledge that was probed was not knowledge about the coronavirus or COVID-19 but about government strategy, and the question about social knowledge probed belief about the extent of scientific understanding and seems to overlap with the question about trust in science:

- Personal knowledge. How much do you feel you understand the government's strategy to deal with the coronavirus/COVID-19 pandemic?
- Social knowledge. To what extent do you think scientists have a good understanding of the coronavirus/COVID-19?
- Direct experience. Have you ever had, or thought you might have, the coronavirus/COVID-19?
- Social amplification. Have you come across information about coronavirus/COVID-19 from friends and family?
- Prosociality. To what extent do you think it's important to do things for the benefit of others and society even if they have some costs to you personally?
- Individualistic worldview. The government interferes far too much in our everyday lives.
- Trust in government. How much do you trust the country's politicians to deal effectively with the pandemic?
- Trust in science. How much do you trust each of the following? (Scientists.)
- Trust in medical professionals. How much do you trust each of the following? (Medical doctors and nurses.)
- Personal efficacy. To what extent do you feel that the personal actions you are taking to try to limit the spread of coronavirus make a difference?
- Collective efficacy. To what extent do you feel the actions that your country is taking to limit the spread of coronavirus make a difference?
- Political ideology. Where do you feel your political views lie on a spectrum of left wing (or liberal) to right wing (or conservative)?

4.2.2.2 Results of this study

The results of the study were in terms of a general model of risk perception across all countries and specific models for the different countries.

General model (across all countries)

Regarding the measure of risk perception, the study found that it was rather high in all countries, varying between 4.78 and 5.45 on a 7-point scale.

Regarding the search for predictors across all countries, it found that personal knowledge, experience with the virus, social amplification through information received from family and friends, prosociality, individualistic worldview, all trust variables, personal as well as collective efficacy were all significantly associated with risk perception, but not in the same ways.

Higher scoring on the measure for risk perception was correlated with higher scores on direct personal experience with the virus, receiving information on the virus from family or friends, thinking that it is important to do things for the benefit of others or society, belief in personal efficacy, trust in science, and trust in medical professionals.

Lower scoring on the measure of risk perception was correlated with higher scores on individualistic worldview, collective efficacy, trust in government.

The only significant demographic variable was gender: men generally displayed lower risk perception than women.

Country-specific models

The study found that different countries had different sets of significant predictors, but also that many predictors emerged to have an effect in several countries.

For instance, holding *individualistic views* was the most important predictor on the general model (the linear regression across all countries) and in five out of the ten countries surveyed (United Kingdom, Germany, Sweden, Spain, and Japan). And it was an important predictor in other countries, too, except for South Korea.

Prosociality was the second most important predictor on the general model, as well as in Italy, Australia, and Mexico. And it was important in other countries, except, again, for South Korea.

Direct experience with the virus was the third most important predictor on the general model. It was also the most important predictor in the US, and important in the other countries except for Australia and Sweden.

The different *trust variables*, and especially trust in medical professionals, had some importance on the general model but only some importance in South Korea and in the US.

Personal efficacy had some importance on the general model and was a strong predictor for Sweden and Germany. But it had low importance for other countries.

Collective efficacy was of low importance on the general model and also for most countries but was a strong predictor for the US and for Mexico.

4.2.2.3 Conclusion

The study that we just discussed used a sophisticated combination of very different kinds of questions to measure the level of perceived risk and to search for predictors of the perception of the risk of being affected by COVID-19.

The questions used to measure the level of risk perceived combined cognitive, emotional, and temporal-spatial dimensions. The questions asked whether people are "worried" (emotional dimension), how they "think" about the likeliness of being affected (cognitive dimension), and it formulated the question with a specific time window (six months) and also with an open-ended one ("I will probably get sick").

The questions looking for predictors were probing different dimensions: personal experience, knowledge, social and political values, trust in different kinds of institution, belief in personal and collective efficacy.

The selection of those different questions reflects the development over several decades of studies that have investigated these dimensions separately and what was learned through those studies about what influence risk perception. In the next sections, we will look at the different kinds of study and theories that have paved the way for such multidimensional approach.

4.3 Approaches to risk perception

A person's perception of risk is a function of many factors which contribute to the result of that perception. Regarding what those factors are and how they contribute to risk perception, there have traditionally been two kinds of approaches.

One kind of approach focuses on the individuals' cognitive processes, assuming that those processes involve immediate and unconscious evaluations of a variety of characteristics of the activity, hazard, or technology. Within this approach, so-called *psychometric studies* attempt to put those evaluations in measurable quantitative form.

Another kind of approach focuses on the social-cultural context and the influence of the social, cultural, and moral beliefs and values that are supposed to characterize this context.

But other approaches have also investigated the influence of emotion, trust, or social interactions.

4.3.1 Psychometric approach

4.3.1.1 The method

The investigation of risk perception by trying to find some predictors, as done in the COVID-19 study presented earlier, started in the late 1970s with the development of a psychometric method. This method was introduced by Baruch Fischhoff, Paul Slovic, and colleagues with the aim of understanding on what basis people who have no expertise form an opinion about a variety of risks.[2] The method assumes that there is a quantifiable cognitive underpinning to the judgments people form about risks. Its name, "psychometric," indicates that risk perception is viewed as a psychological, cognitive phenomenon and that it aims at quantifying, producing a measure of this phenomenon.

One basic hypothesis that motivated the development of the psychometric paradigm is that the perception of risk involves the evaluation of a variety of characteristics. The aim of the studies using this method was to test this hypothesis and to try to identify which factors were influencing the perception of risk.

In this kind of study, respondents are presented with a list of hazards (such as nuclear power, motor vehicles, handguns, smoking, pesticides, hunting, mountain climbing, swimming, skiing, x-rays, home appliances, vaccinations, etc.). The subjects are then asked to evaluate quantitatively the riskiness and the desired level of regulation for each, by attributing a number inside a given interval.

To try to understand how they form their judgments about the riskiness and desired level of regulation, the subjects are then also asked to rate a number of features the risk may have. Firstly, to what extent is it controllable, voluntary, known to the person exposed, known to science, catastrophic, novel, or old? Does it have immediate or delayed effects? How severe are the possible consequences? Does it trigger dread? Are the effects observable? Is it a risk for future generations? Secondly, what are the benefits of these hazards, for themselves and for the society? And thirdly, how extensive are the fatalities related to these hazards?

The next sections will present the main results of psychometric studies:

1. The result that there are significant relations between perception of risk, perception of benefit, and judgments of acceptability.
2. The result that, whereas experts' risk assessments are based on the expected number of injuries or fatalities, people's judgment about risk is, in general, strongly influenced by other characteristics of the hazards.
3. The result that a reduction of the relevant factors to two or three factors is possible, which allows the hazards to be mapped out in a two- or three-factor space, the *risk factor space*.

4.3.1.2 Benefit perception, trust, and acceptability

The seminal study by Chauncey Starr (1969) had found that people's attitude toward risks is generally influenced by their perception of benefits. It was noted that, for better or for worse, these results could be useful to risk communication, suggesting that it may be possible to change perceived risks by changing the perception of benefits (cf. Frewer et al. 1996).

This study was based on the "expressed preferences" method, which examines existing data about activities and technologies to infer those preferences. By contrast, the psychometric paradigm uses a "revealed preferences" method that analyzes responses to questionnaires.

These studies mostly confirmed the correlation between perception of risk and perceived benefits. For example, people rank cigarette smoking and alcohol as very low in benefit and very high in risk, while they rank antibiotics, airplane travel, and vaccines as having high benefit and relatively low risk (Alhakami & Slovic 1994). But this inverse relationship is much stronger for some risk items than for others. The hazards for which risk is perceived are generally the same as those for which the benefit is perceived as lowest, and hazards for which the risk is perceived as lowest are generally the same as those for which the benefit is perceived as highest. For the hazards that are in between those two groups, however, the correlation between perceived risk and perceived benefit is not as clear (Slovic, Kraus et al. 1991).

But the perception of risk, and of benefit, as we will see, is under the potential influence of so many factors that the variation is not surprising, and the negative correlation is still robust enough to motivate the search for an explanation.

Risk and benefit

The hypothesis proposed to explain the negative correlation between perception of benefit and perception of risk was that both evaluations are influenced by the affective reaction, positive or negative feelings, to the hazard or technology under evaluation (Finucane et al. 2000). But further studies have shown that the relation between perception of risk and perception of benefits is not a simple one.

A study by Alhakami and Slovic (1994) found that the negative correlation between the perception of risk and perception of benefit across respondents can be represented as an inverse U-shape curve with two distinct regions[3]:

> When risk level is perceived to be low or moderate, the perception of benefit varies between moderate and high, but with no apparent systematic relationship between perception of risk and perception of benefit.

But . . .

> When risk is perceived as higher, a clear correlation appears between increase of perceived risk and decrease of perceived benefit.

One way to explain these results is to appeal to theories in social psychology according to which people have *a strong need for consistency among their beliefs and attitudes* (Abelson et al. 1968). This consistency theory would predict that hazards, technologies, or activities that receive a positive affective evaluation will also be viewed as having high benefit and moderate to low risk.

But the consistency explanation seems too simple compared to the complexity of the results that it is supposed to explain.

Social trust

Another explanation offered for the inverse relationships between perceived risks and perceived benefits is social trust.

A meta-analysis of 34 empirical studies on public perception of benefits, risk, and acceptance of nuclear energy found that trust in experts or institutions substantially affected public perception of benefits (Ho et al. 2019), even though the influence of trust on perceived benefits seems stronger on benefits that are direct and personal, like the benefit of a secure energy supply, by contrast with the perception of benefit for the climate (Visschers et al. 2011; Earle & Cvetkovich 1995).

But it was also found that the effect of trust varies with the level of familiarity with the hazard or technology (Siegrist 1999; Siegrist & Cvetkovich 2000). There is little to no effect of social trust when people report familiarity with the technology. But for hazards about which people report low personal knowledge, trust is positively correlated with perceived benefit and negatively correlated with perceived risk: the effect of more trust is to perceive benefit as higher, and the effect of less trust is to perceive risk as higher, like for biotechnology, food preservatives, nuclear power, and by contrast with home appliances or smoking.

Acceptability

What is the relation between the perception of risk and benefit and the judgment of acceptability of diverse risks? Not surprisingly, people are willing to tolerate higher risks from activities seen as highly beneficial. But the exact relation between the two depends on a variety of factors.

A study on the effect of trust and knowledge on the perception of risk and benefit associated with gene technology (Siegrist 2000) found that, whereas trust *influences* risk and benefit perceptions, perceptions of risk and benefit *directly determine* judgments of acceptability.

Several studies found that perception of higher nuclear risks is associated with less acceptance for nuclear technology (Whitfield et al. 2009). But numerous studies found that perception of benefits was a more important predictor for the acceptability of the technology than risk perception (Ho et al. 2019; De Groot et al. 2020). This may be because benefits of these energy technologies impact people's lives more directly than do the risks associated with these energy technologies. It was also found, though, that perceived risk is much more important than perceived benefit for acceptance of nuclear energy when it is produced in the area where one lives, where the impact of the risk would be more direct.

Whether it is the perception of the risk or the perception of the benefit that is a stronger predictor of acceptability depends also on the familiarity with the risky item. The perception of risk is a stronger predictor *when the risk is unfamiliar rather than familiar*, like nanotechnology (Cobb 2005), or fracking (extraction of gas or oil by hydraulic fracturing) (Thomas et al. 2017).

Another relevant circumstance is whether the benefits are an abstract possibility or *already a reality*. A study compared the views of the population about the use of nuclear power in France, which produces 80% of its energy with nuclear power, and in the US, which produces only about 20% of its energy with nuclear power (but is the largest producer of commercial nuclear power) (Slovic, Flynn et al. 2000).

The results show that concerns about nuclear power and nuclear waste were no less important in France than in the US. But the French 1) "saw greater need for nuclear power and greater economic benefit from it," 2) had greater trust in scientists, industry, and government officials who are in charge of nuclear power plants, and 3) were a little more likely to express support for nuclear power. Those results are consistent with other results showing that, among member states of the EU, those already relying on nuclear energy show higher support for it.[4]

Although the correlation between perception of benefit and acceptance is a robust result, it was found that it is stronger for some benefits than for others (Ho et al. 2019). Benefits for a secure energy supply seem to have more effect on acceptance of nuclear energy than benefit for the climate, probably because it is perceived as more direct and personal.

4.3.1.3 Risk factor space

Riskiness

When making judgments of risk assessment, experts use the quantities of *likeliness* and *severity* of outcomes, with severity often being the expected number of injuries or fatalities. However, studies using the psychometric method have made clear that this is not what laypeople do.

A study asking people to rate 13 activities or technologies according to "riskiness," "Fatalities," and "injuries" showed that ratings for "fatalities" and "injuries" are closely correlated, and so probably not well distinguished, but neither is well correlated with "riskiness" (Marris et al. 1997).

For instance, nuclear power and ozone depletion are rated high on the riskiness scale but relatively low on the fatalities and injuries scales. Ozone depletion is regarded as a higher risk than home accidents, but the estimated fatalities and injuries are ranked lower; alcoholic drinks are relatively low on the scale of riskiness, but their expected fatality and injury rates are relatively high.

So if people, in general (remember, this is a table showing the means of the ratings), do not understand riskiness in terms of fatalities or injuries, if they are not evaluating risks simply by considering probability and/or severity/fatalities, what else do they use, then?

An array of risk characteristics

Risk perception studies have found that individuals (in general) are actually influenced by a wide array of considerations when they form positions on risks. Judgment of riskiness was found to be correlated with their judgment about other characteristics of hazards. These include judgments about dread, voluntariness, immediacy of effects, knowledge of those exposed, controllability, whether it is novel or familiar, catastrophic potential, known to science, severity of consequences (Slovic 2000). And it was found that "weighted combinations of three or four risk characteristics led to highly accurate predictions of perceived risk (multiple correlations between 0.90 and 0.95) for each of the three groups of laypersons" (Slovic et al. 1985: 102).

In follow-up studies, other characteristics were found to be relevant, like harm for future generations, observability of consequences, equity, social and personal exposure, natural versus man-made hazards, or tampering with nature.

Hazards such as nuclear power, war, and terrorism, which are generally perceived as high on riskiness, were also perceived as high on the scales of dread, catastrophic potential, involuntariness, severity, and harm to future generations. Sunbathing, food coloring, microwave ovens are low on dread and also relatively low on catastrophic potential and severity (Marris et al. 1997).

Risk factor space

A factor analysis of the intercorrelations of the means ratings for the different characteristics found that many of the characteristics' ratings were in fact correlated with each other (Fischhoff et al. 1978). As a consequence, two major factors explained most of the variance (about 75%): *dread* (which explained about 25% of the variance) and *novelty/unknown* (which explained about 50% of the variance).

Characteristics can then be grouped along two dimensions:

- **Dread risk factor**, which includes feeling of dread and other perceived attributes, such as controllability, perceived catastrophic potential, voluntariness, risk for future generations.

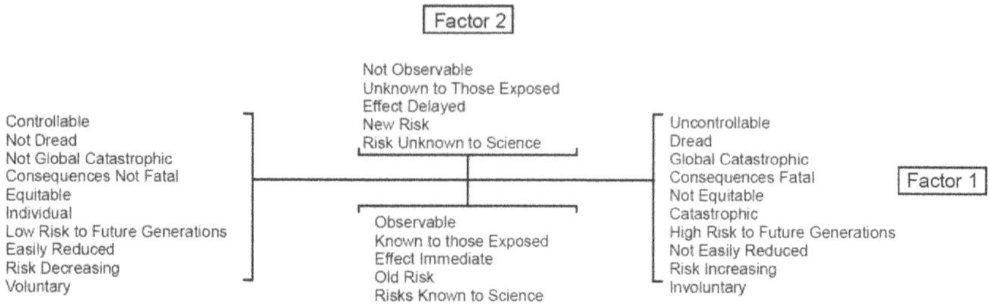

Figure 4.2 Diagram showing how the characteristics used to study the perception of risk with the psychometric paradigm can be grouped along two dimensions. (Picture from Slovic 1987.)

- **Novelty / unknown risk factor**, which includes perception of novelty and other perceived attributes, such as observability, whether it is known, and how immediate or delayed the effects are.

The reduction of the relevant factors to two factors makes it possible to map out hazards in a two-factor space, called the risk factor space.

Similar findings were obtained by studies conducted in different countries intended to investigate differences between perception of risk in the USA and in other countries (Sivak et al. 1989; Hayakawa et al. 2000; Teigen et al. 1988).

Based on those results, the correlation that was more recently found, between perception of seriousness of the risk of COVID-19 and belief in collective efficacy, could be anticipated from the known correlation between perception of risk seriousness and judgment of controllability of the hazard.

Is the risk factor space adequate?

As we saw, the factors used to account *both* for the correlation between characteristics *and* for the level of risk perceived are the "dread risk" factor and the "unknown risk" factor. Another factor that is typically used is "number of exposed." It may not be too surprising that those two or three factors would account well for the correlation between the rated characteristics, because many of the characteristics are cognitively related.

But the real test of the explanatory power of the psychometric approach is whether the factors explain equally well the level of risk perceived. It is not always clear that they do. The data that were used in early studies to calculate how well the risk factors explained the level of risk perceived were mean ratings, not individual data. When individual data are used instead, the levels of risk perceived are not as well accounted for by the typical risk factors as when mean ratings are used (about 20–30% instead of 70–80%) (Sjöberg 2000). We will come back to this result later in the section on ecological fallacy.

Figure 4.3 A group of hazards represented as a dot in the risk factor space whose position reflects the ratings obtained for the dread factor and the novelty factor. We can see that hazards that are generally associated with high perceived risk are rather high on both dimensions, like radioactive waste. By contrast, hazards that are generally associated with low perceived risk are rather low on both dimensions, like bicycles or downhill skiing. (Picture from Slovic 1987.)

This suggests that new characteristics need to be introduced. In fact, one would even expect that, as the research on risk perception developed, researchers would discover that some characteristics not yet considered influence the level of risk perceived. As new kinds of risk appear and new technologies develop, new characteristics would become relevant that were not even conceivable before.

- Natural versus human cause

One such "new" characteristic that was shown to have a substantial influence on risk perception is the distinction between *unnatural versus natural risks* (Sjöberg 1996).

Several studies found that risk perceived as unnatural, as being of human origin, are perceived as more serious. For instance, people, in general, prefer natural to artificial food, even when they are told that they are equally healthy or chemically identical and technologies applied to food production are associated with higher levels of risk perception, potentially because they are perceived to be unnatural (Kaptan et al. 2018).

In two experiments, a hazard was described to one group of participants as having a human cause and to another group as having a natural cause. In the first experiment, the hazard was a release of sulfur dioxide in a town, attributed either to a nearby factory or to a volcano. Participants were randomly assigned to one of the two scenarios, and the outcome was perceived as significantly more severe and with higher negative impact on the population, in the case of the factory. In the second experiment, the hazard was a forest fire destroying a natural park, attributed either to a person who "lit a fire even though there was a drought" or to a lightning strike. Participants were randomly assigned to one of the two scenarios, and the outcome was perceived as having a significantly higher negative impact on nature in the case of the person lighting the fire (Siegrist & Sütterlin 2014).

- Tampering with nature

Another characteristic, related to the idea of unnatural origin of hazard, that was found to influence perception of risk is *tampering with nature*.[5]

An online study with US individuals found that the support for different carbon dioxide removal (CDR) strategies was, in part, a function of how much the strategy is perceived as "tampering with nature" (Wolske et al. 2019). Support for bioenergy with carbon capture and storage and direct air capture was lower than support for afforestation and reforestation, and the former was also rated higher on the "tampering with nature" scale.

The perception of risk related to several climate engineering technologies and the perception that it was tampering with nature were found to be correlated (Jobin & Siegrist 2020). Afforestation was the strategy that received the highest support, and supported biomass-based technology and soil carbon sequestration received more support than did the deployment of mirrors in space and stratospheric aerosol injection. The latter two strategies were perceived as the ones most tampering with nature, while afforestation was perceived as the least tampering with nature.

"Aversion to tampering with nature" (ATN) has been found to correlate with other psychological constructs, such as "trust in science," preference for what is "natural," and environmental concerns (Raimi et al. 2020): the correlation is negative with trust in technology, and it is positive with "aversion to playing God," a naturalness bias, and environmental concerns and values (e.g., "Humans are severely abusing the environment"). There is a weak positive correlation between ATN and the values of autonomy and community, as well as with moral judgments about harm and fairness. No association was found between ATN and general religious values (religiosity or valuing divinity), but a weak relationship was found between ATN scores and political ideology, suggesting that liberals are somewhat more concerned about tampering with nature than conservatives are.

4.3.1.4 Personal vs. general risk

Early studies using the psychometric paradigm presented participants with a list of hazards and asked participants simply to rate the risk. But studies have shown that people make different risk assessments depending on whether the risk is to themselves or to people in general, that is, whether they are considering a personal risk or a general risk (Sjöberg 2000).

Optimism bias is a person's tendency to rate their own risks as lower than the risks to other people and to believe that they are more likely than other people to experience positive events. This is a well-documented tendency (Weinstein N. D. 1980; Weinstein N. 1984; Jefferson et al. 2017). For instance, most people believe that their risk of being involved in a car crash is smaller than for other people (McKenna 1993).

This form of bias is influenced by a variety of factors. In particular, the bias increases when the risk is phrased in more specific and personally relevant way, and it decreases when the comparison target is psychologically close to the respondent instead of being a distant, vague comparison target, such as "the average person" (Perloff & Fetzer 1986).

Optimistic bias can be seen as a coping mechanism that protects individuals from the emotional reaction to a threat. In some cases, it could be an effective strategy. But in other cases, it may result in a harmful or even fatal delay in responding to the threat. Optimistic bias has been proposed as an explanation for governments' and individuals' delayed response to the COVID-19 virus epidemic in the spring of 2020 (Bottemanne et al. 2020).

As previously mentioned, optimistic bias is reduced when the risk is described in more specific and personally relevant ways. It is also reduced when it is felt as more immediate (Garrett et al. 2018). A study conducted in the USA showed that within the next few days after COVID-19 was declared a pandemic by the World Health Organization, there was a sharp increase in the perceived risk of getting infected (Wise et al. 2020).

4.3.1.5 The ecological fallacy

The psychometric approach purports to explain how individuals form an opinion about risks: people make judgments about a variety of characteristics, and there are 1) some correlations between these judgments and their judgment of riskiness and 2) correlations among these judgments of the characteristics themselves so that the variety of characteristics can be reduced to two or three factors.

But one may question whether conclusions about how individuals form an opinion about risk are warranted by these correlations. The problem with that inference is that the conclusions are about individuals, whereas the data used as premises are generally averages. The data are these: for each characteristic, a mean across participants is obtained for each hazard, which represents the rating of this hazard by the group as a whole, and that is done for all the hazards and all the characteristics. It is tempting to infer that the conclusion reached from these data applies equally to the individuals, but this sort of inference is often referred to as the *ecological fallacy* or *population fallacy.*

The problem is twofold: 1) what is true at the average level is not always true at the individual level, and 2) a correlation at the level of averages does not mean correlation at the level of individuals (Marris et al. 1997).

- What is true for the average is not always true for the individuals.

If the average grade of a group is 52, it is not necessarily the case that for a random individual from the group, the likeliest grade is 52.

Imagine the following situation.

Group A: 70% of people got 35 points, and 30% of them got 95 points. The mean score is 53 points.

Group B: 50% of people got 45 points, and 50% got 55 points. The mean score is 50 points.

If you take a random individual from group A and one from group B, is the former more likely to have a higher grade? No. A random individual from group A is actually much more likely to have less than 40 than a random individual from group B, even though the average for group A is higher than for group B.

- A correlation at the level of averages does not mean correlation at the level of individuals (Robinson 1950).

That is sometimes called *Simpson's effect*, after the statistician who first drew attention to it.

FRAME 1: An example of Simpson's effect

In a certain factory, there are some complaints about lighting conditions in the workshops. The management conducts a statistical study and finds that there is no overall correlation between productivity in the workshops and lighting conditions. But then a new study is done, and it turns out that, for women working in there, better lighting conditions mean greater productivity. And similarly, for men working there, better lighting conditions mean greater productivity.

Is that possible? If so, what could explain it? The answer is that the women are more productive in general, but it is overwhelmingly the women who work in poor lighting conditions. There are 100 women and 100 men working there. In the well-lit areas, each man completes 2 tasks per hour, while each woman completes 7 tasks per hour. In the poorly lit areas, each man completes 1 task per hour, while each woman completes 3.5 tasks per hour. Therefore, every worker is twice as productive in well-lit areas than in poorly lit areas.

However, 80 of the men work in the well-lit areas, while only 20 of the women do. And that means that the women are mainly in the poorly lit areas.

Now we can calculate: in the well-lit areas, the number of tasks completed per hour is 2(80) + 7(20) = 300. And in the poorly lit areas, the number of tasks completed per hour is 20 + 3.5(80) = 20 + 280 = 300, the same number.

Compared to the kind of data obtained with psychometric studies, the factory illustration of the Simpson's effect is a very simple example. But it does raise one question: are psychometric studies really saying much about the individual psychology of risk perception?

Some studies found that the correlations that had been observed at the aggregate level, using the average of the ratings, were still present at the individual level, but not so strong. A comparison by Marris and colleagues (1997) between psychometric correlations obtained at the aggregate level and at the individual level found that 1) individuals vary in their rating of riskiness, 2) individuals vary in their rating of the same risk characteristics on the same risk issue, and 3) some of the strong intercorrelations observed between risk characteristics at the aggregate level do not appear at the level of individuals. But the correlations between risk perception and risk characteristics are still present at the individual level.

A similar conclusion was reached by a study in Chile where participants were asked to rate both hazards and risk characteristics (Bronfman & Cifuentes 2003). The researchers compared the correlations between risk characteristics at the aggregate and at the individual levels and found that the correlations had the same sign but most of them were greater at the aggregate level (correlation of averages) than at the individual levels (average of correlations).

So there is still reason to give weight to the results based on mean ratings. But the fact that the correlation between risk characteristics and perception of riskiness is much weaker at the individual level strongly suggests that *other factors are just as important* as those typically used in psychometric studies (Sjöberg 2000). Other factors that have proved to be significant are, as we saw, the natural versus human origin of hazards, or the aversion to tampering with nature. The next two sections will explore still other kinds of factors that may also have an influence on risk perception: sociocultural factors and moral factors.

4.3.1.6 Conclusion

The psychometric approach to risk perception was born from the assumption that with the appropriate design of the survey instrument, risk perception can be quantified and measured. The project was to design a method to measure, through self-assessment, *firstly*, the level at which risk and other characteristics of the hazards were perceived and, *secondly*, to identify some characteristics whose perceived level would explain the level of risk perceived.

Correlations between the characteristics made it possible to construct two or three factors that could account for a large part of the variance in risk perception. The significance of this achievement is that:

> It has allowed risk researchers to map out a number of hazards in two-factor space. Such taxonomy is useful for two purposes. The first value is that it explains differences in risk perceptions across hazards. In fact, the perceived risk of a hazard is related to its position in the two-factor space. The second value is that it explains discrepancies between lay and expert estimates of risk. While lay perceptions of risk are consistently tied to dread risk, expert ratings are not.
>
> (Jenkin 2006: 9)

The psychometric study of risk perception of COVID-19, introduced at the beginning of this chapter, found that stronger belief in collective efficacy and trust was correlated with lower risk perception. This result is consistent with previous psychometric studies that have shown that judgment of controllability and trust often had an influence on the perception of risk.

But this study also found that social-political values were predictors of risk perception. The psychometric approach did not at first try to account for the influence of social-political values, because it considers risk perceivers merely as cognitive subjects making judgments independently of one another. This conception of the risk perceivers has been one of the main criticisms directed at the psychometric approach, with the objection that risk perception does not occur in a social vacuum and that the role of the broader social and cultural context, how it influences risk perception, should be investigated (Boholm 1996).

4.3.2 Social-cultural approach

> People select risks as being important or trivial because in so doing they reinforce the established social relations within the culture in which they are located.
>
> (Jackson et al. 2006)

4.3.2.1 Social-cultural theory

The social-cultural theory stemmed from the anthropological work of Mary Douglas (1966) and was developed by Douglas, Wildavsky, Dake, and colleagues (Douglas & Wildavsky 1982; Wildavsky & Dake 1990).

According to this theory, risk perception is not governed by personality traits, needs, preferences, or properties of the risk objects. It is a socially, or culturally, constructed phenomenon (Oltedal et al. 2004). The rise in the late 1970s of a social opposition to new technologies, which the psychometric approach was trying to explain at the individual level, is here explained by social-cultural changes more than the emergence of new kinds of risk Taylor-Gooby and Zinn (2006). On that view, how people perceive and respond to risk varies depending on how their social relations are organized and on the worldview that this organization reflects through the shared beliefs and values of its individuals.

The cultural theory characterizes different forms of social organization in terms of two dimensions, called "grid" and "group":

- Grid (regulation). Refers to the degree of regulation of individuals' behavior, to how much a social context is regulated and restrictive about the individuals' behavior/interactions. It is high for organizations that have a hierarchical or egalitarian worldview, and low for those that have an individualistic worldview.
- Group (incorporation). Refers to the degree of social identification/incorporation, to how much an individual is member of bonded social units. The greater the incorporation, the more individual choice is subject to group determination. It is low in organizations that have an individualistic or egalitarian worldview, and it is high in organizations that have a hierarchical worldview.

Within this framework, the theory defines four worldviews, social-cultural archetypes, that will result in different ways of conceiving of nature and of human's responsibility toward nature, different ways of perceiving risk in general, and different attitudes toward risk (Thompson et al. 1990).

- Hierarchists: strong group boundaries/incorporation and strong binding prescriptions/regulation (high group / high grid).

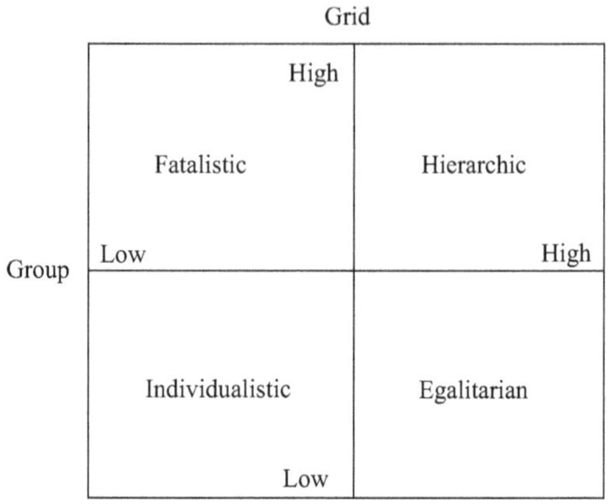

Figure 4.4 Douglas's grid-group model.

    - Fear of social commotion, faith in strong government; emphasize the "natural order," see nature as forgiving to most events but vulnerable to an occasional disaster; see risk as something that can and should be controlled; are skeptical of claims of environmental risks because they see nature as essentially resource for human development.
- Egalitarians: strong group boundaries, but low on regulation in that no one person is granted authority by virtue of their position (high group / low grid).
    - Sense of solidarity and responsibility; fear of inequalities among people, skeptical of experts; see nature as vulnerable to human interventions, something that needs to be taken care of; receptive to claims of environmental risk: they are inclined to believe that activities they associate with inequity and selfishness (commerce and industry) cause environmental harm.
- Individualists: low on incorporation and also on regulation, where individuals are bound by neither group boundaries nor prescribed roles. Boundaries and interactions are subject to negotiation (low group/low grid).
    - Value individual freedom and economic liberalism; see nature as self-preserving and able to return to its natural equilibrium whatever mankind does to it; see risk as opportunity; dismiss claims of environmental and technological risks, societal recognition of which would threaten markets, and other forms of private ordering.
- Fatalists: low on regulation but high on incorporation; there is not much structure or boundaries bounding individuals, but there is a prescribed role or attitude (high group / low grid).
    - Take little part in social life; feel powerless in the face of change, which is always perceived as being imposed from the outside; are quite indifferent about risk.

The cultural theory argues that, within each worldview, attitudes about risks and how they should be managed will seem entirely rational and that recognizing that will help to understand why risk controversies persist and to conceive of new approaches to risk management.

Evaluation of social-cultural theory

As we saw, the proponents of the theory have claimed that hierarchical, egalitarian, and individualistic worldview will be correlated with patterns of risk perception. They conducted an empirical study to calculate correlations between risk perception and cultural adherence to one of the fours worldviews defined by the theory (Wildavsky & Dake 1990; Dake 1991). To calculate these correlations, it has to be possible to "measure" adherence to one of the worldviews (cultural adherence) in a way similar to the way risk perception is measured, that is, the cultural theory needs to be operationalized. To operationalize the theory, Dake (1991) used, for each worldview, a series of statements that are taken to express important aspects of the worldview and asked people their agreement with the statements.

Hierarchical, 15 statements, including:

- There should be more discipline in the youth of today.
- We should have stronger armed forces than we do now.
- The police should have the right to listen to private phone calls when investigating crimes.

Individualist, 9 statements, including:

- In a fair system, people with more ability should earn more.
- A free society can only exist by giving companies the opportunity to prosper.

Egalitarian, 11 items, including:

- If people in this country were treated more equally, we would have fewer problems.
- The government should make sure everyone has a good standard of living.

Fatalist, 11 items, including:

- Cooperating with others rarely works.
- The future is too uncertain for a person to make serious plans.

Compared to other predictors (personality, economy, knowledge), adherence to a worldview appeared to be the best predictor of risk perception. In particular, egalitarianism was correlated with high scores for technological and environmental risks, hierarchy was correlated with high scores for risks associated with social deviance, and individualism was correlated with high scores for risks associated with economic troubles. And individualist and hierarchical worldviews were negatively correlated with risk scores for technological and environmental items.

These results have not been strongly replicated, and critics have offered different explanations: 1) the theory is weak, 2) the operationalization of the theory is flawed, and 3) the theory is not making quantitative predictions.

Empirical studies conducted to test the correlation between worldviews and risk ratings have found only weak correlations (Sjöberg 1997, 1998, 2000). The four worldviews did generate distinct patterns of risk perceptions, and the pattern of correlations between risk perception and cultural biases was consistent with the predictions of cultural theory. But only 11%, at most, of the variation in risk perceptions could be explained by worldviews, and the psychometric theory was found to better correlate with risk perception (Marris et al. 1996, 1998).

Some critics have expressed doubts that the theory's operationalization, in the form of the questionnaires designed by Dake (1991), allows for a meaningful empirical measure of cultural adherence. One major issue is that the theory entails some conditions on the different worldviews, given how they are defined, that are not satisfied (Rippl 2002). For instance, the theory implies that individualism and hierarchism (and respectively fatalism and egalitarianism) should be negatively correlated since they are opposite on both the grid and the group dimensions. Instead, a positive correlation was found between hierarchy and individualism and no significant negative correlation was found between egalitarianism and fatalism. This result suggested that what is measured is not what is supposed to be measured and that the theory should be operationalized differently, with some modifications in the statements used to measure adherence to a worldview to reflect the distinctions assumed to exist between the worldviews themselves.

Also, even if the different worldviews were more distinctly characterized, the mobility view of culture states that the same individual may embrace several worldviews dependent on the social context. It was found that only 14% of respondents could be allocated to a single worldview. At best, then, cultural theory seems limited to make predictions about individuals in a particular context: context that values egalitarianism, context that values hierarchy, etc. As individuals move from one context to another context, it is not clear that their attitude toward risk (or nature) will remain the same: "If someone is hierarchical at home but individualistic at work, how will this be captured by a questionnaire that presupposes people to adhere to only one culture?" (Oltedal et al. 2004: 28).

On the other hand, these objections may be deflected with a different interpretation of the theory. It is possible to conceive of aspects of worldviews as *cognitive factors*, among others, that may influence risk perception. This approach has been embraced by researchers that view the cultural approach complementary to other approaches (Marris et al. 1996; Peters & Slovic 1996;

Leiserowitz 2006). For instance, a study on climate change used a comprehensive model to explore the influence on risk perception of demographic, cognitive, and experiential factors, and also social-cultural factors (Van der Linden 2015). The social-cultural factors were represented by different kinds of characteristics: lifestyle values (like caring about nature and the biosphere) as well as descriptive and prescriptive social norms. To measure adherence to descriptive norms, respondents were asked to answer questions about whether they think others are taking personal action to help tackle climate change; to measure adherence to prescriptive norms, respondents were asked to answer questions about whether they feel pressured to personally help reduce the risk of climate change. The study showed that the overall influence of those social-cultural factors accounted for 15% of the variance in risk perception.

4.3.2.2 Cultural cognition hypothesis

The cultural cognition hypothesis goes even further than adding social-cultural factors to other kinds of factors that may influence risk perception. It argues that the cognitive and the cultural approaches to risk perception are not only complementary but also need to be integrated. There are cognitive processes, including heuristics and evaluation of characteristics, involved in forming an opinion about the risks. But what information is selected or is dismissed, in those processes, depends on values people have and the beliefs congenial to these values, that is, their social-cultural worldview (Kahan 2010, 2012). Their social-cultural values influence what people notice and remember and even what they believe they have experienced (Akerlof et al. 2013).

So social-cultural factors do not have an influence on risk perception *in addition* to the influence of cognitive factors; they have an influence on the cognitive process itself, on what and how cognitive factors will influence risk perception. That is, cognition is cultural. And to take into consideration this influence of values on the cognitive processes involved in risk perception might be crucial to really understand people's reaction to scientific evidence on societal risks, like climate change or nanotechnology (Kahan et al. 2009).

According to the cultural cognition hypothesis, people with individualistic or hierarchical worldviews will tend to dismiss evidence of environmental risk because admitting climate change would pressure them to recognize the need for restrictions on activities that they value, activities favorable to the development of commerce and industry. By contrast, people with an egalitarian worldview are much more inclined to accept the evidence because they already view commerce and industry as a possible source of unjust disparity (Kahan 2010: 296). People will also be more inclined to believe experts that they perceived to share their values. In a study (Kahan et al. 2010) on the perception of risk and benefit of HPV vaccination,[6] respondents were presented with arguments for and against the vaccination that were matched with fictional experts whose appearance made them look as if they were either hierarchical and individualist or egalitarian. The results show that the respondents were more inclined to believe the experts that they perceived as sharing their own values, even when those experts argue against what the respondents were originally inclined to believe. If values influence what people are ready to believe, it may very well influence also how they process information in general, including what characteristics on a situation are selected as significant. And through that selection, it could influence their perception of risks.

4.3.2.3 Social network

The social-cultural approach criticized the cognitive approach for considering individuals as isolated cognitive systems. It can be argued, though, that the social-cultural approach that we just discussed is still considering individuals as isolated cognitive systems. The difference is only that now the cognitive processes are construed differently, as complemented or influenced by social-cultural factors or values.

By contrast, approaches based on the study of social network, and in particular the *social network contagion theory*, really turn their back on the presupposition of individuals as isolated cognitive systems. They view the social group one belongs to and social relations with other members of this group not as a source of information but as having a direct impact on attitudes and behaviors of the individuals.

Social network contagion

According to the network theory of social contagion, individuals that are part of a social network become groups or communities of like-minded individuals. They will share knowledge, attitude, and behavior, so much so that the network can be seen as a social unit characterized in terms of those shared knowledge, attitude, and behavior. Applied to risk perception, this theory suggests that individuals that are part of a social network will be inclined to have similar risk perceptions, and not just because they are processing the same information, but as a result of a direct relational influence. The risk perception of an individual in a network will influence others in the network, and the similarity of the perception between two individuals will be a function of the strength of the network tie between them.

Scherer and colleagues tested this hypothesis with individuals of a community involved in an environmental conflict over the cleanup of a lagoon contaminated with toxic materials (Scherer & Cho 2003). The state agency overseeing the cleanup projected to discharge the toxic material in an inlet of a large lake that was the drinking water supply for the community. The county legislature and the residents objected. The interviews started with the state legislators and included questions about where the respondent had obtained information about the controversy. The individuals named in the first round of interviews became the respondents for the second round of interview, and this process was repeated until no new individuals were named. The interview also included a measure of the strength of the network tie through a question about the frequency of their interactions with that individual and a measure of risk perception, through eight questions combined into one scale.

Results show that the strength of the tie between two individuals is positively correlated with the similarity of their perceived level of risk: "individuals are more likely to share similar risk perceptions if they have frequent interactions with each other" (Scherer et al. 2003: 266). Of course, the existence of a correlation does not show the direction of influence: it is possible that an individual will seek out other individuals they believe share their perceived level of risk, what is referred to homophily. But based on other studies on social cognition, it seems more likely that the network ties are based on social proximity, past interactions, and that the social tie influences risk perception (Fiske & Taylor 1991; Weenigh & Midden 1991).

Similar evidence for social network contagion was obtained in a study on the risk perception of catching AIDS in rural Kenya and Malawi (Kohler et al. 2007). The results of the study in the two countries were different in some respects. But in both cases, having social network partners had a significant influence on respondents' risk perceptions about AIDS. Greater contact with AIDS prevention programs resulted in greater worry, and 18% of the effect of AIDS programs was shown to come from social interactions. Each additional network partner with high-risk perceptions was correlated with a significant increase in the respondents' risk perceptions. By contrast, network partners with moderate or low risk perceptions were correlated with a decrease in the respondents' own risk assessments.

The way in which the social network influences someone's risk perception is not merely a function of the risk perception of the network partners.

A study on the perception of risks faced by the Cormorant population in Northern Lake Huron compared the effect of social networking for three social networks of different kind: one made of experts, one made of laypersons, and one including both experts and laypersons. The results of the study supported the social contagion model: "the more frequently two individuals communicate, the more likely they were to share similar perceptions about an environmental risk (in our case, cormorant management)" (Muter et al. 2012: 1496). But it was found that the contagion effect was the strongest in the latter group, including experts and laypersons, and according to the authors, it is probably the result of a mutual influence between experts and laypersons. The fewest, and weakest, contagion effects were found in the case of layperson-to-layperson interactions. The authors suggest that similarity among laypersons could instead be explained by homophily: people seek out, and form ties with, others who are similar to themselves.

4.3.2.4 Conclusion

When it entered the field of risk perception studies, the social-cultural approach was standing as a competitor of the psychometric approach, viewing the perception of risk as the product of a social-cultural worldview rather than the product of individual cognitive processes. The perception of risk was still construed as the product of a cognitive process, and this cognitive process was still viewed as that of an individual. However, it was the adherence to a social-cultural worldview that was supposed to determine the way in which different risks were perceived rather than characteristics of the risk situation.

The attempts to test this theory and the idea that adherence to a social-cultural worldview accounted for at least a large part of risk perception were disappointing. Probably, it is in part because of methodological difficulties, but also because it overlooked the complexity of risk perception and of the diversity of factors susceptible to have an influence on it. The idea that social-cultural beliefs and values have an influence on risk perception remained, though, and has been fully integrated to the study of risk perception. Adherence to some social-cultural values has become one kind of factors among many others probed for their effect on risk perception. As an example, the study of COVID-19 presented earlier included, in the search for predictors, questions measuring adherence to prosocial and individualistic values. And it found that, overall, holding an individualistic view was the most important predictor, whereas holding a prosocial view was the second most important predictor.

That the social-cultural approach could be integrated in that way to the psychometric approach suggests that it was not as fundamentally different from the cognitive approach as it was presented to be. In both cases, the influence on risk perception that was investigated was *intrapersonal*, coming from a person's beliefs, whether those beliefs were descriptive beliefs about some characteristics of a risk situation (activity or technology) or normative beliefs about social behaviors.

By contrast, approaches based on the study of social network have revealed the interpersonal influence on risk perception of belonging to a social network. Studies have shown that the strength of the tie between two individuals is, in general, positively correlated with the similarity of their perceived level of risk.

4.3.3 Influence of moral judgments

As we saw, a study of risk perception of COVID-19, discussed in §4.2, found prosocial values correlated with as significantly higher perceived risk compared with individualistic values.

That sociocultural values would affect risk perception is not so difficult to understand, because general or societal risks are risks that will affect others and sociocultural values shape the way we conceive of the well-being of others and of the well-being of social organization. It is not too surprising that those values would influence what possible negative impacts on others or the social order we will perceive as more or less significant. But moral values are generally understood as a system of evaluation of human behaviors from the ones we admire and aim to replicate to the ones that make us feel uncomfortable and even evoke some form of disgust. How could they have an effect on the perception of the degree of riskiness of a hazard or a technology?

4.3.3.1 Moral values in risk perception

That our moral judgment of a risk situation influences our acceptability of its riskiness was first evidenced in a study by Sjöberg and Winroth (1986). They also had an insightful explanation for why moral value had not been considered before among the predictors for risk judgment.

Typically, studies on risk perception ask respondents to rate negative outcomes, like being struck by lightning or drowning. But first, it is difficult to see why someone would ever find such outcomes, considered in and by themselves, acceptable. When we do consider the possibility of negative outcomes acceptable (as we actually do constantly), it is because we do not just consider the possible negative outcome, in isolation, but reflect on a course of action of which it is one element. The idea of a choice, expressed in the judgment of acceptability, makes sense: the degree to which we find the risk acceptable is the degree to which we would be willing to take that risk. By contrast, in what sense would we take it to be "acceptable" to drown or be struck by lightning?

This consideration is relevant to the study of the influence of moral judgment, because to find a certain course of action acceptable is to have a certain attitude toward it, being more or less willing or reluctant toward it. And studies have shown that attitudes toward actions are functions of beliefs and values.

In their study, then, Sjöberg and Winroth ask respondents to rate the acceptability of risk *activities*, some of them being individual activities, such as "driving a car immediately after having drunk a bottle of wine" or "trying to save a person who is about to drown in a hole in the ice," "smoking in bed," and some of them being societal activities, such as "allowing food substances whose effects are not fully known" or "building a school in an earthquake area." And they also ask them to evaluate, on the same scale, the extent to which the action is according to their moral values.

The results of the study show a high correlation between judgment of acceptance and judgment of moral value. Societal activities were generally judged to be riskier, in terms of severity of consequences or degree of probability, than individual activities. But there was a quasilinear relation between acceptability and moral judgment (the activity is all the more acceptable than it concurs with moral values) for both types of activities. And for individual activities, moral judgment appeared as the strongest predictor, above severity or probability of consequences: that is, the correlation between acceptability and moral judgment was the strongest.

In a later study, Lennard Sjöberg and Britt-Marie Drottz Sjöberg investigated risk tolerance with respect to nuclear waste in two empirical studies. The levels of the nuclear waste risk and acceptance (voting intention) were correlated with the morality dimension (whether the risk was immoral and unfair). The correlations were high enough to show that morality had an important role in explaining variance of risk perception and risk acceptance (Sjöberg & Drottz-Sjöberg 1993). The importance of the morality dimension has also been demonstrated in studies of the perception of climate change (Bostrom et al. 2012) and, more generally, the perception of environmental risks (Böhm & Pfister 2001).

Those results suggest that the two-factor space, dread and unknown, arrived at in psychometric studies might be too simple. A more recent study (Bassarak et al. 2017), using the psychometric approach, investigated the influence of morality, alongside that of dread, unknown, and disputed, on the perception of societal risks, such as new technologies, genetic engineering, racism, child abuse, financial crisis, global warming. The authors expected to find that morality constitutes a distinct dimension of the risk factor positively correlated with judgment of riskiness such that "an individual who regards a societal risk as morally reprehensible will also judge its overall riskiness as large and severe" (Bassarak et al. 2017: 303).

In actuality, the results showed morality and dread as so strongly correlated that morality was not identified as a distinct dimension of the cognitive representation of societal risks. Rather, morality and dread formed one dimension explaining most of the variance. But morality was not redundant with dread. Morality was found to be the strongest predictors of the perception of riskiness, followed by dread and then disputed. Perceived morality and perceived dreadfulness, when mutually controlled for each other, were found to contribute significantly and independently to the prediction of riskiness. These results suggest that morality and dread are conceptually distinct and that the strength of the correlation between the two may vary from one risk domain to another.

The results of this study showed that moral judgments may be more important in risk perception than the evaluation of harmful consequences. Does that mean that the influence of moral values introduces a bias in the perception of risk, leading to a judgment unsensitive or poorly sensitive to the facts?

4.3.3.2 Moral values in factual and interpretative judgment

When experts refer solely to known statistics and recorded fatalities or injuries in their risk assessment, the practice is designed to exclude affect and value judgments from entering the calculation. It is clear from what we have seen so far in this chapter that the characteristics that influence risk perception are not restricted to such features as fatalities or injuries. But when participants in a study are asked about some of the other relevant characteristics, their reply may – or sometimes must – involve some interpretation on the part of the subject. For example, whether an action is voluntary rather than compelled or constrained by circumstances is, to some extent, a matter of judgment, and different subjects may perceive the action differently. The same can be said of judgments as to whether an effect is natural or the result of tampering with nature.

But we should be clear that in such a study, the participants are still being asked about what the facts are. They are not being asked about how they feel. That two participants give different answers does not imply that their answers are "subjective" in any sense connected with an expression of feelings. To give a simple example, suppose that one of Uncle Jack's nephews, Tim, says that he is bald, and another nephew, Tom, says, "No, Uncle Jack has a receding hairline, but he is not bald!" Their disagreement may just signal that they understand *baldness* differently. Perhaps for Tom the criterion of baldness is not to have hair on the crown of the head, and for Tim it is to have less than half one's head covered in hair. Neither is egregious with respect to what everyone thinks, and they are not using the words in ways that are at odds with common usage. The criteria for baldness are not completely settled, and as a result, there is leeway in what it means to be bald.

The example is simple, because the concept of baldness is not a thick concept. When several people disagree in the application of a thick concept, which clearly involves values (such as the concepts of *kindness, cruelty, arrogance*), the case is more complex. In this respect, though, it is not essentially different: the difference in judgment may just be showing that the same leeway in interpretation, for typically the accepted criteria, is not altogether precise.

But then we can still ask, given this leeway, "Are there factors that affect how a subject will apply it in a specific case?" And specifically, is it possible that the subject's values play a role in such factual but interpretative judgments?

This question was put to empirical test in the newly developing field of *experimental philosophy*.

Joshua Knobe investigated the effect of moral considerations in judgments attributing or denying intentionality to action (Knobe 2003a, 2003b, 2004; Feltz 2007). In several studies, participants were shown the following scenarios:

> **Scenario 1.** The vice president of a company went to the chairman of the board and said, "We are thinking of starting a new program. It will help us increase profits, but it will also harm the environment."
>
> The chairman of the board answered, "I don't care at all about harming the environment. I just want to make as much profit as I can. Let's start the new program."

> They started the new program. Sure enough, the environment was harmed.
>
> **Scenario 2.** The vice president of a company went to the chairman of the board and said, "We are thinking of starting a new program. It will help us increase profits, but it will also help the environment."
>
> The chairman of the board answered, "I don't care at all about helping the environment. I just want to make as much profit as I can. Let's start the new program."
>
> They started the new program. Sure enough, the environment was helped.

After being shown the first scenario, participants were then asked whether the chairman harmed the environment intentionally or unintentionally. After being shown the second scenario, participants were asked whether the chairman helped the environment intentionally or unintentionally.

Given the symmetry between the two scenarios and the similarity of the questions, one could expect the same answer in the two cases about whether the action was intentional. Instead, most participants who were shown the first scenario (about 82%) said that the chairman harmed the environment intentionally, whereas most of those shown the second scenario (about 77%) said that the chairman did not help the environment intentionally. That difference makes it appear that moral considerations play a role in reaching this interpretative judgment about the facts. But it is not obvious how they do so.

If they do, the moral considerations for blame and credit must not be the same. Knobe offered a model that fits these results: the judgment is reached in two stages. First, the action envisaged is subject to moral evaluation, as good or bad. Then, secondly, *specific criteria come into play.* For example:

> For blame, foresight of the effect may be enough; for moral credit, something more than foresight, perhaps intention or purpose, is required.

Interestingly, some results of studies on the role of moral values on judgments of riskiness seem to show an effect analog to the one revealed in the Knobe experiment.

One study investigated whether moral judgments about parental responsibility affected estimates of risk to children. Playing unsupervised in a park is generally judged as much riskier than car accidents, but children are actually much more likely to be hurt in a car accident than when playing unsupervised in the park (Thomas et al. 2016a, 2016b). To explain this attitude toward children playing unsupervised, the authors hypothesized that when they are free to do so, people adopt and/or modify their factual beliefs (e.g., regarding the amount of danger posed to a child by a given situation) so as to better rationalize their intuitive moral judgments (e.g., that this mother did something morally wrong).

In an experiment, participants were asked to read brief vignettes in which a child spends a brief period of time unsupervised. The vignettes differed only in the reason for a parent's absence:

- "Unintentional" condition. The parent was involuntarily separated from the child by an accident.
- "Work" condition. The parent intentionally left the child in order to work.
- "Volunteer" condition. The parent intentionally left the child in order to volunteer for charity.
- "Relax" condition. The parent intentionally left the child in order to relax.
- "Affair" condition. The parent intentionally left the child in order to meet an illicit lover.

After reading each vignette, participants were asked to estimate how much danger the child was in during a parent's absence. The results showed a significant effect of moral judgment about the reasons for a parent's absence on the risk estimates. Specifically:

- A mother's unintentional absence was seen as safer for the child than a mother's intentional absence for any reason.
- A mother's work-related absence was seen as more dangerous than an unintentional absence but less dangerous than if the mother left to pursue an illicit sexual affair.

These results are prima facie puzzling. After all, children who are left alone in circumstances anticipated by their parents are likely to be safer than children who find themselves alone by accident. If it is anticipated, parents can take steps to ensure their child's well-being in their absence (e.g., making sure the baby is securely buckled into a car seat, that the car is parked in a shady spot, that an older child has a cell phone, etc.).

In a modified form, the same experiment was conducted with an extra question: "Did the mother do something morally/ethically wrong by leaving her child alone?" Participants' moral judgments followed a very similar pattern to their risk judgments: a mother's unintentional absence was seen as more immoral than a mother's intentional absence for any reason, and a mother's work-related absence was seen as less immoral than if the mother left to pursue an illicit sexual affair.

The experiment included a test of whether the envisaged dangers were perceived as different when the parent was absent for different reasons. Participants listed the same dangers in all conditions with no evidence that participants imagined different dangers to children in the different conditions.

So an explanation for the participants' judgment that children left alone by accident are safer than those left alone on purpose, given also the result of the follow-up experiments, is that the participants' moral condemnation of parents skewed their risk estimates. And the same explanation would apply for why people view playing unsupervised as a higher risk than car crashes.

In the Knobe experiment, despite the facts being the same in the two scenarios, the participants evaluate the same action (starting the program) differently (as having intentional versus nonintentional effect) because of the difference in moral value attached to the actions of the chairman (harming versus helping).

We already noted Knobe's suggestion that a moral judgment will come first, and the subsequent putative judgment of fact will apply different criteria for intentionality depending on the content of that moral judgment.

In the case of the children left alone, participants evaluate the same physical situation (children left alone) differently (as being more or less risky) because of the difference in moral value attached to the actions leading to this situation (child left alone because parents work versus because parent has an affair). They do not see the situations as being differently dangerous, but their criteria for what counts as more or less risky changed.

4.3.4 Affects and emotions

> Having had visceral contact with the virus strongly engages the affective experiential system.
>
> (Dryhurst et al. 2020)

The questionnaire used to measure how seriously people perceive the risk of COVID-19 asked not just what people *think* about the likeliness that they or people and friends will be affected by but also about whether they are *worried* about coronavirus or COVID-19, that is, about how they *feel* about it. The inclusion of this kind of question reflects a prevalent belief in the field of risk perception that the perception of risk has an important affective component.

This has been supported by studies of the role of affect in decision-making and in the perception of risk. For example, in one study, people were asked to freely evoke images and thoughts related to the concept of a nuclear waste repository and then to rate the affective quality of these images or thoughts (Slovic et al. 1991). It was found that in the large majority of the cases where the first image was rated very negatively, people would also say that they would vote against the repository, as opposed to less than 50% of the people whose first image was rated positively.

The *feelings-as-information view* states that feelings that are triggered by a situation and accompany the cognitive processing of the situation will directly affect the decision people make about how to act. These feelings will enter the decision-making process directly as source of information rather than by eliciting memories or concepts (Clore et al. 1994; Schwarz 1990).

4.3.4.1 A controversy about risk and feeling

The feeling-as-information view still allows for two different views of how feelings and risk perception are intertwined. One school of thought, centered on the work of Melissa Finucane and Paul Slovic, introduced the notion of affect heuristic and views the role that emotions play as analogous to the role played by judgments of representativeness or similarity, modifying or altering the cognitive assessment of risk (Finucane et al. 2000). Another school, led by George Loewenstein, views the role of emotions as more direct, driving the reaction to risk independently of thought and calculation.

- *The affect heuristic*

> Using an overall, readily available affective impression can be easier and more efficient than weighing the pros and cons of various reasons or retrieving relevant examples from memory, especially when the required judgment or decision is complex or mental resources are limited. This characterization of a mental shortcut has led us to label the use of affect a "heuristic."
>
> (Slovic et al. 2004)

This view begins with the hypothesis, of long standing in the field, that expectation of benefits would produce a positive effect and that this would be correlated with a reduced estimate of risk. This was in line with some of the earliest research on risk perception (Starr 1969).

An experimental test of this hypothesis found that information stating that the benefit is high (respectively, low) for a technology such as nuclear power results in risk perceived as lower (resp. higher), whereas information stating that the risk is high (resp. low) results in benefit perceived as lower (resp. higher). The explanation offered, under the *affect heuristic* model, was that the information received created a positive or negative affect, which then had a direct effect on the perceived risk or benefit: if people have a positive (versus negative) feeling toward a certain risk, they will be inclined to perceive the risk as low (versus high) and the benefit as high (versus low).

The affect heuristic model is consistent with numbers of experiments that have shown that people will reach different judgments on the same situation depending on whether they think about it in more intuitive or analytic way, with these two ways of thinking being viewed as two modes of information processing: an emotionally driven experiential system and a rational system (Sloman 1996).

Most of the studies in this area concentrate on the impact of negative feelings. We should note, however, that positive feelings, though studied less often in this context, also play a role. A study of the highly contentious case of nuclear energy in Saskatchewan, Canada, showed results that suggest that positive emotions, like negative emotions, are related to nuclear energy risk perceptions. These findings were similar for risk perception among both supporters and opponents (Bourassa et al. 2016).

- *Risk as feelings*

The affect heuristic model seems to suggest that how people feel about a risk and what judgment they make about it will be consistent. But some research suggests that emotional reactions to risky situations may actually diverge from the cognitive assessment of those situations in terms of severity and likelihood.

Loewenstein and colleagues make a distinction between two kinds of emotions that may influence attitudes toward a risk (Loewenstein et al. 2001). *Anticipated emotion* is an emotion that is expected by the agent to be experienced *in the future* in response to a certain outcome. *Anticipatory emotion* is an immediate affective response to the risky situation itself as it presents itself (Mellers & McGraw 2001). The difference in the effects was shown in an experiment where students were offered $1 in exchange for telling a joke in front of a class the following week. When the appointed time arrived, 67% of those who initially volunteered to tell a joke decided not to do it, while none of those who had initially declined the offer changed their mind.

Taking into account anticipatory emotions, the risk-as-feelings hypothesis postulates that responses to risky situations result in part from the direct influence of feelings, such as worry, fear, or dread.

This hypothesis can explain risk-related behaviors that cannot be well explained when perception of risk is understood as simply a cognitive process. The reason is that emotions often produce behavioral responses different from what individuals view as the best response, that is, when the emotional reaction to risky situations diverge from its cognitive assessment, it is the emotional reaction that tends to drive the behavior. So a measure of risk perception, based on what people think about the likeliness of being affected by the risk, may not be a good indicator of how they will *act* toward the risk. The risk-as-feelings hypothesis can explain what happened in the experiment with the students: the increase in fear when someone is just about to perform a risky action that they had voluntarily decided to perform several days beforehand may lead them to the decision to not perform the action.

- *Do these views conflict?*

Are the "affect heuristic" and "risk-as-feeling" explanations inconsistent, then? Not necessarily. The kind of judgment of perception of risk referred to by Slovic and collaborators is an intuitive, immediate one, not involved with an assessment in terms of severity and likelihood.

But let's admit that emotional reaction and cognitive assessment may diverge and that, in such a case, emotions drive the behavior. Then a measure of risk perception using only questions about the likeliness of being affected by the risk may not reflect how people feel about or indicate how they will act.

4.3.4.2 Effect of fear on risk perception

It will come as no surprise that people experiencing fear will have a more pessimistic perception of risk and will risk adverse behavior.

One of the numerous studies illustrating the effect of fear uses the anticipation of a stressful examination as the source of anxiety. The perception of risk of failure at the exam was measured on two occasions, one month before and one day before the examination date (Butler & Matthews 1987). Increases in anticipatory anxiety as the examination approached were associated with higher perceived risk of examination failure.

Similar results were found in a study measuring the perception of risk related to terrorism (Lerner et al. 2003). The study was conducted in the aftermath of the September 2011 terrorist attack and measured the perception of three types of risk related to terrorism: for the United States, for self, and for the average American. Higher reported fear was found to be correlated with higher risk perception. Women reported more fear than men, and also perception of higher risk, with the gender difference in self-reported emotion explaining most of the variance in the gender risk perception.

Since risk is a matter both of uncertainty and possible negative outcome, is it possible that the effect of fear bears on one of those aspects of risk more than the other? A recent study (Hengen & Alpers 2019) tried to answer this question by assessing the effect on risk perception of three types of fear domain: *fear of spiders*, *fear of snakes*, and *everyday fear triggers*. The authors of the study found, for all domains of fear, that 1) there was no overestimate of the *likeliness* of encounters but 2) highly fearful overestimates of the *outcomes* of all negative encounters. And they also found the perceived risk of aversive outcomes was most pronounced for an individual's specific fear.

Such results may have implication beyond the study of risk perception itself in clinical and therapeutic contexts. In clinical psychology, cognitive models are used to derive conclusions that will suggest cognitive interventions to target maladaptive risk evaluation. This would seem to require information about what specific component of risk evaluation is actually biased in highly fearful individuals, and it may be relevant that the anticipation of negative outcomes has been found to be one of the main drivers of avoidance behavior in anxiety disorders (Mueller et al. 2010; Alpers 2010). But that the effect of fear would be mediated by an estimate of the outcome does not seem all consistent with the affect heuristic or the risk-as-feelings hypotheses, since they both view the impact of emotions on risk perception as direct and intuitive, which seemingly implies that it is not mediated by a judgment on the probability or the severity of the outcomes.

The studies that we just have discussed so far categorize feelings as being positive or negative. According to some theories of emotions, this distinction is too crude and overlook some differences between feelings that are categorized similarly and similarities between feelings that are categorized differently. As we will see now, those differences and similarities are relevant to the effect of feelings on risk perception.

4.3.4.3 Valence-based vs. appraisal-based approaches

Studies of the role of emotions in the perception of risk do not all share the same model of emotion. Two models in play here are the *valence-based* and the *appraisal-based* approaches.

- *The valence-based approach*

Valence is the affective quality of intrinsic attractiveness, "goodness" (positive valence), or averseness, "badness" (negative valence), of an event, object, or situation. The valence-based approach to emotion assumes that emotions with the same valence produce a similar influence on judgments and choices.

The two schools of thought discussed earlier, affect heuristic and risk-as-feeling, share the valence-based approach. They classify feelings as *positive* or *negative* and contrast their influences on risk perception on the basis of that distinction. But this might be too shallow a classification. For example, fear and anger are both classified as negative emotions. But as we will see, these have actually been found to have opposite effects on the perception of risk.

- *The appraisal-based approach*

The appraisal-based approach attempts a more nuanced classification of emotions, in terms of basic evaluations (appraisals) of features of the situation that triggers them. This approach to the role of emotions in risk perception (Lerner & Keltner 2001) is based on the previously developed psychological appraisal theory (Lazarus et al. 1970) which focused on cognitive aspects of emotion, with two main questions:

1. What is the nature of the cognitions or appraisals which underlie separate emotional reactions (e.g. fear, guilt, grief, joy, etc.)?
2. What are the determining antecedent conditions of these appraisals?

An appraisal consists of a subjective evaluation, whether consciously or unconsciously, of (real, recalled, or fictitious) events or situations, by multiple criteria.

Appraisal theory specifies appraisal profiles for different emotions. For example, the combination of unpleasantness and moral badness of the situation, in conjunction with other appraisals, has been associated with anger, and the combination of unpleasantness of the situation and low power or powerlessness of the individual with sadness (Scherer 1988).

Some features of the situation that are typically used by cognitive appraisal theorists to distinguish emotions are certainty/uncertainty, pleasantness/unpleasantness, responsibility ("Is the agent responsible or others?") / controllability ("Does the agent have some control?"). The set of appraisals that is associated with a given emotion forms what is referred to as *a pattern of appraisal*. Different patterns of appraisal are associated with different basic emotions, such as happiness, fear, anger, surprise, pride, hope, shame, guilt (Smith & Ellsworth 1985).

This way of identifying emotions cuts through the distinction between positive and negative valence. For instance, in terms of these appraisals, fear and anger are similar in that they are both associated with unpleasantness. But they are different in that fear is associated with low certainty and low controllability, whereas anger is associated with high certainty and high controllability. And although anger and happiness differ along the pleasantness dimension of appraisal, they are similar with respect to certainty and controllability.

Especially relevant for the study of risk perception are the dimensions of controllability and certainty: low assessment of these factors was found to be correlated with higher risk perception. Fear and anger, then, can be distinguished along the "certainty" and "controllability" dimensions, and we know that the perception of certainty and controllability play a role in risk perception. So one can expect that fear and anger will have different effects on risk perception, despite being both negative emotions. And in effect, fear (and anxiety) was found to lead to higher risk perception and risk-averse choices, whereas anger leads to lower risk perception and risk-seeking choices (Lerner & Keltner 2000, 2001).

- *Relevance to attitudes toward mandated or advised protective measures*

In an interview for *Science News*, Jennifer Lerner discussed the relevance on her findings to understanding people's attitude toward protective measures related to COVID-19.[7] When the interviewer mentioned a poll showing that the difference in people's attitudes toward protective measures follows partisan lines, Lerner noted that these partisan differences could be the result of emotional differences. People's attitude toward the risk can be manipulated with partisan communication aiming at inducing fear or anger. Induced anger and frustration will result in downplaying the risk of being contaminated and neglecting protective measure or even protesting them: "People can be made angry enough to accept risky policies, such as certainty around when to reopen stores, or scared enough to purchase hoax remedies."

This interpretation seemed to find support in later discussions in the news media. Those attending protest rallies often expressed anger and frustration at states' stay-at-home orders, and another poll, released in May 2020,[8] found that Republicans and Republican-leaning independents were much less worried about becoming seriously ill from COVID-19 than did Democrats and Democrat-leaning independents.

4.4 Is risk perception "badly" subjective?

Now that we have understood the methods and results of scientific studies of risk perception, we are in a better position to understand in what ways risk perception is subjective.

In the first chapter, we discussed the ways in which the concept of risk could be said to be a subjective concept. In this chapter, we are discussing not the concept of risk, not what risk "is," but how we perceive it, that is, we are discussing a way in which we form beliefs about risk, a way that is generally contrasted with the expert or scientific way.

"Badly" can be understood in two ways: in the sense of "a great deal" and in a reprobative sense. Both have been applied to risk perception as subjective (Sunstein 2007). In order to clarify whether risk perception is indeed badly subjective, we will address two questions: one is whether being subjective makes risk perception necessarily arbitrary, mistaken, or irrational. The other one is whether, considered independently of risk assessment, some risk perceptions are better than others and in what sense it could be. Whereas to the first question we will answer "No," to the second question we will answer "Yes." But "better" has to be understood not so much in an epistemic way (in terms of what kind of belief it produces) or epistemological way (in terms of how it produces beliefs) as in an ethical way (in terms of what kind of actions it motivates).

4.4.1 The many meanings of subjectivity

There is an important distinction between the question of whether *risk perception is subjective* and the question of whether *the risk perceived is subjective*. That distinction is not always made clearly. The 1983 report of Britain's Royal Society, called "Risk Assessment," emphasized the distinction between objective risk (risk measured by experts) and perceived risk (risk perceived by laypersons) (Adams 1995). This suggests that what is measured by the experts and what is perceived by laypersons are two different things and that the risk perceived by laypersons is something subjective. But a few years later, in 1992, a new report of the Royal Society stated that "the view that a separation can be maintained between 'objective' risk and 'subjective' or perceived risk has come under increasing attack, to the extent that it is no longer a mainstream position."

The antonym of "subjective" is "objective," and it has the same multiplicity of meaning. In "Let's not talk about objectivity," Ian Hacking even urged that these terms should be dropped altogether because of all the misleading connotations they carry (Hacking 2015). But others, also recognizing that the scientific assessment of risk has a subjective dimension, insist that the words "objective" or "objectivity" should not be abandoned in scientific contexts, that it is doing important work (Zhale 2021; Cartwright et al. forthcoming). It works as a guiding, methodological ideal for both quantitative *and* qualitative research: "Rather than give up on the notion of objectivity, it is better to promote an understanding of objectivity which may serve as a reachable – and useful – guiding ideal in qualitative research" (Zhale 2021: 102).

If there cannot be a strict distinction between scientific assessment of risk and perception of risk, in terms of the objective versus subjective nature of what is apprehended, then what about the distinction between the ways in which it is apprehended, by the means of perception or scientific assessment?

The difficulty to maintain a strict distinction between "objective" and "subjective" seems to apply also at the level of the processes of assessment or perception themselves. Results of the studies of risk perception make clear that risk perception is a process that has some regularity, some systematicity, and can be, to some extent, quantified. And in Chapter 3 on risk assessment, we saw that the scientific process of measuring risk includes a subjective dimension in that it requires some evaluative judgments to be made along the way. But scientific assessment and perception are very different ways to form judgments about risk, so the ways in which they both have a subjective dimension may well be very different.

What does it mean to say that risk perception is "subjective"? Of course, there is a sense in which it is subjective simply because it is the result of a subject's cognitive processes that are not following explicit rules. But is there more to it than just the fact that it is an informal and implicit form of assessment? For instance, is it supposed to imply that risk perception is arbitrary or "irrational"? Does risk perception being subjective imply that risk perception is "mistaken"? If we generally perceive risk as being larger or smaller than what science says it is, does that necessarily mean that we perceive *incorrectly*?

Clearly, the term "subjective" has different contrasts, depending on the context of the question.

Subjective vs. Arbitrary

A typical case of a judgment said to be subjective is a judgment based on "personal preferences." What do we mean by "personal preferences"? Take the case where someone is choosing a car. An objective way of doing it could be to look at the results of performance tests, to compare the results for different cars, and to base the choice on this comparative analysis.

By contrast, someone would make a subjective judgment if the person made the choice on a whim, maybe by tossing a coin, without looking at the results of the performance tests, without knowing much about the cars. It would qualify as subjective in the sense of *arbitrary*.

But a choice that does not accord with the data on performance is not necessarily a choice made on a whim. A judgment might not be objective in the sense just explained, and, in that respect, be subjective, without yet being arbitrary. It could be that the agent uses "personal preferences" in the sense that they use criteria, even if implicit, that are not those defined by the profession. Maybe the agent values the way the car looks from a certain angle, or values the way it reminds her of a car she was in when she was a child.

The point is that she may be able, if pushed to the brink, to explain and justify her choice. Her preferences, her criteria, are personal, but her choice is not arbitrary. It might even be based on quantitative data, some specific, sophisticated measurements of perspective. The difference between her judgment and an objective judgment is simply that her criteria are personal and are not limited to the car's performance.

The studies of risk perception showed that the perception of risk is not necessarily guided by the same criteria as scientific assessment of risk, since, as we will see in the next chapter, scientific risk assessment focuses on the measure of the uncertainty and severity attached to the risk. Risk perception is under the influence of factors that do not play a similar role in scientific assessment. But these studies have also shown that the perception of risk is not necessarily arbitrary.

Subjective vs. Mistaken

A judgment that is mistaken is a judgment that is not correct. That sounds obvious, but it is important: an answer, a judgment, cannot count as mistaken without the presupposition that there is a correct answer, the correct judgment. To speak of a mistake raises the question of what makes an answer or judgment correct.

But to say that risk perception is mistaken simply because it does not produce the same evaluation as scientific evaluation is to beg the question. What we want to know is whether there is something proper to risk perception that makes it inevitably mistaken.

Here is an example of a mistaken judgment: the agent is taking part in a contest to identify the safest car, where "safest" is defined in a way agreed upon by the agent. Then it turns out that instead, the agent used personal criteria (like his favorite color) to select the car and did not select the safest car. This judgment is subjective, in the sense that it is based on personal preferences, but what makes it mistaken – whether unintentionally or deliberately – is something else: that it did not select the safest car.

Being mistaken does not necessarily follow from being subjective. In our example, the same preference for a certain kind of car would not have counted as a mistake if the agent hadn't had the goal of identifying the safest car.

We can adapt our example as follows: imagine someone agrees to rank activities in terms of how risky they are and accepts the measure of risk as the chance of a fatality. Then, if that person actually – whether consciously or unconsciously – ranks the activities by the criteria of how dreadful or uncontrollable they are, she will be making a mistake. But what makes it a mistake is not that she judges by what matters most to her but that she failed at what she was trying to do.

One traditional explanation for risk perception being mistaken, and then conflicting with scientific risk assessment, is that people fail at estimating the correct probabilities, while those probabilities serve as a basis for scientific risk assessment. The argument would be:

1. Risk entails uncertainty.
2. People ***fail*** at estimating the uncertainty.
C. People *mis*perceive risk.

Is this argument sound?

We can take Premise 1 as uncontroversial. There are different uses of the concept of risk that express different conceptions of risk, but all of them include uncertainty.

Premise 2 seems to be supported by evidence from empirical work in cognitive psychology showing that people make mistakes when assessing probabilities. This work in cognitive psychology has shown that, in their assessment of probabilities, people rely on a limited number of heuristic principles, popularly known as "rules of thumb," which reduce the complex task of assessing probabilities to simpler judgmental operations (Tversky & Kahneman 1974; Evans 2012).[9]

The most common heuristics are the *representativeness heuristic* and the *availability heuristic*. The first is that people judge the probability that an object or event belongs to a class on the basis of its similarity with other element of the class. The second is that events which can be more easily brought to mind or imagined are judged to be more likely than events that could not easily be imagined.

In general, these heuristics are quite useful, but sometimes they lead to systematic errors, that is, biases. One problem with the representativeness heuristic is that it is likely to be insensitive to prior probability. Another problem is that when people evaluate probability by using representativeness, they expect a small sample to be as representative as a large sample. The availability heuristic, on the other hand, is associated with a bias due to retrievability and a bias due to imaginability.

So there are some cognitive explanations of why people may not be good at assessing probabilities.

But note that one can only *fail* something that one is trying to do in the first place. A crucial question, then, is:

> When people perceive risk, are they trying to estimate the probabilities of the unwanted events?

As we have seen earlier, the perception of risk seriousness is correlated to the perception of a plurality of other characteristics, such as the perception of the benefits, dread, of tampering with nature. It is influenced by social-cultural values, emotions, trust in institutions, perception of scientific consensus, social networking and does not seem closely correlated with the estimate of fatality or injuries. These results suggest that people are not specifically trying and failing at doing what risk experts do when they assess risk, which is to estimate expected fatalities or injuries. Uncertainty might be relevant to risk perception in some cases, but it is far from being the main consideration.

Subjective vs. Irrational

The typical case of irrational judgment is one that is arbitrary, one that has no reason, and so no rationale, no justification. Risk perception is normally not irrational in that sense. But some judgments that can be justified may still count as irrational, in another way – when the reasons are "bad" reasons. "Bad" in what sense? In the sense that they are not fitted to the goal of the agent. For instance, the agent explicitly wants to buy a safe car and insists on choosing a car on the basis of certain features that have been shown to undermine safety.

But if the agent's aim was not to buy a safe car and valued those other features (such as the power to accelerate from 0 to 60 mph in 2.6 seconds or less), to make this choice would not be irrational. It would be subjective in that it would be based on personal preferences or criteria but would not be irrational because the criteria are adequate to the purpose. Similarly, the cognitive process of risk perception can very well be conducted in a way that is informal, implicit, governed by criteria that are not the same as scientific assessment, but not undermining the goal of the process and, in that sense, would not be irrational.

It is possible to be both irrational and mistaken if your goal is to reach a correct answer and you are using a method that you know is likely to produce a wrong answer and it does produce a wrong answer. In that case, you would be mistaken, since your answer is incorrect, and irrational, for choosing a method that is not fitted to your goal of being correct.

But a judgment could be mistaken without being irrational: we all make lots of mistakes without being deemed irrational. We make a mistake if, for instance, we did not use the right criteria or did not apply them in the right way, where "right" entails being fit to the goal. But if we can recognize that what we did was not appropriate when we are confronted with the results it produces, our being mistaken does not count as being irrational.

Suppose a homeowner takes note of the warnings and regulations issued by the county concerning fire hazard abatement and decides on a minimum of fireproofing of her property. If a wildfire then seriously damages her home, we will say that she had made a mistake, because her precautions turned out not to be adequate. What about the decision itself? Maybe she took note of the county's information about fire hazard abatement but discounted it. Maybe she recognized its importance but procrastinated till it was too late. But even if the county could charge her with culpable negligence, we may still hesitate to call her conduct irrational.

Risk perception could be irrational if the way the process of risk perception is conducted undermines the end of it. Let's assume that the end of risk perception is to make oneself safer by becoming aware of possible dangers and being in a better position to take appropriate measures. It would seem irrational not to take into account the characteristics of the risk situation that are most relevant to evaluate the level of danger and possible harm, in terms of how likely it is and how damaging it can be. It may seem irrational to let one's perception of risk influenced by a consideration such as "tampering with nature."

But what counts as dangerous or harmful will not be exactly the same for everyone, and that will be all the more the case since we do not perceive risks in isolation from other risks. Evaluating risks for oneself is generally evaluating a course of action, and it is generally done in the context of other possible courses of action. For someone who is exposed to the risk of losing their business or being evicted, the risk of getting COVID-19 if the lockdown is avoided may not seem as serious as for someone for whom the lockdown simply means working from home. It might be that Sam and Pam value staying healthy almost as much, with Pam only a little less than Sam. This little difference, if they both were able to work from home, would make hardly a difference in their perception of the risk of getting sick. But if the risk of losing her job is much higher for Pam, she may perceive the benefit of avoiding the lockdown as much higher and, correlatively, the risk of getting sick with COVID-19 as much lower than Sam might.

Also, we have assumed that the end of risk perception is to make oneself safer, probably because estimating safety is the end of the scientific assessment of risk in terms of expected value. But risk perception may well be just as much about making oneself *feel* safer (Jenkin 2006). And what contributes to make one feel safer is not so individual-centered as what makes one safe. It would not be surprising if the feeling of safety was more sensitive to social and environmental impacts, real or even symbolic, like the idea of "tampering with nature," and more so for some people than for others.

4.4.2 Not all risk perceptions are equal

We have seen that risk perception is not necessarily arbitrary, irrational, or mistaken. At that point, we might be inclined to think that what makes risk perception subjective, then, is simply that there are no external norms of correctness, because the perception of risk will depend on each individual's interpretation of "negative consequence." But that seems too easy, because there does seem to be a sense in which risk perception can be better or worse, especially when we are wondering whether risk perception can be a valid input for decision-making. And there are actually social efforts invested in modifying risk perceptions, for instance, the perception of the risk of COVID-19, the risk of climate warming, the risk of smoking, or the risk of unhealthy diet. What can be the justification for such efforts?

Epistemic rationale

It is very tempting to think that the justification for modifying some risk perceptions is epistemic. The rationale would be that if responsible decision-making, at the social or personal level, is not just about increasing the feeling of safety but also about increasing safety itself, we want risk perception as an input for decision-making to be responsive, at least to some extent, to the objective dimension of the concept of risk. So risk perception can be better or worse depending on how responsive it is to the objective dimension of the concept of risk. What are the ways in which it could become less responsive to this objective dimension?

First, risk perception would be more responsive to the objective dimension of risk if it is less influenced by factors that are not characteristics of the hazard, or of its possible consequences.

This might be a fine line to walk, however. First, we saw that personal experience, which might include experience with other hazards, may have an influence. Even though that will be something different from the current hazard, it does not seem that it would undermine the validity of the perception. A large part of our understanding of the world and how it affects us comes from experience. Of course, the hazards experienced in the past would have to have enough relevant similarity with the current hazard to count.

However, what is relevantly similar will be, to some extent, different for different persons. Also, risk perception may be partly influenced by the perception of benefits or the perception of other risks. The perception of the economic benefit of avoiding a lockdown or the perception of the risk of losing one's business may have influenced some people toward a lower risk perception of infection by the coronavirus and have no relevance for others. But it would be odd to think that risk perception goes astray because it does not consider its objects in isolation. Risks are actually not experienced in isolation, and we do not make sense of any source of experience in isolation from others.

Another way in which risk perception could become unresponsive to the objective dimension of risk is simply as a result of ignorance or misunderstanding of the situation, of the conditions of exposure to the effects it can generate, of the effects themselves. For instance, one may not find the risk of being exposed to COVID-19 as very serious because they believe, and may be right about so, that they will recover after a few days. But this perception is not responsive to the social effect of the virus, with COVID-19 epidemic bringing the health-care system into a crisis state, with sick patients crowding hospitals, nurses and doctors being overwhelmed, physically and psychologically, scheduled surgeries being canceled, ambulances having to wait hours to offload patients, and critically ill patients being then kept in emergency rooms.

But there is a fine line here, too, because there is no general way to decide exactly what people *should* know without assuming that the risk perception should match expert assessment, which is simply to dismiss the relevance of risk perception in decision-making. If it is not dismissed, there is no general way to decide what people should know to form an opinion that deserves to be heard. And what is relevant information may not be exactly the same for expert's assessment and lay public perception, since, after all, experts do not, in their formal, probabilistic assessment of risk, integrate the considerations that matter to people in their perception of risks, like controllability, familiarity, or delay of consequences. And whatever information is provided may be interpreted differently, for instance, in terms of how it affects the controllability of the unwanted effects of the risky situation rather than in terms of how it affects their probability.

Still another way in which risk perception may become unresponsive to the objective dimension of the concept of risk is through the influence of value judgments (Cross 1998). While for some value judgments, their influence seems legitimate, for others it does not.

Here is an example where the influence of value judgments on risk perception seems legitimate: people who have liberal social-cultural values are more inclined than those with conservative social-cultural values to perceive the risk of climate warming as serious. Of course, social-cultural values have no effect on the nature and probability of harmful consequences of climate warming. But when it comes to deciding how severe these consequences are, it will be a matter of how much we care about the protection of the environment, the survival and well-being of other species, or the inequity in the distribution of harm among the populations, versus how much we care about preserving some economic and industrial interests or a certain form of life.

That social-cultural values would play a role in this evaluation seems legitimate, even if we disagree on the values. How else, after all, could we evaluate – ascribe a value to – the severity of the consequences if not on the basis of what we value and disvalue?

But for some other values, that they would play a role in perception of risks does not seem legitimate. For instance, one may be influenced in their perception of some risks by egoistic, racist, sexist values and that would not seem legitimate. These values would make the person emphasize some aspects of a situation and discard others in a way that would be perceived as unacceptably biased. For instance, sexist values may lead someone to view hiring a woman as much riskier than hiring a man even though the woman is more competent or experienced.

Why exactly would we see this influence as illegitimate? The answer lies in the way values operate. In the case of climate warming, social-cultural values influence the evaluation of, say, the effect on the environment of reducing fossil fuel consumption, with the uncontroversial presupposition that fossil fuel consumption does have an effect on the environment. In the case of hiring someone, the possible unwanted consequences could be that the person will be absent, or unproductive, or uncooperative. But we don't think that sex or gender, per se, has an effect on being absent, or unproductive, or uncooperative. And that is what makes the influence of sexist values, which would make one see hiring a woman as riskier than hiring a man, illegitimate: a lack of connection between what is evaluated (severity of unwanted effects of new hiring) and what is valued (sex/gender). Similarly, negative racial stereotypes would make someone see hiring some people as riskier than others on the presupposition that the color of the skin has an effect on being absent, unproductive, or uncooperative. It is this fallacious presupposition that makes the influence of such values illegitimate.

Egoistic values, too, may be illegitimate. They would lead someone to see personal, and in general, immediate, interests as much more important than collective and long-term interests. Note that this would not be an illegitimate influence for the perception of personal risks. For instance, one driving behind a truck full of junk loosely fastened may choose to slow down and let someone else go between them and the truck. But it is different with societal risks. To perceive a societal risk as such is to perceive its unwanted effects as affecting not just oneself but a community, and not just in the present but possibly in the long-term. Egoistic values may prevent someone from this kind of perception. In the same way as racist or sexist values do, egoistic values will lead someone to form a belief about the risk on the basis of considerations largely irrelevant to the way unwanted consequences are produced. Whereas the considerations will focus on one's personal interest, the unwanted consequences would affect the community with a diversity of interests that may or may not overlap with one's personal interests.

But if the justification for trying to modify some risk perceptions is to counter the effect of some values, it is doubtful that this justification is epistemic. It is not so much about imparting information or correcting misinformation as it is about modifying actions. And if it is so, the justification is not epistemic; it is ethical.

Ethical rationale

It will be helpful to clarify the distinction between individual risks and societal risks. Societal risks are risks to which we all potentially contribute through our actions and are all potentially exposed to through our actions. Paradigmatic examples of societal risks are COVID-19 or climate change. Paradigmatic examples of individual risks are solo rock climbing, smoking when done solely in a private space, dangerous driving on an isolated road, unhealthy diet. Smoking in private or dangerous driving on an isolated road affect society through the health-care costs it may generate, but it is still individual in that only the smoker or driver is exposed to the effects of smoking or driving and no one else contributed directly through their action to the seriousness of the risk.

We are generally tolerant of diversity in the perception of individual risks and much less so regarding the perception of societal risks: individuals will argue, clash, break relationships over disagreement in the perception of societal risks. This difference is difficult to explain if we take the justification for trying to modify others' perceptions of a risk to be epistemic, but it makes sense if we take it to be ethical, directed at the actions rather than the perceptions.

As said earlier, societal risks are such that through our actions, we are all potentially contributing and being exposed to the risks. How people personally act makes a difference to such a risk and has an effect on others' conditions of life, degree of safety. When efforts are made to modify the perception of such risks, it is not so much how people perceive the risk that we are trying to modify as *how they act*. In such examples as COVID-19 or climate warming, if we take those risks seriously, we tend to think that others should act a certain way, not in their own interest, as would be the case if the risk was individual, but in the name of social/environmental values, for the sake of a mass of others, humans or nonhumans. Someone who perceives the risk of climate warming or COVID-19 as very serious is likely to think that others should see it as very serious too, or at least that they should act in the way those who see it that way act, in supporting policies that limit green gases emissions and promote the development of renewable forms of energy or in practicing distancing and wearing a mask. If we think that the actions that conflict with those values are not okay, it is an ethical judgment. When we try to modify the perception of the risks, it is in an effort to modify the actions that contribute to this risk, under the intuition, evidenced by some studies, that the perception has an influence on the action. Those actions are seen as unethical in that they contribute to increasing the seriousness of the risk for others. We can aim at changing some perceptions not because they are illegitimate in the sense of incorrect but because they are more likely to motivate actions that we view as ethically unattractive or even condemnable. Then even though a perception is not in general correct or incorrect, it makes sense to say that it can be *improved*: it can be changed so as to motivate actions that are seen as ethically better.

There is no similar motivation to modify the perception of individual risks, because one's exposure to such risk is not directly related to others' actions, and others' actions do not directly contribute to the seriousness of this risk for others who are exposed to it. Still, in some cases we do try to modify the perception of some individual risks. We will try to convince a friend that they are too drunk to drive, even if they would be driving on an isolated road, and we recognize, at the social level, the value of trying to modify the perceptions of someone who has PTSD or phobia. In those cases, too, the justification can be seen as ethical, but not in the same sense as for modifying the perception of societal risks. The justification here is that some perceptions of individual risks may lead to action harmful to the perceiver and we may feel, for better or worse, that we have an ethical obligation to try to prevent them to be harmed.

4.5 Conclusion

The birth story of the concept of risk, as it appears in scientific risk assessment, locates its origin in the solution in the seventeenth century, by French mathematicians, of a puzzle related to games of chance: how do you fairly distribute the prize pot among the players when the game is suddenly interrupted (Bernstein 1996)? It would not be fair to divide it equally if some players have, by that point, a much better chance of winning. The solution, to put it in our modern terms, introduced the concept of expected value.

From there on, the development of the concept of risk is intertwined with the development of mathematical and statistical concepts and techniques. These provided increasingly refined methods to model uncertainty and expected value, and through the development of insurance companies, we became familiar with the representation of the future in terms of weighted options.

But the earlier story of the origin of the concept of risk locates this origin in the perception of dangers, when these, be they sickness or natural catastrophe, were perceived not just as one's own but as societal dangers, a threat to the stability of a social organization (Douglas 1992). Here the concept of risk is intertwined with the concepts of blame and transgression, and the perception of risk is steered by moral values and societal norms.

From that point of view, scientific assessment of risk addresses an abstraction. For it focuses on a limited range of considerations, of great practical use to be sure, but it does not tell the whole story of what it is like to experience risk. In particular, it omits what decades of studies of risk perception have now brought to light. We experience risks not in isolation but in relation with other risks. We may perceive some ways of dying or being harmed as worse than others, despite a similar result, because we take other characteristics into account. These include such features as controllability, delay of consequences, whether it is natural or man-made, our overall emotional state, or emotions triggered by the exposure to the risk, our social-cultural values, and the opinion of others in our social network.

An early explanation for the difference between risk perception and expert assessment was that people are bad at estimating probabilities. The rationale was that the seriousness of a risk is a function of the probability of the occurrence of the "bad," undesirable, unwanted, possible outcomes. Expert assessment in general involves statistical methods, and lay people are not trained in those methods.

But studies on risk perception have shown that whereas experts' assessment of risk is a function of probability, people's perception is not based or not solely based on an estimate of probability. It is based on many other factors. So even if it were possible to teach everybody how to take into consideration correct probabilities, it would not suffice to arrive at a shared perception. For there would still be other individual factors leading different people to perceive the riskiness of the same activity or phenomenon in different ways.

One explanation that has been suggested to explain differences between results of risk assessment and of risk perception is that laypeople are using *a different conception* of risk, even if it is an implicit one (Slovic & Weber 2002). Thus, Paul Slovic writes:

> Many conflicts between experts and laypeople regarding the acceptability of particular risks are the result of different definitions of the concept of risk and thus often different assessments of the magnitude of the riskiness of a given action or technology, rather than differences in opinions about acceptable levels of risk.
>
> (Slovic 2002: 10)

It is a very attractive proposal. But this way of thinking of risk in terms of distinct concepts for the experts and for the public makes it a bit difficult to make sense of the reality of public discussions of risk, between experts and the public. It also suggests that the experts' perception of the risks either would not exist or could be kept separate from their assessment, and that has been shown to be false, as we will see in the next chapter.

Another way to understanding the disagreement between individuals' perception and between perception and experts' assessment is to settle on one general concept of risk in terms of uncertainty and exposure to unwanted consequences. But what counts as negative consequence is much more strictly defined, and much narrower, for experts' assessment than for informal, laypeople perceptions.

That risk perception is a reflection of personal experience and of other personal factors, such as social-cultural beliefs and values or emotional reaction to the situation, is sometimes given as a reason to doubt the possibility of reasonable disagreement. Is any risk perception, then, just as legitimate as any other?

Our practice speaks against this. In some cases, if we differ, we may take the other's position as a matter of legitimate personal judgment. Someone might find eating meat, or fish, or eating in restaurants, too risky because of the danger of food poisoning, and we might not contest that, even if we do not share that judgment. But this is not always how we react toward others' risk perceptions. Disagreement around the risk of COVID-19 or climate change, for instance, has been not just vocal but supported by evidence both about the nature of the phenomenon and its current and expected impacts. This is typical in a case where risk perception has social implications, where the relevant actions have consequences for others and for a society as a whole, and so we care about what other people will do to lower the risk, and so we care about how they perceive it.

Risk perception is something that expresses one's personal outlook; it is a product of one's personal experience, social-cultural worldview, values, and social interactions. Taken as such, someone's risk perceptions are their own and a fortiori legitimate. But from this it is not to be inferred that they cannot be disputed or corrected.

It makes sense to try to correct them because this is a way to modify the way people will act toward the risk. And it is also possible to modify them because, as studies in risk perception have shown, there are *reasons* for how people perceive risk.

The reasons for how people perceive risk may not all be explicit to the perceiver. But the reasons that are explicit (e.g., one may think that climate warming is totally under control or mostly independent of human activity) can be discussed, and some that are implicit could be brought to light in the course of the discussion (one may realize that their perception is influenced by some fear or anger that is, in fact, not appropriate). The factors influencing risk perception are possible topics of discussion and topics about which some people may come to change their mind. So risk perception can be both a subjective judgment in that it is based, at least in part, on some personal factors and also something that can be changed. And it can be changed in ways that may be beneficial to the perceiver because the process of reflecting on one's perception of certain risk can be an opportunity to question beliefs, values, or emotional reactions.

Review questions

The psychometric approach

Q1

Studies of risk perception using the psychometric paradigm have found that people often perceive risk differently from experts mostly because . . .

A. They make an erroneous estimate of the uncertainty or the severity associated with the risk situation.
B. They are influenced by characteristics of the risk situation other than those taken into account by experts.
C. Experts' evaluation of risk is influenced by hidden value judgments.

Q2

About "unrealistic optimism." The comparison between ratings of general risks (risks for others) and ratings of personal risks (risks for oneself) shows that . . .

A. General risks tend to be rated higher than personal risks.
B. General risks tend to be rated lower than personal risks.
C. General risks tend to be rated about the same as personal risks.

Q3

A criticism of the conclusions from studies based on the psychometric paradigm is that:

A. Those conclusions are based on averages and so might not be indicative of the risk perception of individuals.
B. Those conclusions are not based on empirical data but only on hypothetical data.
C. Those conclusions cannot be replicated because the procedure to obtain the data is unclear.

The sociocultural approach

Q4

On what basis are the sociocultural contexts of the cultural theory characterized?

A. Education and income.
B. Organization and interaction.
C. Race and gender.

Q5

According to the social-cultural theory, perception of risk . . .

A. Cannot be studied scientifically because it depends on sociocultural values.
B. Cannot be quantified because it depends on the sociocultural context.
C. Is not an individual phenomenon but depends on the social group an individual belongs to.

Q6

According to the social-cultural theory, the social-cultural context influences perception of risk and perception of nature. Which of the following claims is true?

A. Egalitarians see risks as a possible source of injustice and nature as vulnerable.
B. Individualists see risks as opportunities and see nature as having to be protected.
C. Hierarchists try to eliminate risks and see nature as unpredictable.

Q7

According to the cultural cognition hypothesis:

A. Social and cultural values have an effect on perception of risk that is distinct and independent from how different characteristics of the situation are perceived.
B. Social and cultural values influence cognitive processes, including how different characteristics of the risky situation are perceived.
C. The perception of different characteristics of the risk has an influence of which cultural values are embraced by the perceiver.

Q8

What is an important difference between the social-cultural approach and the social network approach?

A. The social network approach, but not the sociocultural approach, construes interaction with other individuals as having no direct effect on risk perception.
B. The social network approach, but not the sociocultural approach, construes other individuals in the social group as simply source of information.
C. The social network approach, but not the sociocultural approach, construes social relations as having a direct effect on risk perception.

Feelings and emotions

Q9

On the influence of feelings and emotions on risk perception. What does it mean that affect heuristic is based on a valence-based conception of feelings?

A. It represents feelings as patterns of more basic evaluations of the aspects of the situation.
B. It uses a categorization of feelings as being either positive or negative.
C. It assumes that some feelings have more or less significance than others.

Q10

According to the appraisals-based conception of emotions . . .

A. Emotions are appraised as positive or negative depending on their effect on risk perception.
B. Different emotions may have the same valence without having the same effect on risk perception.
C. Risk is appraised as positive or negative depending on emotions.

Discussion topics

Topic 1

Do you think that sometimes the way some people perceive certain risks needs to be corrected? Why do you think they should or should not be corrected, using some specific examples of social risks and individual risks? If you think that sometimes risk perceptions should be corrected, what should be the perception reference used to correct them? If you do not think risk perceptions need to be corrected, does that mean all risk perceptions are equally valid?

Topic 2

Do you know of some examples where the public's perception of a risk and the experts' assessment of the risk are, for a large part, dissonant? What do you think explains the dissonance, and what do you think may hamper, on each side, a mutual understanding?

Notes

1 Van der Linden et al. 2015; Spence et al. 2012. And there are also studies that produced evidence that high risk perception does not necessarily translate into action. See Haynes et al. (2008) and Wachinger et al. (2013).
2 Fischhoff et al. 1978; Slovic et al. 1980, 1985; Slovic 1987.
3 In this study, respondents were also presented with another questionnaire measuring their affective reaction to the item and their perception of different characteristics typical of the psychometric paradigm (known, unknown; familiar, unfamiliar; old, new; dread, not dread; voluntary, compulsory; fatal, not fatal; controllable, uncontrollable).
4 European Commission, 2008. *Attitudes towards Radioactive Waste*. TNS Opinion & Social, Brussels.
5 See, for instance, Vandermoere et al. 2010; Dragojlovic & Einsiedel 2013; Tenbült et al. 2005.
6 HPV is a sexually transmitted virus that causes cervical cancer. Public health officials have recommended, in 2006, that all girls aged 11 or 12 be vaccinated, but political controversy, with critics claiming that the vaccine causes harmful side effects and will increase unsafe sex among teens, has blocked adoption of mandatory school-enrollment vaccination programs in all but one state (Kahan et al. 2010).
7 Sujata Gupta, *Science News*, May 14, 2020 (interview with Jennifer Lerner).
8 *The Washington Post*, University of Maryland poll released May 13, 2020.
9 See the discussion of prospect theory in Chapter 2 (we perceive small losses more acutely than we perceive small gains, and that goes for their chances too).

References

Abelson, R. P., Aronsnn, E., McGuire, W. J., Newcomb, T. M., Rosenberg, M. J., & Tannenbaum, P. H. (eds.). (1968). *Theories of cognitive consistency*. Chicago: Rand McNally.

Adams, J. (1995). *Risk*. New York: Routledge.

Akerlof, K., Maibach, E. W., Fitzgerald, D., Cedeno, A. Y., & Neuman, A. (2013). "Do people 'personally experience' global warming, and if so how, and does it matter?" *Global Environmental Change*, 23: 81–91. https://doi.org/10.1016/j.gloenvcha.2012.07.006.

Alhakami, A. S., & Slovic, P. (1994). "A psychological study of the inverse relationship between perceived risk and perceived benefit." *Risk Analysis*, 14: 1085–1096.

Alpers, G. W. (2010). "Avoiding treatment failures in specific phobias." In M. W. Otto & S. G. Hofmann (eds.), *Series in anxiety and related disorders* (pp. 209–227). New York: Springer Science and Business Media.

Bassarak, C., Pfister, H. R., & Böhm, G. (2017). "Dispute and morality in the perception of societal risks: Extending the psychometric model." *Journal of Risk Research*, 20(3): 299–325. https://doi.org/10.1080/13669877.2015.1043571.

Bernstein, P. L. (1996). *Against the gods. The remarkable story of risk*. New York: John Wiley & Sons.

Böhm, G., & Pfister, H.-R. (2001). "Mental representation of global environmental risks." *Research in Social Problems and Public Policy*, 9 (Special Issue: Environmental risks: Perception, Evaluation, and Management): 1–30. https://doi.org/10.1016/S0196-1152(01)80022-3.

Boholm, Å. (1996). "The cultural theory of risk: An anthropological critique." *Ethnos*, 61: 64–84.

Bostrom, A., et al. (2012). "Causal thinking and support for climate change policies: International survey findings." *Global Environmental Change*, 22(1): 210–222. DOI: 10.1016/j.gloenvcha.2011.09.012.

Bottemanne, H., Morlaàs, O., Fossati, P., & Schmidt, L. (2020). "Does the coronavirus epidemic take advantage of human optimisim bias?" *Frontiers in Psychology*. https://doi.org/10.3389/fpsyg.2020.02001 www.frontiersin.org/articles/10.3389/fpsyg.2020.02001/full.

Bourassa, M., Doraty, K., Berdahl, L., Fried, J., & Bell, S. (2016). "Support, opposition, emotion and contentious issue risk perception." *International Journal of Public Sector Management*, 29(2): 201–216. DOI: 10.1108/IJPSM-10–2015–0172.

Bronfman, N. C., & Cifuentes, L. A. (2003). "Risk perception in a developing country: The case of Chili." *Risk Analysis*, 23(6): 1271–1285. DOI: 10.1111/j.0272–4332.2003.00400.x.

Butler, G., & Matthews, A. (1987). "Anticipatory anxiety and risk perception." *Cognitive Therapy and Research*, 11: 551–565.

Calsyn, M., Gee, E., Waldrop, T., & Rapfogel, N. (2020). "Social distancing to fight coronavirus: A strategy that is working and must continue." Center for American Progress. www.americanprogress.org/issues/healthcare/news/2020/03/25/482278/social-distancing-fight-coronavirus-strategy-working-must-continue/.

Cartwright, N. D., Hardie, J., Montuschi, E., Soleiman, S., & Thresher, A. (forthcoming). *The Tangle of Science*. Oxford University Press.

Clore, G. L., Schwarz, N., & Conway, M. (1994). "Affective causes and consequences of social information processing." In R. S. Wyers & T. K. Srull (eds.), *Handbook of social cognition* (pp. 232–417). Mahwah, NJ: Lawrence Erlbaum Associates.

Cobb, M. D. (2005). "Framing effects on public opinion about nanotechnology." *Science Communication*, 27: 221–239. ISSN: 1075–5470, 1552–8545.

Cohen, B. (1998). "Public perception versus results of scientific risk analysis." *Reliability Engineering & System Safety*, 59(1): 101–105. https://doi.org/10.1016/S0951-8320(97)00130-0.

Cori, L., Bianchi, F., Cadum, E., & Anthonj, C. (2020). "Risk perception and COVID-19." *International Journal of Environmental Research and Public Health*, 17(9): 3114. DOI: 10.3390/ijerph17093114.

Cross, F. (1998). "Facts and values in risk assessment." *Reliability Engineering and System Safety*, 59: 27–40. https://doi.org/10.1016/S0951-8320(97)00116-6.

Dake, K. (1991). "Orienting dispositions in the perception of risk: An analysis of contemporary worldviews and cultural biases." *Journal of Cross-Cultural Psychology*, 22: 61–82.

De Groot, J. I. M., Schweiger, E., & Schubert, I. (2020). "Social influence, risk and benefit perceptions, and the acceptability of risky energy technologies: An explanatory model of nuclear power versus shale gas." *Risk Analysis*, 40(6): 1226–1243. DOI: 10.1111/risa.13457.

Douglas, M. (1966). *Purity and danger: An analysis of concepts of pollution and taboo*. London: Routledge.

Douglas, M. (1992). *Risk and blame. Essays in cultural theory*. New York: Routledge.

Douglas, M., & Wildavsky, A. (1982). *Risk and culture: An essay on the selection of technological and environmental dangers*. Berkeley: University of California Press.

Dragojlovic, N., & Einsiedel, E. (2013). "Framing synthetic biology: Evolutionary distance, conceptions of nature, and the unnaturalness objection." *Science Communication*, 35: 547–571. https://doi.org/10.1177/1075547012470707.

Dryhurst, S., Schneider, C. R., Kerr, J., Freeman, L. J., Recchia, G., van der Bles, A. M., Spiegelhalter, D., & van der Linden, S. (2020). "Risk perceptions of COVID-19 around the world." *Journal of Risk Research*, 23(7–8). DOI: 10.1080/13669877.2020.1758193.

Earle, T. C., & Cvetkovich, G. (1995). *Social trust: Toward a cosmopolitan society*. Westport, CT: Praeger.

Evans, D. (2012). *Risk intelligence: How to live with uncertainty*. New York: Free Press.

Feltz, A. (2007). "The Knobe effect: A brief overview." *The Journal of Mind and Behavior*, 28(3/4): 265–277.

Finucane, M. L., Alhakami, A., Slovic, P., & Johnson, S. M. (2000). "The affect heuristic in judgments of risks and benefits." *Journal of Behavioral Decision Making*, 13(1): 1–17. https://doi.org/10.1002/(SICI)1099-0771(200001/03)13:1 < 1::AID-BDM333 > 3.0.CO;2-S.

Fischhoff, B., Slovic, P., Lichtenstein, S., & Read, S. J. (1978). "How safe is safe enough? A psychometric study of attitudes towards technological risks and benefits." *Policy Science*, 9: 127–152.

Fiske, S. T., & Taylor, S. E. (1991). *Social cognition*. New York: McGraw-Hill.

Frewer, L. J., Howard, C., & Shepherd, R. (1996). "Effective communication about genetic engineering and food." *British Food Journal*, 98: 48–52.

Garrett, N., González-Garzón, A., Foulkes, L., Levita, L., & Sharot, T. (2018). "Updating beliefs under perceived threat." *Journal of Neuroscience*, 38: 7901–7911. DOI: 10.1523/JNEUROSCI.0716-18.2018.

Hacking, I. (2015). "Let's not talk about objectivity." In J. Y. Tsou, A. Richardson, & F. Padovani (eds.), *Objectivity in science* (pp. 19–33). Berlin: Springer Verlag.

Hayakawa, H., Fischbech, P. S., & Fischhoff, B. (2000). "Traffic accident statistics and risk perceptions in Japan and the United States." *Accident Analysis and Prevention*, 32(6): 827–835.

Haynes, K., Barclay, J., & Pidgeon, N. (2008). "Whose reality counts? Factors affecting the perception of volcanic risk." *Journal of Volcanology and Geothermal Research*, 172: 259–272. DOI: 10.1016/j.jvolgeores.2007.12.012.

Hengen, K. M., & Alpers, G. W. (2019). "What's the risk? Fearful individuals generally overestimate negative outcomes and they dread outcomes of specific events." *Frontiers in Psychology*, 10: 1676. DOI: 10.3389/fpsyg.2019.01676.

Ho, S. S., Leong, A. D., Looi, J., Chen, L., Pang, N., & Tandoc, E., Jr. (2019). "Science literacy or value predisposition? A meta-analysis of factors predicting public perceptions of benefits, risks, and acceptance of nuclear energy." *Environmental Communication*, 13(4): 457–471. https://doi.org/10.1080/17524032.2017.1394891.

Ibuka, Y., Chapman, G. B., Meyers, L. A., Li, M., & Galvani, A. P. (2010). "The dynamics of risk perceptions and precautionary behavior in response to 2009 (H1N1) pandemic influenza." *BMC Infectious Diseases*, 10: 296. https://doi.org/10.1186/1471-2334-10-296.

Jackson, J., Allum, N., & Gaskell, G. (2006). "Bridging the levels of analysis in risk perception research: The case of the fear of crime." *Forum: Qualitative Social Research*, 7(1): 20. [On-line Journal]. https://doi.org/10.17169/fqs-7.1.63.

Jefferson, A., Bortolotti, L., & Kuzmanovic, B. (2017). "What is unrealistic optimism?" *Consciousness and Cognition*, 50: 3–11. DOI: 10.1016/j.concog.2016.10.005.

Jenkin, C. M. (2006). "Risk perception and terrorism applying the psychometric paradigm." *Homeland Security Affairs*, 2, Article 6. www.hsaj.org/articles/169.

Jobin, M., & Siegrist, M. (2020). "Support for the deployment of climate engineering: A comparison of ten different technologies." *Risk Analysis*, 40(5): 1058–1078. https://doi.org/10.1111/risa.13462.

Johnson, B. P. (1993). "Advancing understanding of knowledge's role in lay risk perception." *Risk – Issues in Health and Safety*, 4: 189–211.

Kahan, D. M. (2010). "Fixing the communications failure." *Nature*, 463: 296–297. https://doi.org/10.1038/463296a.

Kahan, D. M. (2012). "Why we are poles apart on climate change." *Nature*, 488(7411): 255. DOI: 10.1038/488255a.

Kahan, D. M., Braman, D., Cohen, G. L., Gastil, J., & Slovic, P. (2010). "Who fears the HPV vaccine, who doesn't and why: An experimental study of the mechanisms of cultural cognition." *Law and Human Behavior*, 34(6): 501–516. DOI: 10.1007/s10979-009-9201-0.

Kahan, D. M., Braman, D., Slovic, P., Gastil, J., & Cohen, G. (2009). "Cultural cognition of the risks and benefits of nanotechnology." *Nature Nanotechnology*, 4(2): 87–90. DOI: 10.1038/nnano.2008.341.

Kaptan, G., Fischer, A. R. H., & Frewer, L. J. (2018). "Extrapolating understanding of food risk perceptions to emerging food safety cases." *Journal of Risk Research*, 21(8): 996–1018. https://doi.org/10.1080/13669877.2017.1281330.

Kerr, J. R., & Wilson, M. S. (2018). "Changes in perceived scientific consensus shift beliefs about climate change and GM food safety." *PLOS ONE*, 13(7): e0200295. https://doi.org/10.1371/journal.pone.0200295.

Knobe, J. (2003a). "Intentional action and side-effects in ordinary language." *Analysis*, 63: 190–194. https://doi.org/10.1093/analys/63.3.190.

Knobe, J. (2003b). "Intentional action in folk psychology: An experimental investigation." *Philosophical Psychology*, 16: 309–323.

Knobe, J. (2004). "Intention, intentional action, and moral considerations." *Analysis*, 64: 181–187. https://doi.org/10.1093/analys/64.2.181.

Kohler, H.-P., Behrman, J. R., & Watkins, S. C. (2007). "Social networks and HIV/AIDS risk perceptions." *Demography*, 44(1): 1–33. DOI: 10.1353/dem.2007.0006.

Lazarus, R. S., Averill, J. R., & Opton Jr., E. M. (1970). "Toward a *cognitive theory* of *emotion*." In M. Arnold (ed.), *Third international symposium on feelings and emotions*. New York: Academic Press.

Leiserowitz, A. (2006). "Climate change risk perception and policy preferences: The role of affect, imagery and values." *Climatic Change*, 77(1–2): 45–72. https://doi.org/10.1007/s10584-006-9059-9.

Lerner, J. S., Gonzalez, R. M., Small, D. A., & Fischhoff, B. (2003). "Effects of fear and anger on perceived risks of terrorism: A national field experiment." *Psychological Science*, 14: 144–150. DOI: 10.1111/1467-9280.01433.

Lerner, J. S., & Keltner, D. (2000). "Beyond valence: Toward a model of emotion-specific influences on judgement and choice." *Condition and Emotion*, 14(4): 473–493.

Lerner, J. S., & Keltner, D. (2001). "Fear, anger, and risk." *Journal of Personality and Social Psychology*, 81(1): 146–159.

Loewenstein, G. F., Weber, E. U., Hsee, C. K., & Welch, N. (2001). "Risk as feelings." *Psychological Bulletin*, 127(2): 267–286. https://doi.org/10.1037/0033-2909.127.2.267.

Marris, C., Langford, I. H., Saunderson, T., & O'Riordan, T. (1997). "Exploring the 'psychometric paradigm': Comparisons between aggregate and individual analyses." *Risk Analysis*, 17(3): 303–312. https://doi.org/10.1111/j.1539-6924.1997.tb00868.x.

Marris, C., Langford, I. H., & O'Riordan, T. (1996). "Integrating sociological and psychological approaches to public perceptions of environmental risks." CSERGE Working Paper GEC 96–07. Centre for Social and Economic Research into the Global Environment, Norwich.

Marris, C., Langford, I. H., & O'Riordan, T. (1998). "A quantitative test of the cultural theory of risk perception: Comparison with the psychometric paradigm." *Risk Analysis*, 18(5): 635–647.

McKenna, F. P. (1993). "It won't happen to me: Unrealistic optimism or illusion of control?" *British Journal of Psychology*, 84: 39–50.
Mellers, B. A., & McGraw, A. P. (2001). "Anticipated emotions as guides to choice." *Current Directions in Psychological Science*, 10(6): 210–214. https://doi.org/10.1111/1467-8721.00151.
Mueller, E. M., Nguyen, J., Ray, W. J., & Borkovec, T. D. (2010). "Future-oriented decision-making in generalized anxiety disorder is evident across different versions of the Iowa gambling task." *Journal of Behavior Therapy and Experimental Psychiatry*, 41(2): 165–171. https://doi.org/10.1016/j.jbtep.2009.12.002.
Muter, B., Gore, M., & Riley, S. (2012). "Social contagion of risk perceptions in environmental management networks." *Risk Analysis*, 33(8): 1489–1499. https://doi.org/10.1111/j.1539-6924.2012.01936.x.
Okrent, D., & Pidgeon, N. (eds.). (1998). "Special issue: Risk perception vs. risk analysis." *Reliability Engineering and System Safety*, 59.
Oltedal, S., Moen, B. E., Klempe, H., & Rundmo, T. (2004). "Explaining risk perception: An evaluation of cultural theory." *Rotunde* (85). Trondheim: Norway: Norwegian University of Science and Technology, Department of Psychology (p. 28).
Perloff, L. S., & Fetzer, B. K. (1986). "Self-other judgments and perceived vulnerability to victimization." *Journal of Personality and Social Psychology*, 50: 502–510.
Peters, E., & Slovic, P. (1996). "The world of affects and worldviews as orienting dispositions in the perception and acceptance of nuclear power." *Journal of Applied Social Psychology*, 26(16): 1427–1453.
Raimi, K. T., Wolske, K. S., Sol Hart, P., & Campbell-Arvai, V. (2020). "The aversion to tampering with nature (ATN) scale: Individual differences in (dis)comfort with altering the natural world." *Risk Analysis*, 40(3): 638–656. DOI: 10.1111/risa.13414.
Rippl, S. (2002). "Cultural theory and risk perception: A proposal for a better measurement." *Journal of Risk Research*, 5(2): 147–165. https://doi.org/10.1080/13669870110042598.
Robinson, W. S. (1950). "Ecological correlations and the behavior of individuals." *American Sociological Review*, 15: 351–357.
Rohrmann, B. (2008). "Risk perception, risk attitude, risk communication, risk management: A conceptual Appraisal." *The International Emergency Management Society (TIEMS) 2008 Annual Conference in Prague*. www.tiems. info/dmdocuments/events/TIEMS_2008_Bernd_Rohrmann_ Keynote.pdf.
Rudisill, C. (2012). "How do we handle new health risks? Risk perception, optimism and behaviors regarding the new H1 virus." *Journal of Risk Research*, 16(8): 959–980. https://doi.org/10.1080/13669877.2012.761271.
Scherer, C. W., & Cho, H. (2003). "A social network contagion theory of risk perception." *Risk Analysis*, 23(2): 261–267.
Scherer, K. R. (1988). *Facets of emotion: Recent research*. Hillsdale, NJ: Erlbaum.
Schwarz, N. (1990). "Feelings as information: Informational and motivational functions of affective states." In T. Higgins & R. Sorrentino (eds.), *Handbook of motivation and cognition: Foundations of social behavior* (vol. 2, pp. 527–561). New York: Guilford.
Siegrist, M. (1999). "A causal model explaining the perception and acceptance of gene technology." *Journal of Applied Social Psychology*, 29: 2093–2106.
Siegrist, M. (2000). "The influence of trust and perceptions of risks and benefits on the acceptance of gene technology." *Risk Analysis*, 20: 195–203. DOI: 10.1111/0272–4332.202020.
Siegrist, M., & Cvetkovich, G. (2000). "Perception of hazards: The role of social trust and knowledge." *Risk Analysis*, 20(5): 713–719. https://doi.org/10.1111/0272-4332.205064.
Siegrist, M., & Sütterlin, B. (2014). "Human and nature-caused hazards: The affect heuristic causes biased decisions." *Risk Analysis*, 34(8): 1482–1494. DOI: 10.1111/risa.12179.

Sivak, M., Soler, J., Trankle, U., & Spagnhol, J. M. (1989). "Cross-cultural differences in driver risk-perception." *Accident Analysis and Prevention*, 2(4): 355–362.
Sjöberg, L. (1996). "Risk perceptions by politicians and the public." RHIZIKON: Risk Research Reports, 23, Center for Risk Research, Stockholm School of Economics.
Sjöberg, L. (1997). "Explaining risk perception: An empirical evaluation of cultural theory." *Risk Decision and Policy*, 2(2): 113e130.
Sjöberg, L. (1998). "World views, political attitudes and risk perception." *Risk: Health, Safety and Environment*, 9: 137–152.
Sjöberg, L. (1999). "Risk perception by the public and by experts: A dilemma in risk management." *Research in Human Ecology*, 6(2): 1–9.
Sjöberg, L. (2000). "Factors in risk perception." *Risk Analysis*, 20(1): 1–11. https://doi.org/10.1111/0272-4332.00001.
Sjöberg, L., & Drottz-Sjöberg, B. M. (1993). "Moral value, risk and risk tolerance." RHIZIKON: Risk Research Report, 11, Center for Risk Research, Stockholm School of Economics.
Sjöberg, L., & Winroth, E. (1986). "Risk, moral value of actions, and mood." *Scandinavian Journal of Psychology*, 27: 191–208.
Sloman, S. A. (1996). "The empirical case for two systems of reasoning." *Psychological Bulletin*, 119: 3–22.
Slovic, P. (1987). "Perception of risk." *Science*, 236(4799): 280–285.
Slovic, P. (2000). *The perception of risk*. London: Routledge.
Slovic, P., Finucane, M., Petrs, E., & MacGregor, D. G. (2004). "Risk as analysis and risk as feelings: Some thoughts about affect, reason, risk, and rationality." *Risk Analysis*, 24(2): 1–12. https://doi.org/10.1111/j.0272-4332.2004.00433.x.
Slovic, P., Fischhoff, B., & Lichtenstein, S. (1980). "Facts and fears: Understanding perceived risk." In R. Schwing & W. A. Albers, Jr. (eds.), *Societal risk assessment: How safe is safe enough?* (pp. 181–214). New York: Plenum.
Slovic, P., Fischhoff, B., & Lichtenstein, S. (1982). "Why study risk perception?" *Risk Analysis*, 2(2): 83–93.
Slovic, P., Fischhoff, B., & Lichenstein, S. (1985). "Characterizing perceived risk." In R. W. Kates, C. Hohenemser, & J. X. Kasperson (eds.), *Perilous progress: Managing the hazards of technology* (pp. 91–125). Boulder, CO: Westview.
Slovic, P., Flynn, J. H., & Layman, M. (1991). "Perceived risk, trust, and the politics of nuclear waste." *Science*, 254(5038): 1603–1607.
Slovic, P., Flynn, J. H., Mertz, C. K., Poumadere, M., & Mays, C. (2000). "Nuclear power and the public: A comparative study of risk perception in France and the United States." In O. Renn & B. Rohrmann (eds.), *Cross-cultural risk perception* (pp. 55–102). Boston, MA: Kluwer Academic.
Slovic, P., Kraus, N. N., Lapp, H., & Major, M. (1991). "Risk perception of prescription drugs: Report on a survey in Canada." *Canadian Journal of Public Health*, 82: S15S20.
Slovic, P., & Weber, E. U. (2002, April 12–13). "Perception of risk posed by extreme events." Paper prepared for discussion at the conference "Risk Management strategies in an Uncertain World," Palisades, New York.
Smith, C. A., & Ellsworth, P. C. (1985). "Patterns of cognitive appraisal in emotion." *Journal of Personality and Social Psychology*, 48(4): 813–838.
Spence, A., Poortinga, W., & Pidgeon, N. (2012). "The psychological distance of climate change." *Risk Analysis*, 32(6): 957–72. DOI: 10.1111/j.1539-6924.2011.01695.x.
Starr, C. (1969). "Social benefits versus technological risks." *Science*, 165(3899): 1232–1238.

Sunstein, C. (2007). "Moral heuristics and risk." In T. Lewens (ed.), *Risk: Philosophical perspectives* (pp. 156–170). New York: Routledge.
Taylor-Gooby, P., & Zinn, J. (2006). "Risk in social science." In P. Taylor-Gooby & J. Zinn (eds.), *The challenge of managing new risks*. Oxford: Oxford University Press.
Teigen, K. H., Brun, W., & Slovic, P. (1988). "Societal risks as seen by the Norwegian public." *Journal of Behavioural Decision Making*, 1(2): 111–130.
Tenbült, P., de Vries, N. K., DrEezens, E., & Martijn, C. (2005). "Perceived naturalness and acceptance of genetically modified food." *Appetite*, 45: 47–50. DOI: 10.1016/j.appet.2005.03.004.
Thomas, A. J., Stanford, P. K., & Sarnecka, B. W. (2016a). "No child left alone: Moral judgments about parents affect estimates of risk to children." *Collabra*, 2(1): 10. https://doi.org/10.1525/collabra.33.
Thomas, A. J., Stanford, P. K., & Sarnecka, B. W. (2016b). "Correction: No child left alone: Moral judgments about parents affect estimates of risk to children." *Collabra*, 2(1): 12. http://dx.doi.org/10.1525/collabra.58.
Thomas, M., Partridge, T., Harthorn, B., & Pidgeon, N. (2017). "Deliberating the perceived risks, benefits, and societal implications of shale gas and oil extraction by hydraulic fracturing in the US and UK." *Nat Energy*, 2: 17054. https://doi.org/10.1038/nenergy.2017.54.
Thompson, M., Ellis, R., & Wildavsky, A. (1990). *Cultural theory*. New York: Routledge.
Tversky, A., & Kahneman, D. (1974). "Judgement under uncertainty: Heuristics and biases." *Science*, 185(4157): 1124–1131.
van der Linden, S. L. (2015). "The social-psychological determinants of climate change risk perceptions: Towards a comprehensive model." *Journal of Environmental Psychology*, 41: 112–124. https://doi.org/10.1016/j.jenvp.2014.11.012.
van der Linden, S. L., Leiserowitz, A. A., Feinberg, G. D., & Maibach, E. W. (2015). "The scientific consensus on climate change as a gateway belief: Experimental evidence." *PLOS ONE*, 10(2): e0118489. https://doi.org/10.1371/journal.pone.0118489.
van der Weerd, W., Timmermans, D. R., Beaujean, D. J., Oudhoff, J., van Steenbergen, J. E. (2011). "Monitoring the level of government trust, risk perception and intention of the general public to adopt protective measures during the influenza A (H1N1) pandemic in the Netherlands." *BMC Public Health*, 11(1): 575. https://bmcpublichealth.biomedcentral.com/articles/10.1186/1471-2458-11-575.
Vandermoere, F., Blanchemanche, S., Bieberstein, A., et al. (2010). "The morality of attitudes toward nanotechnology: About God, techno-scientific progress, and interfering with nature." *The Journal of Nanoparticle Research*, 12: 373–381. https://doi.org/10.1007/s11051-009-9809-5.
Visschers, V., Keller, C., & Siegrist, M. (2011). "Climate change benefits and energy supply benefits and acceptance of nuclear power stations: Investigating an explanatory model." *Energy Policy*, 39: 3621–3629.
Wachinger, G., Renn, O., Begg, C., & Kuhlicke, C. (2013). "The risk perception paradox – implications for governance and communication of natural hazards." *Risk Analysis*, 33: 1049–1065. https://doi.org/10.1111/j.1539-6924.2012.01942.x.
Weenigh, M. W., & Midden, C. J. H. (1991). "Communication network influences on information diffusion and persuasion." *Journal of Personality and Social Psychology*, 61(5): 734–742.
Weinstein, N. D. (1980). "Unrealistic optimism about future life events." *Journal of Personality and Social Psychology*, 39: 806–820.
Weinstein, N. D. (1984). "Why it won't happen to me: Perceptions of risk factors and susceptibility." *Health Psychology*, 3: 431–457.

Whitfield, S. C., Rosa, E. A., Dan, A., & Dietz, T. (2009). "The future of nuclear power: Value orientations and risk perception." *Risk Analysis*, 29: 425–437. DOI: 10.1111/j.1539–6924.2008.01155.x.

Wildavsky, A., & Dake, K. (1990). "Theories of risk perception: Who fears what and why?" *Daedalus*, 119: 41–60.

Wise, T., Zbozinek, T. D., Michelini, G., Hagan, C. C., & Mobbs, D. (2020). "Changes in risk perception and protective behavior during the first week of the COVID-19 pandemic in the United States." *Royal Society Open Science*, 7: 200742. http://doi.org/10.1098/rsos.200742.

Wolske, K., Raimi, K. T., Campbell-Arvai, V., & Sol Hart, P. (2019). "Public support for carbon dioxide removal strategies: The role of tampering with nature perceptions." *Climatic Change*, 152: 345–361. https://doi.org/10.1007/s10584-019-02375-z.

Zhale, J. (2021). "Objective data sets in qualitative research." *Synthese*, 199: 101–117. https://doi.org/10.1007/s11229-020-02630-2.

5 Risk management

Contents

DOI: 10.4324/9780429023521-6

In Chapter 2, we discussed how an individual might come to recognize and make decisions about taking or accepting a personal risk. The focus was therefore on *individual* decision-making. "Risk management," on the other hand, is a kind of catchall term that encompasses efforts to make *societal* decisions, which are informed by a great number of individual opinions (Shrader-Frechette 1985: 401).[1] Such opinions include the assessments of experts (Chapter 3) and the perceptions of nonexperts (Chapter 4). They are geared toward risks that affect the health and safety of significant portions of the public or that have implications for human welfare in general. Economists Scott Farrow and W. Kip Viscusi (2011) offer the following list of areas that pertain to public safety and thus may expose people to risks of this nature (6):

1. Security: crimes, terrorism, defense
2. Safety: traffic, building codes
3. Natural hazards: waterway control, fire, wind, flood, earthquake, tsunami
4. Environment: water, hazardous waste, pollution, climate change
5. Public health: disease, sanitation
6. Products: food, motor vehicles, tobacco, drugs, and other consumer products
7. Employment: occupational risks

Scanning this list, the COVID-19 pandemic naturally comes to mind as a recent and profound example of a public health concern whose management has necessitated policy decisions at nearly all scales of government worldwide. Later in this chapter, we will describe and discuss the model for managing the early stage of the pandemic that was adopted by the US and other countries, namely, the "social distancing" model, along with some of the critical decisions that managing agencies faced when adopting this model.

One note before we proceed: risk management is a practice that pertains to many domains, including universities, trade industries, manufacturing plants, hotels, resorts, utilities providers, and private businesses. For practical reasons, we will limit our attention primarily to the management of risks by public offices charged with overseeing areas like those appearing in the list above. But keep in mind that much of what we discuss in this chapter is applicable to those other domains.

This chapter has three parts. In the first part, we summarize the main method by which decision makers select among different policy options – i.e., *cost-benefit analysis*. In the second part, we discuss an alternative approach that relies on the *precautionary principle*. In the third part, we discuss challenges faced by analysts and decision makers when attempting to communicate important messages about public risks and the policies meant to manage them.

5.1 Cost-benefit analysis (CBA)

Governments and regulatory agencies have a crucial role to play in making decisions about public safety that require analyzing risks and assessing options to manage them. Cost-benefit analysis (CBA)[2] is the standard economic method for performing the latter tasks and arriving at actionable decisions. US agencies that utilize the method include:

> Local police and health departments [;] state offices and national agencies such as the Federal Emergency Management Agency (FEMA), the U.S. Coast Guard, the Transportation Security Administration (TSA), the U.S. Environmental Protection Agency (EPA), the Consumer Product Safety Administration (CPSC), the Food and Drug Administration (FDA), the U.S. Army Corps of Engineers, and the U.S. Department of Transportation (DOT).
>
> (Farrow & Viscusi 2011)

The Centers for Disease Control (CDC) and the World Health Organization (WHO) also rely on the method and have used it most notably to investigate trade-offs and inform decisions about how best to manage the COVID-19 crisis. While cost-benefit analysis offers a framework for exploring a diverse range of issues, *its essential function is to determine whether and to what extent the aggregate benefits of a policy exceed its costs.* This enables the selection of options that are likely to be the most economically efficient (Robinson & Hammitt 2013). The focus on efficiency draws criticism from philosophers and others, because efficiency ignores ethical considerations, such as the distribution of positive and negative impacts across members of society.

We will consider such criticisms later in this chapter. (See sections titled "Distributional analysis" and "Democratizing the procedure.")

One attractive feature of cost-benefit analysis is that it ostensibly mirrors the informal deliberative process that individuals use to make decisions about accepting or taking risks. To judge whether an action is "worth the risk," we look for trade-offs between the benefits of the action and its potential for unwanted outcomes. But CBA excels over individual decision-making in its appearance as a highly rational and purportedly "objective" approach to decisions about risks. Users who see it this way tend to emphasize the "expert's role" in risk management and insist that the acceptability of a risk should be decided according to scientific facts. However, as we will see, the method inevitably requires practitioners to make choices and value judgments. Thus, CBA invokes the now-familiar tensions between experts and nonexperts, objectivity and subjectivity, facts and values, etc., that have appeared throughout this book and that, indeed, must appear in any substantive conversation about risk. These tensions must be acknowledged and allowed to guide philosophical, political, or economic critiques of CBA. But we will not regard them here as inherently detrimental to the method, since no decision about risk, be it individual or societal, can be made in their absence. Suffice it to say that the only initial danger is failing to recognize or accept the existence of these tensions.

In the following section, we describe the method of cost-benefit analysis in a series of steps. This allows us to point out some of the many difficulties that analysts and decision makers face when trying to determine which actions can be realistically expected to reduce adverse social risks and improve public safety and welfare (at acceptable costs). Some of these difficulties are "on the ground," or practical in nature (Nardinelli 2018). Others are theoretical or philosophical in nature. While we will discuss both kinds of difficulties, we may not always identify them by type.

5.1.1 The method

Governments at all levels enact policies and focus resources so as to maximize social welfare. As mentioned, cost-benefit analysis is the main method used by economists and others to achieve this aim. It delivers a measure of the net benefits of a project or action by summing its potential rewards and subtracting from this the sum of its costs. Law professor Daniel H. Cole describes cost-benefit as a six-step process (Cole 2009):

1. Identify the collective action problem[3] and determine the goal.
2. Identify policy alternatives, including no action.
3. Determine foreseeable impacts, including nonmarket impacts, of each of the alternatives over their expected life spans.

4. Assign values to those impacts,
   a. Favorable impacts = benefits.
   b. Unfavorable impacts = costs.
5. Discount future costs and benefits to present day dollars, and calculate the net present benefits or costs for each alternative.
6. Finally, compare the net benefits/costs of all alternatives and choose the alternative with the greatest net benefits or lowest net costs.

Note that these six steps represent merely a simplified overview of CBA. The method is continually evolving, and we can expect considerable variation in conduct and complexity among real cases. We cannot hope to provide a comprehensive discussion of these variations, nor can we rigorously explain every step of the overview. Thus, in what follows, we focus our descriptions and explanations on the steps most relevant to our purposes in this chapter, namely, Steps 1 to 4. We expect our exposition to deliver the message that actual cost-benefit analysis is hard but very worthwhile.

Step 1: Identify the problem and determine the goal

Although Step 1 is listed as part of the CBA, it can be thought of as partly exogenous to method because it describes a process that regulating agencies responsible for managing public risks will have to undertake regardless of approach. Nevertheless, its inclusion suggests an ordering of events whereby societal risks are identified and evaluated prior to (or at least alongside) the development of regulations to manage them.[4] These stages where risks are being selected for intervention present numerous challenges. Governments tasked with distributing public goods and mitigating public health risks face a potentially endless array of issues but possess only so many funds/resources. For this reason, they cannot chase every issue and must make choices about which risks to accept and which to abate. Moreover, they must make decisions about the scale and priority of the risks so they can budget funds accordingly. This imposes an additional burden of selecting among differing principles and standards of prioritization (Hermansson 2010).

General difficulties. Decisions at this stage have drawn criticism from both economists and philosophers, which is understandable in light of the weighty demands. Philosopher Hélène Hermansson, for instance, is troubled by the fact that no consistent set of principles and standards exists for the assessment of risks by the many agencies responsible for public safety. For her, this absence disposes regulators to an "unsystematic management of risks" such that "societal resources are allocated arbitrarily between different risk-reducing areas," leading to inefficiencies and fewer lives saved (Hermansson 2005: 558).[5] This problem is compounded by influence from media, who "exaggerate one risk at the expense of another – putting exotic and sensational risks on the front-page while ordinary but far larger risks go unnoticed" (ibid., 557). Risk analysts and decision makers who are sensitive to these headlines can end up "devot[ing] large amounts of resources and attention to alleged dangers that are speculative (at best) and probably small (or even nonexistent)," while regrettably allocating too few resources to the reduction of significant social risks (Graham 1996, quoted in Hermansson 2005: 557).

Some have summarized these managerial pitfalls (be they real or potential) as resulting from too much deference on the part of decision makers to the irrational perceptions of nonexperts regarding risks that may require collective action. However, we have shown in Chapter 4 that there is little ground to dismiss these public perceptions as "irrational" *tout court*, even if they are heavily subject to manipulations by media. And it seems misguided to suggest, either explicitly or implicitly, that arbitrariness and inefficiencies surrounding the identification of societal risks and the distribution of resources to combat them could be solved by means of assessment that takes no account of public perceptions. For, as Hermansson suggests, "laypeople contribute with important aspects to risk issues by seeing things that the experts miss" (Hermansson 2010: 502). They are also, presumably, "the best judge of their own interests";[6] thus, including their views in risk decisions might "make them more legitimate and lead to better results" (Fiorino 1990, quoted in Hermansson 2010: 502). We will explore these and similar suggestions at the end of this chapter, in the section titled "Democratizing the procedure."

Dynamics of assessment and management. Step 1 of our simplified overview urges consideration of something we first discussed in our chapter on risk assessment – namely, the dynamic, mutually informative relationship between the assessments of experts and the decisions of management. The existence of this relationship makes the process of identifying problems and setting goals all the more challenging to delineate and enact. This is largely because it resists conclusive resolutions, even as decisions are made and policies are implemented. Theoretically, concrete data from the assessment of public risks is necessary for, and thus should precede, the determination of management goals. This might look something like steps a to c in the following idealized scenario.

Risk Assessment

a. Scientists working independently of federal policy makers identify carcinogenic properties of an ingredient used to make a popular consumer product.
b. Experts then assess health risks associated with exposure to the ingredient.

Risk Management

c. Federal policy makers and analysts consider a possible ban on the ingredient to reduce exposure.

Those responsible for assessing the risks in step b of this story may require more or different data than was initially gathered by the scientists, and the scientists may thus need to do further research. But however much back-and-forth occurs between the researchers and the assessors, these exchanges are construed as part of an "assessment" process that will conclude prior to (and thus motivate) the development of regulatory aims.

Ongoing assessments. This simple sequence and associated explanation might represent a plausible narrative for how some public health risks are identified and managed. However, for larger or more enduring public health problems, the progression to regulation/solution is less linear, more complex, and more open to practical and philosophical criticism. Consider, for instance, the recent push in US society to rethink the function and funding of local police departments (Nix 2020). This push is motivated by outrage over events like the police killings of Breonna Taylor and George Floyd, but it is thought to be accompanied by evidence of racial bias in law enforcement, e.g., statistical disparities in the rates at which Blacks and Whites are subject to fatal police violence. Certainly, there must, over time, have been many nonanecdotal assessments that would draw attention to police violence and prompt analysts, decision makers, and the public to regard its occurrence as a most pressing "public health and racial justice problem" (Schwartz & Jahn 2020). However, assessments are still ongoing, and necessarily so, as policy makers and law enforcement agencies across the US struggle to develop clear and manageable goals for addressing the problem.

Variable framing. We explained this issue at the end of Chapter 3. Here we'll add one specific consideration that has general implications for the aims of Step 1 (in CBA). The way that a problem is *framed* at this stage can have an ongoing impact both on the development of policies and on the data required for future decisions. Schwartz and Jahn (2020) may have described police violence as a single problem concerning "public health and racial justice." However, public health and racial justice are different issues, and getting serious about either one will require disciplined framing. Framing the violence as a public health problem encourages thinking about risks to the general public of being shot by police. If so, then following Justin Nix (2020), the data that Schwartz and Jahn collected could prove useful, for instance, for locating "place-specific policy contexts" where incident rates are highest and thus for deciding where it might be best to introduce new initiatives and assign funds/resources. However, if Nix is correct, the disparity figures that appear in their data are insufficient for concluding that "officers disproportionately use deadly force against Black citizens," as we discussed earlier in §3.5.2.3. Thus, framing the issue as a problem of racial justice requires the collection of certain, more probative data along the lines of what Nix suggests in his article. Aims will adjust accordingly.

The general lesson from this example is that the way a risk gets framed will affect decisions at Step 1 (and maybe other steps) of the CBA. We need to recognize that this is a value-guided act, just like many other parts of the method. As such, it is open to ethical criticism and to inputs from the "subjective" perceptions of nonexperts. (For more, see "Democratizing the procedure" at the end of this chapter.)

Step 2: Identify policy alternatives, including no action

Although Step 2 appears as a unique move in CBA, it blends fairly seamlessly with the processes and decisions described beforehand for Step 1. This is because competing policies are a direct outgrowth of these activities. Here we have only to add that it is customary to estimate benefits and costs relative to a baseline. In other words, net benefits are determined by comparing the world with the policy intervention to the world without the intervention (Nardinelli 2018). If the net benefits are negative relative to the world without the intervention, the recommendation is that no action be taken. Societal risks that are sufficiently large or ongoing will typically yield many possible interventions. In these cases, CBA can be used to determine which policy is best.

Step 3: Determine foreseeable impacts

The number of impacts that might result from a risk-reducing initiative is nearly limitless. Thus, analysts must make explicit choices about when to stop conceiving of new outcomes and about which are the most salient and severe. Subjective value judgments inevitably inform these choices. This is because, as Daniel Cole explains, "the determination of foreseeable impacts requires drawing lines that cannot be legitimately tied to neutral principles or presumed consensus" (Cole 2009: 3). This fact may be troubling for governments and their agencies who might hope for a more neutral decision tool, and for critics who are looking for how these tools might be manipulated to serve political ends. What's clear is that determinations at this stage can have a direct effect on calculations of net benefits and can thus make one policy appear more attractive than another or make the status quo more appealing. Risk experts, economists, and others who help choose and rate impacts must therefore be vigilant to ensure outcomes that accurately reflect a society's interests.

Anyone who has participated in an actual CBA will have an acute sense of what such vigilance entails, because they will have needed to make the value judgments that we are describing here in broadest terms. Indeed, political scientists and economists seem intimately aware both of the subjective nature of these judgments and of their limitations for arriving at inarguable results.

Moreover, they are often diligent to provide reasons for their judgments and to offer practical solutions for overcoming the limitations.[7]

Foreseeable impacts of social distancing. To bring readers closer to insights achieved (and challenges faced) by actual practitioners of cost-benefit analysis in Step 3, we offer an example from a cost-benefit analysis led by the economist Linda Thunström from the University of Wyoming in 2020. This study, called "The Benefits and Costs of Using Social Distancing to Flatten the Curve for COVID-19," was among the earliest to assess the net benefits of social distancing measures adopted in the USA to slow the spread of the coronavirus.[8] Due to the urgency of the crisis and the scale of the management model being considered, Thunström's team chose to aggregate all foreseeable impacts into a single cost: decline in GDP. However, they *could* have considered other impacts that would increase the cost side of the equation. We can imagine, for instance, a range of health-related impacts associated with social isolation and economic downturn. Economist Kip Viscusi emphasized this possibility in his April 2020 appearance on the *Two Think Minimum* podcast:

> During times of economic downturn [and] increased unemployment, mortality rates go up. What I've found is for a loss of less than $100 million, anytime we lose that amount of money, there's one expected death across the economy. . . . The reasons for that include suicide by people who've lost their job. And when people have less money, they have less money for safe food, safe housing, and so on . . . . So when we think about the economic costs associated with these policies, we should . . . recognize that we're not just talking about money. If you're imposing a huge economic cost, there's also a health loss associated with that.

The suggestion is that whenever a policy package forecasts huge economic costs, health effects should appear on both sides of its analysis, not just on the benefits side. Indeed, this idea is at the heart of many objections that were raised in opposition to lockdowns and others of the more stringent mandates. We will return to the idea later in our "Distributional analysis." For now, suffice it to say that choosing to avoid such complexities when analyzing policies that could be adopted for this pandemic might have negative ramifications for the degree to which those policies are cost-effective.[9] In fact, Thunström and her team acknowledge this limitation and suggest several other "potentially important consequences" that could be explored in future work, including "[an] associated decline in levels of pollution, a possible spike in domestic violence . . . and other non-market social impacts."

Qualitative impacts. Note, finally, that because CBA is a quantitative method, any impact that absolutely cannot be quantified (in Step 4) will be excluded from consideration. These qualitative impacts, as they are sometimes called, may include impacts on the ecosystem, impacts on endangered species, or aesthetic impacts. However, for reasons we briefly discuss in "Valuing other impacts," which follows, conscientious analysts will try to include such effects despite how tough they are to quantify.

Step 4: Assign values to impacts

Once analysts have identified the potential outcomes of a policy and estimated their likelihoods, they must assign values to them. This task is easiest for material impacts that are readily quantifiable, such as the costs imposed on polluters and administrators by environmental protection measures, financial gains or losses to market productivity, or the economic benefits of medical innovations. But difficulties emerge for aspects of human concern and welfare that are not easily quantified and which some may think to be more subjective and "value-laden," if not essentially unmeasurable. These include leisure activities (religious gatherings, etc.), developments in human capital, environmental quality, biodiversity preservation, personal health and longevity, and so on. The list of such "nonmarket" valuables that might be affected by risk management is inexhaustive. We cannot hope to cover all of them or address every difficulty associated with their valuation. Instead, in what follows, we describe a general approach to valuation that is used in CBA to estimate the trade-offs. We also discuss the application of this approach to certain of the more-difficult risk outcomes – most notably, the preservation or loss of human lives.

Units. In order to compare costs with benefits, the two components are usually both estimated in monetary units, e.g., dollars.[10] While this seems sensible for material results, it may appear oddly inappropriate for valuing lives, the environment, or other noncommodity goods. Nevertheless, the usual goal is a series of numerical analyses that help decision makers "understand the impacts of a decision in a monetary or equivalent metric while also being able to view key quantities and values that lead up to the monetization" (Farrow & Viscusi 2011: 7).

Denoting values in monetary terms has clear advantages. For one, it facilitates comparisons and gives information about the degree and the direction of preferences. Moreover, it enables decision makers to assess risks systematically and ensure that the mitigating initiatives are financially sound. The value of some policy outcomes may still be described only in qualitative or nonmonetary terms. Nevertheless, as Farrow and Viscusi warn, too many such descriptions can produce an "unwieldly" analysis and an accompanying danger that the choice of action will be made with disregard for "the overall economic merits of the policy" (loc. cit.).

Denoting values in monetary terms also has disadvantages, some of which we alluded to in the preceding passages.[11] In particular, because it is very difficult to translate certain values into monetary terms, we may be tempted or forced to exclude these features from the analysis.

Willingness to pay. As we explained in Chapter 2, the monetary value of risk outcomes can be derived from individual willingness to pay (WTP). This approach measures the dollars that individuals are willing to pay for reductions to risks associated with their mortality, health, or welfare. Thus, in addition to securing the general advantages of monetization, WTP estimates promise to reflect actual preferences and to carry real information about how individuals think about their safety. Analysts who believe that policies should reflect the real preferences of affected populations thus rely heavily on WTP to inform valuations of costs and benefits. Because changes to mortality rates are a great concern for policy makers and public alike, WTP is commonly used to estimate the value of human lives (saved or lost), which is called the "value of a statistical life," or VSL.

Valuing reductions to risk of death (VSL). To help understand how economists calculate the "value" of lives and incorporate them into their analyses, let's return to the study by Linda Thunström et al. that we introduced in our description of Step 3. In this study, researchers estimated human mortality rates (from the virus) to be 1.5% without social distancing and 0.5% with social distancing (2020: 182, 183).[12] Thus, we would say that, according to estimates, the main benefit of social distancing is a *1% reduction to a person's risk of dying from COVID-19.*[13] What is the economic value of this benefit for US society as a whole? Let's investigate.

Calculation. First, following earlier suggestions, we can insist that the value be significantly determined by the safety preferences of American people. We can accomplish this by measuring the amount of money they are willing to pay (WTP) for the 1% reduction in mortality risk. Ideally, if we could know what each American is willing to pay for this small reduction to their own probability of dying and then sum up all these individual dollar amounts, the result would represent the total economic value of the benefit.

Of course, individuals will vary in this amount, so it will not be possible to collect information about individual WTPs to this level of granularity. Thus, we resort to averages. In other words, we seek a figure that lets us say, "On average, a member of the US population is willing to pay *this many* dollars for a 1% reduction to their mortality risk." We would then multiply that average dollar amount by the size of the US population to get our estimate of the total value of the benefit. This method is summarized in Table 5.1.

This approach may resonate better if we instead describe the benefit in terms of lives saved / deaths averted by social distancing.[14] If, per recent estimate, the US population is 328.2 million,[15] then the number of lives saved would be calculated as 0.01 × 328.2 million, which is 3,282,000. In other words, about 3.3 million fewer Americans are expected to die if social distancing is implemented (in USA).[16]

VSL. All we have done with the latter move is frame the outcome in a different way. We're in the business of "saving lives," not merely reducing certain risks. However, the financial value of the impact remains the same

Table 5.1 Proposed method for describing and calculating the benefits of using social distancing to slow the spread of COVID-19 in USA.

Managerial Model	*Benefit*	
	Description	*Calculation*
Social Distancing (USA)	1% reduction in (virus-related) mortality risk	Average individual WTP for 1% mortality reduction *x* population of USA

Table 5.2 Proposed method for calculating the benefits of using social distancing to slow the spread of COVID-19 in USA. The difference between this and the method in Table 5.1 lies only in the description of benefit.

Managerial Model	*Benefit*	
	Description	*Calculation*
Social Distancing (USA)	3.3 million lives saved/ deaths averted	Average individual WTP for 1% mortality reduction *x* population of USA

regardless of how we frame it. Either way, we calculate it as shown in the rightmost columns of Tables 1 and 2. Then, given our current framing, we interpret the result as a measure of how much money the American people, as a whole, are willing to pay to save 3.3 million lives. If we go one step further and divide that amount by the number of lives saved (3.3 million), we'll get a value that represents the amount of money that the US society is willing to pay to save one life.[17] Economists refer to this amount as the *value per statistical life*, or VSL, which has unit of dollars per statistical life saved.[18]

VSL estimates are useful anytime analysts are trying to quantify the benefits of a policy or regulation that promises to reduce expected number of deaths. It accomplishes the goal of translating lives into "some kind of dollar equivalent," which can then be catalogued for routine use in such analyses. Multiply the VSL by the number of lives saved (or deaths averted) by the regulation and you get the total economic value of that benefit. Thunström and colleagues (2020) used a VSL of $10 million, which they derived from US federal agency guidelines and other literature (183). Their estimate for deaths averted through social distancing was 1.24 million.[19] Thus, by their calculations, the gross benefits of social distancing came to $12.4 trillion.

Guidelines and interpretation. We arrived at the concept of value per statistical life by imagining how we might estimate the gross economic benefit of social distancing to slow the spread of COVID-19. Our strategy relied on information about an individual's willingness to pay for a small reduction to their likelihood of dying from the virus. In practice, analysts do not typically have access to such specific information; instead, they must borrow WTP and VSL estimates from existing valuation studies or, more commonly, from government guidelines developed from these studies. Such guidelines vary by country and agency. In the United States, the Environmental Protection Agency (EPA), Department of Transportation (DOT), and Department of Health and Human Services (HHS) are the main suppliers of estimates. The HSS's most recent (US Department of Health and Human Services 2016) VSL figure of around $10 million is higher than those of many, but it is increasingly favored by analysts of US regulations, including, as we saw, Thunström and colleagues (Robinson 2020; Robinson et al. 2016). Table 5.3 shows a list of VSL estimates from different agencies in America and abroad.

The routine use of VSL estimates for regulatory decision-making has at times received opposition from people who misinterpret the terminology or do not know how the figures are derived. The term "value per statistical life" can produce the mistaken belief that a "price" is being placed on individual lives. However, as should be evident from the preceding discussion, VSL does

Table 5.3 Examples of VSL estimates from different agencies in America and abroad. Adapted from Robinson and Hammitt (2013: 115).

Country/Agency	*VSL Estimates*	*Basis*	*Adjustments*
US Environmental Protection Agency (2010b)	**$7.4 million** (standard deviation: $4.7 million, 2006 dollars)	Primarily revealed preference studies of job-related risks	Inflation and real income growth, latency or cessation lag
US Department of Transportation (2011)	**$6.2 million** (standard deviation: $2.8 million, 2011 dollars)	Primarily revealed preference studies of job-related risks	Inflation and real income growth, averted costs
Canada (Treasury Board, 2007)	**$6.11 million**[a] (2004 Canadian dollars)	Primarily revealed preference studies of job-related risks	Inflation
UK (HM Treasury, 2003)	**£1.145 million**[b] (2000 British pounds)	Stated preference studies plus averted costs	Inflation and real income growth
European Commission (2009)	**1 million to 2 million euros**[c] (Year not reported)	Not reported	May use more context-specific estimates
Organisation of Economic Cooperation and Development (2012)	**$1.5 million to $4.5 million** (2005 dollars)	Stated preference studies	Inflation and real income growth

Notes: [a]6.17 million US dollars based on current exchange rate. [b]1.8 million US dollars based on current exchange rate. [c]1.3 million to 2.6 million US dollars based on current exchange rate.

not reflect the value that a governing agency places on saving an individual's life; instead, it reflects the value that individuals themselves place on small reductions to their own probability of death (Robinson 2020).[20] This fact bears repeating, especially when noting large variations in VSL guidelines among different countries. The fact that the estimates are higher for one country than for another does not mean that the residents of the former are worth more. What it means is that societies vary in their willingness to pay for small changes to mortality rates, which is predictable, given that such willingness is a function of "income as well as social and cultural factors (such as attitudes towards risks and health system characteristics)" (Robinson & Hammitt 2013: 114).

This way of understanding the figures was perhaps inadequately communicated during the COVID-19 pandemic, where, at least in the US, the term "value of statistical life" repeatedly entered the public discourse and provoked earnest rejections from some highly visible critics.[21] The economist Kip Viscusi tried to rectify this disconnect in his appearance on the *Two Think Minimum* podcast:

> If you're looking at the many hotspots for coronavirus – if you're looking at Spain, Italy, China – their value of statistical life would be less than that of the United States. [But] that's because they have different preferences for risk versus money, how much they're willing to spend on greater amounts of safety. . . . It's not that we're saying their lives are worth less from our standpoint; we're saying this is how they think about safety and their policies should reflect their own preferences, which in fact they do.

Reflecting on this point can help avoid the mindset that the use of VSL is incompatible with the deontological intuition that a human life is priceless, or with the fundamental principle that no one (from any nation/populace) is more important than anyone else. That said, there is room for debate over the acceptable risk-reducing contexts for which VSL is as an adequate reflection of relevant preferences.

FRAME I: Pricing the priceless

Scientists are always attempting to put a dollar value on things that seem priceless: an extra day of quality life, an extra year of life, the services provided by salt marshes, the work of bats and bees.[22] In fact, some have even ventured to put a price tag on the Earth itself! It may be common to think this practice is somehow misguided and to question the value of understanding everything we might care about in terms of dollars and cents, but the reality is that we do not have infinite resources to apply when one of these things is threatened, so trade-offs are inevitable, and the prices are a way to help us decide if/when a proposed intervention is actually worthwhile. Imagine, for instance, that the coronavirus outbreak had been projected to kill just one person. In this case, would it have been acceptable for the world's governments to mount such huge efforts to contain the virus? Would it have been okay to suspend operations of schools and day care centers, seal off all playgrounds and other public spaces, cancel cultural events and tourist attractions and sports, ban social gatherings, impose travel restrictions, require vaccinations, and so on, all to save this one life? If not, what scale or type of effort would have been acceptable?

Questions like those raised above help us realize that no one really thinks a human life has *infinite* value, at least not when it comes to making societal decisions about what to do when such lives are at risk. And in fact, it would be impossible to develop measures like the value of a statistical life if there were no limits to what individuals were willing to pay to prevent or reduce deaths. Still, the feeling that it is wrong to put a value on life remains unshakable for many, especially when one sees how the VSL can vary by country or personal characteristic. The statistical value of life is smaller for poorer countries and developing markets; it also decreases with age and, historically, is much smaller for children than for adults. It's hard not to see these facts as suggesting that poor, old, and young people have less intrinsic value – even if we know that this interpretation is based on a misunderstanding of what the VSL is and how it is determined.

Do you believe that human life is priceless or that no one person from any nation, age, or economic status, etc., is more valuable than anyone else? If so, how do you reconcile these beliefs with the use of VSL estimates to decide whether a public policy meant to save lives is worth undertaking? It may help to recall that VSL is a measure of the price people place on small changes to the likelihood (or "risk") of death. (Typically, this translates to reducing the *average* number of deaths in a group by one.) It is not what someone would pay to escape certain death.

Uncertainty. Like other variables in cost-benefit analysis, VSL estimates involve uncertainties that may have ramifications for the decision process. In her article "COVID-19 and Uncertainties in the Value Per Statistical Life," decision scientist Lisa Robinson describes numerous such uncertainties that could significantly affect the evaluation of policies meant to combat the coronavirus (August 5, 2020). For instance, both theory and evidence suggest that VSL varies with age, but the exact relationship between these two variables is uncertain. Uncertainty stems from the fact that the willingness studies underlying VSL recommendations primarily address occupational risks among working adults and thus exclude input from children and the elderly. This lack of age-specific information is regrettable, because most coronavirus deaths occur in older people beyond age 65. In a recent study with Ryan Sullivan and Jason Shogren, Robinson compared the effects of three approaches to adjust for age and found that "when applied to the US age distribution of COVID-19 deaths," population-average VSL estimates varied between $10.6 million, $8.5 million, and $4.5 million. Importantly, further calculations revealed that these differences in value are "substantial enough to alter the conclusions of frequently cited [cost-benefit] analyses of social distancing" in USA.

Earlier, we said that analysts must borrow WTP and VSL estimates from existing valuation studies. This practice of importing estimates, referred to as "benefit transfer," is permissible in principle because WTP is simply about reducing probability of death; theoretically, it seems that details concerning the regulation of interest, including *which risks* are its target, shouldn't affect these values. But this assumption may be inadequate given the recurring revelation that public perceptions are attuned to numerous risk characteristics beyond mere probability. (See Chapter 4 and our later segment on "risk communication," among other parts of this book.)

Conscientious analysts admit this limitation and expect differences in VSL across various types of risks that may increase the values appropriate for more dreadful threats – like COVID-19, for instance. As Robinson explains, whereas typical VSL estimates reflect preferences against immediate death from injury, COVID-19 deaths "may be preceded by a longer period of pain and suffering, including severe breathing difficulties and ventilator use" (Robinson 2020). Likely, this image of protracted suffering will exacerbate already-high associations of dread, novelty, involuntariness, and uncontrollability of COVID-19 risks that, by Robinson's estimation, may increase VSL by as much as a factor of two. That said, the appropriate values for many risks remain uncertain, and valuation research that is better tailored to specific risks and their characteristics may be needed for fairer recommendations.

Despite the implications of these uncertainties, most federal agencies do not adjust VSL for different risks or risk factors. Nor do they adjust for age, income or wealth, morbidity prior to death, or other characteristics of individuals that can affect their willingness to pay for lessening their chance of dying. The latter choice is understandable, considering the uncomfortable alternative of appearing to give greater or lesser weight to individuals with different properties. Nevertheless, it has drawn opposition from philosophers like Hermansson, who believes this disregard for "[t]he separateness of individuals and individual rights" is liable to produce unjust conclusions (Hermansson 2005: 562). Aside from highlighting an area in need of further exploration, this objection elicits a more general desire for equitable management of societal risks.

Valuing reductions to nonfatal health risks. Above, we described the methods and challenges of valuing changes to risk of death in the context of cost-benefit analysis. However, public policies can also affect the risk of injury, illness, and other factors that reduce the quality of life but do not kill. Changes to these risks are no more easily valued and may, in many cases, be more difficult. The techniques used to value changes in nonfatal risks are more diverse than those used for mortality risks, but the analytic framework for valuing changes to health risks still primarily involves estimates of willingness to pay. For illnesses, cardiovascular and respiratory conditions associated with air pollution are among the most studied. For injuries, WTP studies focus either on one type (e.g., spinal cord or brain injury) or on a range of injuries from several categories. For these studies to be applicable to a particular CBA, their target risks should be similar to those affected by the policy.

When suitable WTP estimates are unavailable, analysts sometimes rely on estimates of cost of illness (COI). This quantity is helpful for risk management because it represents the costs of illness or injury that might be avoided by policy interventions. Estimates typically include medical costs for hospital visits, patient care, medication, etc., which would be paid by patients, insurance companies, and/or employers. Many estimates also include "productivity losses," which result from absences or decreased productivity at work.

While WTP and COI are reasonable indicators for cost-benefit analysis, they are unable to capture every health outcome that might concern decision makers. Indeed, as Robinson and Hammitt mention, these figures are somewhat blind to "the value of pain and suffering [and] other quality of life impacts associated with a health impairment and its affects [sic] on work and other activities" (Robinson & Hammitt 2013). It is important for analysts to recognize these limitations and consider their implications for risk management.

Valuing other impacts. We have focused our summary of Step 4 on values associated with the survival and physical health of humans. This is because such values are the primary ingredients of the majority of cost-benefit analyses. Still, these are not the only effects people care about and might wish to include in a calculation of trade-offs. For instance, many humans care deeply about ecosystems and the nonhuman animals that comprise them. Thus, a regulation to reduce risk of ocean disasters like the Exxon Valdez oil spill of 1989 would be remiss not to count the lives of seabirds, sea mammals, and other wildlife among the saved.

These often-called "intrinsic" or "nonmarket" values, however, are difficult to incorporate in CBA – partly because they are less universally affirmed, and partly because they are, by nature, very tough to express in dollar terms. (It would be impossible to generate a VSL for a seagull that reflects the average seagull's willingness to pay for a small reduction to their risk of death.)

Nevertheless, these values should be quantified because, otherwise, they would receive zero weight in the calculation of trade-offs, which is usually worse than assigning an inaccurate positive value (Cole 2009). Indeed, as the Green Facts Initiative warns, "without these value estimates," resources such as clean air and water, healthy fish and wildlife populations, "may be implicitly undervalued[,] and decisions regarding their use and stewardship may not accurately reflect their true value to society" (Glossary at greenfacts.org, "Non-market value").

5.1.2 Distributional analysis

Cost-benefit analysis is a well-established and widely used method for informing policy decisions. It has served this purpose in the COVID-19 context, helping policy makers appreciate the gravity of the crisis and understand key trade-offs (Robinson 2020). As we've seen, many of these analyses use population averages and focus on economic efficiency. However, risk management must also assess the extent to which a policy's effects are equitable and just. So-called distributional analyses, which aim to determine how the positive and negative impacts are distributed across members of society, are integral to this. Among other things, these analyses promise to yield morally conscious decisions about how to modify or implement a policy package.

In what follows, we offer a simplified, broad-stroke analysis of the distribution of impacts of social distancing measures in USA. This will give a sense of what must be added to cost-benefit studies like that from Thunström and colleagues (2020) to better inform choices about how to manage risks associated with COVID-19. As it turns out, distributional analyses may call for additional calculations to assess trade-offs for certain social groups that will be disproportionately affected by the gamut of self-quarantine and other distancing measures. This will enable the development of optimal policies that differentially target such groups.

5.1.2.1 Distribution of impacts of social distancing in the USA

The cost-benefit analysis provided by Thunström et al. (2020) assessed a policy package representing the entire range of social distancing measures being adopted in the USA. The authors measured the benefits of such actions in terms of total value of lives saved ($12.4 trillion, from 1.24 million lives saved and $10 million VSL) and costs to social distancing as lost GDP ($7.21 trillion). The difference yielded an estimated net benefit of $5.16 trillion. Assuming their estimates of disease spread and impacts on the economy were accurate, this result suggests that social distancing is better for the US than does the alternative of taking no measures to control the outbreak. Or as the authors put it, social distancing policies "likely do not constitute an overreaction to COVID-19" (Thunström et al. 2020: 181). However, this suggestion leaves much latitude for judgments about how the policy package should be practically implemented. And these judgments must account for, and be responsive to, the degree to which the costs and benefits are justly distributed among the population.

To analyze this distribution, we ask which people are bearing the economic costs and which are receiving the health benefits. The good news is that we can expect some degree of symmetry between these two camps. The scale of the crisis and of the policy measures makes it plausible to suggest that most Americans would suffer some of the costs while also benefiting from the reduction in mortality risk. But surely, there will be individuals, or groups of individuals, who bear a disproportionately larger chunk of the costs, whereas some, possibly different people groups, will benefit more than others from the slowing of the spread. Let's investigate.

Who bears the costs? Reason suggests that society's most vulnerable groups will be hit the hardest by social distancing mandates. Among those disproportionately affected will be low-income workers in the labor-intensive service industry, where mass layoffs are inevitable. These layoffs will include a higher percentage of women and workers from racial/ethnic minority backgrounds, since these groups are disproportionately represented in service sectors, like restaurants/bars, entertainment, travel and transportation, and certain types of retail and manufacturing (Kantamneni 2020). These predictions are confirmed by a growing collection of data.[23] Thus, socioeconomically disadvantaged groups bear a significant share of the economic and work-related costs resulting from distancing protocols set in the United States. We might add that within these more-affected people groups, financial impact may vary by education level and region (e.g., urban versus rural) (Edwards & Lopez 2021).

The impact on small businesses and entrepreneurial ventures is likely to be severe. Stores, factories, and many other businesses will close by policy mandate. Indeed, according to a July 2020 study by Robert Fairlie, the number of active business owners in the United States dropped by a whopping 3.3 million, or 22%, over the short window from February to April 2020. This reduction in active business owners was the largest on record. Moreover, simulations suggest that industry compositions put immigrants, racial and ethnic minorities, at higher risk of business activity losses – a prediction confirmed by the Fairlie study. Many of these closures may be permanent if owners are unable to pay ongoing expenses and survive the shutdown(s). Thus, negative outcomes of lockdowns for small business owners may be much longer-term than those for, say, service workers who have suffered pay cuts or have been laid off.

Who reaps the benefits? Ostensibly, the people who stand to gain most from coronavirus mitigation strategies like social distancing are those who might suffer the most severe health consequences from COVID-19. By this measure, people aged 65 and older make up the largest percentage of benefiters. (As of October 6, 2021, over 76% of deaths from coronavirus occurred within the 65+ age group. The rate of death in people aged 85+ is 570 times higher than in

Table 5.4 Distribution of impacts from social distancing in USA. *Estimates taken from the 2020 analysis by Thunstrom and colleagues.

	COSTS	*BENEFITS*
Impact	Lost GDP	Saved lives
Estimate*	$7.21 trillion	$12.4 trillion
Groups most affected	Disadvantaged groups and/or people of lower socioeconomic status, including: • Racial/ethnic minorities • Low-income workers • Women Particularly those in the "non-essential" services industry, e.g., restaurants/bars, entertainment, travel, certain types of retail (CDC December 10, 2020; Kantamneni 2020). Small-business owners Adults without college degrees (Edwards & Lopez 2021) Working-age population: ages 15–64; millennials (largest generation in the US labor force as of 2018)	Disadvantaged groups and/or people of low socioeconomic status, including: • Racial/ethnic minorities • Low-income workers • Women Particularly, frontline, essential, and critical infrastructure workers Adults without college degrees Older adults above retirement age, particularly 65–older

people aged 18–29. See Centers for Disease Control and Prevention, April 23, 2021 and September 9, 2021.) Frontline, essential, and critical infrastructure workers also stand to gain from the distancing measurers, because people who work in these settings have more chances of being exposed to COVID-19.[24] And we could also include those who were able to start working from home and maybe, as a result, even move away from the expensive urban centers to areas with lower housing costs.

Many of the disadvantaged groups we've identified as cost-bearers might also benefit from the reduction in mortality risk. In December 2020, the CDC released a report on racial and ethnic disparities that are evident in data from COVID-19 studies. The data show a disproportionate representation of racial and ethnic minority groups among COVID-19 cases, as well as differences in rates of hospitalization and outcomes of hospitalized patients by race and ethnicity. Importantly, these groups also exhibit a disproportionately high incidence of COVID-19 deaths. Thus, they will gain from efforts to slow the spread of the virus inasmuch as those efforts succeed in reducing deaths and other negative health outcomes. We summarize this and other findings in Table 5.4.

5.1.2.2 Discussion

We have analyzed the distribution of costs and benefits of social distancing among the US population. To determine the extent to which this distribution is just or equitable, we look for critical imbalances between the groups that are hit hardest by the costs and those that have the most to gain.

First, note that disadvantaged groups appear on both sides of the summation because they are at high risk of dying from the virus yet will also suffer heavily from the distancing strategies meant to minimize that risk. This makes it difficult to judge how fair the policy is for disadvantaged individuals relative to those who are more privileged (per status quo). We may expect an asymmetry between essential and nonessential service workers within these vulnerable groups: the nonessential workers will bear more of the costs of social distancing, while essential workers will reap more of the benefits as an indirect consequence of the fact that they are at higher risk of dying from COVID-19 due to the nature of their work.

A great imbalance occurs between age groups, with the lost GDP affecting the working population to a much greater degree than the older population (age 65+), and the older population benefiting far more from the reduction in mortality risk. Importantly, the imposition of costs is also heavily lopsided toward owners of small business and budding entrepreneurs.

CBA for cost-bearing groups

Additional cost-benefit analyses should be conducted to estimate the magnitude of impact for those who will be hit hardest by policies and guidelines (federal, state, local) to increase social distance. These cost-benefit analyses will be narrower in scope, as they are directed at specific people groups – particularly those for whom the *net* benefits of social distancing may appear much lower than those calculated for the whole population. Nonessential service workers and small-business owners within the working-age population are chief candidates. For these analyses, benefits must include estimates of the number of lives saved within the target subpopulation, which we expect may be lower in percentage relative to the general population. Additionally, some research suggests that benefit calculations might be more equitable if they incorporated VSLs derived from the unique preferences of these groups, as opposed to population-level VSLs.[25]

Adjustments to costs may prove difficult. One approach would be to estimate the amount of GDP that is lost strictly within the target group or their associated industries. For owners of small businesses, this estimate is likely to be significant; for the working-age population, it may be closer to amounts projected for the general population. However, being such a general and imprecise measure, lost GDP cannot be a sufficient indicator of the costs for these highly affected groups.[26] For some, this may be especially true in light of the short time window associated with GDP projections.

Consider, for instance, the aforementioned possibility that small-business closures may be permanent if owners are unable to pay ongoing expenses and survive shutdowns. Thus, negative outcomes of lockdowns for small-business owners may be much longer-term than those for, say, service workers who have suffered pay cuts or have been laid off. To some extent, this prospect could be mitigated by applying lower discount rates to the sum of costs (Step 5 in CBA). But it seems right to look for additional impacts associated with these longer-term losses. For instance, some owners of lost businesses may drop to a lower economic class and experience a reduced quality of life that persists indefinitely. Moreover, we can imagine that the emotional and psychological toll on those who lose their businesses or whose entrepreneurial ventures fail as a result of cancellations and shutdowns may be significant. Such outcomes may be hard to quantify and valuate, but fairness demands that we try.

Certain nonfatal health risks, such as a decline in mental condition or other determinants of well-being, are absent from studies that look only at GDP for costs and at mortality rates for benefits. This should be rectified in later CBAs, because such declines may be among the most damaging and longest-lasting effects that are not strictly economical in nature. In the prior section called "The method," we summarized some approaches used to valuate such health risks, which will undoubtedly increase as a result of the isolation imposed by social distancing, and of job or business losses, reduced wages, etc. It seems fair to suggest that these valuations be added to analyses performed for any population, not just analyses for cost-bearing ones. However, these additions will be more crucial, and valuations likely higher, for the more vulnerable groups we've identified and discussed. In fact, we might expect social distancing practices to exacerbate long-standing inequities in social determinants of health[27] that affect racial/ethnic minorities or other disadvantaged groups (e.g., low-education, low-income). The subsequent decline in health, well-being, or quality of life for individuals within these groups may well exceed any beneficial reductions to their nonfatal risks associated with COVID-19 (e.g., exposure, illness and severity of illness, hospitalization). Thus, in CBAs for such groups, the balance for changes to nonfatal health risks should lie on the cost side of summation.

Remedies

The goal for assessing distribution of impacts is to better inform management decisions, given the expectation that some version of the social distancing model is implemented in USA. We've seen that additional cost-benefit analyses tailored to cost-bearing groups are a crucial first response. Based on our findings, it seems likely that the net benefits may be significantly lower or even negative for certain groups – especially, perhaps, small-business owners. We cannot hope to describe all the decisions that might stem from this realization, but the general goal is for government agencies at all levels to offset imbalances as much as possible.[28] Part of this offset may include changes to the policy package, e.g., concerning the locale, type, duration, degree, or extent of distancing mandates and guidelines.[29] Agencies must also make decisions about how to allocate funds, resulting in the generation of bills (e.g., CARES Act), subsidies, grants, and programs. For instance, the federal government has responded to concerns over longer-term effects on small businesses through programs like the Paycheck Protection Program (PPP), which allocated over $650 billion by July 2020, and the Economic Injury Disaster Loan program by the Small Business Administration, which provided over $150 billion by the same month (Fairlie 2020).

Decision makers who are concerned for justice should keep in mind that some people for whom the net benefits of social distancing are lower are not disadvantaged in the status quo. These include wealthier, working-age adults, and/or racial majorities who are generally healthy and face little risk of dying from the virus. For this reason, government agencies could aim to provide extra compensation to people within the cost-bearing population who are otherwise already vulnerable or underprivileged. This may be easier at the state or local levels, where loans and grants can be tailored more precisely to Black-owned businesses, e.g., or to small companies owned by women, Latinos, and other small minority-owned businesses. For instance, on May 5, 2021, the city of San Francisco, California, pledged to redirect $3.75 million from its policing budget to support local Black-owned businesses. This move can be thought of not only as an attempt to rectify the heavy impact of COVID-19 distancing policy but also as part of an initiative to reallocate police funding in response to the police shootings and protests that occurred amid the pandemic.

Finally, it's worth reminding that the increased susceptibility of certain disadvantaged groups to the ill effects of COVID-19 results heavily from underlying social conditions that affect health more generally and influence numerous quality-of-life risks and outcomes (CDC, December 10, 2020). The most successful strategy for reducing deaths from COVID-19 would be one that aggravates inequities in these conditions to the least extent possible.

5.1.3 Democratizing the procedure

5.1.3.1 More deliberation

In order to be less abstract, we have considered the distribution of impacts as well as net benefits of an actual policy package that was aimed at a particular crisis and implemented in the USA. It proved important for analysts to explicitly address both who bears the costs and who receives the benefits so that the need for policy adjustments and programs to address inequities becomes evident. Such considerations are especially important for managing COVID-19, since many disadvantaged groups are disproportionately affected both by COVID-19 risks and the economic consequences of policy actions. However, the need to accompany cost-benefit analysis with analysis of the distribution of impacts is not limited to this particular public health concern, and many government and other guidelines require this accompaniment for a wide range of issues and proposals (ibid.).

These tools bring us a long way toward a fair and ethical procedure for managing public risks, especially when they include finer-scale analysis of a proposal's net benefits (or costs) to those who are most susceptible to its negative outcomes. However, the fact remains that cost-benefit analysis, distributional analysis, and other methods used by decision makers remain the tools of "experts." Elsewhere, we have suggested that to make risks an area solely for experts might undermine citizens' trust in their government and agencies.

Some critics who recognize this problem and its normative implications are advocating for an enlarged model for risk management that focuses on the procedure for decision-making instead of just the outcome. Philosophers like Hélène Hermansson, for instance, call for risk decisions to be "made in a more public and deliberative manner." The idea is to democratize key parts of the decision process by creating opportunities for risk analysts, decision makers, and laypeople to openly discuss how they perceive the risk and why. The goal would not be to undercut the crucial role of experts in estimating risks and choosing among proposals but rather to ensure that they "co-operate with, i.e. discuss and listen to, other parties who may not share their point of view" (Hermansson 2010).

Various stages of the existing model (CBA) are amenable to expansion in such hopeful directions. For instance, the task of identifying collective action problems and determining management goals (if any) can be structured to facilitate open discussions of the sort just described. These discussions will continue to be useful when it comes to determining foreseeable impacts, as risk analysts tend to overlook features that cannot be easily translated into dollars.[30] Moreover, we expect these deliberations to produce fairer and more informed valuations of those impacts. They can, for instance, illuminate characteristics that may increase or decrease the value of reducing a risk. Such characteristics include psychometric factors associated with risk perception, which we discussed in Chapter 4. Because these factors source many of the discrepancies between lay beliefs and the assessments of experts, it is reasonable to demand we give them special consideration and to expect them to have a significant impact on the assignment of values to outcomes.

As we mentioned in Chapter 3, the differences between the ways in which the public perceives certain risks and in which experts assess them is sometimes attributed to people being not only uninformed but also highly emotional. On this view, a layperson's emotional reaction to a risk can prevent them from making rational judgments about it, thus rendering their perception irrational and unreliable. For instance, according to Cass Sunstein, a well-known legal scholar who worked for President Obama, many risk-related judgments can be explained by an "anti-tampering with nature" heuristic (Sunstein 2005b). And the use of heuristics is typically associated with reasoning that is intuitive, unreflective, and driven by emotion, in contrast with reasoning that is analytic, reflective, and responsive to facts (Slovic, Finucane et al. 2004). Probabilities would surely be among these "facts," and it is notable that, in early 2020, Sunstein decried our human proclivity to neglect probabilities as responsible for making "[a] lot more people" be "more scared than they have any reason to be" about their risk of contracting COVID-19 (Sunstein 2020). The resulting suggestion is that we should interpret disagreements between experts and the public as a clash between an emotional reaction to the risk and a rational assessment of it.

However tempting this reductive suggestion may be, it is ridden with problematic assumptions about the brain and about good decision-making. It assumes, for instance, a strict dichotomy between cognitive processes and emotional reactions, but as we discuss in the next section, this popular conception of how the brain works has become scientifically untenable. Moreover, emotions, as we are going to see, can be redeemed as a source of knowledge crucial to risk management and one that traditional forms of cost-benefit analysis do not necessarily provide.

FRAME 2: GMOs and tampering with nature

In one thought experiment from *The Pig that Wants to Be Eaten*, Julian Baggini asks us to imagine a chicken-like bird that has been genetically modified to live the life of a vegetable "with no awareness of self, environment, pain or pleasure" (Baggini 2006: 13). Baggini's focus is on the moral permissibility of eating this so-called "decerebrated" chicken. We, however, can ask whether there might be any risks associated with such an action.

If Cass Sunstein is right, the people who would find it too risky to eat a decerebrated chicken but who would otherwise eat a normal chicken may be applying an "anti-tampering with nature" heuristic to their judgment. But are we really any more likely to get sick from the decerebrated chicken than from one reared by ordinary farming methods? Moreover, as Baggini himself asks, "aren't even organic arable farmers, who have selected and bred varieties to grow on a mass scale, tampering with the natural order anyway?" (ibid. 15) Perhaps it is just the "yuck factor" that makes the engineered bird seem so unnatural, and thus riskier to consume, but there is nothing in this visceral feeling to suggest that one is being reflective and responsive to facts. In short, is there any good reason that we should consider it overly risky to engineer and eat an animal who, by design, has no more awareness than an onion? What do you think?

5.1.3.2 A role for emotions

As we saw in Chapter 3, Heather Douglas makes a strong case for regarding social-ethical value judgments as necessary for the process of assessing risks. In an argument that can be viewed as an extension of Douglas's, ethicist Sabine Roeser contends that we must take into consideration risk-related emotions when attempting to make such judgments (Roeser 2006).

Roeser begins by challenging the old notion that cognitive and emotional processes run in parallel and are strictly independent of each other. Neurobiological research has shown that, in reality, these two processes are deeply interconnected. "The distinction between the 'emotional' and the 'cognitive' brain is fuzzy and context-dependent," Roeser explains. "[E]motion and cognition are deeply interwoven in the fabric of the brain, suggesting that widely held beliefs about the key constituents of 'the emotional brain' and 'the cognitive brain' are fundamentally flawed" (Okon-Singer et al. 2015). On the one hand, cognitive processes such as attention, rationalization, and memory can help regulate some emotional reactions. On the other hand, emotion can have the effect of making us more attentive, more perceptive, and more focused – effects we normally associate with cognition. Things that evoke feelings of fear, awe, or love are more attention-grabbing and enhance our ability to selectively respond to some aspects of the environment.

Following contemporary theories of emotions (Scherer 1984), Roeser construes certain emotions each as having an *intentional object* and a *cognitive function*. The intentional object is the specific thing that the emotion has in focus. For instance, spiders are the objects of arachnophobia, wrongdoers are objects of anger, people and pets are objects of love, and sunsets inspire awe. Cognitive functions help guide actions and ensure judgments that are appropriate for those objects. For instance, when we seek to judge the moral acceptability of a situation, we rely on cognitive processes that enable us "to know or to be able to imagine how it feels to be in a certain situation, to be treated by others in certain ways, to know how it feels when one is hurt or happy" (Roeser 2006: 695). Emotions of this sort exist for some duration, which distinguishes them from the immediate, transient physiological reactions we typically associate with *feelings*. Such emotions also differ from *dispositional emotions*, which are underlying tendencies to behave in a certain way. For example, we may say of some people that they are caring or that they are anxious.

Roeser applies this conception of emotions as having both intentional objects and cognitive functions to discussions about risk perception and risk assessment. The pretense, as we've learned, is that when assessing risk, experts focus on measuring probability and severity, and emotions play no role in this assessment. If an expert allows themselves to be influenced by emotions, this will undermine the objectivity of their assessment. Risk perception, on the other hand, is almost inevitably influenced by our emotional relation to different risks. This is why risk perception has many more dimensions than just the estimate of probability and severity, like whether the exposure is controllable or the consequences observable.

Indeed, it is not hard to see how emotions can get generated and involved in the perception: the mere idea of being forced to do something (e.g., compulsory vaccinations to remain employed), especially if there might be unwanted consequences, might well arouse anger. The idea of being exposed to a situation with possible unwanted and unobservable consequences might well trigger fear toward the risky technology or activity. However, on Roeser's view, the anger and fear in these cases are appropriate, not irrational. After all, what would we make of a person who is involuntarily exposed to a risk and yet cares little about this fact? Wouldn't we decry this lack of concern as irrational? Or maybe this person just doesn't understand the injustice that is done to them. Either way, the absence of emotion appears in this case to be an indication not that everything is right but that something is amiss. Studies of risk perception also found that individual perceptions can be influenced by awareness of how harms and benefits of the exposure are distributed. Again, it is not difficult to see how emotion could play a role in this influence. One may feel outrage at the idea of being forced to undertake risks without much to gain, while others suffer less risk and have more to gain. And such outrage is quite evidently reasonable.

Emotions, then, according to Roeser, help us react to some aspects of risks exposure in the same way as emotions of fear or compassion are reactions to dangerous or unjust situations. And they have a cognitive function because they are not just side effects of a detached evaluation of the situation but actually help us realize the danger or the injustice of the situation. So emotions should not be excluded from discussions about the moral acceptability of risks for the sake of being objective. Emotions are a source of moral insight in a way that scientific methodology is not. In a debate about the acceptability of risks, especially when there is a clear moral dimension to the exposure, there should be room for the perspective that emotional reactions have to offer. And this is especially so since experts are not likely to be immune, in their evaluation, to their own emotional relation to the risk. Experts may feel enthusiasm toward a certain technology or worry that if a risk is not taken seriously, they will lose their funding. And as we saw, Douglas goes further than that by showing that social-ethical judgments are and should be involved in risk assessment, from the choice of a methodology to the interpretation of the data to the selection of a course of action that may have social-ethical consequences. Considering that emotions are a source of moral knowledge, if social or ethical judgments have a role to play in decision-making about risk, then emotions have a role to play too. Because emotions are always already there, they should not be hard to elicit and openly integrate in debates between the public and the experts about acceptability of risks that have possible social or ethical consequences.

Roeser acknowledges that emotions are not infallible as a guide for action or for managing risks. Some emotions, like fear, anger, and enthusiasm, could make us focus so much on some aspects of the situation that we become oblivious to other aspects that are also relevant to decision-making. For instance, fear of a new technology (e.g., mRNA vaccines) could make it hard to recognize its potential benefits,[31] anger about unfair distribution of risk and benefits could prevent us from seeing how this distribution could change in the future, and enthusiasm could make us dismiss the way other people will be affected. Our emotional reaction could also be based on a lack of information about a technology or hazard or on a misunderstanding of the available information. But Roeser insists that this is not a reason to dismiss reactions based on emotions. Emotional reactions are legitimate informants of the acceptability of a risk, even if they are not to be the main dictators of decisions. They should be included in procedural debates about societal risks and in such a way that they are respected and shared alongside factual information in a "genuine dialogue" among the public, experts, and policy makers (Roeser & Pesch 2016).

This emotional deliberation approach, as Roeser calls it, gives us an ideal to strive for. But it is difficult to imagine specifics for how it might actually work in practice. We have portrayed it here as a process that is somewhat orthogonal to CBA, but perhaps that isn't right. Already we have suggested that CBA is amenable to expansion in various democratic directions, and surely, our emotional reactions to risks could help direct and participate in the expansion. They may prove instrumental for identifying collective action problems and for determining which risks must be managed and which can be left alone. They can, of course, help determine foreseeable impacts and decide on values that are appropriate for those impacts. Moreover, it is possible to imagine the emotions themselves as counting among the potential impacts to be valued. It was possible, for instance, to anticipate the anger that people felt over certain mandates that their governments imposed on them in response to the COVID-19 pandemic (e.g., lockdowns, compulsory wearing of face masks, vaccinations). This anger led to protests, demonstrations, and strikes in various countries across the world.[32] It is not unreasonable to suggest that government analysts might have conceived a way to quantify this anger (say, using WTP for some adjacent, nonfatal health risk) and add it to the costs of their proposals for containing the virus.[33]

As we will see in the next two sections, to take into account such nonmonetary impacts – emotional, moral, psychological impacts – that may result from risk exposure and risk management is at the center of recent models of risk management, like the alternatives assessment model. The alternatives assessment model for risk management presents itself as an alternative to the cost-benefit analysis model that was presented earlier. But the reason for that is not that it forsakes the use of a cost-benefit analysis; rather, it is that it rejects the use of cost-benefit analysis as an absolute principle for decision-making and makes room for the precautionary principle as a possible basis for decision-making.

5.2 The precautionary principle

5.2.1 The precautionary principle: numerous versions

In 1992, in the Dutch city of Maastricht, the ruling monarchs and presidents of 12 European nations signed the Treaty on Union (now generally referred to as the Treaty of Maastricht), which created the European Union. This treaty included a section on environment, with this text:

> Community policy on the environment . . . shall be based on the precautionary principle and on the principles that preventative action should be taken, that environment damage should as a priority be rectified at source and that the polluter should pay.
>
> (Luxembourg 1992: Article 130r)

In the last 20 years, the precautionary principle, hereafter PP, has found its way into national and international legal documents and policy statements in diverse areas of health and environmental protection in risky situations. To speak of *the* precautionary principle is misleading, though, because there are numerous versions of "the" principle. For instance, in the 1992 Rio Declaration, it says:

> In order to protect the environment, the precautionary approach shall be widely applied by States according to their capabilities.
>
> Where there are threats of serious or irreversible damage, lack of full scientific certainty shall not be used as a reason for postponing cost-effective measures to prevent environmental degradation.

And in the Conference on the North Sea, The Hague (1990), it says:

> [T]he precautionary principle, that is to take action to avoid potentially damaging impacts of substance that are persistent, toxic and liable to bioaccumulate even when there is no scientific evidence to prove a causal link between emissions and effects.

In 1998, a conference that brought together academics, farmers, environmental consultants, physicians, and environmental advocates representing Greenpeace, among others, was held at Wingspread, a historic home which is the headquarters of the Johnson Foundation in Wisconsin. The statement issued, the *Wingspread Statement*, spells out the motivations for adoption of PP.

Wingspread Statement on the precautionary principle (Wingspread Consensus 1998)

The release and use of toxic substances, resource exploitation, and physical alterations of the environment have had substantial unintended consequences on human health and the environment. Some of these concerns are high rates of learning deficiencies, asthma, cancer, birth defects and species extinctions; along with global climate change, stratospheric ozone depletion; and worldwide contamination with toxic substances and nuclear materials.

We believe existing environmental regulations and other decisions, particularly those based on risk assessment, have failed to adequately protect human health and the environment, as well as the larger system of which humans are but a part.

We believe there is compelling evidence that damage to humans and the worldwide environment, is of such magnitude and seriousness that new principles for conducting human activities are necessary. . . .

Therefore, it is necessary to implement the Precautionary Principle: Where an activity raises threats of harm to the environment or human health, precautionary measures should be taken even if some cause and effect relationships are not fully established scientifically.

In this context the proponent of an activity, rather than the public, bears the burden of proof.

The process of applying the Precautionary Principle must be open, informed and democratic, and must include potentially affected parties. It must also involve an examination of the full range of alternatives, including no action.

Source: The Wingspread Conference, January 15, 1998. www.gdrc.org/u-gov/precaution-3.html

The PP was not defined in the Treaty of Maastricht, but in 2002, the European Commission issued the clarification:

> The precautionary principle applies where scientific evidence is insufficient, inconclusive or uncertain and preliminary scientific evaluation indicates that there are reasonable grounds for concern that the potentially dangerous effects on the environment, human, animal or plant health may be inconsistent with the high level of protection chosen by the EU.[34]

In this form, the principle has informed much of EU policy, and not just on the environment: other applications were in the regulations concerning chemicals and food, for example Regulation (EC) No 1907/2006, known as REACH, and Regulation (EC) No 178/2002.

What is common to all the formulations of the principle are the ideas of threats or potential damage to health or the environment, inconclusive scientific evidence / lack of conclusive evidence regarding cause-and-effect relationship, precautionary measures to be taken, and actions suspected of having potentially damaging effects to be avoided. This role, of guiding risk management when there is high level of uncertainty regarding some effects, was described in detail by the European Commission in a publication in 2017, "The Precautionary Principle: Decision Making Under Uncertainty" (Science for Environment Policy 2017).

In Germany, this approach first found its voice as a principle: the principle of *Vorsorge*, literally "care beforehand" (Martuzzzi & Tickner 2004). Before the formation of the European Union, this principle was invoked in Germany in vigorous policies to tackle acid rain as well as river pollution and pollution in the North Sea. It is easy to see the adoption of the PP by the EU as growing out of the example of German governmental risk management.

While the PP does not play the same role in, for example, American jurisprudence, it has been important in other parts of the world. But it has also been the subject of severe criticisms.

5.2.2 *Different interpretations of the PP*

There are different versions of the principle and considerable disagreement about what it means, or should mean, and about how it should be used.

It is helpful, in order to try to clarify what the principle means, to consider three possible interpretations as distinguished by Sandin (2007):

1. As a rule of choice
2. As epistemic principle
3. As procedural requirement

5.2.2.1 As a rule of choice

In particular situations, with different possible courses of action, the PP provides a rule to choose one of them:

> When an activity raises threats of harm to human health or the environment, precautionary measures should be taken, by *avoiding this activity*, even if some cause and effect relationship are not fully established scientifically.
>
> (Science and Environmental Health Network 1998)

> [T]he precautionary principle, that is *to take action to avoid* potentially damaging impacts of substance that are persistent, toxic and liable to

> bioaccumulate even when there is no scientific evidence to prove a causal link between emissions and effects.
>
> (Conference on the North Sea, The Hague, 1990)

Under this interpretation, the focus is on the prescription of "avoiding this activity." It could be viewed as an extrapolation of the "better safe than sorry" proverb one would use in ordinary life to justify taking some precautionary measures, including avoiding some activity, like avoiding eating some food that was left on the counter even though it does not look or smell bad.

According to Alan Ryan, the PP expresses our disproportionate aversion for loss compared to our appreciation of gain: "That asymmetry might be thought to represent an intuitive attachment to a 'better safe than sorry' principle" (Ryan 2007: 172). This view on the PP applies to its interpretation as a rule of choice, but maybe not so well to the other interpretations.

The problem with PP interpreted as "rule of choice" is that the principle is supposed to apply not to individual decisions but to governmental decisions. Ryan says:

> [If people decide to] forgo gains to their welfare they might easily have had, but do not mind, then that is up to them. Governments are not in that position; a government—in a modern, liberal-democratic societies at least—is obliged to do its best for the general welfare.
>
> (ibid.: 174)

And if acting on the basis of the PP means "to forgo gains that the public might easily have had" because of fears that do not have a solid scientific ground, it would go against doing what is best for the general welfare.

The principle may even seem self-refuting and incoherent, as Sunstein has argued, because it may lead to the creation of new harms (Sunstein 2005a). Reduction of greenhouse gases emissions, for example, may mitigate the consequences of global warming, but they might cripple the economy. How do we decide which harm is better or worse?

One may reply that the PP says to choose the action where the worst possible outcome is least bad. But when appeal is made to the precautionary principle, it is in situations in which we probably do not know enough to make this determination.

Another common criticism of PP is that it is so vague that it applies everywhere and nowhere. It is meant to be applied if an activity raises threats of harm to human health or the environment. But what is the criterion for raising threats of harm? How do we know that something is a real threat if that has not been scientifically established? Similarly, at what point are there clearly reasonable grounds for concern? Is it enough that some people have become worried or that some groups devoted to some special cause raise an alarm? And what counts as a precaution – would crossing your fingers do?

On this reading, the PP can be seen as overreaching, because it requires precautions before there is evidence that there will be harm, and stifling, obstructing progress and innovation. What would have become of the idea of the steam engine when it was introduced, or later, the internal combustion engine, if the PP had been applied? What potentially damaging effects could have been invoked that would have held back their development?

By insisting on precautions when the evidence is mixed and the case has not been scientifically established, the principle has been perceived as antiscientific and as giving an apparent justification for actions that have no scientific basis, even for irrational fears. So again, the PP read as a rule of choice seems self-defeating. But it may simply not be the proper way to interpret it.

5.2.2.2 As epistemic principle

Maybe, instead, the PP should be understood as a principle about *what evidence is sufficient to believe a claim* – a claim about whether a course of action (the use of a drug, of a technology) is not safe. As the European Commission put it in 2002:

> The precautionary principle applies where scientific evidence is insufficient, inconclusive or uncertain and preliminary scientific evaluation indicates that there are reasonable grounds for concern that the potentially dangerous effects on the environment, human, animal or plant health may be inconsistent with the high level of protection chosen by the EU.[35]

As an epistemic principle, the PP requires that, in some conditions, we should need very little evidence to accept that an activity is not safe, much less than science would normally need to accept a claim.[36]

As we discussed in Chapter 3 on risk assessment, the priority in science is to avoid forming false beliefs, type-1 error. For instance, consider the belief that a drug is efficient against a disease. In a scientific context, we do not want to form the false belief that the drug is not efficient just because it may have harmful side effects. It is true that in policy contexts, as we also saw in Chapter 3, when the consequences of making an error include that some people will be harmed or put at risk of being harmed, the priority is generally different: it is safety. But to reject the drug because it is not safe is not the same thing as believing that it is not efficient, even if the course of action is the same.

The problem, then, with such an epistemic principle is that it would lead to include a large number of false beliefs in our belief system, and that makes this interpretation of PP very unappealing. But here, too, it may simply not be the proper way to interpret it.

5.2.2.3 As procedural requirement

The understanding of the PP as a procedural requirement views it as a reaction to earlier bad decisions and a deep dissatisfaction with those earlier decisions. And the dissatisfaction is not only with the past chosen courses of action and their consequences but also with *how* the decisions were made.

> Millions of children worldwide have suffered from neurological damage, diminished mental capacity and thus the ability to make a living as a result of exposure to lead from smelters, in paint and in petrol. Tobacco, asbestos and numerous other agents provide ample evidence of the high costs associated with waiting for convincing proof of harm. These cases exemplify the failure of science and policy to prevent damage to health and ecosystems and the resulting impacts on health and the economy.
>
> (Martuzzi et al. 2004: 2)

But the motivation for a different form of risk assessment and management is not just what has happened in the past; it is also the societal and technological developments that have multiplied both the size of the impact that human activity can have and the uncertainties about what it actually is.

Take as an example the production of animal feed that relies on large-scale acquisition of components. The large scale increases the risk of contamination, and the feed is distributed to thousands of food-producing animals kept in CAFOs. The animals may all ingest the same contaminants before their meat is distributed to many different stores in different parts of the country to be sold to thousands of people (Crawshaw 2012). And the same CAFOs are producing tons of waste that can run off into surface waters, contaminate groundwater, rivers, and finally, drinking water systems of distribution that serve hundreds of thousands of people. Scientific studies have shown adverse health effects on CAFOs workers (Douglas, P. et al. 2018) and children (Pavilonis et al. 2013) living in proximity of an operation, such as a multitude of respiratory and allergic symptoms (Schultz et al. 2019), effects and stress from the noise and the odors, as well as "the growth of antibiotic-resistant bacteria, which have the potential to harm populations nationwide" (McElroy 2010).

Yet in 2017 the EPA signed an agreement with industry groups limiting the information on the operations that EPA was allowed to make public (National Resources Defense Council 2019). The EPA was required under the Clean Air Act to regulate the pollution due from CAFOs operations, but in 2017, a review from the EPA itself reported that the EPA had not developed the methods to estimate emissions from the CAFOs and so was not able to determine whether the operations complied with the regulations (Environmental Protection Agency 2017).

5.2.2.4 Role of the PP as a procedural rule

What the precautionary principle is then supposed to provide is not a rule for choosing a particular course of action but a set of requirements for how such decisions are to be made and for what arguments are relevant to decision-making.

For instance, the 1992 Rio Declaration says:

> In order to protect the environment, the precautionary approach shall be widely applied by States according to their capabilities. Where there are serious threats of serious or irreversible damage, **lack of full scientific certainty shall not be used as a *reason*** for postponing cost-effective measures to prevent environmental degradation. (emphasis ours)

This interpretation of the PP puts the emphasis on what should or should not count as a reason to decide on a certain course of action. But it might be a mistake to make the principle rejecting the use of scientific uncertainty regarding damages as a reason not to take measures to prevent degradation. Lack of full scientific certainty is too common to be a good reason for anything. Sandin points out that this interpretation has been called the "most cautious and weak." A stronger understanding of the procedural requirement would be as a requirement of reversal of the burden of proof, as it is said explicitly in the formulation from the Wingspread Conference:

> Where an activity raises threats of harm to the environment or human health, precautionary measures should be taken even if some cause and effect relationships are not fully established scientifically.
>
> In this context the proponent of an activity, rather than the public, bears the burden of proof.

On this understanding, the proponents of an activity would be required to show that it is safe for the activity to be permissible. And it may seem that the requirement that an action be proven safe is sending us back to the first interpretation of the principle, the self-defeating one, because no course of action can be proven to be absolutely safe. The context, however, is different, because under this interpretation the PP is not viewed as a rule of choice; instead, under the present interpretation, to place the burden of proof on the shoulders of the proponents of the activity could be understood as a way to give legitimacy to the concerns of the public and to a debate. If there is no proof that it is safe, there is no proof that *being concerned* is out of place.

In summary, the interpretation of the PP as a procedural rule would thus appear to be the one that makes it both the more defensible and the more practical in application, as well as the more appropriate in a democratic process. And in fact, the statement of the Wingspread Conference continues with:

> The process of applying the Precautionary Principle must be open, informed and democratic, and must include potentially affected parties.

> It must also involve an examination of the full range of alternatives, including no action.

Interpreted that way, the reversal of burden of proof would not be the end point of procedural requirement; it would be the starting point.

5.2.3 The alternatives assessment (AA) approach

5.2.3.1 Difference in aim

One of the aims of applying the PP as a procedural requirement is to create opportunities for debates and debates that include not just specialists but potentially affected parties. And the debates would be open to the consideration of a large range of alternatives, including but not limited to no action.

This interpretation of the PP is the one that is adopted, for instance, in the San Francisco Environment Code in its Chapter 1 on the precautionary principle:

> A central element of the precautionary approach is the careful assessment of available alternatives using the best available science.

And it is also the one that is used as springboard for the defense of a view on risk assessment and management grounded in the consideration of a large scope of alternative options, the alternatives assessment approach.

From the point of view of the alternatives assessment approach (O'Brien 2000; Myers & Raffensberger 2006), the traditional form of risk assessment and management aims to determine, for a given proposal or project, the maximal acceptable impact[37] for a minimal monetary cost. By contrast, this approach views the aim of risk management as creating the least possible impact for a maximal benefit for health and the environment:

> It is not a matter of *whether* we cause damage to each other and other living organisms. Instead, it is a matter of *how much* damage we cause. The major question is whether we and our social institutions (e.g., corporations and legislatures) will approach the world recklessly, causing or permitting as much damage as we can get away with; or carefully, causing or permitting as little damage as possible. If we are going to try to cause as little damage as possible, we (and our social institutions) have to systematically examine options for least damage.
>
> (O'Brien 2000: 12)

As an example, let us take a county's proposal to build an incinerator at a location that is near a school. The incinerator will emit a certain amount of particulate matter into the air, which will affect air quality at the school. Should this project go ahead?[38]

The Environmental Protection Agency has rules for particle pollution, which is a mixture of airborne particles and liquid droplets, composed of acids, water, carbon, metals, organic chemicals, and soil. Particle pollution (PM) is divided in terms of particle size; for example, $PM_{2.5}$ are fine particles, such as are found in smoke, with diameters of less than 2.5 microns.

In 1997, after evaluating hundreds of health studies, the EPA established a national 24-hour standard limiting $PM_{2.5}$ to 35 micrograms per cubic meter. This and other standards "set limits to protect public health, including the health of 'sensitive' populations such as asthmatics, children, and the elderly" (EPA n. d. "What are the air quality standards for PM?").

So, the EPA would approve the building of that incinerator near the school if it could be established that its emissions remained within the limits set by this rule for particulate pollution and similar relevant standards. And the county could then conduct a cost-benefit analysis to determine whether it would be advantageous to build and run the incinerator so that it would meet those standards.

The objection by proponents of the alternatives assessment approach is that the proposal should be considered not with the short-term aim of an acceptable EPA standard of impact but with the long-term aim of the least possible pollution and harmful impacts on health and the environment. The assessment should not just focus on whether the emitted amount of certain particles remains below a certain threshold that has been deemed acceptable but should consider other possible options and thoroughly assess each of them, considering a large range of impacts and benefits.

In light of those assessments, the choice of a course of action should not be based only on the comparison between similar proposals for the county, with options for alternative locations and alternative designs for the incinerator that meet the EPA standards; it should also include the consideration of alternatives to polluting incinerators, including requiring the companies that produce the wastes to safely store them on their premises.

Alternatives assessment approach presents itself as a different way to do risk management, a way other than CBA. What makes it different is not that CBA cannot or never does consider other options; it is that it advocates for systematically considering a larger scope of options. And it is not just more options but more diverse options, with the goal not just of making the risk acceptable but to make it as small as possible and even try to eliminate it. Regarding the contamination of air and water with toxic chemicals, for instance, the goal of the alternatives assessment approach is to look for options that could do without the use of the toxic chemicals.

So the idea of alternatives assessment applies to the assessment of management options, courses of action that could be taken as ways to manage a risk. The justification to replace the traditional costs-benefit analysis approach to risk management with an alternatives assessment approach is based on a criticism of the way in which CBA considers costs and benefits in its analysis.

CBA considers only monetary costs and benefits, but there are some non-monetary costs to pollution (like psychological impacts) and nonmonetary benefits to no pollution (increase in quality of life) that should be taken into account and that CBA does not take into account. When those nonmonetary costs and benefits are taken into account, what looked like acceptable options do not look acceptable anymore, and the pressure for finding new ways of addressing the problems is increased.

But the AA approach to risk management is actually not just about replacing CBA with something else. An indication of this is that the defense of the AA approach is often, for a large part, a critical discussion of how risk *assessment* is conducted. This criticism is developed by someone with firsthand experience in Mary O'Brien's monograph.

Her criticism has two main axes: one is that it is myopic, that it does not see far enough; the other is that it is narrow, that it does not see wide enough. It is myopic in that the assessment of risk is simply focused on keeping risks within the "acceptable" level in terms of degree of contamination. Her objection is, "Who says it is acceptable to have X amount of toxic contaminant released in the air or water?" "Who is to say that it is acceptable for people to drink a water or to breath an air that is contaminated to this or that degree?" "Who knows what the effect of drinking this water or breathing this air will be on people or their children in 10 or 20 years?" "Who knows how an acceptable degree of contamination of X combines with another acceptable degree of contamination of X or of Y, each being assessed as if they were the only ones in the life of people who may be exposed to multiple sources throughout the days?"

It is narrow in that it only looks at some kinds of impacts that are measurable and for which data are actually produced. But it does not consider a whole range of other kinds of impact, like psychological or emotional impacts; impacts on forms of life, like simply walking by the river or having dinner on your patio, which both become impossible when a pig farm moves in a few miles from your home; impact on cultural traditions; impacts on how we relate to our environment and the importance of this relation for our physical, emotional, and ethical well-being; differences in impact for different groups of people. And also, for O'Brien and, in general, those who are defending a precautionary approach, risk assessment should not just be concerned with human life, health, and quality of life but also, and maybe just as much, with the health, life, and quality of life of ecosystems and members of other species.

Given that the AA approach presents itself as a replacement of CBA and that it also criticizes the way in which risk assessment is conducted, it may seem that it is actually proposing a different way of doing things at those two distinct levels, the levels of risk assessment and risk management. At the level of the consideration of courses of action, it promotes the search for alternatives that seek to minimize impacts on health and the environment and, more broadly speaking, on quality of life. At the level of assessment, it promotes the assessment of a larger range of impacts, well beyond the measure of emission of a particular toxic chemical or particle, by taking into consideration different disciplinary perspectives and the inputs of those that may be affected in different ways. And in some ways, as we just explained, the aim of the AA approach does target those two levels. But it is also more than that.

Risk assessment can only find what it is looking for in the first place, meaning, it will not find impacts that it is not looking for. And what risk assessment is looking for is, for the most part, determined by the larger risk management framework it is part of. If risk management is about keeping the contamination of a list of toxic chemicals and particles within what has been deemed acceptable levels, risk assessment will be about measuring the levels of those chemicals and particles. It may then seem that risk management is only happening once the results of risk assessment have been produced, itself produced in total independence from the management level. But in fact, the management framework was always already there and shaping the way risk is assessed, in making possible or impossible some findings by the risk assessment process. Some results are impossible in the sense, as we just said, that one rarely can find what one is not looking for; one cannot assess impacts that one is not even considering as such.

> [R]isk assessment can result in the adoption of a rather narrow perspective in appraisal, often involving only a small subset of the relevant scientific disciplines. Precaution encourages a more broadly based approach, enhancing the ability of science to address complex interactions in complex environmental systems and thus to help detect and investigate early warnings. This may, in turn, identify promising new options that might otherwise be missed in risk management.
>
> (Stirling & Tickner 2004)

Risk management is supposedly about how we should act, whereas risk assessment is about what we know about the situation, and it may seem that management is based on assessment, whereas assessment is prior and independent from management. But how we aim at managing risk determines how we work at assessing them. Given this embedding of risk assessment within risk management, the changes promoted by the AA approach are not, in principle, directed at two distinct levels. It sees taking into consideration a larger scope of impact and aiming at minimizing or even eliminating harmful impacts as what should define the risk management framework. It means that, from the start, in this form of risk management, risk assessment should be interdisciplinary and also receptive to inputs from those who are impacted in different ways (Pellerano & Montague 2006).

5.2.3.2 Difference in method

Taking into account a larger range of costs and benefits

A main argument against the PP is that it does not weigh costs, whether direct (as in the costs of enforcing regulations) or indirect (loss of jobs or of local tax revenue). Some proponents of the PP argue that it is a requirement not to be bound by a monetary assessment of the costs and benefits of engaging or not engaging in a certain activity. Still, a condition that appears in some formulations of the PP, like the 1992 Rio Declaration, and that seems to put some constrains on its application, is for the measures taken to avoid the potential threats to be cost-effective.

To ensure that the measures taken are cost-effective means to assess and compare the costs and benefits of taken precautions with the costs and benefits of not taking the precautions. Such a requirement may undercut the whole point of the PP if it is directed at situations in which precisely it is not yet possible to assess the extent of the potential impacts of an activity.

It is generally easy to produce numbers to answer certain questions and not so easy for others:

- What would be the benefit of engaging in the activity (e.g., increase in productivity)?
- What would be the cost of not engaging in the activity (e.g., loss of additional employment)?
- What would be the cost of engaging in the activity?
- What would be the benefit of not engaging in this activity?

It appears to be generally easier to answer the first and second questions and more difficult to answer the third and fourth. For costs of engaging in the activity will include any collateral damage there might be, not just the financial outlay by those who propose the activity. If it is decided not to engage in the activity, the benefit might not seem to be any gain additional to what we already have, and opponents of the activity might be unable to cite anything but costs to be avoided.

A telling example was the majority opinion written by Justice Scalia regarding a 2012 regulation limiting mercury emissions and other pollutants from coal-fired power plants. "One would not say that it is even rational, never mind 'appropriate,'" said Scalia, "to impose billions of dollars in economic costs in return for a few dollars in health or environmental benefits."[39] Justice Scalia was referring to the calculated financial burden on the industry and to an informal, imprecise estimate of the health benefits of regulation.

FRAME 3: Michigan et al. versus the EPA

The EPA had argued that it was required not to take cost into account when making the decision to regulate emissions of hazardous air pollutants if the regulation was appropriate and necessary. Justice Scalia, delivering the court's majority opinion, argued that unless Congress provides otherwise, an agency acts unreasonably if it ignores economic considerations. The majority opinion rejects the EPA's contention that it need not consider cost when deciding whether to regulate an activity, because it can consider costs later when deciding how much to regulate them. In the dissenting opinion, Justice Elena Kagan emphasized that the EPA conducted a formal cost-benefit study afterward, which found that the quantifiable benefits of its regulation would exceed the costs up to nine times over – by as much as $80 billion each year. Those benefits include as many as 11,000 fewer premature deaths annually, along with a far greater number of avoided illnesses. "[T]he result," Kagan concludes, "is a decision that deprives the American public of the pollution control measures that the responsible Agency, acting well within its delegated authority, found would save many, many lives. I respectfully dissent."

Source: (*Michigan v EPA* 2015)

The real benefits of avoiding loss of health and loss of environmental degradation may not be mostly monetary or measurable in terms of lives saved. The quality of life benefits that health procures not only for the person that is healthy but also for their family are not just physical but psychological, emotional, and existential. Similarly, there are some economic benefits to protecting the environment and the conditions of life of other species, for instance, in maintaining environmental resources, but there are also, maybe mostly, nonmonetary benefits in terms of quality of life, and not only in its physical or psychological aspects but also ethical.

In most cases, the industry might well be able to demonstrate a clear increase in costs of production for alternatives to its established practice. For example, in the long ongoing dispute between the USA and the European Union about hormone-treated beef, the agricultural industry in the USA insists that costs be considered as well as the possible harmful health effects to people and animals (Clemens & Babcock 2002). The EU, adopting a precautionary approach, cites the dangers of meat from animals treated with synthetic sex hormones and, specifically, the evidence that it increases the risk of cancer, though the evidence (when the ban was instituted in 1989) was far from conclusive.

The relevant alternative here is to raise cattle for beef without use of those hormones. But what would that mean for the industry?

The proponents of the AA approach argue that, indeed, the traditional form of assessment favors industry, but by ignoring hidden additional costs not borne by those who receive the benefits. The same objection of not considering costs can be turned against the opponents of the AA approach: there are many costs, and benefits, that are normally not taken into account in a traditional cost-benefit analysis.

CBA may very well consider alternatives and compare the costs and benefits of different options for dealing with a risky situation. But CBA aims at arriving at numbers that represent the total of the different costs and the total of the different benefits so as to be able to compare those two numbers. All costs and benefits have to be converted in monetary value, so CBA only considers costs and benefits that can be assigned a monetary value.

By contrast, the AA approach starts with the principle that a condition for the impacts of an option to be considered in the decision about what to do is that they *matter* to those who would be impacted by the choice of the option.

Table 5.5 Additional costs of producing non-hormone-treated beef for the European Union.

Higher production costs for not using hormones	$15 to $40 per head
Initial NHTC Program documentation processing and audit by USDA/AMS	up to $3,000
Annual NHTC Program audit by USDA/AMS	$500 to $2,000
Labor for maintaining NHTC Program paperwork and documentation	Not estimated
Slaughter plant costs	
Initial plant certification inspection by USDA/FSIS	$500
Annual plant inspection (not required, but recommended)	$500
Plant modifications to meet EU requirements	Not estimated
Onetime validation fee for using Maxxam Analytics (effective until August 31, 2005)	$30,000[a]
Additional residue testing for product from steers and heifers	$1,950[b]
Other costs	
Shipping small volumes and using air freight	Not estimated
Marketing the remainder of the carcass	Not estimated

[a]This fee is $10,000 for companies associated with the original export group who invested in the validation costs for Maxxam Analytics.

[b]Tests are conducted randomly based on total slaughter volume. The reported cost is based on the price schedule effective through August 31, 2002.

In the case of hormone treatment, some costs are the effects on the human health, including in the US, ingesting the hormones when they eat the meat. The alternative, the shift to nonhormonal production, could reduce those costs and yield benefits not considered in the prior table.

Allowing different perspectives on the impacts may produce different evaluations of the costs and benefits from people who are impacted in different ways. For instance, the disappearance of salmon in the Columbia River Basin because of dams may be an inconvenience for some grocery shoppers, but for some members of Native American nations, it is a loss of cultural identity; for some others who fish for a living, it is the loss of a job.

> The cultural emotions connected to a given alternative, for instance, can be a pro or a con, and may be both, depending on which sector of the community you inhabit. And advantage or a disadvantage of a given alternative can be social, religious, economic, scientific, or political.
>
> (O' Brien 2000: 1).

FRAME 4: EPA and the Columbia River

In a decision on February 25, 1991, the EPA established a total maximum daily loading (TMDL) limit for the amount of dioxin released in the Columbia River. The same amount of contaminants found in the river was found to impair reproduction in some species, and the population of bald eagles living along the river was declining.

Dioxin/Organochlorine Center and Columbia River United (DOC) went to court on January 11, 1993, contending that the TMDL fails to implement adequate water quality standards because it 1) inadequately protects aquatic life and wildlife, 2) inadequately protects certain human subpopulations, 3) fails to consider the cumulative effect of dioxin-related pollutants in the water system, and 4) that the EPA abused its discretion by arbitrarily and capriciously considering only the risk to human life and failing to consider the effect of dioxin on animal life.

In this and other disputes, the courts found in favor of the EPA. But in a series of decisions, based in part on consultation with the public, the EPA has modified the original regulations.

What do you think could explain why the court originally found in favor of the EPA? What do you think could explain why the EPA modified the original regulations?

Sources: National Service Center for Environmental Publications (NSCEP), US Court of Appeals 9th Circuit Nos.93–35973, 93–3600.

United States Environmental Protection Agency Reanalysis (2010): *Federal Register* vol. 75, number 120, June 23, 2010.

So the AA approach is open to considering all kinds of costs and benefits. What should be considered when choosing between options is not just physical health but also quality of life, with its cultural, psychological, emotional, and ethical components:

> The consequences (i.e., the pros and cons, or the costs and benefits) of alternatives assessment, however, can include issues of democracy, aesthetics, spiritual values, ethnic values, uncertainty, sense of community, and personal feeling as well as monetary consequence.
>
> (O'Brien 2000: 143)

And what should be taken into account are not just positive and negative impacts of the options on human lives but also the life and conditions of life of members of other species and of ecosystems. In our earlier example, an alternative location for the incinerator, while having the same impact on human health, might be less damaging to wildlife and forests in the area. If the damage to wildlife and environment is taken into account, what could have appeared as similar alternatives will appear as importantly different ones.

Fostering scientific interdisciplinarity and innovation

The goal of taking into account a larger range of impacts is served by fostering interdisciplinary cooperation. For instance, since 2012 the University of California, Berkeley, offers an interdisciplinary course called Greener Solutions that gathered "graduate students in chemistry, environmental health, and engineering to understand each other's discipline, and to work together to develop safer alternatives to hazardous chemicals and manufacturing processes" (Schwartzman & Buckley 2019). What this initiative and other collaborative initiatives (Kokai et al. 2020) show is that the idea of interdisciplinary cooperation and assessment of alternatives is not limited to situations of great scientific uncertainty; it is an especially adequate strategy, according to Ashford (2005), when there are concerns about the fairness of the distribution of costs and benefits of hazardous activities and persistent and/or bioaccumulative toxic substances.

Since the goal of alternatives assessment is to support an informed transition to safer chemicals by comparing a range of options, it demands an action-oriented process. Since what it demands goes beyond quantifying the risk of a chemical for a specific hazard end point (e. g., cancer) associated with a given level of exposure, it requires new and innovative research designed to produce relevant decisions about adoption (Tickner et al. 2017). In contrast to a reactive, "problem-centered," risk-based approach to risk, the AA approach requires answers to further questions: are there other products, processes, or tools that fulfill the same function? If so, which are safer by your criterion? Could we do without fulfilling that function? What would be lost, and what would be gained, very broadly speaking?

While the demand for additional, innovative research makes for greater cost to industry, it can be seen as stimulating novelty in scientific research, with longer-term contributions both to society and to scientific knowledge. Moreover, to generate the range of alternatives to be considered, input is required from scientific areas outside the chemical industry, and that fosters interdisciplinary collaboration and public involvement in environmental health policy and practice.

As a result, new communities of practice have been emerging, and this, in turn, requires the development of new information infrastructure to reach across disciplinary lines. An example is the Data Commons, part of the Pharos Project, to provide access and interaction with many different sources of information (Kokai et al. 2020). It also appears that business and industry have begun to see the advantages that may accrue from this new scientific activity.[40]

5.2.4 *Is AA an alternative to CBA?*

The alternatives assessment approach to risk assessment and management, which can be seen as an application of the precautionary principle as a procedural requirement, presents itself as an alternative to CBA. But the difference between CBA and AA is not that AA excludes consideration of costs and benefits or that CBA excludes the consideration of alternatives.

From the perspective of the AA approach, the traditional form of risk assessment and management is narrow in focus and myopic. It only assesses specific, predefined kinds of impacts and from sources considered in isolation; when considering alternative options, it only aims at keeping pollutants within a certain threshold; it is bound to only consider monetary value when comparing options for management.

By contrast, the AA approach aims at eliminating polluting or making it the least possible and encourages the consideration of innovative options, emerging from different perspectives; it aims at considering all kinds of particular impacts for a given project and also the cumulative scope, in space and time, of those impacts given that other sources than the one under study may contribute to it too; it rejects the requirement to only consider monetary values. To the question "How, then, can we decide among the alternatives if we have to consider numerous groups and numerous factors, some of them financial, some cultural, some spiritual?" O'Brien answers, "The same way each of us makes decisions each day" (O'Brien 2000: 144).

Of course, when we make everyday decisions, we often do not need to account for how exactly we made the decision; we do not need to demonstrate that it was done in a fair and systematic way. And it seems that to consider only monetary values for the costs and the benefits is the best way we have to make the choice between options accountable and systematic and, in that sense, fair. But one may just as well object that it actually does not really account for all that we care about. Or that when it does assign a monetary value to impacts that are not monetary, it cannot be done fairly, because how much one would pay for silence or clean air will depend on many personal and contextual factors independent from how much one really cares about silence or clean air.

Balancing costs and benefits when they have not all been converted into a monetary equivalent and there is no systematic way of doing it is very challenging and requires making choices that are expressing value judgments. The AA approach promotes choices that are situated, are deliberative, and involve those who may be affected by the consequences of the choice. And one may even argue that it is, in fact, more transparent not to force a monetary value on all the factors that can be regarded as costs and benefits because, decision makers are then obliged "to make explicit their value judgments and tradeoffs, thereby preventing them from abdicating responsibility for their decisions" (Ashford & Caldart 1991: 145).

5.3 Risk communication

5.3.1 Introduction

On May 13 of 2021, the Centers for Disease Control and Prevention (CDC) updated their COVID-19 guidelines on mask wearing: people who had been fully vaccinated could shed the mask, both outdoors and indoors. They could "start doing the things that [they] had stopped doing because of the pandemic," said the CDC director Rochelle Walensky.[41]

This update was presented as an evidence-based decision: newly published studies on the efficiency of the vaccine (see CNN article) led public health authorities to revise their recommendation. But the decision was very coldly received by the media and many in the health-care community. The evidence about the efficacy of the vaccines wasn't really that new or surprising, critics argued: we very much expected that they would drastically reduce transmission of the virus, given the prior data from early clinical trials that supported the vaccines' emergency use authorization months earlier. At that time in the pandemic, the vaccination rate in the United States was still much too low for comfort, they thought. Worse perhaps, they claimed, this recommendation was unfair to the most vulnerable: since mask-wearing was still highly polarized, a message associating being mask-free with being vaccinated would give the immunocompromised, who can't get vaccinated themselves, a false sense of security around the unmasked. But we had to trust each other and count on everyone's sense of collective responsibility, the CDC implied. Yet the shift in messaging itself, the critics argued, would affect the CDC's reliability and, in turn, the public's trust in public health organizations.

Months later, after the dramatic rise of more transmissible variants in the summer of 2021, the CDC recanted that recommendation. New evidence – data on the delta variant's prevalence – justified a new recommendation:[42] "When you get information about risks and how to mitigate risks, there's a public health obligation to let people know about it," administration officials said. This newer recommendation would give local authorities "cover" to implement new mandates.[43]

The May 13 recommendation, however, represented a true shift in communication strategy. We knew in 2020 that virus transmission was airborne: frequent handwashing was mostly irrelevant to stop an aerosolized virus, spraying disinfectant in the subway wouldn't stop contracting COVID, and plastic shields wouldn't protect cashiers – they could even make things worse. Yet there was no major announcement inviting people to "go back to not caring about washing your hands so much." CDC, NIH, or White House officials didn't go on TV saying people could stop cleaning surfaces. Wasn't there a public obligation to let people know about this information about risk and how to mitigate it? Wasn't there a need to give local authorities cover to mandate the most efficient risk-management strategies rather than wasteful measures?

To be fair, when we learned that the virus was airborne, public health messaging shifted and emphasized ventilation and masking over mere physical distancing and surface cleaning. But the CDC did not go on TV all but asking people to drop any health safety measure. Frequent handwashing would still prevent infections other than COVID-19, after all. But so would mask-wearing. So what changed in this messaging from the CDC? It wasn't just new evidence, if at all.

The tone of the messaging changed too: ditching the mask was "exciting and powerful," the CDC director said. It was powerful probably because it demonstrated an achievement but also because it would signal the benefits of vaccination; it would show the vaccine hesitant what they were missing out on. The vaccinated *should* – not just could – shed the mask, or so it seemed. Indeed, in a surprising twist in communication, public health officials now had to address the issue not of too little compliance with safety recommendations but that of *too much* risk aversion! NIH director Antony Fauci's measured and personable voice now had to cajole mask wearers rather than the vaccine hesitant:

> There's absolutely nothing wrong with an individual who has a certain level of risk aversion, as we know the risk [after vaccination against COVID-19] is extremely low of getting infected whether you're indoors or outdoors. But there are those people who don't want to take that bit of a risk and there's nothing wrong with that and they shouldn't be criticized. (same CNN article)

This May 13 announcement was a true shift in style, substance, and goal: the message was no longer "Wear a mask and go get vaccinated; it's the right thing to do for yourself and those around you"; it was now, "If you're already vaccinated, stop wearing a mask, we should accept some risk, we all have different risk attitudes and we should accept that, and let's just get the vaccine and enjoy life." Interestingly, much of that new message was already what the mask noncompliant and the vaccine hesitant were proclaiming.

The CDC's shift was one of communication, in a deep sense: not just a change of a message's content because the information had changed, but a change in whom it addressed, whom it involved as being part of the conversation, and whom it empowered as decision makers. The messaging went from top-down transfer of information (from experts to laypeople on the safest practices) to a conversation, a multifaceted deliberation that would take into account people's perceptions, attitudes toward risk, and concern for others. One could say that with the May 13 perceived recommendation *not* to adopt safety precautions, the CDC gave all US residents – risk averse and risk seekers, those trustful of public institutions and those distrustful – a common language to discuss risk assessment and management.

Whether or not that announcement succeeded, this shift in messaging illustrates that risk communication is, of course, about experts conveying information to a lay audience. And we'll see that conveying information successfully has its specific challenges. But the example about the CDC's shift in communication also shows that there is much more at play in risk communication than conveying information.

Risk communication is complex: effective communication depends, for, instance on each party's goal (e.g., what nonscientist stakeholders expect from experts or what public health officials expect from the public); it depends on people's risk perception, although, as we will see, not in a straightforward way; it depends on a message's framing; and it depends on the relationship among the parties and, crucially, how well they trust each other.

5.3.2 Challenges of risk perception for risk communicators

As we saw in previous chapters, what counts as a risk or not and how acutely it is perceived may vary widely from one individual to another, or from one interest group to another. Consequently, even assuming that perceiving a risk entails a willingness to act on it, effective risk communication cannot just be about communicating effective mitigation strategies. Indeed, assuming further that those who give and those who receive information about a risk agree on the nature of specific risks (i.e., agree, for instance, that smoking is unequivocally bad with unwanted consequences), risk communicators have to take into account the psychology of risk perception to tailor their message so that they make the most of people's heuristics, tell a relatable story with relevant numbers free of jargon and that emphasize how, for instance, controllable a risk is.

"Only you can prevent forest fires," says the friendly but authoritative, fatherlike Smokey the Bear familiar to US drivers. This is an example of straightforward risk communication whose efficiency rests on a direct, jargon-free, and personal message on a risk we can all agree on: wildfires are bad, and they're preventable.[44] But risks are often more ambiguous than wildfires. Lead is a dangerous poison that can greatly affect young children's development. Its presence in decades-old residential building, whether as plumbing or in the paint, can constitute either a very manageable risk if left mostly untouched (for instance, by painting over chipping lead-based paint) or made much worse if poorly managed (improperly removing paint may produce hazardous dust). Effective communication must then be more specific than "Lead is dangerous for your child" or "Stay away from lead," as such simple messages could do more harm than good.[45]

Food itself is a risk: it is full of yummy fats and sugars, pesticides, synthetic components that may or may not affect our health. Medicine itself is a risk: drugs as common as antidepressants may lead to nausea, weight gain, sleep problems, or even suicidal thoughts, as black box labels may warn its consumers.

In many cases, the relationship between knowledge and risk perception is straightforward, and so is that between risk perception and risk-mitigating behavior. Studies interested in a population's level of risk perception, knowledge, and readiness to adopt risk-mitigating behaviors can at times observe a straightforward relationship among all three variables; see for instance Arslanca et al. (2021) on health-care workers in Turkey at the beginning of the COVID-19 pandemic, or Anthonj et al. (2019) on Kenyan wetland communities' risk perception, knowledge, and behavior of water-related infectious disease exposure. In both cases, findings support the idea that heightened risk perception go along with improved knowledge about the risk, which in turn may result in better preparedness and actions. People may not always act as their level of risk perception and knowledge would suggest (otherwise, we wouldn't do things we know are "bad for us"). But there is still, as often studies such as those find, a positive relationship between perception, knowledge, and behavior. If that model is true and generalizable, then risk communication, if it aims at improving preparedness and behavior, should be to increase risk perception and knowledge.

Yet in another study about risk perception, knowledge, and behavior about COVID-19, Grima and collaborators (Grima et al. 2021) found that knowledge about a risk was clearly associated with risk-mitigating behavior but that the relationship was inconclusive between perception and behavior. Worse, an increase in risk perception may result in a decrease in preparedness. Indeed, catastrophist media announcements on climate change may result in general apathy; people may be numbed into inaction out of overwhelming anxiety and fear. Hence, this general conclusion:

> Risk communication can be considered effective if it alerts the target audience (whether the public in general or particular at-risk populations)

> as to what is hazardous, the extent of the danger and what should be done to protect oneself. It should do this without arousing unnecessary anxiety.
>
> (Breakwell 2000: 111)

Risk perception may then both help and hinder effective risk management. Effective risk communication should then be done in a way that empowers rather than paralyzes or desensitizes an audience.

Psychometric studies[46] suggest that risk perception is affected by some of the risk's characteristics: whether it's voluntary (risks taken voluntarily, such as with extreme sport, are more acceptable), controllable (we find more acceptable risks we control ourselves or that are perceived as more natural), or limited in time and space (we react less acutely to more diffused risks). We also saw that people are less likely to act on dreadful, novel, complex risks (such as irreversible, all-powerful climate change or a suddenly appearing, life-threatening meteorite) or very familiar risks (such as a sugar-rich diet) than on manageable, well-understood risks (such as ozone-depleting chemicals). And we saw that risk perception is also affected by people's social identity (partisan affiliation, racial or gender identity) as well as their worldview (such as their individualism or authoritarianism).

All such factors shape risk perception, which in turn is associated with different attitudes and behaviors about risk (for an example of an overview on risk perception and how it might shape behavior about COVID-19, for instance, see Cori et al. 2020).

Knowing about how risk perception affects an audience matters for communication, because such psychological effects are in part detached from more direct characteristics of risk. That is, these psychological effects don't depend on a rational or fact-based assessment of risk – of the audience's knowledge about a risk or the assumed value attached to the potential loss of our health, well-being, belongings, etc., and the assumed frequency of a given unwanted event.

Indeed, much of our collective response to the COVID-19 pandemic was driven by factors of risk perception that had little to do with our knowledge of the risk. Little was known about the transmission of the COVID-19 disease early in the spring of 2020. Yet attitudes about mask-wearing were sharply polarized, to the point where, in the US, for instance, political partisan affiliation was the *strongest predictor* of mask-wearing, not income, education, nearby mortality from the disease, or knowledge about the virus (see, e.g., Allcott et al. 2020; Gadarian et al. 2021).

This disconnect between knowledge and risk perception – and then, hopefully, behavior – may occur even when knowledge is more clearly identified than for a novel pandemic. In the context of risk communication about flood management, when communities are consulted on how to manage flooding risks, Miceli and collaborators (2008) found that the likelihood of a disaster was barely taken into account when making judgments about perceived risk levels – and therefore decision-making about mitigation (see Wachinger et al. 2013; Haimes 2004).

The relationship between risk communication and risk perception, then, is not straightforward. If risk communication should aim to both alert and empower the target audience to make informed decision, it may not be able to maximize both at the same time. If one wants to maximize the audience's awareness and therefore the acuity of its risk perception, one could, at the same time, overwhelm the audience and either numb it into passivity (think of inefficient, catastrophist climate change communication) or trigger overreactions (such as blank bans on nuclear energy that result in more death from fossil fuels).

Conversely, if one wants to maximize an audience's ability to make informed decisions, then it should provide it with expert knowledge, including transparent assessments of uncertainty. This, however, is unlikely to provoke much reaction if it overwhelms the audience with complexity or else is likely to result in haphazard risk management decisions if not accompanied by a good management of the audience's perception of the nature of the risk.

This is the sort of concerns the United States Food and Drug Administration had in mind when it sent a warning in 2013 to the personal genomics company 23andMe, who was selling a personal genome service as intended for use in the diagnosis of disease.[47] In its marketing, the genomics company claimed that it could provide its customers, from genetic information obtained from a small saliva sample, a personalized analysis of risk factors (phrased in percent of chance to develop such and condition) and carrier status for as many as 254 diseases and conditions, called a "health report," which would constitute a "first step in prevention" that enables users to "take steps toward mitigating serious diseases" such as diabetes, coronary heart disease, and breast cancer. Patients, the FDA ruled, were likely without expert guidance to over-interpret these results and start pursuing treatment on their own, some of which may be harmful.

There is, as Wachinger and colleagues (2013) put it:

> [A] complex relationship between risk perception and social responses: some studies assume that individuals with low risk perception are less likely to respond to warnings and undertake preparedness measures than individuals with a high risk perception. . . . However, this is not always the case. Many studies provide evidence that even though individuals have experience and high risk perception, they seldom take appropriate preparedness actions. . . . Haynes et al. (2008) argue in the same direction: "it is now understood that there is not necessarily a direct link between awareness, perceived risk and desired (by risk managers) preparations or behavioral responses." Miceli et al. (2008) noted that "most

empirical evidence suggests that the link between these two variables [risk perception and preparedness actions] is quite weak or even null."

Referring to this state of affairs as a risk perception paradox, Wachinger and colleagues explain that this complex relationship is mediated by such factors as audience members' previous personal experience with a given risk, their trust toward the agency recommending risk mitigation efforts and their own liability, and their personal ability to act. Such factors, these authors report, can be addressed by adopting participatory forms of risk communication and management strategies.

So, some ways in which risk perception challenges communication are that 1) it is affected by factors not most relevant to experts' risk assessment, 2) heightened perception can both enable and hinder action, and 3) at the same time, communication's success (its ability to enable people to act on what they agree are risks) requires taking risk perception into account.

Put differently, 1) it's not enough when communicating about risks to tell an audience what is at stake for them and how much they might lose if they don't adopt such and such measure, 2) it's not enough to phrase it in a way that will create the most alarm and, therefore, the most heightened perception, and yet 3) communication that only addresses the most factual elements of risk judgments (how much one could lose and how likely it is) and doesn't engage with the factors of risk perception (such as voluntariness, fairness, immediate versus delayed risk, its controllability, etc.) sets itself for failure.

5.3.3 Information-deficit model of risk communication

As one can see on such polling visual tools as those of the Yale Program on Climate Change Communication,[48] only 55% of Americans in 2020 believed that scientists thought that global warming is happening when in fact the reality of global warming is undisputed among scientists – regardless of its cause. Only 64% in Massachusetts, 63% in New York, and 62% in California believed so. After all, less than two-thirds of millennials in America in 2018 believed that the Earth was flat (Foster & Branch 2018), so such numbers maybe shouldn't be surprising.

Scientists, when asked about their role in engaging the public and policy makers, respond that "the public is uninformed about science and therefore prone to errors in judgment and policy preferences" (Besley & Nisbet 2013). As a consequence, to the extent that they are willing to engage in communication, scientists view it as aiming to increase science literacy.

This model of science communication, labeled "deficit model of communication," implies that behavior follows from attitude, which itself follows from knowledge. On that view, if people knew what the scientists knew, they would make the "right" decision. This is particularly pertinent to scientific communication about risks. It is a view of science communication that addresses only the public deficit in knowledge.

This view, which gives scientists a central role in risk communication, may run counter to the intuition that lay audiences will respond better to a message from someone they like or identify with rather than experts they may not have any strong feelings toward. Public service announcements – such as "Get out the vote" or public health campaigns – often rely on popular celebrities, actors, or athletes. But for instance, at the beginning of the COVID-19 pandemic, a large study on more than 12,000 respondents in over six countries showed that celebrities were the least effective public health spokespersons, worse than elected officials, and that scientists were the most efficient spokespersons (Abu-Akel et al. 2021).

Studies have shown, however, that information-centered communication can backfire, to the point where *more information* can lead to *more polarization*, for instance, on the need to mitigate the effects of global warming. Dan Kahan and collaborators (2012) surveyed 1,500 Americans about their science literacy, knowledge about climate change, worldviews (egalitarian, hierarchical, individualist, or communitarian), and political preferences; they found that science literacy had a *negative* effect on their views on climate change! In other words, the more people knew about science, the less they agreed on the view that climate change was a risk and on the need to mitigate it. These findings were replicated even after controlling for what respondents thought scientists knew about climate change (Kahan 2012).

Indeed, most – almost two-thirds, even – adult Oklahomans in 2020 thought that climate change is happening, a majority of them (55%) perceived it as a risk,[49] yet they just re-elected to the Senate James Inhofe, a vocal climate science denier and opponent of climate regulations,[50] in line with their weak support (42%) for the claim that global warming should be a high priority for the next president and Congress.

The results from Kahan et al. (2012) suggest that education provides one with the ability to pick out the information that confirms one's preferences:

> People with different values draw different inferences from the same evidence. Present them with a PhD scientist who is a member of the US National Academy of Sciences, for example, and they will disagree on whether he really is an 'expert', depending on whether his view matches the dominant view of their cultural group.
>
> (Kahan et al. 2011)

> The positions on climate change of both groups track their impressions of recent weather. Yet their impressions of what the recent weather has been are polarized, too, and bear little relationship to reality (Goebbert et al. 2012). But is this sort of cultural polarization evidence of irrationality? If it is, then how can we explain the fact that members of the lay

> public who are the most science literate, and the most proficient at technical reasoning, are also the most culturally polarized.
>
> (Kahan, Peters et al. 2012)

> If anything, social science suggests that citizens are culturally polarized because they are, in fact, too rational – at filtering out information that would drive a wedge between themselves and their peers.
>
> (Kahan 2012)

Because it attributes disagreement between experts and the general public to a lack of information, the information-deficit model of science communication overstates information deficit. It also dismisses human psychology: people don't reason to get the right answer but rather to get the answer they want to be right – called motivated reasoning.

Building on the observation that the audience is complex and segmented along interests and differing psychological attitudes to a given risk, studies have suggested adopting different risk communication strategies depending on the circumstances.

Acknowledging the paradox of risk perception we saw earlier, agencies such as the World Health Organization recommend different risk communication strategies depending on the public's sense of outrage to a risk on one

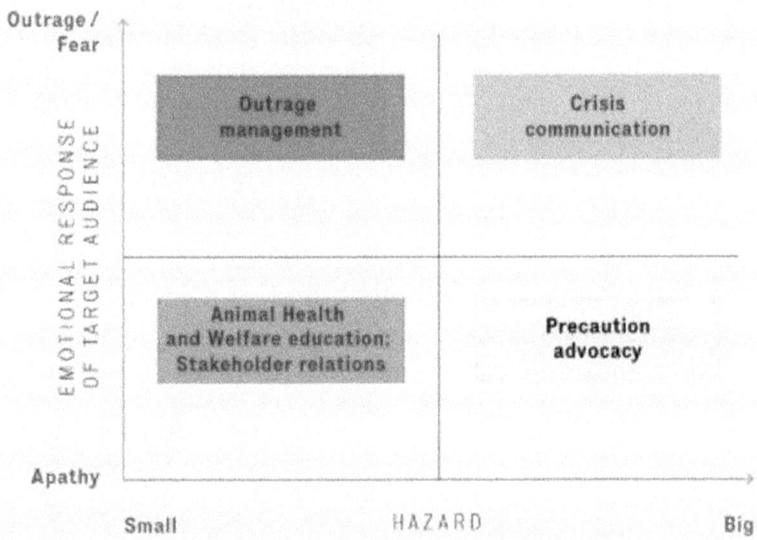

Figure 5.1 Risk communication strategies according to hazard and the emotional response of the target audience, from Sandman, http://psandman.com.

hand and its perception of risk (i.e., chance of harm), following the work of Peter Sandman.[51]

On that view, scientists can tailor their communication strategy to the public's risk perception and level of interest: they can either be empathetic and acknowledge uncertainty, in the case of crisis communication (high hazard and high fear), or be provocative, blunt, and by using compelling storytelling when facing an audience apathetic to acute hazard ("precaution advocacy" in the previous graph).

Recent work from the Yale Program on Climate Change Communication and the George Mason Center for Climate Change Communication revealed how the public is segmented into six distinct groups who respond differently to climate change: the alarmed, concerned, cautious, disengaged, doubtful, and dismissive (Leiserowitz et al. 2021).

These groups differ in how likely they are to accept or reject the science of climate change (this is the attitudinal valence in the previous graph) and in how involved they are on this issue. These results suggest that scientists should tailor their communication to the specific group they are addressing: they can help the disengaged see how climate change may affect them personally, they can provide the alarmed with specific recommendations on how to mitigate the effects of climate change, and they should probably not waste much time engaging anti-climate-science activists.

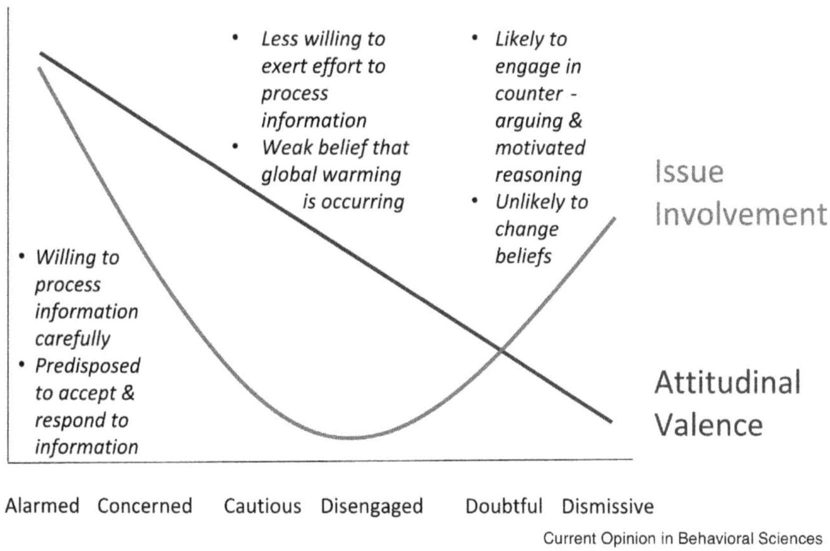

Figure 5.2 Information-processing propensities among the six Americas, from (Leiserowitz et al. 2021).

5.3.4 From the public to the experts: participatory model

What different audiences may respond to, how they will "reason to get the answer they want to be right," as we saw earlier, depends in a large part on their values and identity. As Daniel Hicks (2017) argues, for such scientific controversies as mandatory vaccination, the acceptability of genetically modified food, or climate change, science serves as a *proxy* for such political and philosophical debates as the relationship between capitalism and the environment, the meaning of risk, or the role of expertise in a democracy. And as Hicks shows, taking the example of how their co-op debated the merit of genetically modified food, such controversies may occur among scientists *even when there's little debate about the scientific evidence* (see also Hicks 2015).

Scientists are experts about the science, but they're not necessarily value and identity experts. As Michael Sandel put it in his critique of technocracy and the meritocracy:

> If the primary source of opposition to action on climate change were a lack of information or a refusal to accept science, one would expect opposition to be stronger among those with less education and scientific knowledge. But this is not the case. . . . The technocrat's belief that, if only we could agree on the facts, we could then have a reasoned debate about policy, misconceives the project of political persuasion. . . .
>
> What would it take to counter the outsize influence of the fossil fuel industry on democratic politics? Should we reconsider the consumerist attitudes that lead to treat nature instrumentally, as a dumping ground for what Pope Francis has called our "throwaway culture"? And what about those who oppose government action to reduce carbon emissions, not because they reject science but because they do not trust government to act in their interest, especially in a large-scale reconfiguration of the economy, and do not trust the technocratic elites who would design and implement this reconfiguration?
>
> These are not scientific questions to be answered by experts. They are questions about power, morality, authority, and trust, which is to say they are questions for democratic citizens.
>
> (Sandel 2020: 110–112)

Yet at we saw earlier, scientists, to the extent that they are interested in communication, merely do so to increase science literacy; "few scientists view their role as an enabler of direct public participation in decision-making through formats such as deliberative meetings" (Besley & Nisbet 2013)

To see what that may mean in practice and why it matters, consider the case of nuclear waste management in the Yucca Mountain (see Shrader-Frechette 1994). Experts assessed that permanent geological disposal in the Nevada desert was the best approach, as it reduced transportation risk, minimized harm, and addresses a collective responsibility to future generations (since it is a permanent solution). It minimized harm because the assessed fatality rate (calculated on the basis of yearly exposure) was below an acceptable threshold, and because the remote site chosen minimized the number of people who exposed to radiation.

This risk management choice, however, was deeply unpopular. As Shrader-Frechette argues, the experts thought that the goal for risk communication toward the public was to address "perceived" (as opposed to "real") risk to assuage irrational fears that would explain any disagreement with this policy.

Shrader-Frechette argues that such expert reasoning is already debatable strictly on technical grounds as, for instance, it neglected small short-term harm despite unknown long-term effects of exposure. But by dismissing future local residents' right to consent to their exposure (since this was a permanent solution) and by discarding potential concerns about the unfairness of the uneven geographic distribution of exposure, experts made decisions that should arguably have been adjudicated by the citizenry.

This case illustrates ethical questions and dilemmas about risk assessment and management that would warrant a deliberative decision-making process between experts and the public: how to assess cumulative risk and its acceptability when each contributing risk taken on its own is acceptable? How to define acceptable thresholds for harm when they are calculated based on average effects? What is a fair compensation to those who depart from the average if the decision is based on an average? How to define consent to take a risk when those most likely to face a risk are the least likely to be able to provide informed consent? (See Shrader-Frechette 1986).

Experts can *help* address such questions, but they cannot decide them as experts; they also *need* such dilemmas to be resolved to carry out their expert assessment. This requires deliberation and mutual exchange, not simply a one-way transfer of information from scientists to a lay audience. As Daniel Sarewitz – a geologist who spent years working for Congress – put it about environmental policy, it will suffer from an excess of objectivity if scientists are the only or main source of policy prescriptions (Sarewitz 2000). Instead, he advocates a participatory form of decision-making

> [that] accepts that various stakeholders legitimately see reality in different ways; that there is no ultimate source of knowledge that can dictate the "correct" action under conditions of natural and societal complexity; and that the characterization of a problem, and consequences of any particular course of action aimed at addressing the problem, must always be uncertain. Policies are experiments; science can assess the success of the experiments and thus provide additional information that decision makers can integrate as they pursue longer-term goals. This feedback process is often called" adaptive management. . . . This view honors the reality of

> democratic politics and complex natural phenomena, and places science not outside this reality, but squarely within it.
>
> (Sarewitz 2000: 95)

Such participatory decision-making process leaves a central role for scientists, but one that is quite different from the risk communication strategies evoked earlier. Crucially, it requires a very different understanding of communication: from a one-way transfer of information (from experts to a lay audience) to a conversation.

This echoes Baruch Fischhoff's summary of the field of risk communication's developmental stages (Fischhoff 1995):

1. All we have to do is get the numbers right.
2. All we have to do is tell them the numbers.
3. All we have to do is explain what we mean by the numbers.
4. All we have to do is show them that they've accepted similar risks in the past.
5. All we have to do is show them that it's a good deal for them.
6. All we have to do is treat them nicely.
7. All we have to do is make them partners.

We have seen that improvement in risk communication cannot just rely on communicating more information to the public. First of all, what counts as the relevant information for the experts is not all that is relevant for the public. And second, the relationship between knowing, perceiving, and acting is either not a very systematic one or not yet sufficiently well understood to be treated as such. Basically, communication about risk cannot be a one-way process; it cannot be impervious to what the audience cares about.

Risk communication has to be a two-way process that includes listening to those who are or might be exposed to the risk. The expert side of the communication needs to be open to learning about people's concerns about 1) the possible impacts of the exposure, beyond those impacts that are normally part of a scientific assessment, and about 2) what a management project may require from them in terms of change in behavior, since people's behavior is not always aligned with their perception and their actions. If risk communication needs more information, it is, at least in part, more information from and about the public.

But something needs attending also in the other direction, from the experts to the public. Here, it is not so much more information, though, as better information or better form of conveying information.

5.3.5 From the experts to the public: making uncertainty meaningful

Studies on the discrepancy between expert and lay risk perception are often interested in how lay audiences misperceive probabilities: typically, we overestimate rare events and underestimate frequent ones, and consequently, we "overperceive" the risk of nuclear power plant accidents and "underperceive" that of car crashes. As a consequence, much of recent risk communication effort has been spent on how to clearly explain, in plain language, probabilities and uncertainty (see, for instance, Patt & Schrag 2003 on the IPCC's efforts to dejargonize probabilities in its risk assessment reports). An example of the overestimation is seen in the reaction to learning of the risk of blood clots that affected those who had received the Johnson & Johnson or the AstraZeneca COVID-19 vaccine shot. In the case of the Johnson & Johnson vaccine, it seemed to affect about 2 individuals per 1,000,000 people who had received the vaccine; for AstraZeneca, it was about 1 per 100,000 (Wallis 2021). The case fatality rate, in 2020, for the COVID-19 reached the world average value of 7.34% for a few months and then stabilized around 2% (Ritchie et al. 2020).

It is difficult and controversial to determine the probability that someone infected with COVID-19 would die from the infection. The main reasons are, first, that the odds of dying from COVID-19 are very different, depending on a person's age, sex, health, and standard of care received. The other reason is that there is great uncertainty as to the number of people who were infected with the disease. But even with those considerations in mind, there was little doubt for the experts that the chance of dying from COVID-19 if infected was much greater, in general, than the chance of dying from a blood clot if vaccinated with Johnson & Johnson or AstraZeneca (*Science News* 2021).

Public health authorities interrupted the distribution of the vaccine for ten days in the US, and the European Commission decided not to renew its contract for the following year with AstraZeneca and Johnson & Johnson (Reuters, April 13, 2021). Both the pause in the US and the nonrenewal in Europe might have been a wise political decisions, given the actual or expected reaction of the public to the news of the blood clotting issue. But the J&J vaccine, as a one-dose vaccine, was especially used to vaccinate hard-to-reach populations, like rural populations or houseless populations, and it made it very unclear that the pause in the distribution prevented more harm than it created. For some experts in risk communication, the incident was evidence of a failure in risk communication. The failure in this case, according to Fischhoff, is that health officials should have been clearer in explaining the consequences of the possible choices, in particular, the possible harm of interrupting versus continuing the distribution of the vaccine (Wallis 2021).

Another, deeper reason for the failure has to do with the way communication about uncertainty is usually framed, in particular, whether it uses numerical probability language or words such as "likely," "unlikely," "probably," "almost impossible" (Patt & Schrag 2003):

> Presenting risk probabilities in numbers as opposed to words could lead the public to have different levels of uncertainty, which in turn could lead them to perceive a risk with differing levels of severity.
>
> (Hove & Paek 2015: 164)

Some risk communication experts have argued that communication about uncertainty should be presented in words rather than numbers because it is easier to read and remember (Wardekker et al. 2008). A study tested women's understanding of a claim that mammography screening is associated with a 25% reduction of breast cancer mortality: "92% of about 5,000 women overestimated the benefit 10-fold, 100-fold, and more, or they did not know" (Gigerenzer et al. 2010: 791). And it was shown, in a study about the perception of the risk related to mad cow disease, that of two communication formats that both communicate fear and uncertainty, the one that used verbal communication of uncertainty generated a risk perception more aligned with the experts' than the one using numerical format (Hove & Paek 2015).

Interestingly, confusion around the interpretation of probabilities is not limited to the lay audience. When some gynecologists were asked to explain the meaning of the claim of a 25% reduction of breast cancer mortality, 31% of them thought it meant that for every 1,000 women who were screened, 25 or 250 fewer would die (Gigerenzer et al. 2010). The truth is that it amounts to a reduction from about five to four in every 1,000 women, that is, 0.1%.

In order to address what they see as a problem of statistical illiteracy, Gigerenzer and colleagues (2008) urge risk experts to make the communication of risk more transparent. That is achieved by "using frequency statements instead of single-event probabilities, absolute risks instead of relative risks, mortality rates instead of survival rates, and natural frequencies instead of conditional probabilities" (loc cit. 53).

For example, if a patient is told that, if they take Prozac, they have 30 to 50% chance of developing sexual problems, there is an ambiguity about the reference class that could lead the patients to believe that in 30 to 50% of the times they have sex, they will have problems. The misinterpretation can be avoided by saying that three to five persons out of ten who take Prozac will experience issues.

Similarly, the expression of relative risks can easily be misinterpreted, as the example of the mammography screening showed. Instead of saying that undergoing mammography screening reduces their risk of dying from breast cancer by 25%, the same information can be made clearer by saying that "of 1000 women who do not undergo mammography about four will die from breast cancer within 10 years, whereas out of 1000 women who do three will die" (Gigerenzer & Edwards 2003: 743). The advantage of using natural frequency to express uncertainty is that it makes the class of reference class clear: "1,000 women who do not undergo mammography screening" versus "1,000 women who do undergo mammography screening."

The way the outcomes of a risk policy are framed also matters. For instance, being screened for cancer can be framed in terms of positive or negative outcomes: 97% chance of survival is also 3% chance of dying. And how it is framed makes a difference on how it is received. Positive framing is more effective at persuading people to take a risky treatment option, whereas negative framing is more effective at persuading people to accept some measure, like screening, to reduce the risks. But presenting only the rate of survival can be misleading, because it is inflated by the number of those who survived after being screened and did not have the disease to start with.

Even more misleading is mismatching forms of representation of the costs and benefit of a given treatment. According to Gigenrenzer and colleagues (2010), the costs are typically reported in small numbers, whereas the benefits are reported in big numbers. Imagine, for instance, a treatment that reduces the probability of getting a disease A from 10 to 5 in 1,000 and that, also, increases the probability of getting a disease B, as side effect of the treatment, from 5 to 10 in 1,000. Mismatched framing consists in representing the benefit as a 50% decrease of the probability of getting disease A and representing the cost as a 5 in 1,000, 0.5% increase of the probability of getting disease B. The mismatched representation of the statistics about the effect of the treatment is in the interest of the pharmaceutical industry because it "is most likely to impress the readers and, particularly, the doctors who receive the reprints" (Gigerenzer et al. 2008: 78). But the lack of clear understanding on the part of the public, and also sometimes the experts, of the information that is conveyed undermines the possibility of a shared and enlightened, more democratic form of decision-making in risk management.

5.4 Conclusion

Risk management based on cost-benefit analysis has been criticized for being too technocratic in its reliance on scientific risk assessment, on a principle of rationality that requires to select the course of action with maximal expected value, and on the condition that the costs and benefits to be included in the analysis be monetizable. Critics have advocated more democratic forms of risk management, allowing a diversity of perspectives in the assessment of the risk and more open to how the lay public perceives the risk they are exposed to.

But even those more democratic forms of risk management do not eschew the use of a cost-benefit analysis: possible impacts still have to be identified, they have to be distinguished in terms of "good" or "bad" and how good or how bad, and the management of the risk can still be seen as a form of cost-benefit analysis. The difference, however, is that the decisions as to what the goal of the management should be, what impacts should be taken into account as such, what significance they should receive are the results of a different process. In a more democratic form of risk management, those decisions are made in the context of a deliberative procedure where those who are exposed and might be affected by the possible consequences of a risk situation are given opportunities to be heard and to influence the way in which the risk is managed.

The shift from a technocratic form of risk management to a more democratic one brings to the fore the central role of risk communication. For a technocratic form of risk management, what is needed from the public is that it abide by the management policies. Assuming, then, that how people act is, at least in part, a result of how they perceive the risks, the central function of risk communication is to modify people's perception of the risk so that it aligns well enough with the experts' so as to help produce the behaviors needed for the success of risk management policies.

For a democratic form of risk management, the public is expected to contribute its perspective on the risk and the management of the risk in the context of a deliberation with experts. That means that risk communication has to be a two-way system of communication; what is at stake now is for both sides to be heard by the other. On the one hand, there needs to be avenues for the public to express its perception of the risk and of the costs and benefits associated with different forms of management of the risk; on the other hand, the experts' understanding of the situation needs to be part of what is informing the public's perspective. And as we saw, recent work on risk communication precisely focuses on representing statistical information in terms that make it clear, unambiguous, so as to help create a shared understanding.

Review questions

1. CBA

Q1

Cost-benefit analysis is a method that:

A. Transforms the costs of a project into benefits.
B. Justifies the costs and the benefits of a project.
C. Calculates and compares the costs and benefits of an intervention to determine whether it's worth pursuing.

Q2

One advantage of using cost-benefit analysis as a basis for regulatory decisions is that:

A. It is objective and value-free, because all the costs and benefits are expressed in monetary terms.
B. It is transparent: the procedure follows from steps that can be made explicit.
C. It is essentially democratic: the choice of the relevant costs and benefits of the project results from a public process.

Q3

Another advantage of cost-benefit analysis is that it:

A. Automatically gives highest priority to saving lives.
B. Simplifies complex decisions and provides a common scale for comparing different risk-reducing measures.
C. Systematically takes into account all aspects of a situation.

Q5

What is a common difficulty in applying cost-benefit analysis?

A. Not all the costs and benefits are easily quantifiable.
B. It is a method difficult to explain to the large public.
C. Because of its complexity, different users may understand the method differently.

Q6

How are value judgments involved in a cost-benefit analysis?

A. Value judgments are involved in the selection of what count as costs and as benefits.
B. Value judgments are involved in comparing the values of the costs and of the benefits.
C. Value judgments are involved in assigning a quantitative value to monetary costs.

Q7

The value of a statistical life (VSL) is:

A. The value that governments place on saving an individual life.
B. A measure of the intrinsic worth of a human being.
C. An estimate of how much a population is willing to pay for small reductions to their risk of death.

2. Alternatives assessment

Q8

A crucial difference between traditional CBA form of risk management and alternatives assessment (AA) form of risk management is that:

A. AA takes into account costs and benefits that are nonmonetary.
B. AA does not consider costs and benefits.
C. CBA does not consider alternative options for how to manage a risk.

Q9

A crucial difference between the traditional CBA form of risk management and the alternatives assessment (AA) form of risk management is that:

A. AA considers several options for risk management of a certain activity (like how to manage the risk created by the construction of an incinerator), but CBA only considers one option.
B. AA considers a large range of options, including the precautionary option of not engaging in the risky activity under consideration.
C. AA does not take into account the costs when selecting an option for risk management.

Q10

A crucial difference between traditional CBA form of risk management and alternatives assessment (AA) form of risk management is that:

A. AA does not rely on the opinion of risk experts but only on the opinion of the public.
B. CBA does not take into account impacts of risky activity on the environment.

C. AA aims at taking into account a larger range of perspectives on the impact of the risky activity, from experts and also from people exposed in different ways to the risk.

Q11

Interconnectedness of natural resources can be a source of unfair distribution of the costs because:

A. The use of natural resources by someone in one place can create natural costs in terms of pollution or depletion in a different place or in the same place at a different time.
B. Some natural resources are not renewable or exchangeable.
C. We don't really know what the need of future generations will be, and the need of different societies, different cultures might be different.

Q12

It can be argued that more sustainability requires more democratic forms of management of environmental risks:

A. Because more democratic forms of decision-making are easier and faster to put in place than technocratic forms of decision-making based on experts' assessment.
B. Because to be more involved in the discussions and decisions regarding the mitigation of environmental risks makes people more aware of the risks, more concerned, and so more motivated to address them.
C. Because more democratic forms of decision-making generate choices for managing risks that everybody can agree on

Discussion topics

Topic 1

For more than a year after the beginning of the 2020 school year, schools have operated with various combinations of remote learning strategies and in-person instruction in order to balance risks from COVID-19 against the costs of school closures to students and families. Due to increases in infections that came with the new variants (delta, omicron), policy makers began adjusting their school reopening plans. Imagine you are among the analysts who will prepare the cost-benefit analysis to help policy makers make good decisions. What are some possible costs to students and parents of school closings and virtual instruction? On the other hand, what are the costs (or increased risks) associated with in-person schooling? How might you attempt to quantify these negative outcomes to measure against the benefits? For instance, if virtual education will lead to reduced learning outcomes, how could you decide on a dollar amount to reflect the magnitude this "learning loss"?

Topic 2

Cost-benefit analysis can be thought of as both a precursor and a major contributor to the explosion in volume and production of data that is now being called the "data revolution." Numbers have become more valuable than ever for making impactful decisions in nearly every industry, especially when they can be gathered up into a single bottom-line stat with clear implications for action. In CBA, that stat is the net benefit of a policy action, and the recommendation is to select whichever policy gives the biggest sum. In baseball, WAR, or "Wins Above Replacement" stats attempt to express a player's value in a single number, often for the purposes of deciding whether a team should keep them. VAR, or "value at risk," is a single measure invented by quantitative analysts in the late 1980s, which enables a Wall Street CEO to see how much money their traders could lose in a certain time frame.

The advantages of such values for reducing uncertainty and intellectual fatigue when faced with big decisions are easy to see. But there may be downsides. Michael Lewis, author of *The Fifth Risk*, suggests we too often use these figures as substitutes for real understanding, and this can blind us to their limitations and to other sources of wisdom or insight – sometimes to our peril. "CEOs began to trust VAR over the advice of their own traders," Lewis recalls. "After all, VAR was a number that claimed 99% accuracy" (2022, April 12). This worked for the Wall Street firms "right up to 2008, and then the risks that the traders took blew up the global financial system." Lewis points out that the numbers themselves aren't the problem; the problem is what people do with them. These figures "start out as tools for thinking" but "wind up replacing thought."

Recalling how cost-benefit analysis is conducted and used to manage societal risks, do you find yourself with similar concerns? Do you think there is any danger that risk analysts and policy makers who rely on the method might deceive themselves into thinking they know more about the problem than they actually do or might follow the method blindly without giving enough thought to its limitations? It might help to think of a concrete example. In this chapter, we discussed a study which concluded that the benefits of social distancing in USA outweighs economic impact by about $5.2 trillion. Does this figure tell us the full story about the goodness of this intervention strategy? If not, what else is there to say?

Notes

1 N.b., with many of the examples discussed in this chapter, risk *management* is effectively synonymous with risk *mitigation, abatement, reduction*, etc. However, "management" is the preferred term because sometimes it turns out that a problem may not be worth resolving (Cole 2009: 2), in which

case nothing is done and a risk is thereby accepted. In other cases, the risk being considered is not being mitigated but *taken* by the government or agency, such as the risk of "reopening" a city or state's economy after the pandemic lockdowns (i.e., moving to a less-srestrictive tier, etc.).

2 The method goes by various names in the literature, including regulatory cost-benefit analysis, risk-cost-benefit analysis, and risk-benefit analysis, to name a few.

3 For Cole, such problems include the provision of public goods and other services. We focus more narrowly on the mitigation of risks that are significant/extensive enough to merit collective action.

4 For instance, risk assessments are needed to develop National Air Quality Standards, which in turn get utilized in proposals for regulating the industries that generate particulates.

5 One notable example is related by the economist Kip Viscusi in his April 2020 interview on the *Two Think Minimum* podcast. A certain hazardous waste cleanup program initiated by the EPA selected targets and allocated resources extremely inefficiently such that the statistical cost per cancer case prevented was a trillion dollars. Sadly, for the same budget, the EPA could have cleaned up a remarkable 95% of all the hazardous waste sites across the United States.

6 Here is not the place for us to vet this claim. But note that it is contested by many psychologists and behavioral economists, among others. It is a premise of neoclassical welfare economics that some see as a problem for CBA to address, because it can affect the content and measure of foreseeable impacts (Steps 3 and 4). For instance, it serves as part of the theoretical basis for using willingness to pay as a measure of one's utility, which in turn affects judgments about the severity of impacts.

7 See "Towards Principles and Standards for the Benefit-Cost Analysis of Safety" by Farrow and Viscusi (2011) for good examples of such efforts.

8 The authors took "social distancing" to include all policies and guidelines (federal, state, local) to increase social distance, including urging citizens to avoid gatherings of a certain size; suspending operations of schools, universities, day care centers; sealing off playgrounds and other public spaces; canceling cultural events; closing tourist attractions, including Broadway and Disneyland; suspending or canceling national sports leagues; imposing travel restrictions; urging or requiring use of masks in certain contexts; and many others (Thunström et al. 2020: 180).

9 Consider Casey Mulligan's discovery in "Economic Activity and the Value of Medical Innovation during a Pandemic" that exclusive focus on lost GDP is liable to significantly understate the costs of a shutdown (Mulligan 2021).

10 This is a strategy that we first described in the section titled "Defining and measuring utilities," Chapter 2.

11 We also discussed this in Chapter 2, in the section titled "Can money provide the universal utility unit?"

12 This isn't quite right. The higher mortality rate of 1.5% was predicted only to apply to individuals who become infected and seek treatment at peak periods when the US health-care system is overwhelmed. The model suggested that social distancing measures would avoid overwhelming the health-care system and keep the average mortality rate at the lower level of 0.5% for all infected individuals. Conversely, in the uncontrolled scenario with no social distancing, the health-care system would become overwhelmed. But this would only be true while there are too many infected people requiring treatment, which would not be all the time. This means that not everyone who gets the virus in the uncontrolled scenario will face a higher likelihood of death, and it means that the average reduction to mortality risk for controlled vs. uncontrolled cannot be calculated as the simple difference between the higher and lower rates (i.e., 1%). So at the cost of some accuracy, we are simplifying the narrative to make it easier for the reader to grasp the basic methods and concepts.

13 Again, the authors of this study would not have calculated or framed the benefit exactly this way, but we are doing so to help readers understand the fundamental ways of thinking that underlie VSL estimates.

14 Note that the phrase "lives saved" is euphemistic because everyone eventually dies. As Robinson and Hammitt explain, "policies extend lives rather than saving them; the deaths prevented by the policy are delayed to a later date and possibly shifted to another cause" (Robinson & Hammitt 2013: 111).

15 Sources include US Census Bureau, Eurostat, World Bank, Google.

16 This assumes, quite unreasonably, that everyone in the US would be infected by the virus and thus be subject to its associated mortality risks. In reality, not everyone will be infected, and in fact, the number of infections will differ depending on whether social distancing is enacted. The real way to calculate the number of lives saved is to make projections about the number of infections in

the controlled vs. uncontrolled scenarios, multiply these by their respective mortality rates, then subtract the smaller product from the larger. Dispensing with these complexities, as we've done here, would only hinder our message if we were striving for accuracy, but in this case we are merely trying to show an alternative way of framing the benefit.

17 The standard way to calculate this value is to divide average WTP by the change in mortality rate, which has the advantage of not requiring a population estimate. A dimensional analysis of the lengthier procedure that we've just described will confirm that both approaches yield the same number.

18 The word "statistical" is used because the measure results from averages and involves uncertainties about whether and which life is ultimately saved by the policy. It is common, though incorrect, to think the VSL could denote the worth of particular individuals (Robinson & Hammitt 2013: 111).

19 This figure is significantly lower than the 3.3 million we estimated prior. This is for reasons discussed in previous footnotes: Thunström and collaborators limited their scope to the infected population, which they predicted to reduce from 287 million without social distancing to 188 million with social distancing (Thunström et al. 2020: 185). And they did not apply the higher death rate of 1.5% to the entire 287 million in the uncontrolled scenario, but rather just to the portion who would become infected and seek treatment at peak periods when the US health-care system is overwhelmed.

20 This misunderstanding is so common and problematic that numerous government agencies are now advocating changes to the terminology. The United States Environmental Protection Agency has proposed "value of mortality risk reduction," or VMR, to replace VSL, as this term "more accurately describes the health risk changes that are being analyzed" and thus conveys the less alarming interpretation more clearly (EPA, Nov. 20, 2020).

21 Consider the now-famous assertion by (then) New York Governor Andrew Cuomo: "To me, I say the cost of a human – a human life is priceless, period." Curiously, Cuomo offered this line in answer to a "hard" and "controversial" question that he believed no one was openly asking, namely, "How much is a human life worth?" In fact, everyone was asking this question, hence the great need for clarity about the meaning and use of quantities like VSL.

22 *Worth: Radiolab*. WNYC Studios. (2014, December 23). Retrieved from www.wnycstudios.org/podcasts/radiolab/episodes/worth.

23 For instance, one PEW research study (Edwards & Lopez 2021) suggests that Hispanic and Black Americans have been hardest hit by COVID-19 wage and job losses, and these groups also tend to have fewer/no emergency funds.

24 It's worth noting that racial and ethnic minority groups are disproportionately represented in such settings, e.g., "healthcare facilities, farms, factories, food production and processing, grocery stores, and public transportation" (Centers for Disease Control and Prevention April 19, 2021).

25 Consider, for instance, the well-documented fact that VSL increases with income. So if the costs of a regulation fall mostly on the poor but a population-average VSL is used to calculate benefits, the regulation may appear cost beneficial even though the poor suffer costs that may outweigh the value they place on the benefits they receive (Robinson 2020: para. 14). Using income-adjusted VSLs to analyze such policies might yield a more accurate understanding of the trade-offs for such people.

26 This is partly because GDP measures only averages, but the direct effects of a shutdown are unequally distributed (See Mulligan 2021).

27 The CDC provides a list of such determinants, which include socioeconomic status, education level, access to health care, poor living conditions, and certain occupation and job conditions (December 10, 2020).

28 This is a point acknowledged by Thunström et al.: "In principle, the asymmetric impact of the epidemic and economic burdens of the policy responses can be mitigated with appropriate redistributions of resources" (193).

29 Consider that suspending operations of schools, universities, and day care centers will undoubtedly yield more punishing costs for a greater section of the population than urging or requiring use of masks in certain contexts. Yet both actions belong to the proposed policy package.

30 Hermansson suggests several such features, including "the value of silence, a clear blue sky, closeness to nature or the absence of social conflicts" (2005: 562).

31 Some adults in the US were reluctant to get the Moderna or Pfizer vaccines due to their use of emerging mRNA technology, and were grateful that Johnson & Johnson offered an alternative that used more traditional, virus-based technology. This reluctance could be seen as problematic if the

mRNA vaccines were demonstrably more effective, or if the Johnson & Johnson vaccine carried with it major health risks that the mRNA vaccines did not.

32 These countries include, but aren't limited to, Kenya, Hong Kong, China (Mainland), Indonesia, Philippines, Thailand, Bulgaria, France, Germany, Canada, Mexico, the United Kingdom, Argentina, Brazil, Australia, and the United States. Some of these protests are ongoing as of the writing of this book, in year 2022.

33 Note that our goal here is not to endorse or vindicate the anger but to acknowledge its reality and suggest it as a factor that could reduce the net benefits of certain methods for managing the pandemic. Caution and fairness would therefore urge us not to automatically dismiss the emotional cost from consideration.

34 Cited by the European Institute at the University of Maryland <www.europeaninstitute.org/index.php/ei-blog/84-november-2009/895-qprecautionary-principleq-often-riles-us\>.

35 Cited by the European Institute at the University of Maryland <www.europeaninstitute.org/index.php/ei-blog/84-november-2009/895-qprecautionary-principleq-often-riles-us\>.

36 For a discussion and criticism of the precautionary principle understood as epistemic principle, see Harris and Holm (2002).

37 For instance, regarded as acceptable is 10 micrograms of lead per deciliter of blood, breathing air that contains 50 $\mu g/m^3$ of particulate matter, 500 μg herbicide Dacthal per liter of drinking water.

38 O'Brien cites a real example of this sort: an incinerator in East Liverpool, Ohio, that is located a few hundred yards from a school has been allowed to emit "9400 pounds of lead, 2560 pounds of mercury, and 157,400 pounds of fine particles" (O'Brien 2000: 5).

39 (*Michigan v EPA* 2015, slip op. at 7).

40 See Business-NGO Working Group for Safer Chemicals and Sustainable Materials <http://bizngo.org/>.

41 www.cnn.com/2021/05/13/health/cdc-mask-guidance-vaccinated/index.html.

42 One might argue that at the time of that later announcement, no new evidence justified spending efforts advocating mask-wearing rather than vaccination: whether in May or in July, mass vaccination was still the main tool to end the COVID-19 epidemic in the US, at least for a time. As such, for either announcement, it is not clear that new evidence was the main reason behind a change in recommendation.

43 www.cnn.com/2021/07/27/health/cdc-mask-guidance-vaccinated-people-bn/index.html.

44 Smokey the Bear's familiarity, however, may diminish the message's effectiveness. Indeed, as we saw in Chapter 4 (section 4.3.1.2), familiarity with a hazard reduces risk perception.

45 Removing lead-based paint, if not done by trained technicians, may pose much greater risk – by creating dangerous dust from sanding – than leaving it untouched.

46 We are here taking these results at face value and leaving aside limitations and doubts about the validity of these results and their applicability and meaningfulness both at the individual and collective levels (see infra, Chapter 4 on risk perception).

47 See the full letter reproduced at www.wsj.com/articles/BL-234B-3035].

48 https://climatecommunication.yale.edu/visualizations-data/ycom-us/.

49 This number corresponds to the share of respondents who said they were "worried" about it.

50 https://time.com/3725994/inhofe-snowball-climate/.

51 www.who.int/risk-communication/introduction-to-risk-communication.pdf www.psandman.com/col/4kind-1.htm.

References

Abu-Akel, A., Spitz, A., & West, R. (2021). "The effect of spokesperson attribution on public health message sharing during the COVID-19 pandemic." *PLOS ONE*, 16(2): e0245100.

Allcott, H., et al. (2020). "Polarization and public health: Partisan differences in social distancing during the coronavirus pandemic." *Journal of Public Economics*, 191: 104254. DOI: 10.3386/w26946.

Anthonj, C., Diekkruger, B., Borgemeister, C., & Kistemann, T. (2019). "Health risk perceptions and local knowledge of water-related infectious disease exposure among Kenyan wetland communities." *International Journal of Hygiene and Environmental Health*, 222(1): 34–48. DOI: 10.1016/j.ijheh.2018.08.003.

Arslanca, T., Fidan, C., Daggez, M., & Dursun, P. (2021). "Knowledge, preventive behaviors and risk perception of the COVID-19 pandemic: A cross-sectional study in Turkish health care workers." *PLOS ONE*, 16(4): e0250017.10.1371/journal.pone.0250017.

Ashford, N. A. (2005). "Incorporating science, technology, fairness, and accountability in environmental, health, and safety decisions." *Human and Ecological Risk Assessment: An International Journal*, 11(1): 85–96. https://doi.org/10.1080/10807030590919918.

Ashford, N. A., & Caldart, C. (1991). *Technology, law and the working environment*. New York: Van Nostrand Reinhold.

Baggini, J. (2006). *The pig that wants to be eaten: 100 experiments for the armchair philosopher*. London: Penguin.

Besley, J. C., & Nisbet, M. (2013). "How scientists view the public, the media and the political process." *Public Understanding of Science*, 22(6): 644–659. DOI: 10.1177/0963662511418743.

Breakwell, G. M. (2000). "Risk communication: Factors affecting impact." *British Medical Bulletin*, 56(1): 110–120. DOI: 10.1258/0007142001902824.

Centers for Disease Control and Prevention. (2020, December 10). *COVID-19 racial and ethnic disparities*. Centers for Disease Control and Prevention. www.cdc.gov/coronavirus/2019-ncov/community/health-equity/racial-ethnic-disparities/index.html#print.

Centers for Disease Control and Prevention. (2021, April 19). *Health equity considerations and racial and ethnic minority groups*. Centers for Disease Control and Prevention. www.cdc.gov/coronavirus/2019-ncov/community/health-equity/race-ethnicity.html.

Centers for Disease Control and Prevention. (2021, April 23). *NVSS – provisional death counts for COVID-19 – executive summary*. Centers for Disease Control and Prevention. www.cdc.gov/nchs/covid19/mortality-overview.htm.

Centers for Disease Control and Prevention. (2021, September 9). *Risk for COVID-19 infection, hospitalization, and death by age group*. Centers for Disease Control and Prevention. www.cdc.gov/coronavirus/2019-ncov/covid-data/investigations-discovery/hospitalization-death-by-age.html.

Clemens, R. L. B., & Babcock, B. A. (2002). "Why can't U.S. Beef compete in the European union?" MATRIC Briefing Papers. 10. http://lib.dr.iastate.edu/matric_briefingpapers/10 DOI: 10.22004/ag.econ.18712.

Cole, D. H. (2009). "Regulatory cost-benefit analysis and collective action." *Institute for Policy Integrity Working Paper*, 1.

Cori, L., Bianchi, F., Cadum, E., & Anthonj, C. (2020). "Risk perception and COVID-19." *International Journal of Environmental Research and Public Health*, 17(9): 3114. DOI: 10.3390/ijerph17093114.

Crawshaw, R. (2012). "Animal feeds, feeding practices and opportunities for feed contamination: An introduction." In J. Fink-Gremmels (ed.), *Animal feed contamination: Effects on livestock and food safety* (pp. 11–32). Oxford: Woodhead Publishing 2012. DOI: 10.1533/9780857093615.11.

Douglas, P., Robertson, S., Gay, R., Hansell, A. L., & Gant, T. W. (2018). "A systematic review of the public health risks of bioaerosols from intensive farming." *The International Journal of Hygiene and Environmental Health*, 221: 134–173. DOI: 10.1016/j.ijheh.2017.10.019.

Edwards, K., & Lopez, M. H. (2021). *Black Americans say coronavirus has hit hard financially, but impact varies by education level, age*. Pew Research Center. www.pewresearch.org/fact-tank/2021/05/12/black-americans-say-coronavirus-has-hit-hard-financially-but-impact-varies-by-education-level-age/.

Environmental Protection Agency. (2017). Report NO. 17-P-0396. https://www.epa.gov/sites/default/files/2017-09/documents/_epaoig_20170919-17-p-0396.pdf.

Fairlie, R. W. (2020). "The impact of COVID-19 on small business owners: The first three months after social-distancing restrictions." Working paper 27462. National Bureau of Economic Research. DOI: 10.3386/w27462.

Farrow, S., & Viscusi, W. K. (2011). "Towards principles and standards for the benefit-cost analysis of safety." *Journal of Benefit-Cost Analysis*, 2(3): 1–25. DOI: 10.2202/2152–2812.1033.

Fiorino, D. J. (1990). "Citizen participation and environmental risk: A survey of institutional mechanisms." *Science Technology & Human Values*, 15(2): 226–43. DOI: 10.1177/016224399001500204.

Fischhoff, B. (1995). "Risk perception and communication unplugged: twenty years of process." *Risk Analysis*, 15(2): 137–145. DOI: 0272-4332/95/0400-0137$07.50/1.

Foster, C. A., & Branch, G. (2018, August 21). "Do people really think earth might be flat?" *Scientific American*.

Gadarian, S. K., Goodman, S. W., & Pepinsky, T. B. (2021). "Partisanship, health behavior, and policy attitudes in the early stages of the COVID-19 pandemic." *PLOS ONE*, 16(4): e0249596. DOI: 10.1371/journal.pone.0249596.

Gigerenzer, G., & Edwards, A. (2003). "Simple tools for understanding risks: From innumeracy to insight." *BMJ*, 327: 741–744. DOI: 10.1136/bmj.327.7417.741.

Gigerenzer, G., Gaissmaier, W., Kurz-Milcke, E., Schwartz, L. M., & Woloshin, S. (2008). "Helping doctors and patients making sense of health statistics." *Psychological Science in the Plubic Interest*, 8(2): 53–96. DOI: 10.1111/j.1539–6053.2008.00033.x.

Gigerenzer, G., Wegwarth, O., & Feufel, M. (2010). "Misleading communication of risk." *BMJ*, 341: 791–92. DOI: 10.1136/bmj.c4830.

Goebbert, K., Jenkins-Smith, H. C., Klockow, K., Nowlin, M. C., & Silva, C. L. (2012). "Weather, climate, and worldviews: The sources and consequences of public perceptions of changes in local weather patterns." *Weather, Climate, and Society*, 4(2): 132–144. DOI: 10.1175/WCAS-D-11–00044.1.

Graham, J. D. (1996). "Making sense of risk: An agenda for congress." In R. W. Hahn (ed.), *Risks, costs, and lives saved: Getting better results from regulation* (pp. 183–207). New York: Oxford University Press.

Grima, S., et al. (2021). "The relationship between risk perception and risk definition and risk-addressing behaviour during the early COVID-19 stages." *Journal of Risk and Financial Management*, 14: 272. https://doi.org/10.3390/jrfm14060272.

Haimes, Y. Y. (2004). "Risk of extreme events, reliability, and the fallacy of the expected value." In Y. Y. Haimes (ed.), *Risk modeling, assessment and management* (pp. 297–345). Hoboken: John Wiley & Sons. DOI: 10.1002/9780470422489.ch8.

Harris, J., & Holm, S. (2002). "Extending human lifespan and the precautionary paradox." *Journal of Medicine and Philosophy*, 27: 355–368. DOI: 10.1076/jmep.27.3.355.2983.

Haynes, K., Barclay, J., & Pidgeon, N. (2008). "Whose reality counts? Factors effecting the perception of volcanic risk." *Journal of Volcanology and Geothermal Research*, 172: 259–272.

Hermansson, H. (2005). "Consistent risk management: Three models outlined." *Journal of Risk Research*, 8(7–8): 557–568. DOI: 10.1080/1366987050008 5189.

Hermansson, H. (2010). "Towards a fair procedure for risk management." *Journal of Risk Research*, 13(4): 501–515. DOI: 10.1080/13669870903305903.

Hicks, D. J. (2015). "Epistemological depth in a GM crops controversy." *Studies in History and Philosophy of Science Part C: Studies in History and Philosophy of Biological and Biomedical Sciences*, 50: 1–12. DOI: 10.1016/j.shpsc.2015.02.002.

Hicks, D. J. (2017). "Scientific controversies as proxy politics." *Issues in Science and Technology*, 33(2): 67–72.

Hove, T., & Paek, H-J. (2015). "Effects of risk presentation format and fear message on lay people's risk perceptions." *Journal of Public Relations*, 19(1): 162–182. DOI: 10.15814/jpr.2015.19.1.162.

Kahan, D. M. (2012). "Why we are poles apart on climate change." *Nature*, 488(7411): 255. DOI: 10.1038/488255a.

Kahan, D. M., Jenkins-Smith, H., & Braman, D. (2011). "Cultural cognition of scientific consensus." *Journal of Risk Research*, 14: 147–174. DOI: 10.1080/13669877.2010.511246.

Kahan, D. M., Peters, E., Wittlin, M., Slovic, P., Ouellette, L. L., Braman, D., & Mandel, G. (2012). "The polarizing impact of science literacy and numeracy on perceived climate change risks." *Nature Climate Change*, 2(10): 732–735. DOI: 10.1038/nclimate1547.

Kantamneni, N. (2020). "The impact of the COVID-19 pandemic on marginalized populations in the United States: A research agenda." *Journal of Vocational Behavior*, 119: 103439. DOI: 10.1016/j.jvb.2020.103439.

Kokai, A., Blake, A., Dedeo, M., & Lent, T. (2020). "Building shared information infrastructure for chemical alternatives assessment." *Elementa Science of the Anthropocene*, 8: 26. https://doi.org/10.1525/elementa.422.

Leiserowitz, A., et al. (2021). "Global warming's six Americas: A review and recommendations for climate change communication." *Current Opinion in Behavioral Sciences*, 42: 97–103. DOI: 10.1016/j.cobeha.2021.04.007.

Lewis, M. (Host). (2022, April 12). Field of Ignorance (Episode 3) [Audio podcast episode]. In *Against the Rules*. Pushkin. www.pushkin.fm/show/against-the-rules-with-michael-lewis/.

Luxembourg: Office for Official Publications of the European Communities, Article 130r. (1992). https://op.europa.eu/en/publication-detail/-/publication/93920455-e8d5-4937-bcd1–11bdb91a443b.

Martuzzi, M., Tickner, J. A., & World Health Organization. (2004). *The precautionary principle: protecting public health, the environment and the future of our children*. World Health Organization. Regional Office for Europe.

McElroy, K. G. (2010). "Environmental health effects of concentrated animal feeding operations: Implications for nurses." *Nursing Administration Quarterly*, 34(4): 311–319. DOI: 10.1097/NAQ.0b013e3181f5649c.

Miceli, R., Sotgiu, I., & Settanni, M. (2008). "Disaster preparedness and perception of flood risk: A study in an alpine valley in Italy." *Journal of Environmental Psychology*, 28(2): 164–DOI: 173.10.1016/j.jenvp.2007.10.006.

Michigan v EPA. (2015). October Term 2014, 576 US 743.

Mulligan, C. (2021). "Economic activity and the value of medical innovation during a pandemic." *Journal of Benefit-Cost Analysis*, 12(3): 420–440. DOI: 10.1017/bca.2021.5.

Myers, N., & Raffensberger, C. (eds.). (2006). *Precautionary tools for reshaping environmental policy*. Cambridge, MA: MIT Press.

Nardinelli, C. (2018). "Some pitfalls of practical benefit-cost analysis." *Journal of Benefit-Cost Analysis*, 9(3): 519–530. DOI: 10.1017/bca.2018.18.

National Resources Defense Council. (2019). "CAFOs: What we don't know is hurting us." https://www.nrdc.org/sites/default/files/cafos-dont-know-hurting-us-report.pdf.

Nix, J. (2020). "On the challenges associated with the study of police use of deadly force in the United States: A response to Schwartz & Jahn." *PLOS ONE*, 15(7): e0236158. DOI: 10.1371/journal.pone.0236158.

O'Brien, M. (2000). *Making better environmental decisions: An alternative to risk assessment*. Cambridge, MA: MIT Press.

Okon-Singer, H., Hendler, T., Pessoa, L., & Shackman, A. J. (2015, February 17). "The neurobiology of emotion-cognition interactions: Fundamental questions and strategies for future research." *Frontiers in Human Neuroscience*. DOI: 10.3389/fnhum.2015.00058.

Patt, A. G., & Schrag, D. P. (2003). "Using specific language to describe risk and probability." *Climatic Change*, 61(1): 17–30. DOI: 10.1023/A:1026314523443.

Pavilonis, B. T., Sanderson, W. T., & Merchant, J. A. (2013). "Relative exposure to swine animal feeding operations and childhood asthma prevalence in an agricultural cohort." *Environmental Research*, 122: 74–80. DOI: 10.1016/j.envres.2012.12.008.

Pellerano, M. B., & Montague, P. (2006). "Democratic tools: Communities and precaution." In N. Myers & C. Raffensperger (eds.), *Precautionary tools for reshaping environmental policy* (pp. 69–79). Cambridge, MA: MIT Press.

Ritchie, H., Mathieu, E., Rodés-Guirao, L., Appel, C., Giattino, C., Ortiz-Ospina, E., Hasell, J., Macdonald, B., Beltekian, D., & Roser, M. (2020). "Coronavirus pandemic (COVID-19)." *Published online at OurWorldInData.org*. Retrieved from: https://ourworldindata.org/coronavirus.

Robinson, L. A. (2020, August 5). "COVID-19 and uncertainties in the value per statistical life." *The Regulatory Review*. www.theregreview.org/2020/08/05/robinson-covid-19-uncertainties-value-statistical-life/.

Robinson, L. A., & Hammitt, J. K. (2013). "Skills of the trade: Valuing health risk reductions in benefit-cost analysis." *Journal of Benefit-Cost Analysis*, 4(1): 107–130. DOI: 10.1515/jbca-2012–0006.

Robinson, L. A., Hammitt, J. K., & Baxter, J. R. (2016). "Guidelines for regulatory impact analysis." ASPE: Office of the Assistant Secretary for Planning and Evaluation.

Roeser, S. (2006). "The role of emotions in judging the moral acceptability of risks." *Safety Science*, 44: 689–700. DOI: 10.1016/j.ssci.2006.02.001.

Roeser, S., & Pesch, U. (2016). "An emotional deliberation approach to risk." *Science, Technology, & Human Values*, 41(2): 274–297. DOI: 10.1177/0162243915596231.

Ryan, A. (2007). "Risk and terrorism." In T. Lewens (ed.), *Risk: Philosophical perspectives* (pp. 171–189). New York: Routledge.

Sandel, M. (2020). *The tyranny of merit: What's become of the common good*. New York: Farrar, Straus and Giroux.

Sandin, P. (2007). "Common-sense precaution." In T. Lewens (ed.), *Risk: Philosophical perspectives* (pp. 99–112). New York: Routledge.

Sarewitz, D. (2000). "Science and environmental policy: An excess of objectivity." In R. Frodeman & V. R. Baker (eds.), *Earth matters: The earth sciences, philosophy, and the claims of community* (pp. 79–98). Upper Saddle River: Prentice-Hall.

Scherer, K. R. (1984). "On the nature and function of emotion: A component process approach." In K. R. Scherer & P. Ekman (eds.), *Approaches to emotion* (pp. 293–317). London: Lawrence Erlbaum Associates.

Schultz, A., Peppard, P., Gangnon, R. E., & Malecki, K. M. C. (2019). "Residential proximity to concentrated animal feeding operations and allergic respiratory disease." *Environment International*, 130: 104911. DOI: 10.1016/j.envint.2019.104911.

Schwartz, G. L., & Jahn, J. L. (2020). "Mapping fatal police violence across U.S. Metropolitan areas: Overall rates and racial/ethnic inequities, 2013–2017." *PLOS ONE*, 15(6): e0229686. DOI: 10.1371/journal.pone.0229686.

Schwarzman, M., & Buckley, H. (2019). "Not just an academic exercise: Systems thinking applied to designing safer alternatives." *The Journal of Chemical Education*, 96(12): 2984–2992. DOI: 10.1021/acs.jchemed.9b00345.

Science and Environmental Health Network. (1998). *The Wingspread consensus statement on the precautionary principle*. Retrieved August 10, 2022, from https://www.sehn.org/sehn/wingspread-conference-on-the-precautionary-principle.

Science for Environment Policy. (2017). *The precautionary principle: Decision making under uncertainty*. Future Brief 18. Produced for the European Commission DG Environment by the Science Communication Unit, UWE, Bristol. http://ec.europa.eu/science-environment-policy.

Shrader-Frechette, K. (1985). "The real risks of risk-cost-benefit analysis." *Technology in Society*, 7(4): 399–409. DOI: 10.1016/0160–791X(85)90007–7.

Shrader-Frechette, K. (1986). "The conceptual risks of risk assessment." *IEEE Technology and Society Magazine*, 5(2): 4–11. DOI: 10.1109/MTAS.1986.5010007.

Shrader-Frechette, K. (1994). "Expert judgment and nuclear risks: The case for more populist policy." *Journal of Social Philosophy*, 25: 45–70. DOI: 10.1111/j.1467–9833.1994.tb00348.x.

Slovic, P., Finucane, M., Petrs, E., & MacGregor, D. G. (2004). "Risk as analysis and risk as feelings: Some thoughts about affect, reason, risk, and rationality." *Risk Analysis*, 24(2): 1–12. DOI: 10.1111/j.0272–4332.2004.00433.x.

Stirling, A., & Tickner, J. A. (2004). "Implementing precaution: Assessment and application tools for health and environmental decision-making." In M. Martuzzi & J. Tickner (eds.), *The precautionary principle: Protecting public health, the environment and the future of our children* (pp. 181–208). Copenhagen: World Health Organization.

Sunstein, C. (2005a). *Laws of fear: Beyond the precautionary principle*. New York: Cambridge University Press.

Sunstein, C. (2005b). "Moral heuristics." *Behavioral and Brain Sciences*, 28: 531–573. DOI: 10.1017/S0140525X05000099.

Sunstein, C. (2020, February 28). "The cognitive bias that makes us panic about coronavirus." *Bloomberg*. www.bloomberg.com/opinion/articles/2020-02-28/coronavirus-panic-caused-by-probability-neglect.

Thunström, L., Newbold, S. C., Finnoff, D., Ashworth, M., & Shogren, J. F. (2020). "The benefits and costs of using social distancing to flatten the curve for COVID-19." *Journal of Benefit-Cost Analysis*, 11(2): 179–195. DOI: 10.1017/bca.2020.12.

Tickner, J., Weiss, C. P., & Jacobs, M. (2017). "Alternatives assessment: New ideas, frameworks, and policies." *Journal of Epidemiology and Community Health*, 71(7): 655–656. DOI: 10.1136/jech-2016–207810.

US Department of Health and Human Services. (2016). "Guidelines for regulatory impact analysis." US Department of Health and Human Services.

Wachinger, G., Renn, O., Begg, C., & Kuhlicke, C. (2013). "The risk perception paradox – implications for governance and communication of natural hazards." *Risk Analysis*, 33: 1049–1065. DOI: 10.1111/j.1539–6924.2012.01942.x.

Wallis, C. (2021). "Few would fear Covid vaccines if policy makers explained their risks." *Scientific American*. www.scientificamerican.com/article/few-would-fear-covid-vaccines-if-policy-makers-explained-their-risks-better/.

Wardekker, J. A., Van der Sluijs, J. P., Janssen, P. H. M., Kloprogge, P., & Petersen, A. C. (2008). "Uncertainty communication in environmental assessments: Views from the Dutch science policy interface." *Environmental Science & Policy*, 11(7): 627–641. DOI: 10.1016/j.envsci.2008.05.005.

Conclusion

In the first chapter, "What is risk?" we set about clarifying what risk is by clarifying the conditions of use for the concept of risk. Our leading question was how the concept of risk could be understood as being both subjective and objective. We found that someone is facing a risk or, rather, more frequently, engaged in a risk situation or a risk activity, when that person is exposed to the possibility of unwanted consequences from their engagement in this situation or activity.

Exposure, uncertainty, and negative evaluations are the three main conditions that we identified for the application of the concept. We also saw that a person or being can be said to be exposed to a risk situation even when she is not the one making or even able to make the negative evaluation, as in the case of a young child, a fetus, or a dog.

Exposure and uncertainty are attached to something that could happen, something "out there," so to speak, even if this something is a psychological occurrence: it is something that can be the object of a third-person description. On the other hand, the negative evaluation of this something, which is also essential to the concept of risk, constitutes a normative and, in that respect, subjective dimension of the concept of risk. We saw that the concept of risk generally has a prescriptive function which also contributes to its normative dimension.

Thus, we identified the concept of risk as a "thick" concept, a concept with both objective and normative components.

In the second chapter, "Decision-making under risk," we asked how to make a rational decision when we are facing a risk situation. We investigated models of rational decision-making that a person could use, at least as guidance, when making personal decisions about risks.

Using models of rational decision-making requires that we represent the different options in terms of their pros and cons, benefits and costs, and that we express those costs and benefits in terms of a unique measure, called a utility measure. Identifying the costs and the benefits and assigning a value to them leave much room for interpretation, discussion, and value judgments.

These models require complete information. This requirement, in general, is difficult to satisfy. It is even difficult to imagine what a clear indication

DOI: 10.4324/9780429023521-7

could be that this condition is satisfied: how can we really know that there is not something relevant still that we do not know about? We found that it is not possible to have a framework of decision-making that is both perfectly rational and psychologically realistic.

But in the process of investigating those models, we became acquainted with a framework for representing a risk situation when a decision has to be made. It may not be possible to live up to the exacting standards of rationality that are presupposed in the models, but the framework gives us a systematic way to represent the situation, a systematic representation that can then be reflected upon, adjusted, shared, discussed, criticized, modified, improved.

And our investigation also alerted us to aspects of the situation that precisely resist rational modeling and will be most sensitive to interpretation and evaluation. That framework is the one that we discussed in its practical application in the later chapter, "Risk management," where we examined more in-depth the aspects that are open to interpretation and evaluation.

In the third chapter, "Risk assessment," we investigated the scientific assessment of risk with a specific focus on how normative judgments that express values are integrated with this assessment. We considered separately, on the one hand, the assessment of the uncertainty, the measure of the probability of the unwanted consequences, and, on the other hand, the assessment of the severity, the measure of the (possible) negative impacts of the risk situation, be it from climate warming, the production of nuclear energy, an epidemic, or the use of an incinerator.

An important finding of this chapter concerned the role of experts and the conditions for expertise. A risk expert is not just someone who is educated or skilled at estimating uncertainty, and not even simply someone who is a specialist in the field of the risk situation. Risk expertise requires calibration, an ability to estimate one's own uncertainty about one's assessment of the uncertainty attached to the risk situation, and this ability is acquired through receiving feedback on the assessments.

Another important result of our discussion was the central role of the selection of a reference class in the process of estimating probabilities. This central role shows the role, just as central, of normative judgments, because the selection of a reference class is mostly guided and warranted by the purpose of estimating the probability, the purpose of assessing the risk. And a purpose is an expression of values; it is an expression of what we care about. There is another way in which the selection of a reference class shows the importance of normative judgments in the assessment of risk: what reference class can be selected, in practice, depends on what data are available. And what data are available depends, for a large part, on what data we cared about gathering, even though it depends also on what data we allow ourselves to gather and on what data we are able at all to gather.

We highlighted the importance of normative judgments in the assessment of the severity of the risk situation. That this assessment would involve normativity is not surprising, since severity is an evaluative concept. To ask about the severity is to ask how bad it is. But our discussion underscored some ways in which normative judgments are active in assessing severity that may easily go unnoticed. What will be counted as unwanted effects will reveal not only what kinds of things we care about but also whom we care about, how much effort we invest in finding out the diverse impacts of a given risk situation, and how much effort we invest in finding out who is impacted. Here again, then, availability of information, information about some possible impacts, and the decisions that are behind this availability or lack of availability determine, for a large part, the results of the assessment of the severity.

In the fourth chapter, "Risk perception," we discussed studies of the perception of risk and of what influences this perception. Our leading question was to clarify what it could mean, if anything, to say that a perception is incorrect and/or needs to be corrected. The practical motivation behind this question is whether risk perception could have a productive role to play in risk management. It is an important and lively issue, because one traditional view on how to integrate risk perception to the process of management is that it needs to be corrected through the communication of more information or through manipulation. A better understanding of what influences risk perception could be instrumental in manipulating it. For instance, it was found that the perception of benefits may have an influence on the perception of risk. So one way, for instance, to try to influence the perception of a risk, say, toward a lower risk perception, might be to highlight the possible benefits associated with taking the risk. Tools for manipulation can, be misused or abused, for example, to install a mistaken sense of risk to our culture, heritage, or way of life for political purposes, but equally, they can be used to impart information ensuring health and the possibility of continuing life, liberty, and the pursuit of happiness.

But what studies on risk perception have shown is that there is actually a multitude of factors that are influencing risk perception: some are related to physical or practical characteristics of the situation, some to the cultural context of the perceiver, some to the moral appreciation of the risk situation, some to one's social network.

Second, because there are many factors that influence risk perception, and because many of them are not taken into account in risk assessment, it seems inappropriate to judge whether risk perception is correct or incorrect by reference to risk assessment. That would presuppose that only the factors that are taken into account in risk assessment can have a legitimate influence on risk perception. As we saw, there is no ground for this claim. There is no ground for the claim that risk perception is, in general, arbitrary, irrational, or mistaken.

But it would be dishonest to claim that risk perception never needs to be corrected. Most of us probably have had the experience of correcting our perception of some risks and felt that we benefited from it. A great deal of social effort is made to correct the perception of some risks, such as, for example, campaigns for recycling plastic or saving water or using condoms to lower the risk of STDs. One explication for this kind of effort that does not depend on taking scientific assessment as an epistemic reference for risk perception is to view the need to correct some risk perceptions as an attempt to correct the practical consequences they seem to have.

In the fifth chapter, "Risk management," we carefully examined three components of risk management: cost-benefit analysis, precautionary attitude, and risk communication. We investigated the traditional process of cost-benefit analysis used as framework for risk management and highlighted the role of normative judgments at different moments of this process. We also discussed the criticisms directed at this framework for risk management for not being sufficiently democratic, not taking sufficiently into consideration the perspective of the stakeholders. Our analysis showed, however, that there are different moments in the process that could, in principle, be modified so as to make the process more open to deliberations.

We discussed the approach to risk management that is based on upholding the so-called precautionary principle and illustrated this kind of approach by explicating the approach called alternatives assessment. We saw that this approach appears as an alternative to the traditional form of cost-benefit analysis. But we also discovered that it does not really eschew cost-benefit analysis. Instead, it enlarges the consideration of management options by including the precautionary option, which aims at preventing rather than mitigating harmful impacts and actively promoting the search for alternatives. And it also aims at considering a much larger range of impacts, rejecting the requirement that those impacts be well evidenced or monetizable: cultural impacts, psychological and emotional impacts, impacts on quality of life are all viewed as legitimate considerations for decision-making. This kind of approach makes deliberation an integral part of the framework of risk management.

But constructive deliberation about risk management calls for efficient communication about risk. A traditional model for risk communication, the information-deficit model, is based on the presupposition that the aim of risk communication is to convey information, information based on risk assessment. Newer approaches that view deliberation as pertaining to risk management promote a bidirectional form of risk communication, back-and-forth between the stakeholders and the experts. What is required for this form of communication to function is for the public to be heard, for risk perception and concerns outside the scope of risk assessment to be accepted as a legitimate part of the conversation. But the experts, too, need to be heard. And we saw that an important condition for that has to do with how, in what form, they represent and express their knowledge. The use of statistical language is doomed to create misunderstanding, confusion, or frustration because not only it is, to many people, esoteric but it also is filled with ambiguities. Using a language in terms of natural frequencies fosters communication because it uses ordinary terms, which makes is more appealing, and it is more transparent, which facilitates understanding.

Looking back over these chapters, we can see how the simple question "What is risk?" led to a large array of subsequent questions to be answered. Assessment and management of risk, of great importance both to the individual and to society, are possible only on the basis of an accurate understanding of the concept of risk. This is a "thick" concept, with both subjective and objective aspects; attributions of risk involve both factual and normative judgments. To make these judgments requires knowledge of, and competence with, all the tools that have been developed for rational decision-making. They require in addition respect for those values and interests that are apparent in their effect on risk perception and go beyond what is easily quantifiable. And in practice, the management of risk requires shared information, between individuals and between experts and the public, hence effective forms of accurate and truthful communication.

Index

For Product Safety Concerns and Information please contact our EU representative GPSR@taylorandfrancis.com
Taylor & Francis Verlag GmbH, Kaufingerstraße 24, 80331 München, Germany

www.ingramcontent.com/pod-product-compliance
Ingram Content Group UK Ltd.
Pitfield, Milton Keynes, MK11 3LW, UK
UKHW021308260926
475702UK00048B/920
9780367086435